T0305901

Experiment Design for Environmental Engineering

Experiment Design for Environmental Engineering
Methods and Examples

Francis Hopcroft and Abigail Charest

CRC Press
Taylor & Francis Group
Boca Raton London New York

CRC Press is an imprint of the
Taylor & Francis Group, an **informa** business

First edition published 2022
by CRC Press
6000 Broken Sound Parkway NW, Suite 300, Boca Raton, FL 33487-2742

and by CRC Press
2 Park Square, Milton Park, Abingdon, Oxon, OX14 4RN

Library of Congress Cataloging-in-Publication Data
Names: Hopcroft, Francis J., author. | Charest, Abigail, author.
Title: Experiment design for environmental engineering : methods and
examples / Francis Hopcroft and Abigail Charest.
Description: First edition. | Boca Raton, FL : CRC Press, 2022. |
Includes bibliographical references and index.
Identifiers: LCCN 2021037281 (print) | LCCN 2021037282 (ebook) |
ISBN 9781032017044 (hbk) | ISBN 9781032026183 (pbk) | ISBN 9781003184249 (ebk)
Subjects: LCSH: Environmental sciences—Experiments. | Environmental
engineering—Experiments. | Pollution—Measurement—Experiments. | Experimental design.
Classification: LCC GE77 .H66 2022 (print) | LCC GE77 (ebook) |
DDC 666/.14—dc23/eng/20211014
LC record available at https://lccn.loc.gov/2021037281
LC ebook record available at https://lccn.loc.gov/2021037282

ISBN: 9781032017044 (hbk)
ISBN: 9781032026183 (pbk)
ISBN: 9781003184249 (ebk)

DOI: 10.1201/9781003184249

Typeset in Times
by codeMantra

Contents

List of Figures...ix
List of Tables...xi
Preface... xiii
Acknowledgments.. xv
Authors...xvii

Chapter 1   Introduction 1

Chapter 2   How to Design an Engineering Experiment 3

    2.1   Defining the Question to Be Answered................................3
    2.2   Defining the Variables Involved in a Question.................... 4
    2.3   Measuring and Controlling the Variables 5
    2.4   Evaluation of Potential Interferences That Can Occur............7
    2.5   Minimizing, Avoiding, or Accounting for the
           Effects of Interferences 7
    2.6   Sensitivity Analyses of Experimental Data..........................8
    2.7   Safety Considerations in Experiment Design...................... 12

Chapter 3   Sampling Source Media... 15

    3.1   Sampling Water and Other Liquids..................................... 15
    3.2   Sampling Soil or Other Solids... 18
    3.3   Sampling Air and Other Gases.. 19
    3.4   Sampling Health and Safety Plans 21

Chapter 4   Expected Outcomes and Interpretation of Data................. 23

    4.1   Expected Outcomes.. 23
    4.2   Interpretation of the Data 24
    4.3   Uncertainty Considerations 25
    4.4   Estimating Future Parameter Values.................................... 25
    4.5   Probability 25
          4.5.1   Probability as Basis of Statistics 26
          4.5.2   Estimating Probabilities in Experimentation............ 29
          4.5.3   Misuse of Probability Data...................................... 30
          4.5.4   Number of Data Points Needed................................ 31
          4.5.5   Selective Use of Data 32
          4.5.6   Cause and Effect vs. Correlation............................. 36
    4.6   Risk... 41

Chapter 5   Model Design Methodology..43

      5.1   Discussion..43
      5.2   Model Format 43
      5.3   Experiment Design Format Model...46

Chapter 6   Laboratory Report...49

      6.1   Conversion of Theory to Experimental Output Data 49
      6.2   Compare and Contrast Experimental Output Data to
              Existing Literature...49
      6.3   Suggested Laboratory Report Template 50

Chapter 7   Effective Presentation of the Data in Outcome Reports 55

Chapter 8   Designing Research Experiment Projects...59

      8.1   Research to Assess Standard Sample Drying Protocols 59
      8.2   Research to Assess Standard Indicator Organisms.................61
      8.3   Research Recommendations..62

Chapter 9   General Experiments...63

      Experiment 9.1: Turbidity Meter Calibration.....................................64
      Experiment 9.2: Calibration of Spectrophotometers...........................70
      Experiment 9.3: Jar Test Procedure..75
      Experiment 9.4: Duct Tape Permeability Test.....................................82
      Experiment 9.5: Determination of Specific Heat Capacity 89
      Experiment 9.6: Determination of Insulation R-Values for
                     Various Materials..95
      Experiment 9.7: Headspace Analysis for the Presence of Volatile
                     Organic Compounds 104
      Experiment 9.8: Surface Runoff Rate Determination and Volume
                     Calculation..109
      Experiment 9.9: Water Filtration Media Evaluation 114
      Experiment 9.10: Water Filtration Media Evaluation Remote
                     Area Options..120

Chapter 10 Oil and Petroleum-Based Experiments...129

      Experiment 10.1: Solubility of Oil in Water as a Function
                     of Salinity 130
      Experiment 10.2: Gasoline Fingerprinting.......................................135
      Experiment 10.3: Determination of Porosity and Void
                     Ratio in Soil...140

Chapter 11 Oxygen and BOD Experiments... 147

Experiment 11.1: Calibration of DO Meter by Winkler Method 148
Experiment 11.2: Oxygen Transfer Rate Determination................. 152
Experiment 11.3: Maximum DO Concentration in Water as a
                 Function of Temperature and Salinity 160
Experiment 11.4: 5-Day BOD Test with Determination of
                 Exertion Rate k 165

Chapter 12 Environmental Microbiology Experiments...................................... 179

Experiment 12.1: Total Coliforms and *E. coli* By IDEXX
                 Quantitrays® and Colilert® Most Probable
                 Number Methodologies 180
Experiment 12.2: Field Testing and Quantification of Total
                 Coliforms and *E. coli* by Colilert and
                 Petrifilm Methodologies 187
Experiment 12.3: Viral Indicators Coliphage Quantification
                 Based on Easyphage Method............................. 195
Experiment 12.4: Comparison of Disinfection Methods................. 201
Experiment 12.5: Comparison of Disinfection Methods: Remote
                 Area Options... 209

Chapter 13 Water Quality Experiments... 217

Experiment 13.1: Introduction to Water Quality Parameters 218
Experiment 13.2: pH As a Function of Acid/Base Concentration
                 With pH Neutralization Calculations................... 224
Experiment 13.3: Determination of Mean Cell Residence Time
                 in a Dispersed Plug Flow Reactor 231
Experiment 13.4: Determination of Surface Water
                 Evaporation Rate 237
Experiment 13.5: Characterization of Pond, Lake, or
                 Stream Foam..247

Chapter 14 Contaminant Removal Experiments 253

Experiment 14.1: Determination of Contaminant Removal Rate 254
Experiment 14.2: Technique for Metal Ion Precipitation
                 from Water.. 260
Experiment 14.3: Separation of Liquid Phase Components
                 through a Distillation Process............................. 268
Experiment 14.4: Technique for Potable Water Softening.............. 274
Experiment 14.5: Coagulation, Flocculation, and Sedimentation
                 for the Removal of Organic and Inorganic
                 Water Contaminants 282

Experiment 14.6: Determination of Granular Media Suitability
                for Use in Granular Media Filters........................ 289
Experiment 14.7: Analysis of Suspended Solids in Water 297
Experiment 14.8: Analysis of Total Solids in Water....................... 303

Appendix..313

Bibliography 343

Index...347

List of Figures

Figure 4.1 Average annual temperature over 10-year period (Fictitious Data from Table 4.1). (Hopcroft, Francis J., *Engineering Economics for Environmental Engineers*, Momentum Press, LLC, New York, NY, 2016.) 33

Figure 4.2 Average annual temperatures based on data from Table 4.2 (even months February through December). (Hopcroft, Francis J., *Engineering Economics for Environmental Engineers*, Momentum Press, LLC, New York, NY, 2016.) 35

Figure 4.3 Average annual temperature over a 10-year period (odd months, January through November). (Hopcroft, Francis J., *Engineering Economics for Environmental Engineers*, Momentum Press, LLC, New York, NY, 2016.) 35

Figure 4.4 Charts of variation of Anscombe's Quartet. (Hopcroft, Francis J., *Engineering Economics for Environmental Engineers*, Momentum Press, LLC, New York, NY, 2016.) 39

Figure 4.5 Charts in Figure 4.4 with trend lines shown. (Hopcroft, Francis J., *Engineering Economics for Environmental Engineers*, Momentum Press, LLC, New York, NY, 2016.) 40

Figure 4.6 Y4 from Figure 4.5 with the outlier ignored; the trend line is vertical at 9.0. (Hopcroft, Francis J., *Engineering Economics for Environmental Engineers*, Momentum Press, LLC, New York, NY, 2016.) 40

Figure 11.1 Typical BOD curve. (Hopcroft, F. J. (2015). *Wastewater Treatment Concepts and Practices*, Momentum Press.) 174

Figure 11.2 Log-normal plot of BOD data from Figure 11.1. (Hopcroft, F. J. (2015). *Wastewater Treatment Concepts and Practices*, Momentum Press.) 174

Figure 14.1 Form for plotting soil grain size distribution curves 294

Figure A.1a R-value determination test box plan 313

Figure A.1b R-value determination test box details (1) 314

Figure A.1c R-value determination test box details (2) 315

Figure A.2a Runoff coefficient measurement device plan 316

Figure A.2b Runoff coefficient measurement device details (1) 317

Figure A.2c Runoff coefficient measurement device details (2) 318

Figure A.2d   Runoff coefficient measurement device details (3)....................... 319

Figure A.2e   Runoff coefficient measurement device details (4) 320

Figure A.2f   Runoff coefficient measurement device details (5)....................... 321

Figure A.2g   Runoff coefficient measurement device details (6)....................... 322

List of Tables

Table 2.1 Potential Interferences for Example Experiment 7

Table 2.2 Potential Interferences for Example Experiment with Management Plan..9

Table 4.1 Average Air Temperatures by Month and Year (Degrees F) (Fictitious Data)...33

Table 4.2 Six Months of Average Annual Temperature Data Even Months........34

Table 4.3 Six Months of Average Annual Temperature Data Odd Months.........34

Table 4.4 Data Sets for Variation of Anscombe's Quartet...................................37

Table 4.5 Statistical Equivalency Values for the Original Anscombe's Quartet and the Variation of Anscombe's Quartet Shown in Table 4.4 38

Table A.1 Collection, Preservation, and Holding Times for Selected Liquid Environmental Samples..323

Table A.2 Collection, Preservation, and Holding Times for Selected Soil and Sediment Environmental Samples 329

Table A.3 Specific Heat Capacity of Selected Materials....................................332

Table A.4 Thermal Conductivity of Selected Materials at 25°C (77°F)............334

Table A.5 Typical Soil Porosity and Void Ratio Values for Selected Soils 335

Table A.6 Density Estimates for Various Soil Types..336

Table A.7 Maximum DO Concentration in Water by Temperature...................337

Table A.8 Density of Water at Selected Temperatures 339

Table A.9 Typical Surface Stormwater Runoff Coefficients.............................340

Preface

Designing experiments for environmental engineering projects differs from designing experiments for social science studies and other disciplines where experimental design is more commonly encountered in the context of social research projects. With environmental engineering designs, the interconnectedness of nature and the interaction of environmental factors with the outcome data can significantly affect the decisions made on the bases of those outcomes – and not always for the better. This book describes a method for preparing an environmental engineering experiment to demonstrate specific environmental phenomena or to document expected environmental outcomes. It includes the methodology, the background, and potential interferences. The final six chapters provide some successful experiments that can be implemented to demonstrate specific environmental topics. These experiments are specifically geared to a university laboratory but are also applicable to commercial or municipal applications or field experimentation.

Acknowledgments

The work and contributions to the success of this book by the Wentworth Institute of Technology students who tried out many of them in the laboratory over the years are greatly appreciated and gratefully acknowledged. In particular, Ms. Emma Loughlin contributed to the drawing of specific diagrams in CAD and sorted them into separate sheets for inclusion in the book. Her work was invaluable to the success of the writing.

Authors

Prof. Francis J. Hopcroft recently retired from teaching civil and environmental engineering after 23 years in the classroom and about 40 years of consulting in the field. He is the author of six environmental engineering and hazardous waste management books, the coauthor of 22 such books, and a contributor to a dozen or more professional manuals of practice. He was registered as a Professional Engineer in all six New England states and as a Licensed Site Professional in the Commonwealth of Massachusetts. Before starting his teaching career, he spent 25 years in professional practice as a consultant, an EPA regulator, and as the President of several consulting firms doing site assessment for the presence of hazardous materials. He continued his consulting work while teaching to maintain currency in his field and to bring current concepts into the classroom.

Dr. Abigail Charest is an Associate Professor and Dean of the School of Management at Wentworth Institute of Technology (WIT) in Boston, Massachusetts. She is currently the Blittersdorf Endowed Professor and utilizes the professorship to address topics of sustainability in the curriculum. She is an avid researcher, experimenter, and innovator in the laboratory. She is focused on the biological nature of environmental work and developed the biological experiments in this book, among others. She has also been the lead faculty member in the redevelopment of a graduate program in civil engineering at Wentworth. She earned her doctorate from the Worcester Polytechnic Institute, and prior to entering into academia, she worked in the field of environmental consulting in the New England area. During this time, she received her Professional Engineering license in the Commonwealth of Massachusetts.

1 Introduction

The desire to change and shape the world is at the heart and soul of engineering. The art of effective experimentation is an invaluable function to learn if the engineer is going to excel at their profession, regardless of the specialty or the subspecialty an engineer chooses. This does not mean that every engineer needs to be proximate to a laboratory. Experimentation takes many forms and can involve intellectual experiments as well as physical ones. In fact, physical experimentation almost always requires some intellectual exercises before the experiment is designed and then again after the data are generated to properly evaluate and explain the outcomes.

How, then, should one go about designing an experiment?

Experimental design is as much an art as a practice. Elegant experiments exist, but not nearly as often as mundane exercises of practical judgment superimposed on some physical phenomenon. Indeed, most experiments do not work, at least not the first time. If they did, there would be limited need to do them. It is the failure of experiments and the iteration of design from which the most is often learned, and this new knowledge allows us to narrow the scope of subsequent experiments to better define, describe, or demonstrate the outcomes the initial experiment was designed to demonstrate in the first place. It is a noble goal, of course, to minimize the number of iterative experiments needed to resolve an issue or question, but it should not be considered a bad thing if more than one or two tries are needed to get something complex right. The more complex the issue, of course, the more difficult it will be to get the experiments right from the beginning.

This book is about designing experiments, and it is also a book of complete and detailed experiments. Experiments that have been designed to demonstrate specific environmental phenomena. The experiments in this book are for teaching various physical traits of common engineering basics so that the novice engineer can begin to see how the world works and begin to develop necessary skills for the effective design of new experiments.

Chapter 2 looks at how to design an experiment; Chapter 3 describes the most effective ways to sample media under different sample purity requirements; Chapter 4 examines how to establish the expected outcomes from an experiment, how to collect data for effective evaluation of actual results, how to interpret the data generated by an experiment, including what to do when the data do not coincide with the expected outcome, and considerations of uncertainty in the experimental outcomes, including a discussion of how probability plays into evaluating data; Chapter 5 evaluates some considerations for preparing the outcome data for effective presentation to others; Chapter 6 provides a Model Design Methodology and format; Chapter 7 provides a suggested template for a laboratory report that mirrors the data and information in the experiment outline with actual results, discussions, recommendations, and conclusions; Chapter 8 discusses the differences between the experiments described in this book and the type of experimentation needed in a research project, and discusses

DOI: 10.1201/9781003184249-1

how to develop appropriate research projects; and Chapters 9–14 provide a series of successful experiments designed to show engineering students some of the basics of environmental engineering.

Each of the experiments in Chapters 9–14 provides an introductory section on the basic theory behind the experiment. Where more than one experiment relates to the same basic theory, the theoretical background is provided only once, and subsequent experiments that are based on the same theory refer the experimenter back to the appropriate section of a previous experiment. These are not intended to be detailed theses on the underlying theory, but rather a reminder of the engineering basics underlying the experiment. It is assumed that the student has a sufficient educational background to grasp the fundamentals outlined in the experiment introductions and to understand the context for the data to be developed during the experiment.

2 How to Design an Engineering Experiment

The fundamental design of an experiment contains several distinct design elements. Those include the question to be answered; the variables involved; how the variables will be adjusted; the potential interferences that can occur; how the investigator intends to minimize or avoid the effects of those interferences, or to account for them in the experimental data; and what theoretical outcomes are expected. Once the data are generated, how those data are interpreted and how the results are presented will go a long way to validating the outcomes.

Note that not all experiments succeed. If they did, there would be no need to do an experiment because the outcome could be accurately predicted. It is important, therefore, to recognize that failure *is* an acceptable component of investigation. That recognition will minimize the tendency to interpret data in a way that supports the expected outcome and to reject data that do not support that outcome. *If the data are not what is expected, it should be assumed that the data are correct and that the theory is wrong or that there was an error in the experiment design or conduct.* The investigator then needs to try to figure out why the theory or the experiment was wrong and how to redo the experiment to account for the new thinking.

Certainly, equipment will occasionally fail, people will do things in a manner inconsistent with the planned protocol of the experiment, reagents will become contaminated, and all sorts of other things will go wrong with experiments. The data that are generated are *always* correct for the experiment that was done. If those data do not reflect the expected outcome, either the theory is wrong or the experiment incorporated some unknown flaw. Either way, it is imperative to accept the data as real and to adjust the experiment or the theory, or both, to incorporate what was learned from the unexpected outcome.

2.1 DEFINING THE QUESTION TO BE ANSWERED

It is axiomatic in engineering that in order to solve a problem, it is first necessary to define the problem accurately and completely. Much of what is done in experimentation is aimed at defining the basic problem. That implies that the initial question posed may not be the intended question the investigator is attempting to answer. Sometimes, an intermediary question is required to define the underlying details of the ultimate question.

In either case, the question posed needs to be as clear and concise as possible. Ambiguous questions lead to ambiguous results. For example, "How does temperature affect water quality?" might be an interesting question, but there are too many variables in the question that are not defined. For example, is the question intended to look at ambient air temperature above the water or the temperature of the water

DOI: 10.1201/9781003184249-2

itself, or both? Does it intend to examine water quality from a reservoir, a pond, a lake, a stream, or the ocean? At what depth? How is water quality defined in the question? How much time variation and temperature variation are allowed? Multiple other questions will also quickly arise as the experiment is designed and any attempt is made to run it.

A clearer, more concise question might be "What is the effect of water temperature on the concentration of oxygen in a shallow (less than the average depth of 1 m (3 feet)) natural stream with a flow velocity less than 2 m (6 feet) per second?" By identifying a suitable water body for study, using continuous reading temperature, dissolved oxygen, flow rate, and water depth probes, all the pertinent data can be simultaneously measured over an extended period of time. Note that, as usual, there are some uncontrolled variables that may be at play here that must be considered, discussed, and assessed.

2.2 DEFINING THE VARIABLES INVOLVED IN A QUESTION

Very few things in engineering are simple. Engineering questions are driven by physics, chemistry, biology, mathematics, mechanics, geology, and a host of other "ologies". Those subjects all form engineering basics to which engineers routinely turn to find answers. How those basics interact with each other in any specific instance or circumstance is not always clear, but can be significant. Defining the variables at work in any experiment, whether those variables are to be controlled, and how to account for those not being controlled is important.

There are generally three kinds of variables involved in experiments and knowing which kind is being discussed is important. *Independent variables* are those that the experimenter controls. *Dependent variables* are those that respond to the changes made to the independent variables. *Controlled variables* are those that are kept constant throughout the experiment. The ideal experiment will be designed so that only one independent variable is changed at a time and the results in all the dependent variables can be observed. Occasionally, more than one variable may need to be changed at the same time, but that should be avoided to the maximum degree possible.

Note, too, that an important characteristic of a variable is that it can be reliably measured. Time, temperature, velocity, mass, and similar characteristics are measurable and are good quality variables. Emotions, feelings, opinions, judgments, and similar characteristics are not measurable and therefore are not suitable experimental variables.

In the question posed regarding the effects of water temperature on the concentration of dissolved oxygen in a natural shallow stream, there are many potential variables. Four independent variables have been identified as key to the selected question: water temperature, flow velocity, dissolved oxygen concentration, and stream depth. All four have been defined as measurable variables in the statement of the question. Stream depth is defined for the experiment within the experimental statement, and the stream velocity is restricted. The question statement would require removal of data generated when the stream velocity or depth exceeded the stated parameters, although data from outside the stated parameters might well suggest further areas for additional study.

It is noted, however, that a lot of variables exist in a natural stream that have not been identified or considered in the question statement. For example, natural water bodies typically contain a wide variety of dissolved minerals and organics that can vary in concentration with water temperature and velocity, along with the underlying soil and rock strata, and animals discharge organic waste products into the environment at random locations and random times, without concern for any effects this might have on the engineer's experiments. Silt or soil particles may be suddenly mixed into the streamflow by a land animal entering the water or an aquatic animal swimming near the probes. Sunlight hitting a probe might inadvertently elevate the temperature readings above the actual water temperature at any time during the experiment, or aquatic debris could temporarily clog or block a probe receptor, generating false readings that are not inherently obvious. Rain could occur during the experiment that could change the dissolved oxygen concentrations sharply over a short time interval. None of these variables are proposed to be measured or controlled by the experimenter, but each could, alone or in conjunction with one or more of the others, significantly impact the data.

2.3 MEASURING AND CONTROLLING THE VARIABLES

Clearly, there are lots of things that could go wrong with this experiment. Minimizing those negative effects takes some planning. In the stream example experiment, the experimenter is not actually controlling anything; not even the four independent variables that are the basis for the question. The question presupposes a natural stream and a measurement of four variables over time. Those data would then be correlated to generate an analysis of the effects of water temperature on dissolved oxygen in a natural stream defined by the four stated parameters. Note that because only those four variables are being measured and there are so many other variables that are not being measured, the data generated would apply only to the specific stream measured at the specific location of the measurements. This experiment would not generate universally applicable data (but may identify applicable trends).

There is usually more than one way to do everything in engineering, and there are three general ways to conduct this experiment. The first is to find a suitable natural stream meeting the stated flow and depth parameters, inserting the necessary probes, and collecting data. All the uncontrolled and unmeasured parameters cited earlier would be potential problems for data analysis. The measurements would then be taken by the probes and the data analyzed, noting the potential impacts of the unmeasured variables.

A second way to conduct this experiment is to create a streamflow in a suitably long manufactured trough in the lab. The trough would need to be designed to recreate natural stream bed conditions of soil, rock, depth variations, roughness, stream width variations, and other factors to replicate the natural stream conditions to which the data are intended to be applied. In this case, the water temperature could be artificially adjusted by the experimenter and the dissolved oxygen concentration measured directly. The stream depth and flow could be held constant and most of the external parameters could be eliminated. This would eliminate many of the other unmeasured variables, but would not account for their impact, alone or in conjunction with each other, on the outcome data from a natural environment. The resulting data would directly provide the answer to the stated question, but only for the limited controlled conditions under which the experiment was conducted; not in regard to an actual, natural stream.

A third possibility is to construct some form of dam across a suitable stream with an automated variable depth weir controlled by a downstream depth gauge and flow rate monitor such that the flow rate and water depth are maintained within a very narrow range during the experimental period. Additional real-time monitoring probes could be installed for a variety of organic constituents, suspended solids concentrations, and other parameters of concern to determine whether there were significant changes in those parameters sufficient to warrant further experiment for their effects. The water temperature and dissolved oxygen concentrations would then be measured continuously for some appropriate period of time and the data analyzed, noting the potential interferences from all the other measured and unmeasured parameters.

Regardless of the experiment design employed, there are several factors that would need to be measured or controlled during this experiment, including the water temperature, dissolved oxygen concentration, flow rate, and water depth. In this case, direct measurement of the four defined parameters using in-stream, real-time probes may be beneficial. The alternative is regular unique probe readings at specific time intervals, typically the same time every day or two over an extended period of time. Either way, an extended timeline is necessary in a natural setting to identify the effects of high and low temperatures and the time delays between temperature changes and dissolved oxygen concentration changes. A laboratory experiment could adjust water temperatures at will and greatly accelerate the experimental timeline, while greatly reducing the ability to understand the effects of the unmeasured parameters. The experimenter needs to weigh the costs of doing a field study with the loss of fidelity in the data from a laboratory study; in this case, weighing the need for information about the specific parameters against the need to identify charasteristics of that specific river.

Controlling the experiment for potential effects of unmeasured parameters is more difficult. Over a short period of time, it may be assumed that the other water quality parameters do not change dramatically and that their effects are negligible. Over longer periods of time, this assumption might well be false. Over a very long time frame, the effects of the unmeasured variables may average out and become negligible again, even if they are significant in the magnitude of their variability. Again, the experimenter needs to weigh the costs of the long-term data collection effort with the benefits of short-term data collection that may not well represent the long-term natural environment outcomes.

Note that this does not mean that a researcher or experimenter can assume or state that the time frame is sufficiently short or long as to render unmeasured impacts negligible. A short time period in the water quality analysis example being discussed is typically measured in minutes – usually fewer than 5. A long time frame is typically measured in years – often decades. Most analyses are done using a time frame that is not within either set of guidelines and those guidelines are not relevant to many other types of engineering analyses.

2.4 EVALUATION OF POTENTIAL INTERFERENCES THAT CAN OCCUR

The unmeasured interferences do need to be considered in the analysis of data. Since they are unmeasured, they are, by definition, unknown and cannot be numerically applied to the data. In order to rationally consider their potential impacts on the data, it is first necessary to determine what those interferences are, and what possible impacts they could have on the experimental data. It is necessary to ask the pertinent question: "What could possibly go wrong?" A lot of things, it turns out.

Tabulation of potential interferences is a useful exercise to start to focus the mind on what could go wrong. Table 2.1 is a possible table of potential interferences for the example problem. This table is expanded shortly to show how these potential interferences may be considered and managed.

This table does not represent a comprehensive list of all possible interferences related to the example experiment, but is sufficient to indicate the broad range of potential problems that the investigator should consider when designing an experiment.

2.5 MINIMIZING, AVOIDING, OR ACCOUNTING FOR THE EFFECTS OF INTERFERENCES

Given that unmeasured interferences are likely to create issues with any experiment, it is useful to give considerable thought to how those effects on the data will be determined or measured. The easiest way to account for those effects, of course, is to actually measure them during the experiment. While it may be the intent of the

TABLE 2.1
Potential Interferences for Example Experiment

Interference	Possible Cause
Unmeasured chemicals in water column	Dissolved by flowing water from natural sources
Unmeasured chemicals in water column	Introduced randomly from animal waste discharges
Changes in suspended solids in water column	Bottom disturbance from animal, fish, or people in the water
Increased suspended solids in water column	Runoff from upstream areas due to increased recent rainfall, flooding, or irrigation
Temporary clogging of one or more probes	Floating organic matter in the water column
Temporary clogging of one or more probes	Silt or sand infiltration into probes or temporary burying of probes in bottom sediments
Rainfall changes to dissolved oxygen concentrations	Light, heavy, or variable rainfall over short or long period of time causing short-term fluctuations in dissolved oxygen concentration
Significant short-term (minutes) variation or change in barometric air pressure	Significant air pressure variation due to storm approaches that could affect the dissolved oxygen concentration
Probe failure	Loss of power to the probe
Probe failure	Probe becomes dislodged and is damaged or destroyed

experiment to determine the effect on dissolved oxygen concentration resulting from changes in water temperature, this objective does not prohibit the simultaneous measurement of other parameters. There are continuous real-time probes available, with data loggers, to measure a wide range of common water quality parameters. Things such as nitrogen concentration, metals concentrations, various gas concentrations, suspended solids concentrations, and general turbidity, along with the dissolved oxygen, flow rate, and water depth, are readily available (at some monetary cost, to be sure). Adding as many probes as possible to the array provides a lot of useful data for the current and potential future experiments. It is far easier to obtain extraneous data during the experiment, than to try to backtrack and account for those factors later.

Note that there are a lot of unintended consequences that can occur from trying to mitigate identified interferences. In the sample experiment, for example, protecting the probes from clogging or damage is useful but may introduce potential turbulence around the probes that could alter the output data. Care would need to be taken to provide protections that would minimize damage to the probes while avoiding interference with the data. It could also prove useful to examine the study location for a few minutes to determine whether there is likely to be a layer of silt or sand moving close to the bottom, for example, or floating organic matter near the surface. Judicious placement of the probe array in the water column can reduce a lot of risk in this regard. By placing more than one array, at varying, but specific depths, can indicate whether there is a temperature variation with depth and what that variation looks like – a potentially serendipitous addition to the output data that was not initially considered as likely. Moreover, if one probe array is compromised, but the data that are developed indicate good, consistent correlations between the probes, careful mathematical adjustment to the data set can reasonably predict the missing data provided that those data manipulations are clearly identified in the data reports.

In many cases, consideration of how to manage unmeasured interferences is usefully tabulated in an expansion of Table 2.1, as shown in Table 2.2. When the number of interferences is expected to be small (<5, for example) and easily managed, the use of tables like these is suggested. See one or more of the completed experiments in chapters 9 through 14 for how this procedure is done without cumbersome tables. A literature search may be conducted on any of the interferences and possible ways to mitigate them. It is best not to reinvent the wheel, but to learn from others.

2.6   SENSITIVITY ANALYSES OF EXPERIMENTAL DATA

When looking at a series of independent variables and their combined effect on one or more dependent variables, complications can arise. Most independent variables interact with each other as well as with the dependent variables being measured. It is not always clear how a particular change in one variable is affecting the other independent variables (which are then acting as dependent variables) and what those changes are doing to the dependent variable being measured. To try to get a handle on that issue, a sensitivity analysis is conducted.

To conduct a sensitivity analysis, it is first necessary to identify the things that are causing changes in the dependent variables. These are generally going to be the previously identified independent variables but could include a few other variables,

TABLE 2.2

Potential Interferences for Example Experiment with Management Plan

Interference	Possible Cause	Management Plan
Unmeasured chemicals in water column	Dissolved by flowing water from natural sources	Add probes to the array to the extent possible (principally metals and organics) and minimize the time of study
Unmeasured chemicals in water column	Introduced randomly from animal waste discharges	Add probes to the array to the extent possible (principally nitrates, phosphates, and bacteria) and minimize the time of study
Changes in suspended solids in water column	Bottom disturbance from animal, fish, or people in the water	Monitor with suspended solids or turbidity probe during study
Increased suspended solids in water column	Runoff from upstream areas due to increased recent rainfall, flooding, or irrigation	Set up rainfall gauge at study location and then monitor upstream watershed rainfall conditions during study. If rainfall occurs, develop or access a hydrograph for the stream at the study location to correlate with suspended solids and turbidity data
Temporary clogging of one or more probes	Floating organic matter in the water column	A screen with moderate openings, sufficient to catch large debris, but large enough to allow smooth flow through the screen, can be erected far enough upstream of the probes to reduce the danger while allowing normal flow conditions to reestablish prior to the probe location (perhaps 15–20 feet upstream, depending on flow rates)
Temporary clogging of one or more probes	Silt or sand infiltration into probes or temporary burying of probes in bottom sediments	Prior observation of the study location and design of the probe array support system should minimize the closeness of bottom sediments to the probes. Judicious location of the probes within the water column is useful to minimize this risk, along with setting multiple probe arrays at different depths
Rainfall changes to dissolved oxygen concentrations	Light, heavy, or variable rainfall over short or long period of time causing short-term fluctuations in dissolved oxygen concentration or flow rate unrelated to water temperature changes	Establish rain gauge at study location to monitor rainfall events and correlate to existing rainfall dissolved oxygen concentration data developed by others or set up a separate rainfall collection and DO probe at the study site
Significant variation or change in barometric air pressure or humidity	Significant air pressure variation or humidity due to storm approaches could affect the dissolved oxygen concentration	Establish a weather monitoring station at study location to monitor air pressure and humidity to a data logger for the duration of the study

(Continued)

TABLE 2.2 (*Continued*)
Potential Interferences for Example Experiment with Management Plan

Interference	Possible Cause	Management Plan
Probe failure	Loss of power to the probe	Install fresh batteries at the start of the study, inspect water seals around probe bodies to minimize leakage risks, and change batteries at predetermined intervals to reduce power failure potential
Probe failure	Probe becomes dislodged and is damaged or destroyed	Consult with others on the design of the probe array, the station establishment criteria, and probe attachments. This is a risk management issue more than an unmeasured interference issue, but one that needs to be considered early in the experiment design

as well. Any characteristic of the system in which the variables under consideration reside, which could affect the dependent variable, should be viewed as a possible factor to be included in the sensitivity analysis. Then a set of standards must be established by which the sensitivity of the data will be measured.

For the example problem described in this chapter, the independent variables will be accepted as the only causative factors for change in the dependent variable. That is not an entirely valid assumption, but since nothing else is being measured, and the intent is only to determine the sensitivity of the dependent variable to the three measured independent variables, that assumption will work in this case. The assumptions upon which the sensitivity analysis is based are the following:

1. Percent change in DO as a function of a percentage change in water temperature
2. Percent change in DO as a function of a percentage change in water depth
3. Percent change in DO as a function of a percentage change in stream velocity

To conduct the analysis, each independent variable is changed *while all the other independent variables are held constant*. The change in the dependent variable as a function of the measured change in the varied independent variable will yield a sensitivity curve. It is possible for the dependent variable to change linearly with a constant change in the specific independent variable. It is also possible for any other form of change to occur, such as a parametric curve, a nonlinear change, and so forth. Until the controlled changes are made and the data plotted, the effects will not be known.

In this example, the change in maximum DO as a function of water temperature is a well-established physical property of water. Tables, such as Table A.7 in the Appendix, provide those data. The assumption, however, is based on the percentage of water temperature change, not on the absolute temperature change. Therefore, it is necessary to recalculate the percentage change represented by each one degree of temperature change at each temperature within the range of interest. Water temperature in streams (at least in New England) usually varies from 0°C (32°F) to about 22°C (72°F). Plotting the percent change in DO on the y-axis over that range versus the percent change in water temperature on the x-axis will yield the desired curve. The time over which the percent changes are calculated is important to note. All the parameter changes need to be measured over the same time frame. The consistency of the terms of measurement, here percentage changes in everything, is also important so that the outcomes can be properly compared.

Water depth is an issue when the water becomes so deep that an isocline develops causing water temperatures to vary significantly with depth. The problem stated here has a maximum depth of approximately 3 feet and it is moving. Isoclines are created where movement is limited and flushing of the water does not readily occur, such as in a deep pool within a lake or pond. A moving stream such as that contemplated here does not allow for such isoclines to be created. However, the turbulence associated with the streamflow will be variable depending on the depth of flow. Turbulence will also be affected by the bottom conditions such that a rougher bottom (rocky or rutted, for example) will generate greater turbulence than a smooth one (sand or hard smooth rock, for example). Greater turbulence is expected to be associated with higher DO concentrations than less turbulence in the same water depth and temperature. Turbulence is not being measured in this experiment, but water depth is. Therefore, the percentage change in water depth should be plotted on the x-axis against the percentage change in DO for this parameter on the y-axis.

Finally, streamflow is being measured in this experiment. As with the other parameters, the percent change in DO as a function of percent change in water flow rate is plotted for the same time interval as for the other two parameters. The percent change in DO is plotted on the y-axis and the percent change in streamflow rate is plotted on the x-axis.

When all the plots have been completed, overlaying them on a single graph will yield a graphic representation of how the DO is affected by the change in each of the three independent variables being measured. Ideally, each of the three lines will be flat, meaning that the percent changes are linearly correlated and a singular linear equation to predict the DO at any set of those three variables may be reliably developed. If that is not the case, which is more common, then a nonlinear equation will need to be developed to better predict the impact of the various independent variables on the singular dependent variable of interest. Moreover, the relative effect of each of the three measured independent variables will be clear, and if one is significantly different from the others, it will indicate a need to more closely and carefully monitor that parameter in the field.

It is instructive to note that all data may be assessed as statistics. Statistics are subject to analysis by statistical analysis techniques. This generally includes the various analytical tools described in Tables 4.4 and 4.5. The derivation and use of those analytical tools is not done here for two significant reasons. The first is that they can be complex to understand and there are dozens of excellent texts available for review, should a reader choose to pursue them.

The second reason is that all of those tools assume that all data are random. On the other hand, there is nothing truly random about nature. All things in nature are connected in some form or fashion to everything else in nature. Therefore, while the application of statistical analysis tools that rely on randomness is often done with measured *environmental* data, it is not appropriate for most *experimental* data since the changes in the dependent variable are presumed to be a direct result of changes in the independent variable, and thus, not random.

2.7 SAFETY CONSIDERATIONS IN EXPERIMENT DESIGN

Safety is paramount in the design of experiments, just as it is in the conduct of professional civil and environmental engineering, in general. It is, therefore, important to incorporate appropriate safety considerations into every experiment design. All college and university laboratories, private laboratories, and rooms or spaces in which experiments are carried out contain a wide variety of physical, chemical, and biological agents that can seriously harm or kill inattentive, experimenters.

Acids, alkalis, and other caustic substances can cause serious burns to the skin and blindness in the event of eye contact. Some organic chemicals can cause toxic reactions to anyone, but particularly to those with sensitivities to allergens. For example, volatile organic compounds (VOCs) can cause respiratory distress when inhaled, cancer in the long run, and death at high concentrations. Biological agents used to grow or enhance the growth of bacteria and other organisms can be toxic to humans. Most of the bacteria and other organisms grown in laboratories are harmful to humans, which is why they are being researched, and those effects can lead to gastrointestinal symptoms, dehydration, and death. Samples studied in environmental engineering laboratories can include industrial wastes, human sewage and surface water contaminated with human sewage, animal wastes, and the potentially toxic chemicals used to treat them.

Common considerations:

- There is no reason to believe at any time that the tables and counters in any laboratory are germ free. The principal route of exposure to harmful organisms is through ingestion and touching a contaminated surface, then touching the face or mouth, even just to scratch an itch, can cause accidental ingestion or subcutaneous infection.
- Ovens, incubators, and hotplates can achieve temperatures from 20°C (68°F) to 500°C (932°F). It should be assumed that they are very hot at all times and that severe burns can result immediately on contact from accidentally touching the sides or edges when inserting or removing samples.
- Personal protective equipment consisting of safety glasses, latex or vinyl gloves (or heat resistant gloves when working with ovens, incubators, or hotplates), and lab coats should be required for all people entering a research laboratory or experiment space, including nonparticipatory observers.
- No fewer than two persons should be present at all times in any space in which an experiment is being conducted or data are being collected or read.

- There should be a direct way to contact emergency response personnel available, such as a dedicated telephone line to the public safety office inside the laboratory space, to summon aid when needed.
- No work should be allowed to proceed without those safety protections in place for everyone present. Accidents do happen in laboratories and preplanning for safety will minimize the risks of harm when accidents do happen.

In addition, when accidents happen, it is important not to be cavalier about the consequences. Even what appears to be a minor scrape or burn can result in the introduction of serious toxic agents to the bloodstream with significant health consequences. *All* accidents and injuries, however minor or major, must be reported to the laboratory supervisor immediately and recorded in a logbook. The log should contain the date and time of the incident, a list of those present at that time, a description of what happened, and the immediate effects of any actual, suspected, or potential exposure. Open wounds, puncture wounds, or second- or third-degree burns require medical attention immediately. Any eye exposure requires immediate eye washing and medical attention.

Safety is everyone's responsibility. There should always be at least two people in a laboratory or experiment space at all times that experiments are being conducted and there should be a direct way to contact emergency response personnel available, such as a dedicated telephone line to the public safety office inside the laboratory space, to summon aid when needed. It is not possible to be *too* safe, and safety plans are an important part of every experiment design.

3 Sampling Source Media

Engineering experiments often involve some form of testing of materials. Those materials may be natural, such as water, soil, or air, or they may be manufactured materials. This chapter examines the accepted ways to sample the various forms of the selected materials to provide the most reliable outcomes.

It is noted that not all experiments require absolute purity of the media or materials being sampled. It often happens that the outcomes of an experiment are never going to be precisely correct because the media are constantly changing and their parameters are highly variable. The characteristics of wastewater, for example, change constantly, and before a sample can be returned to a laboratory adjacent to the sampling location, the composition of the wastewater at the sampling location may well have subtly changed. The procedure for sampling the wastewater, then, is more a matter of not significantly changing the value of the parameters to be measured, without regard for what happens to other parameters. Similarly, soil does not change as rapidly as liquid in terms of chemical or mineral composition during sampling events. The key with soil and other solids is only to avoid contamination of the sample from outside sources such that the test data represent only the soil or solids conditions at the sampling location at the time of sampling and nothing else. Soil gases, however, are very difficult to maintain even over short periods, and careful consideration of how to avoid agitation of samples during sampling and how to stabilize the gas content is important in sampling those soil conditions where soil gases are an important component being tested.

3.1 SAMPLING WATER AND OTHER LIQUIDS

The sampling of liquids for experimentation presents some interesting challenges for environmental engineers. Liquids tend to be subject to component concentration changes based on surface pressures, temperatures, and short time frames during which reactions of internal components can occur. It is imperative, then, to ensure that samples are collected in such a way as to minimize the opportunity for such changes to occur. It is also useful in many cases to add a preservative to a sample to reduce chemical reactions within the sample between the time of sampling and the time of testing.

Liquids are generally amenable to in situ testing of various parameters using portable testing equipment. Dissolved oxygen, temperature, pH, suspended solids concentration, electrical conductivity, and some chemical concentrations, such as ammonia, ammonium, nitrite, nitrate, chlorides, and phosphate, can be measured in real time by inserting probes into the liquid, whether flowing or still, to generate accurate, real-time data. When possible, this is the preferred method of sampling and testing liquids.

DOI: 10.1201/9781003184249-3

When in situ testing of liquids is not possible for any reason, samplers must consider ways to minimize changes between the sampling and the testing.

Table A.1, in the Appendix, provides several useful columns of information relative to the sampling and testing of liquids. This table is provided by the U.S. Environmental Protection Agency (EPA) as a guideline for collecting, preserving, and testing samples that are potentially going to be subject to court challenge and to provide a mechanism for consistent sample collection and handling. In most cases, undergraduate students in university laboratories do not need to be quite so precise in their sampling and handling methods. However, the discussion that follows does provide guidance on how routine samples are collected and handled for consistent laboratory results. The following data are provided in Table A.1.

- Column 1 – a selected list of parameters for which liquid environmental samples are frequently tested.
- Column 2 – suggested sample testing methodologies defined by U.S. EPA test protocol numbers with which all commercial laboratories are familiar and which are described in various Standard Methods of Analysis manuals. Note that not all laboratories use the same test procedure for each compound or chemical and that it is important to know which test method is being used for consistency of results.
- Column 3 – a type of recommended sample containers and sample volumes to be collected.
- Column 4 – recommended preservatives to be used to prevent or minimize changes over short time periods after sampling or preservation.
- Column 5 – accepted transport and holding conditions recognized as essential for minimizing changes over short time frames.
- Column 6 – accepted holding times for samples which have been preserved as recommended in the previous columns. Data from a sample which is not tested within the recommended holding times should be regarded as suspect.

Where the table calls for the addition of a preservative, it is usually considered appropriate to ask the laboratory providing the sample jars to add the preservative in advance. The sample jar then needs to be carefully filled, using a nonturbulent filling method, to avoid overfilling and losing any of the preservative. It is common to use a secondary container to collect the sample and to fill the transportation container slowly from the collected sample. Note that when grease and oil components are being measured, the use of a secondary container is strongly discouraged due to the potential for various components of the oil and grease mixture to adhere differently to the walls of the secondary container, thereby changing the concentrations in the tested sample.

Nonturbulent sampling means that the sample is collected slowly in a jar or vial by submerging the sampling jar into the liquid and allowing it to slowly fill when not using a sample container with preservative pre-entered. This usually implies laying the jar into the liquid sideways, slowly lowering it into the liquid, then turning it upright, slowly removing it from the liquid, and immediately screwing a tight lid on top. If the sample requires a preservative, the preservative may be added by inserting an eyedropper or pipette with the appropriate volume of preservative to the bottom of the filled sample jar and slowly injecting the preservative, allowing the excess liquid to spill out of the top of the jar. The cap is then screwed on tightly as soon as the preservative has been added. There should be no air trapped above the sample inside the sample jar – a condition referred to as leaving no headspace. If a sampling container does have preservative pre-added, it is usually best to use a secondary container to collect the sample and to then fill the transport container slowly from the secondary one such that a small meniscus appears above the lip of the container to prevent air entrapment when the lid is immediately screwed on tightly. As noted above, when grease and oil components are being measured, the use of a secondary container is strongly discouraged due to the potential for various components of the oil and grease mixture to adhere differently to the walls of the secondary container, thereby changing the concentrations in the tested sample.

It is not uncommon to require samples of liquids to be collected from various depths at the same sampling location. Inserting a sampling jar at the surface and lowering it to the desired depth before pulling it out and then capping it generally causes cross-contamination of the sample from the shallower depth to the deeper one. To avoid this, sampling devices are available commercially that allow a sealed container to be lowered to the desired depth, then opened at the selected depth. The container is resealed in situ, at depth, after the container is filled, and then retrieved. This helps to mitigate the cross-contamination issue.

When sampling a monitoring well, the sample is collected in a bailer, typically with a small ball valve at the bottom. The valve ball is lifted with a short tube inserted into the bottom of the bailer after it has been extracted from the well. The tube is inserted slowly enough to avoid rapid discharge of the fluid into the sample jar or vial, and the sample is allowed to run down the side of the container as the container is slowly turned right side up. A small meniscus on top of the liquid should be seen as the cap is tightly placed on the container.

Most tests of liquid samples require only a very small aliquot of sample – typically 1 mL or less. These are typically collected in a 40 mL volatile organic analysis (VOA) vial rather than a larger jar. That allows for preservatives to be used in small quantities when things like petroleum hydrocarbons are being tested, for example, but requires more care when filling the vials to avoid issues such as loss of preservatives, nonturbulence when filling, and the presence of a meniscus on top of the liquid before applying the cap to avoid an air pocket on top of the liquid. Smaller sample jars also conserve space in field coolers and minimize the waste disposal problem at the laboratory. Thus, smaller jars are preferred when they are reasonable.

A special scanning test for volatile petroleum hydrocarbons in water is the Headspace Analysis (see Attachment II in the Massachusetts DEP Guidance Manual at: https://www.mass.gov/doc/wsc-94-400-interim-remediation-waste-management-policy-for-petroleum-contaminated-soils/download). This test is performed on-site when volatile petroleum hydrocarbons are expected to provide an indication of the concentration of those contaminants in the sampled media. An 8 or 16 oz "mason-type" jar of sample is collected half full and immediately sealed with aluminum foil followed by a screw-on lid without the metal insert. The sample is then "vigorously" shaken for 15 seconds and then allowed to rest for about 10 minutes for the headspace concentrations to develop. The sample is then vigorously shaken a second time, immediately before testing. When the ambient temperatures are below 0°C (32°F), headspace development should be done within a heated vehicle or building.

At the end of the 10 minute development period, the probe of a photoionization detector (PID), a flame ionization detector (FID), or a similar testing device is inserted through the foil liner into the interior of the headspace to a depth of about half the depth of the headspace, avoiding direct contact with the sample. The highest reading on the PID or FID device that shows immediately after the probe is inserted (it will decline quickly from the peak reading) is taken as the approximate (*very* approximate) concentration of volatile petroleum hydrocarbons present in the headspace over the sample. Normally, if that initial reading indicates a likely concentration of 10 ppm or higher, a sample is required to be collected for laboratory analysis.

3.2 SAMPLING SOIL OR OTHER SOLIDS

Sampling soils or other solid and semisolid materials requires a somewhat different approach than used for liquid samples. This type of medium includes all soil types, sludges, lees, sediments, and other solid or semisolid materials. Small samples of these materials are generally collected from larger samples that are well mixed to ensure that when a one gram aliquot is later tested in the laboratory, that very small aliquot adequately represents the soil characteristics of the larger mass.

When compositing a sample from a larger mass, several samples of one to two cubic feet of material are collected from various locations throughout the mass of material to be tested. Care needs to be taken to ensure that all components of the mass are represented in approximately the same concentration in the collected samples as they exist in the original mass. The number of samples collected in this manner depends on the mass or area to be tested. Generally, one sample per cubic yard ($0.75 \, m^3$) of material will be adequate. Those samples are then placed on a clean plastic tarp or in a clean mixer and thoroughly mixed so that any sample collected from the mixed pile will likely be a fair representation of the mass as a whole. A sufficient sample for testing is then collected from the composite mix and returned to the laboratory for analysis. Grain size analysis may require a larger sample of several cubic feet, while chemical analysis may better be represented by a smaller, 8–16 oz (250–500 mL) sample from the composite mix. Chemical analyses are done on one gram aliquot from the sample jar, and commercial laboratories seldom remix samples prior to testing unless specifically instructed to do so (and paid for that time and effort).

Note that soil being tested for volatile organic content cannot be sampled and mixed in the manner described for general soil sampling. Doing so would dramatically reduce the volatile component concentrations and destroy the accuracy of any future tests. In that case, a small, one milligram, sample is collected from each of the proposed sampling locations within the mass and carefully placed into a sampling jar or VOA vial. The composite sample is not mixed at that time, but the composite sample is fixed with a preservative, typically methanol in a 1:1 ratio of methanol volume per unit volume of soil, to extract the petroleum components. The methanol is then tested for the concentration of the extracted petroleum components, with the methanol components being subtracted from the results, rather than the soil being tested directly. The Headspace Analysis (MA DEP) test is performed on-site when volatile petroleum hydrocarbons are expected to provide an indication of the concentration of those contaminants in the sampled media. Table A.2, in the Appendix, provides several useful columns of information relative to the sampling and testing of soils and other solids, including:

- Column 1 – a selected list of parameters for which liquid environmental samples are frequently tested.
- Column 2 – suggested sample testing methodologies defined by U.S. EPA test protocol numbers with which all commercial laboratories are familiar and which are described in various Standard Methods of Analysis manuals. Note that not all laboratories use the same test procedure for each compound or chemical and that it is important to know which test method is being used for consistency of results.
- Column 3 – type of recommended sample containers and sample volumes to be collected.
- Column 4 – recommended preservatives to be used to prevent or minimize changes over short time periods after sampling or preservation.
- Column 5 – accepted transport and holding conditions recognized as essential for minimizing changes over short time frames.
- Column 6 – accepted holding times for samples which have been preserved as recommended in the previous columns. Data from a sample which is not tested within the recommended holding times should be regarded as suspect.

3.3   SAMPLING AIR AND OTHER GASES

There are several ways to sample air and other gaseous media besides taking a deep breath and hoping that nothing bad happens. These methods span the continuum from scanning tests that will indicate the presence of a target compound and provide a colorimetric indication of the concentration, to precise, time-based, composite samplers from which samples can later be collected for very precise measurements in the parts per trillion (ppt) range.

Among the least expensive (but also one of the least accurate) methods is a Draeger Tube, a Tenax Tube, or an equivalent system. These devices are thin, clear, glass tubes filled with a specific proprietary resin which is selected to capture the target compound for that tube and to change color in the process. The length of the tube resin which changes color, or sometimes the brilliance of the color, will indicate the approximate concentration of that compound in the tested air. Markings along the side of the tube provide an easy mechanism for determining the approximate concentration. The air is introduced to the tube by breaking off a seal at both ends, inserting one end into a small displacement pump, drawing the handle of the pump to pull a preset volume of air through the tube, allowing a specified amount of time to expire for the reactions to take place, and reading the results from observing the changes in the resin. These are single-use devices, and after use, they are disposed as hazardous waste. They are available, however, for the testing of air for a very wide range of chemicals and petroleum hydrocarbons. These tests are most appropriate as a scanning tool to indicate the probable need for more precise testing.

When testing air for particulates, and certain specific compounds such as oxygen (O_2), carbon dioxide (CO_2), hydrogen sulfide (H_2S), and particulates, including specific sizes of particulates such as $PM_{2.5}$ and PM_{10} particulates, a small pump is employed to draw composite samples over a predetermined time and a set volumetric draw rate. For chemical testing, the air is drawn through a proprietary observation chamber for chemical constituents, which typically uses a specific light source to ionize the target chemical and record the concentration in parts per million (ppm) or parts per billion (ppb) of the volume passed through the device. For particulates, a proprietary filter is used to capture the particulates. The clean filter is weighed before being attached to the pump and weighed again at the end of the preset sampling period. The difference is the mass of the target particulates captured for the volume of air pulled through the filter. Note that this means that a $PM_{2.5}$ filter, for example, will capture everything larger than $2.5\,\mu m$ and that it will be necessary to subtract out all unwanted sizes by simultaneously filtering the air through a prefilter that removes everything larger than the target filter size.

There are a limited number of samplers available for specific air contaminants; however, those of significant concern in certain industries are well developed. H_2S, O_2, and CO_2 samplers, for example, are widely used in the hazardous material (HazMat) responder industry and in those professions which require entrance to confined or potentially hazardous spaces, such as sewers and subsurface electric company access pits.

For sampling air in order to conduct very accurate testing, using things such as gas chromatographs, for example, it is necessary to use a gas sampling bag or a SilcoCan. These are typically stainless steel canisters of various volume capacities that are evacuated to a very high vacuum, connected to a special valve arrangement that can be set to pass a specific volume of air per specified unit of time or to cycle on and off for preset sampling times at preset time intervals. That allows flexibility for the sampler to be able to sample a one-time sample or a time-based composite sample over any time frame up to, typically, 24 hours. The unit then shuts down completely, and the sampler can collect the canister at his or her leisure. The canister is then taken to a laboratory, and the contents are released directly into a gas chromatograph or similar electronic device for testing of various known or unknown compounds in the sampled air.

An alternative to the canister is the use of gas sampling bags. These are typically neoprene bags of standard fixed volume. A specialized valve is attached to a port on the bag, similar to the valves and ports on a SilcoCan. These valves are also programmable for collection options and will allow an attached pump to force a preset volume of air into the bag at preset intervals. At the prescribed end of the test period, the valves shut off completely and the sampler may collect the bag at a convenient future time. The issue with this procedure is that any target compound which could react with the neoprene will not be measured in useable concentrations and occasionally an unknown compound will react with the bag and add or subtract from a target compound even when the reaction of the target compound with the bag is not direct.

Canisters and bags have the advantage of collecting large samples of air and being subjected to electronic analysis can yield data on a wide range of compounds not specifically targeted. The location of a peak on the timeline of the resin used in the gas chromatograph may indicate a specific compound and concentration not expected, or at least indicate the need to test for a few compounds that elute in the same temperature and time range using different resins where problems are potentially observed.

Canisters are quite expensive to buy and difficult to clean and maintain. Accordingly, most samples done using a canister are contracted out to a specialized air quality testing firm that specializes in this equipment and can guarantee the cleanliness of the canisters, the reliability of the valves and programming systems, and the accuracy of the test data.

3.4   SAMPLING HEALTH AND SAFETY PLANS

Health and Safety Plans (HASPs) will vary depending on the site and the materials being tested. The purpose of a HASP is to ensure maximum protection for those doing the sampling and the environment. For work on designated or suspected hazardous waste disposal or release sites, HASPs should follow guidelines provided by OSHA at: https://www.osha.gov/Publications/OSHA3114/OSHA-3114-hazwoper.pdf.

At a minimum, HASPs for hazardous waste disposal or release sites should include instructions and guidelines regarding the following items:

- Names, positions, and contact information for key on-site sampling personnel and for health and safety personnel on-site or available for immediate contact
- Site or incident-specific risk assessment addressing sample collection activities
- Training requirements
- Personal protective equipment (PPE) on-site and usage requirements
- Medical screening requirements (maintain confidential documents properly and securely)
- Site or incident control
- Emergency response plan, containing off-site emergency contact information such as local hazardous materials response teams or additional trained rescue personnel (29 CFR 1910.38)
- Entry and egress procedures
- Spill containment
- Decontamination procedures

Most sites are not going to be hazardous waste disposal or release sites. Accordingly, the extent of sampling is not going to pose sufficient risk to justify the extensive procedures outlined in the cited OSHA standard. In those cases, the HASP needs to address the following items:

- Sampling location
- Sampling plan (what media will be sampled, a map of where to collect samples, a list of sample containers needed, including coolers with ice, sampling tools needed, cleaning supplies, preservatives to be used, and PPE needed)
- Personnel assigned to the site to do the sampling (at least two people are required for all field sampling events)
- A listing of the risks known or suspected to be present on the site, including things like slippery slopes, poisonous plants, bees and hornets, spills of acidic preservatives on a person or to the environment, and any other risks known or perceived
- A plan for minimizing potential exposure to identified hazards
- A plan for what to do if exposed to a hazard on-site
- PPE to be used (generally, vinyl or rubber gloves and eye protection and with respirators if volatile or toxic gases are expected to be present)
- Plan for disposal of contaminated PPE and hazardous wastes at the end of sampling

A HASP is not intended to be a burden or a hindrance to effective sampling, but rather a reasonable evaluation of risks posed, risk management, and exposure response so that safety is properly considered before the team visits the sampling location.

In the laboratory, the same safety concerns encountered in the field are expected to be encountered during testing. A Safety Plan is included as part of every experiment design to ensure that the experimenter has thought through the risks inherent in the work at hand, how to minimize or eliminate those risks, how to protect against exposure, and what to do in the event of accidental exposure.

4 Expected Outcomes and Interpretation of Data

4.1 EXPECTED OUTCOMES

The point of an experiment is to determine whether a predicted or expected outcome from some change in conditions is reasonable or accurate. That implies, therefore, that some expected or desired outcome is known. It may be reasonably predicted, for example, from the sample experiment discussed so far that the water temperature will not affect the dissolved oxygen concentration in a moving stream as much as it would in a sedentary beaker of oxygenated water in a laboratory. There are lots of tables available to indicate the maximum dissolved oxygen concentration possible in pure water at various temperatures (see Table A.7 in the Appendix, for example), and those precise temperatures not shown can be linearly inferred from the laboratory data so tabulated. In that case, however, the water is pure, usually distilled and deionized, carefully controlled to a precise temperature, and very carefully measured for dissolved oxygen multiple times to establish a specific value for the expected oxygen content of water constrained under those conditions. There are very few uncontrolled parameters in that experiment and the data are precisely predictable for similar conditions.

Such is not the case for field experiments or for experiments with water not meeting the sedentary, distilled, and deionized purity upon which the tabulated data are based. It is useful, then, to think through what the likely effects will be from varying the water temperature in the field, adding natural turbulence, allowing for the influence of dissolved minerals and organics not measured, allowing for sediment transport against the probes, and allowing for rainfall upstream of the study area and in the study area directly.

Sometimes, it may not be possible to predict the outcome from the experiment. That is rare, however, and it is a situation that should be avoided whenever possible. Going forward without any idea of the expected outcome can lead to dangerous experimental conditions for which adequate safety precautions have not been taken. No data are worth dying for or being severely injured over.

More normally, a question of "What would happen if...?" has been posed with the desired outcome being a positive one (even if that implies reducing the effects of a negative outcome). A discussion of the likely effects will normally ensue between knowledgeable persons and an expected outcome will be determined. An experiment is then designed to verify, *or refute*, the expected outcome. The reason it is necessary to understand, recognize, and manage this process is that a designer will almost always be predisposed to develop a design to prove his or her point. That design may then actually, although not necessarily deliberately or consciously, eliminate any data that may disprove the expected outcome or minimize its value, even if the basic

DOI: 10.1201/9781003184249-4

theory was correct. The fallacy not found in the data will be discovered by others trying to replicate the data, and the original experimenter will end up being professionally embarrassed. Therefore, the experiment design must assume a stated objective
and expected result before the design is done. This will minimize or eliminate the
interferences discussed earlier, lead to a cleaner outcome data set, and minimize the
potential for flawed experiment design to be shown later by others.

4.2   INTERPRETATION OF THE DATA

Most data are fundamentally useless. As independent numbers or values, data are
meaningless. All data, then, require analysis and interpretation before they become
useful. If the experimenter is interested only in the variation of dissolved oxygen
concentration with water temperature in a specific stream at a specific location over
some period of time, measurement of those two parameters over an extended period
should provide sufficient data to predict the average temperature and dissolved oxygen correlation at that location because nothing else mattered. Whatever unmeasured
parameters were present and how they affected the dissolved oxygen concentration
are unimportant to the resulting value. By plotting the water temperature against dissolved oxygen concentration from the collected data, a reasonably accurate prediction could be made for the dissolved oxygen content in that stream, at that location,
given the water temperature at that location at some time in the future.

A more generalized form of the basic question, as posed at the beginning of
Chapter 2, requires that the dissolved oxygen concentration in any stream meeting
the stated flow and depth characteristics be predictable based on a temperature reading at any time in the future. When the basic question is so broadened, the simplicity of the experimental data used in the first instance is no longer valid. Now the
question involves a consideration of all of the unmeasured parameters previously
discussed. It is incumbent upon the experimenter, then, to measure as many of those
otherwise unmeasured parameters as possible and to relate the change in dissolved
oxygen to temperature by adjusting for the effects of the other parameters. A mathematical formula can then be established in which the concentration or presence of
other factors can be input to generate an expected dissolved oxygen concentration
based on temperature for a given stream or location at which those other parameters
are also known or estimable.

Note that "estimable" is an important concept here. Even where data have been
measured over an extended period of time, they are going to be variable. No matter
what value is then chosen to represent the parameter at any given moment, it is likely
to be wrong. That introduces a parameter of uncertainty into the mix. Uncertainty
can be useful if a broad range of values for the outcome is desired, since that is what
uncertainty forces the experimenter to accept. More commonly, however, the more
precise the answer can be, and therefore the least uncertainty in the data, the better
the experimenter will feel about the results.

Uncertainty is a function of statistics and statistics are a function of probability. To
understand the risks of uncertainty, it is necessary to understand a few fundamental
facts about probability and statistics. While not a treatise on probability or statistics,
the following discussion should help ease the way to evaluating data on a rational basis.

4.3 UNCERTAINTY CONSIDERATIONS

The future is not known. Yet engineering experiments are done all the time as though the future was accurately known and predictable, and those experimental outcomes will always be the same for the same experiment. Clearly, there is a disconnect here. That disconnect is called uncertainty. In fact, what the future will hold and how unmeasured parameters of experiments will change over time are not known, and it is necessary to consider future uncertainty in the analysis of experimental outcomes.

The best way to do that is to begin by making a careful estimate of all the important variables involved in the decision. Then the concept of predicting a range of possible outcomes should be carefully considered. Finally, what happens when the probabilities of the various outcomes are known, or can be reliably estimated, should be incorporated into the experimental design process.

Estimates and their use in experimental design require evaluation of the future consequences of alternatives. The accuracy of these estimates can, and often do, have significant consequences on the decisions made, particularly when the estimates are not made carefully enough at the outset.

4.4 ESTIMATING FUTURE PARAMETER VALUES

It is usually more realistic to describe the future value of parameters with a range of possible values, rather than a single estimated future value. Such a range could include an optimistic estimate, the most likely estimate, and a pessimistic estimate, for example. Then the outcome data analysis can determine whether the decision is sensitive to the range of projected values, and, if so, by how much.

A table can be created with all of the variables listed followed by their individual optimistic, most likely, and pessimistic values. If there are only a couple of such variables, it is easy enough to calculate from the analysis using all the values to see which is most sensitive. When there are a lot of variables, however, this becomes more problematic, and also, because each of the variables is likely affected in some way by all the others, the total range of possibilities gets out of hand quickly.

This can be addressed by using an average or mean value for each parameter to conduct the analysis. The equation for this mean, weights the "most likely" value four times as heavily as each of the other two estimates, as follows:

$$\text{Mean value} = \left[\left(\text{optimistic value} \right) + 4 \left(\text{most likely value} \right) + \left(\text{pessimistic value} \right) \right] / 6$$

4.5 PROBABILITY

Statistical analysis of environmental data is an important tool for understanding the implications of the data over time. It is important to understand the relationship between changes in data over both long time periods and short time periods. Environmental data are not static, and they do change rapidly. They tend to go up and down regularly, and it is the trend over time that matters most. The causes of short-term changes are important, but not as critical as the long-term changes, in most cases. Statistical analyses can smooth out the seasonal and noise variability in the data to indicate to the engineer whether the long-term trends are favorable.

Statistical data, however, are seldom believed or taken at face value by an audience. Even a sophisticated and technically savvy audience will look at statistical data askance and be wary of interpretations made on the basis of those data. Therefore, it behooves the engineer to be as precise and careful as possible with the presentation of statistical data if the engineer is to be believed in the end. People "know" that engineers and mathematicians "lie" with statistics "all the time" and that any outcome derived from statistics must be viewed with severe skepticism.

4.5.1 Probability as Basis of Statistics

One of the least well-understood concepts of statistical analysis is that statistics are based on probabilities, not absolutes. Factual data are developed from which to predict future events and outcomes, but the data set is never complete, and it is a historic data set, not a future data set. Thus, any event predicted by the data for the future will necessarily be subject to doubt and some real probability that the prediction will be wrong. This uncertainty is a paramount parameter of probability analyses and, therefore, also a paramount parameter of statistical analysis.

Probability plays a significant role in the management of risk and uncertainty in engineering data analysis. There are certain logical or mathematical rules for probability. If an outcome can never happen, then the probability is 0, or 0%. If an outcome will certainly happen, then the probability is 1, or 100%. This means that probabilities can neither be less than 0 nor more than 1. They must fall within the range of 0–1.

Probabilities are defined such that the sum of the probabilities for all possible outcomes is 1, or 100%. Summing the probabilities that the value of a specific parameter will remain the same, increase in the future, or decrease in the future, for example, shows that each of these three possible outcomes could have a probability of exactly one out of three, or 0.3333, for a sum of 1.0 for all possible outcomes. They could also each have a range of possible values, but the sum of the three values must always add to exactly 1.0.

For example, a drilling program for a potable water well can have three possible outcomes: a dry hole; water, but not in useable quantities; or water in a useable quantity. The probabilities of these three outcomes must always sum to 100% since one of these outcomes must occur.

In most probability books, many different probability, or frequency, distributions are presented. These distributions describe the results of large numbers of trials yielding large populations of data from which probabilities can be quite easily derived. In engineering experimentation, however, it is more common to use two to five outcomes to determine probabilities, even though two to five outcomes can only approximate the total range of possibilities. This is done for two reasons. First, the data are often estimated from expert judgment, not actual experimentation; so using numerous estimated data values would suggest a false sense of accuracy or precision. Second, each outcome requires additional analysis, and the resources are seldom available to provide those analyses. The use of two to five trials, then, has become a standard, accepted, trade-off between accuracy and efficiency.

There are lots of different probabilities that can be developed. If there is more than one variable present, then the probabilities of any two or more occurring at the same time are called *joint probabilities*.

For example, if a fair coin is flipped and a fair die rolled at the same time, the probability of a head coming up for the coin toss is 1/2. The probability of a 4 coming up when the die is rolled is 1/6. The joint probability, when flipping the coin and rolling the die, of getting both a head on the coin and a 4 on the die is the product of the two probabilities, or $1/2 \times 1/6$ or 1/12. Notice that there are 12 possible outcomes between the head or tail of the coin and any of the 6 numbers on the die. Therefore, each outcome has a probability of 1/12. The sum of all the possibilities is still equal to exactly $12 \times 1/12 = 1$ or 100%. Note here that the order in which the results are determined is not important and that there is only one unique set of data possible for each data point.

This simple example clearly demonstrates the concept of determining the probability of an outcome based on *permutations*, rather than *combinations* of the options. The difference between *combinations* and *permutations* is the order in which the outcomes are selected. With *permutations* the order in which the outcomes are selected matters, whereas with *combinations* it does not matter. For example, if a lock "combination" were made up of four numbers, 1–4, there are 12 possible combinations that could be made from those four numbers. If the correct combination is 2143, but 1243 is entered, the lock will not open because the numbers entered are in the wrong order – in essence, the *permutation* selected is incorrect. With "combination locks", the correct sequence is actually a permutation, not a combination, in probability terms.

The equation for determining the number of possible permutations among a set of values is:

$$P = n! / (n - r)!$$

where:

  P = permutation probability of occurrence
  n = the number of things to choose from
  $!$ = the factorial function, which means that the answer is a multiplication of each value in the series together ($3! = 3 \times 2 \times 1$, for example)
  r = the number of things to be selected

This equation assumes no repetition of the selected numbers, but the order of selection *does* matter.

Therefore, the probability of winning a lottery run with permutation rules (which is NOT the way lotteries are run) and which requires the gambler to select 5 numbers from a pool of 69, followed by one number from a pool of 26, would be calculated as:

$$P = 69! / (69 - 5)!$$

or

$$P = (69)(68)(67)(66)(65)(64!) / (64!)$$

which means that $P = 1,348,621,560$.

In this case, however, there is also a need to select a single number from a pool of 26 numbers, so the above quotient needs to be multiplied by 26 to yield a total number of permutations of

$$P = (1,348,621,560)(26)$$

$$P = 35,064,160,560$$

And the odds of winning that lottery are 1 in 35,064,160,560.

Calculating the odds in this fashion implies that the order in which the numbers are selected by the gambler must be identical to the order in which the numbers are selected by the lottery computer. That means that this calculation infers that there are 35,064,160,560 possible combinations of the 5 numbers *when the order in which the numbers are selected is important.*

Lottery games do not rely on selecting the numbers in any specific order, as shown by the order in which they are drawn when watching that event occur live on television. Therefore, the 6 numbers selected by the gambler can be selected in a different order by the lottery computer and the gambler will still win. When the order of selecting the numbers does not matter, the calculation becomes a combination problem, not a permutation problem, and is done in the following manner:

$$C = [n!/(n-r)!] \times 1/r!$$

or

$$C = n!/r!(n-r)!$$

where:

C = combination probability of occurrence
n = the number of things to choose from (in the current lottery problem that would be 69)
! = the factorial function
r = the number of things to be selected (in the current lottery problem that would be 5).

This equation also assumes no repetition of the selected numbers, and that the order of selection does *not* matter. The reason the 26 is used as a separate multiplier is that this value includes the same numbers to select from as the first 26 of the 69 from which the first 5 values are selected. The "replacement" of the value to select the last digit requires a separate multiplication.

Using this equation, the odds of winning the example lottery, a combination problem, rather than a permutation problem, are calculated as:

$$C = (69)!/(5)!(64)!$$

$$C = (1,348,621,560)/(120)$$

$$C = 11,238,513$$

Multiplying that sum by 26 for the number of options for the last number yields:

$$P = (11,238,513)(26)$$

$$P = 292,201,338$$

And the chances of winning this lottery are increased to a mere 1 in 292,201,338. Still not very good, but way better than 35 billion to one against! Those are the odds of winning that would be published by the lottery commission involved in the lottery used for this example. That is also why lottery jackpot winners are rare relative to the number of players.

This concept of probability influences on experimental data starts to become important when the interferences become less well defined but are important to the evaluation of the data. The probability of things happening assumes a random selection of outcomes. When outcomes stop being random, the probabilities change rapidly and often unpredictably.

4.5.2 ESTIMATING PROBABILITIES IN EXPERIMENTATION

The probabilities of interest during experimentation are almost always associated with negative events: the probability that something bad is going to happen. It is usually very difficult, if not impossible, to accurately measure the probability of potential adverse events occurring. It can be instructive to examine past experiments of similar kinds to see what went wrong there and to carefully consider the adverse events occurring with the prior experiment to see what could go wrong with a current experiment. Looking then at what caused the adverse event, and what could have been done to prevent it, can be useful in reducing the risk of that event occurring anew.

A useful process for developing an estimate of the probability of an adverse event can be the use of average probabilities. Consider, for example, the potential failure of a specific probe being used to generate data. A specific probability is unlikely to be available to reflect the potential for this failure. Begin then, with a *range* of possibilities for this event. Consider the most optimistic probability, the most likely probability, and the most pessimistic probability.

Once the three probabilities have been estimated, an average probability is calculated from the following equation previously proposed.

$$P_{avg} = [(\text{optimistic estimate}) + (4)(\text{most likely estimate})$$
$$+ (\text{most pessimistic estimate})] / 6$$

The resulting estimated probability is weighted toward the most likely value, but tempered with the reality that either of the other two probabilities could also occur.

For example, if the most optimistic estimate of the probability of failure of the probe is determined to be 1/100, the most likely estimate is 1/50, and the most pessimistic estimate is 1/20. Then the calculation would be:

$$P_{avg} = [(1/100) + (4)(1/50) + 1/20] / 6$$

$$P_{avg} = [(1/100) + (4/50) + (1/20)] / 6$$

$$P_{avg} = \left[(1/100)+(8/100)+(5/100)\right]/6$$

$$P_{avg} = \left[14/100\right]/6$$

$$P_{avg} = 2.3/100 \text{ or } 2.3\%$$

Notice that the resulting estimate in this case is better than the most likely estimate (2.0%) because the probability of the most likely estimate is better than the most optimistic estimate by much less (1%) than the most likely estimate is better than the most pessimistic (3%). That skews the average estimate toward the better, closer to, most optimistic estimate. The average is still worse than the most optimistic, but better than the most likely.

4.5.3   Misuse of Probability Data

Consider the following concepts and cases in which statistical data were poorly used, or even misused for nefarious purposes. The basic problem facing the statistical analyst is that any three or more data points can be analyzed by statistical methods. But the fewer the number of data points, the louder the noise, or misinformation, that is provided and the shakier the analytical outcome becomes. That causes poor or improper interpretation of the data and that poor interpretation yields incorrect analyses. The number of data points needed for effective prediction into the future depends on what the data represent and the use to which the analyses are intended to be put.

The following examples demonstrate this phenomenon:

Premise: The premise of an analysis presented at a technical seminar was that a new engineering course, based on project-based service-learning ideals, provided added value to the overall engineering program at the presenter's university and that specific design skills, and a broader set of skills for graduates to use to help them thrive within a global environment, were being successfully imparted to the students through this course.

Details: To document the validity of the premise, a survey instrument was sent to all program alumni. The survey was internally tested, first, to eliminate bias and ambiguity. 1,500 electronic requests were sent out, and 1,000 other alumni were sent a postcard with an electronic link to the survey. In addition, to encourage participation, a premium was offered to those who responded, regardless of their feelings or responses. There were approximately 600 respondents.

Findings and Conclusions Drawn: A very high percentage of the respondents found the course to be very helpful to them, individually, and agreed that the results would improve their project management skills going forward. The majority also agreed that this course would provide significant added value to the education offered by this program.

Problem: A total of 600 responses out of 2,500 survey requests is a reasonably large response pool, and a 23% response rate would normally give some fairly reliable data. However, in this case, the pool of respondents was self-selected, probably already felt good about the university (or, conversely, had really bad feelings about the university) and the data were going to have a bias, probably a positive bias, right from the start.

It is further noted that any survey that offers a premium for responding, regardless of the value of that premium, is already biased by the self-selection of the respondents and the generally improved feelings about the surveyors and the survey. Any analyses, then, are going to be unreliable, at best.

Similarly, a professor at a different school conducted a survey on the following basis:

Premise: A specific leadership and service-learning module in the first year of study positively impacted the success of students in subsequent years and increased interest in pursuing leadership careers.

Details: The subject leadership module was well designed and implemented as an elective course for all students who wished to take it, and the course included excellent leadership and service components. The first class of students who took the course, and a similar group of students in the same major and cohort who did not take that course, were surveyed at the end of the course to determine the validity of the premise. There were 87 respondents – 24% of those surveyed who took the leadership module responded (54 of the 87 respondents), and 18% of those surveyed who did not take the module responded (33 of the 87 respondents).

Findings and Conclusions Drawn: Those who did take the course found it very helpful, while those who did not take the course saw limited value in it. It was concluded, therefore, that the premise was correct, and it was predicted that this module would improve the leadership skills of all who took it in the future.

Problem: The course module was voluntary and taking the survey was voluntary. Those who took the course were already predisposed to leadership, and those who did not take the course were predisposed to not be interested in leadership. In addition, while the response rate is fine for statistical analysis, the actual numbers are so small as to be meaningless when projected over a much larger cohort and much further into the future. The data say only that the module may help those who want to lead and that it would likely do nothing for those who do not already want to lead. Any interpretation beyond that is speculative, at best.

4.5.4 NUMBER OF DATA POINTS NEEDED

Finally, it is important to note that the number of data points used in statistical analyses is important. Consider the following case of the traveler and the train:

A traveler who routinely rode a train into the city for work decided one day to accept a ride from a friend who happened to be going into the city on that day. Upon arrival at his office, on time, he noted a report on the radio that the train he normally rode, and the one on which he would have ridden that morning had he not accepted his friend's offer, had broken down, and was long delayed in arriving at the city. He had never experienced a train delay prior to that date and none since.

The statistics say that any time this rider accepts a ride from a friend, the train is going to break down – with 100% certainty – since every time he had taken a ride with a friend the train had, indeed, broken down, and every time he had ridden the train it had arrived on time. That is, of course, a false premise because the data set is nowhere near sufficient to justify either the premise or the conclusions, and there is no conceivable cause-and-effect relationship between the two events.

4.5.5 SELECTIVE USE OF DATA

The selective use of data implies the deliberate omission of data that do not support the hypothesis being tested. For example, if 152 data points were collected, but only 75 supported the hypothesis being tested, selective use of data would indicate that the 77 points that did not support the hypothesis would be ignored. Regardless of how the data are then displayed, ignoring the data that do not support the hypothesis is unethical and wrong.

Consider the case of air temperatures collected at precise intervals every month for 10 consecutive years and then averaged over those months to provide 10 data points for each month of the year; in essence, 10 years of average monthly data. Suppose a hypothesis that average air temperatures at the test site are declining, not increasing, as a result of presumed climate change effects. Assume, further, that the data are tabulated as shown in Table 4.1. This is a hypothetical example, so none of the data are real, but they do illustrate the principle involved.

The change in average annual temperature over the stated time frame is shown in Figure 4.1 on the basis of the Fictitious Data from Table 4.1.

Looking at the data in Table 4.1, it can be argued that the average annual temperature during the entire 10-year period did not change at all at this hypothetical location. The average temperature for the year 1996, shown at the bottom of the second column, is identical to the average of all the years at the end of the 10-year period, as shown at the bottom of the 12th column, and reinforced by the zero-change calculated in the lowest right-hand cell. That would, however, be a false reading of the data.

Notice is called to the linear trend line in the graph in Figure 4.1. There is an initial decline in average annual temperatures from 1996 to 1998. Thereafter, however, the average annual temperatures increase almost every year relative to the previous year, with the exception of 2002–2003. At the end of 2005, the average annual temperature is actually 0.7°F higher than that recorded in 1996 and 1.4°F higher than the lowest point recorded in 1998. Including the 10-year average number as the final data point on the chart skews the data, so that the casual reader may imply a conclusion that is not valid. Figure 4.2 shows this same chart without the 10-year average number, and the trend line increase is more dramatic – and truthful.

A person wanting to promote the concept that global warming has made a big difference in this community by raising the average annual temperatures might show Figure 4.2 without the average value in the calculations and neglect to note the effect

TABLE 4.1
Average Air Temperatures by Month and Year (Degrees F) (Fictitious Data)

Month	\u200b				Year						10-year Average	Change in Value
	1996	1997	1998	1999	2000	2001	2002	2003	2004	2005		
Jan	23.7	23.5	21.0	23.7	22.1	21.3	23.6	24.4	21.9	21.8	22.7	−1.0
Feb	27.5	26.7	26.6	26.7	27.5	28.9	27.6	29.4	32.3	31.6	28.5	1.0
Mar	38.7	38.2	39.4	37.5	39.5	37.7	36.8	35.2	37.3	37.4	37.8	−0.9
Apr	53.6	52.7	50.9	48.3	52.7	58.9	60.1	59.4	58.9	61.3	55.7	2.1
May	58.6	57.5	57.0	57.2	58.1	59.3	58.3	57.2	59.3	58.2	58.1	−0.5
Jun	66.1	66.9	66.4	66.1	65.9	67.8	66.3	65.2	67.7	66.8	66.5	0.4
Jul	72.6	71.2	70.6	69.9	70.5	70.4	71.2	71.9	74.2	72.7	71.5	−1.1
Aug	72.1	73.8	71.6	73.9	75.2	71.6	72.3	72.4	76.8	73.1	73.3	1.2
Sep	67.5	66.5	69.5	69.3	69.0	66.3	67.8	65.9	61.7	65.8	66.9	−0.6
Oct	50.1	51.7	50.8	50.9	50.1	50.3	50.4	50.3	50.1	50.8	50.6	0.5
Nov	32.6	33.7	31.9	30.7	32.6	31.6	30.5	32.9	30.9	31.8	31.9	−0.7
Dec	26.0	25.9	24.8	27.8	26.8	26.6	27.6	25.8	24.7	26.4	26.2	0.2
Avg. for the year	49.1	49.0	48.4	48.5	49.2	49.2	49.4	49.2	49.7	49.8	49.1	0.0

From: Hopcroft, Francis J., *Engineering Economics for Environmental Engineers*, Momentum Press, LLC, New York, NY, 2016.

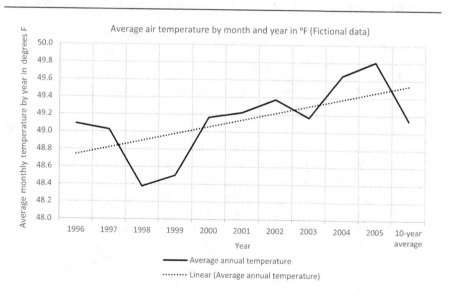

FIGURE 4.1 Average annual temperature over 10-year period (Fictitious Data from Table 4.1). (Hopcroft, Francis J., *Engineering Economics for Environmental Engineers*, Momentum Press, LLC, New York, NY, 2016.)

of averaging the temperatures over the 10-year data period. That person could also show the data for only every second month, as shown in Table 4.2.

From these 6 months of data, it can be argued that average monthly and annual temperatures at this location rose about 1.2°F over the 10-year period and that climate change effects are real. This conclusion is further demonstrated by Figure 4.2.

A person who is a climate change denier might use the other 6 months, as shown in Table 4.3, and argue that the average annual temperatures at that location have actually declined 0.5°F over the same 10-year period. That position would be further demonstrated with Figure 4.3 on which the data from Table 4.3 are plotted.

TABLE 4.2
Six Months of Average Annual Temperature Data Even Months

						Year					
Month	1996	1997	1998	1999	2000	2001	2002	2003	2004	2005	Change in Value
Feb	27.5	26.7	26.6	26.7	27.5	28.9	27.6	29.4	32.3	31.6	4.1
Apr	53.6	52.7	50.9	48.3	52.7	58.9	60.1	59.4	58.9	61.3	7.7
Jun	66.1	66.9	66.4	66.1	65.9	67.8	66.3	65.2	67.7	66.8	0.7
Aug	72.1	73.8	71.6	73.9	75.2	71.6	72.3	72.4	76.8	73.1	1.0
Oct	50.1	51.7	50.8	50.9	50.1	50.3	50.4	50.3	50.1	50.8	0.7
Dec	26.0	25.9	24.8	27.8	26.8	26.6	27.6	25.8	24.7	26.4	0.4
Avg. for the year	24.6	24.8	24.3	24.5	24.9	25.3	25.4	25.2	25.9	25.8	1.2

From: Hopcroft, Francis J., *Engineering Economics for Environmental Engineers*, Momentum Press, LLC, New York, NY, 2016.

TABLE 4.3
Six Months of Average Annual Temperature Data Odd Months

						Year					
Month	1996	1997	1998	1999	2000	2001	2002	2003	2004	2005	Change in Value
Jan	23.7	23.5	21.0	23.7	22.1	21.3	23.6	24.4	21.9	21.8	−1.9
Mar	38.7	38.2	39.4	37.5	39.5	37.7	36.8	35.2	37.3	37.4	−1.3
May	58.6	57.5	57.0	57.2	58.1	59.3	58.3	57.2	59.3	58.2	−0.4
Jul	72.6	71.2	70.6	69.9	70.5	70.4	71.2	71.9	74.2	72.7	+0.1
Sep	67.5	66.5	69.5	69.3	69.0	66.3	67.8	65.9	61.7	65.8	−1.7
Nov	32.6	33.7	31.9	30.7	32.6	31.6	30.5	32.9	30.9	31.8	−0.8
Avg. for the year	24.5	24.2	24.1	24.0	24.3	23.9	24.0	24.0	23.8	24.0	−0.5

From: Hopcroft, Francis J., *Engineering Economics for Environmental Engineers*, Momentum Press, LLC, New York, NY, 2016.

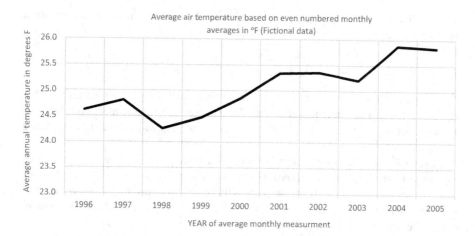

FIGURE 4.2 Average annual temperatures based on data from Table 4.2 (even months February through December). (Hopcroft, Francis J., *Engineering Economics for Environmental Engineers*, Momentum Press, LLC, New York, NY, 2016.)

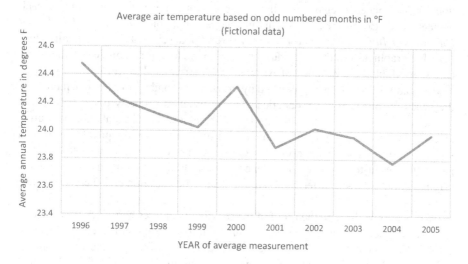

FIGURE 4.3 Average annual temperature over a 10-year period (odd months, January through November). (Hopcroft, Francis J., *Engineering Economics for Environmental Engineers*, Momentum Press, LLC, New York, NY, 2016.)

Clearly, the climate change proponent and the climate change denier cannot both be correct at the same time, but both have selected those data that support their position and ignored that which opposes their position. Both approaches are unethical and wrong. Note that these temperature values have been deliberately selected to illustrate the points being made here, and that data separation is seldom this neat and clean. Careful selection of data, however, without a clear presentation of the known data supporting an alternative view can be used to skew any analysis unfairly and unethically. A presenter only has to be caught at this once to ruin a reputation for a very long time.

4.5.6   Cause and Effect vs. Correlation

Notice, too, that statistics do not denote cause and effect, only a correlation between two presumably independent events. Ascribing cause and effect to mere correlation is an improper use of the statistical analysis tools and a good way to lose the confidence of any audience.

Statistical analysis assumes random samples. Samples that are not random, such as responses from self-selected individuals, are inherently biased, and the outcomes and conclusions based on those analyses will be equally biased. To overcome that, it is necessary to accept that statistical analyses are based on probabilities and to accept the notion that the outcomes are rife with uncertainty. That uncertainty needs to be carefully and clearly characterized as part of the statistics presentation. It is important to recognize and to show the audience that the data are only *perceptions* of reality and *not actual reality*.

To minimize the perception that the engineer or mathematician is not being truthful when presenting statistical data, it is also useful to first understand some additional basic concepts regarding why people do not believe statistics. An approach pioneered by Edward R. Tufte, in his classic book on *The Visual Display of Quantitative Information*,[1] was to display several data sets that are statistically identical, but graphically and numerically very different. See, for example, the following data sets, which are a variation of Anscombe's Quartet used by Tufte.

Anscombe's Quartet was published by Francis Anscombe in 1973[2] to demonstrate the necessity of visualizing statistical data in order to properly understand them. It consists of four sets of paired numbers, *X/Y* values, that are statistically equivalent within reasonable limits of common measures of statistical equivalence. A data set that comprises a variation of Anscombe's Quartet is shown in Table 4.4. The parameters used to evaluate equivalence among the data sets, their values for the original Anscombe's Quartet, and their values for the variation used here are shown in Table 4.5.

Without going through the proof of the statistical analyses here, they were all calculated in Excel by proper formulation, suffice it to be said that these four data sets are statistically identical based on the analytical tools utilized and the values shown in Table 4.4. Most of the accuracy statements in the third column of Table 4.5 come from an anonymous short essay titled *Anscombe's Quartet*, published May 16, 2011, at https://www.vernier.com/innovate/anscombes-quartet/ that describes the original Anscombe's Quartet. Other values shown in that column came from an Excel analysis of the presentation of this quartet by Edward Tufte in his book titled *The Visual Display of Quantitative Information*. The accuracy values shown in Column 5 of Table 4.5 were calculated in Excel on the basis of the values shown in Table 4.4.

[1] Tufte, E. R. (2001). *The Visual Display of Quantitative Information* (Second Edition). Cheshire, CT: Graphics Press.
[2] Anscombe, F. J. (1973, February). Graphs in statistical analysis. *American Statistician* 27, 17–21.

TABLE 4.4
Data Sets for Variation of Anscombe's Quartet

Set	X1	Y1	X2	Y2	X3	Y3	X4	Y4
	12.0	8.05	12.0	6.38	11.70	8.77	20.0	9.40
	8.0	6.81	8.0	8.51	8.05	8.04	9.0	9.00
	14.0	7.35	14.0	8.43	14.05	8.03	9.0	8.70
	7.0	6.85	7.0	7.63	6.81	7.21	9.0	8.58
	13.0	6.75	13.0	7.31	12.80	8.53	9.0	7.68
	15.0	9.71	15.0	9.35	15.29	6.69	9.0	7.78
	9.0	6.59	9.0	9.15	9.22	8.50	9.0	7.40
	5.0	6.12	5.0	5.69	5.11	5.10	9.0	7.98
	11.0	8.96	11.0	7.35	10.95	8.79	9.0	6.20
	10.0	9.16	10.0	8.55	9.99	8.67	9.0	6.01
	6.0	8.36	6.0	6.36	6.06	6.38	9.0	5.98
Average	10.00	7.70091	10.00	7.70091	10.00	7.70091	10.00	7.70091
Sum of squares	110.00	14.58549	110.00	14.59409	110.00	14.58989	110.00	14.59409
Variance	11	1.458549	11	1.459409	11.00418	1.458989	11	1.459409
Correl		0.460866		0.488184		0.483003		0.466471
RSQ		0.212398		0.238324		0.233292		0.217595
Linest		0.167818		0.177818		0.175872		0.169909

From: Hopcroft, Francis J., *Engineering Economics for Environmental Engineers*, Momentum Press, LLC, New York, NY, 2016.

It can be seen directly from the data in Table 4.4 that the numbers in these four sets of data are very different. It may, in fact, be difficult to discern where, or how, the sets of data were altered to make them identical – and they *were* mathematically altered to ensure that they are statistically equivalent – to the degree shown in Table 4.5.

To show these data in a way that allows an understanding of how different they are, in spite of their statistical equivalence, it is necessary to graph the four data sets separately; as shown in Figure 4.4, where it can be seen that the four data sets graph very differently. It is also clear from the graphs, and in hindsight from the data sets, where most of the outliers are that cause the statistical equivalence.

Therein lies a key consideration with the presentation of statistical data. Whether the outliers are used in the statistical analysis of the data is a matter of judgment on the part of the engineer. The decision to use or not use outliers will always be subject to challenge regardless of which decision is made. Generally, a true outlier can be ignored in environmental work, but only if the presence of the outlier is acknowledged, the justification for the decision to ignore it is provided and is cogent, and the effect of including it in the analyses is also acknowledged and described. In this case, for example, ignoring the outliers would dramatically change several of the plots

TABLE 4.5

Statistical Equivalency Values for the Original Anscombe's Quartet and the Variation of Anscombe's Quartet Shown in Table 4.4

Property	Anscombe's Value	Accuracy	Variation Quartet Value	Variation Quartet Accuracy
Number of data points per set	11	Exact	11	Exact
Mean of x (Average in Excel)	9	Exact	10.00	To 2 decimal places and exact in 3 of the four sets
Mean of y (Average in Excel)	7.50005	±0.0005	7.70091	Exact
Linear regression line	$Y = 3 + 0.5 x$	To 2 and 3 decimal places, respectively	$Y = 5.97 + 0.1728$	±0.03 and ±0.005, respectively
Standard error of estimate of slope	0.118	±0.0001	0.1065	±0.05
t	4.24	±0.002	1.6183	±0.06
Sum of squares, X-$\overline{X}$	110.0	Exact	110.00	To 4 decimal places except for 2 decimal places in set 3
Sum of squares, Y-$\overline{Y}$	41	To 0 decimal places	14.59	To 2 decimal places
Regression sum of squares	27.49	± 0.02	3.2880	± 0.19
Residual sum of squares of Y	13.7594	± 0.017	11.3021	± 0.186
Correlation coefficient (Correl in Excel)	0.816	To 3 decimal places	0.5	To 1 decimal place
r^2, or Coefficient of Determination of the linear regression (RSQ in Excel)	0.67	To 2 decimal places	0.22795	± 0.01035
Sample variance of x (Variance in Excel)	11	exact	11	To 3 decimal places
Sample variance of y	4.125	plus/minus 0.003	1.459	To 3 decimal places

From: Hopcroft, Francis J., *Engineering Economics for Environmental Engineers*, Momentum Press, LLC, New York, NY, 2016.

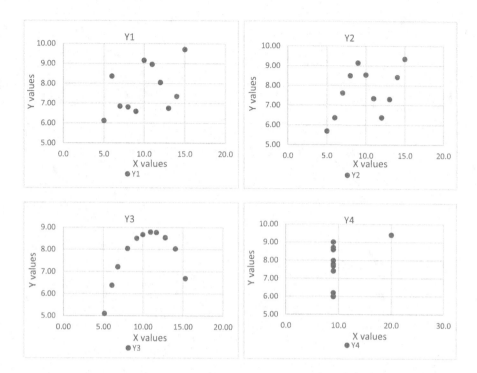

FIGURE 4.4 Charts of variation of Anscombe's Quartet. (Hopcroft, Francis J., *Engineering Economics for Environmental Engineers*, Momentum Press, LLC, New York, NY, 2016.)

and destroy the claim of statistical equivalence among the data sets. The engineer or mathematician can use only the data the analyst believes, *and can demonstrate*, are both relevant and valid, regardless of whether those data support the hypothesis being tested, and that outcome will be acceptable to the majority of reviewers if the justifications for ignoring other data are cogent, clear, and valid.

Figure 4.5 shows the same four charts shown in Figure 4.4, but with a trend line, or linear regression line, provided. In this case, all the outliers are included. Figure 4.6 shows what happens when the outlier in Y4 is ignored; the trend line remains straight but becomes vertical. That dramatically indicates why it is important to understand the effects of outliers.

Notice in the above-mentioned examples that all four data sets are analyzed using a linear regression line. Linear regression lines are typically used on data that are, in fact, linear. It can be seen from the plots of those data that only the first data set is in any way linear. The others would generally, and arguably more correctly, be analyzed using different forms of the regression line, such as exponential, logarithmic, polynomial (in one of several optional ways), power, or a moving average over an optional period length. Using a linear regression line with those data will yield interesting lines, but provide no useful information, particularly when the objective is to predict the future with a reasonable degree of certainty. The results mean exactly nothing; which is exactly what Anscombe was trying to point out in his use of a linear regression analysis on these types of data sets. Nevertheless, for consistency

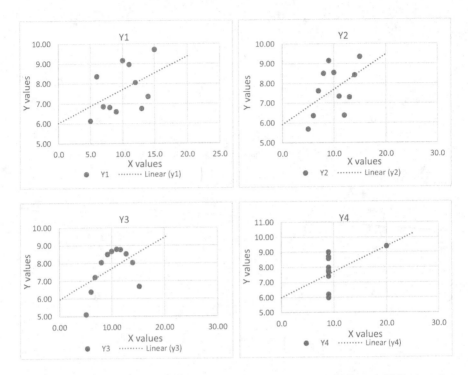

FIGURE 4.5 Charts in Figure 4.4 with trend lines shown. (Hopcroft, Francis J., *Engineering Economics for Environmental Engineers*, Momentum Press, LLC, New York, NY, 2016.)

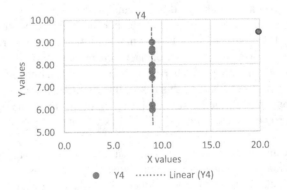

FIGURE 4.6 Y4 from Figure 4.5 with the outlier ignored; the trend line is vertical at 9.0. (Hopcroft, Francis J., *Engineering Economics for Environmental Engineers*, Momentum Press, LLC, New York, NY, 2016.)

with the equivalency calculations, and for consistency with the analyses done by Anscombe, a linear regression line was used here for all the data.

4.6   RISK

Risk can be thought of as the probability of getting an outcome other than the expected outcome, usually with an emphasis on something negative happening. One common measure of risk is the probability of a loss, for example. The other common measure of risk is the standard deviation, which measures the dispersion of outcomes around an expected value. With a Normal Distribution, represented by a standard bell curve, 68% of the values lie within ±1 standard deviation from the mean value and 95% of the values lie within ±2 standard deviations of the mean value.

Mathematically, the standard deviation is defined as the square root of the variance. The variance is defined as the weighted average of the squared difference between the outcomes of the random variable x and its mean. Thus, the larger the difference between the mean and the value, the larger the variance and the larger the standard deviation.

The equation is as follows:

$$\text{Standard deviation} = \left[\text{Expected value} \, (x - \text{mean})^2 \right]$$

Squaring the differences between the individual outcomes and the expected (mean) value ensures that positive and negative deviations all receive positive weights. Consequently, negative values for the standard deviation are not possible. Moreover, the standard deviation equals 0 if there is only one possible outcome. Otherwise, it is positive. Note that this is not the standard deviation formula built into most calculators, just as the weighted average is not the simple average built into most calculators. The calculator formulas are for n equally likely outcomes drawn from a sample of outcomes so that the probability of each outcome is always one. In engineering data analysis, a weighted average is used for the squared deviations since the outcomes are not equally likely.

5 Model Design Methodology

5.1 DISCUSSION

As indicated in several of the previous chapters, the design of an effective experiment requires consideration of many peripheral issues, along with the main question to be answered or observations to be made. It is useful to organize those concepts into a uniform format in order to manage them. This chapter provides an example of a useful format for achieving this goal. This example is a recommended model and not a template, so notice that where spaces are provided for data, the size of the space is irrelevant and sufficient space should be utilized to completely and adequately provide the information requested.

5.2 MODEL FORMAT

The following pages provide the recommended format for experiment design and data collection.

The title of the experiment provides a way to easily refer to the specific experiment design for the convenience of the investigators and others who may be reviewing or approving it. The title should be descriptive but does not need to be as comprehensive as an academic research paper.

The date is shown at the top so that any changes can be identified easily. Whenever a document is modified or adjusted insert a new date so that everyone using the document will be able to ascertain which version is being discussed.

The name and contact information for the principal investigator and any collaborators should be easily available and space is provided for that information.

The objective or question to be addressed needs to be clear and concise, following the guidance in Section 2.1 of this book.

The theory behind the experiment provides background and context to the question being addressed. It is intended to force thinking about why this experiment is being conducted, how it should be done, and the expected outcomes. Good research into this issue prior to initiation of the experiment design will ultimately lead to a much better outcome from the experiment.

The data to be collected section provides a way to focus the investigators on how the experiment will be conducted. It is axiomatic in engineering that in order to solve a problem it is first necessary to fully define the problem. Sometimes, it is just as important to determine what is not a part of the problem or out of scope of the experiment. How data are to be collected is best addressed after the list of desired data has been created, thereby defining the problem to be solved and how data will be collected.

DOI: 10.1201/9781003184249-5

A list of tools, equipment, and supplies is required to be developed to ensure that the procedures have been thoroughly thought through and that everything necessary for the experiment is available and on hand when needed.

Safety is a key consideration in everything an engineer does, including experimental work. In this section, the collaborators need to think through what could possibly go wrong, how to minimize that risk, and how to protect the experimenters and anyone around them in the event something does go wrong,

The next step is to think through the procedures to be followed during the experiment. That includes a discussion of what is included in each step and a plan for how each step will be performed. For example, collection of a water sample usually involves more than sticking an empty bottle into a stream and screwing the cap on after the jar is full. There is often a need to provide some preservative in the bottle before the sample is added, and therefore, overfilling will wash out the preservative and destroy the sample. In addition, rapidly filling a sample container can introduce oxygen during the transfer and invalidate a subsequent DO reading. Filling a sample jar too slowly can allow volatiles to escape, thereby invalidating those analyses later. How the sample is to be collected, then, is dictated by the preservation methods and the planned analysis procedure for the sample. Chapter 3 describes the best methods used to sample various media.

Potential interferences and their resolution are key to a successful set of outcome data. Section 2.4 of this book discusses interferences in more detail and provides a mechanism for identifying and managing the effects of those interferences.

Once the data are collected, they need to be analyzed. How those data are analyzed can dramatically affect the outcomes. For example, consider the measurement of pH and dissolved oxygen, digital meters are generally more accurate than colorimetric methods and pH meters are generally more accurate than pH strips. But Winkler titration analyses for dissolved oxygen are often more accurate than digital meters. It is useful to determine the degree of accuracy required by the experiment, the amount or variance allowed within the expected outcomes, and how often simple tests may need to be calibrated with more precise tests. The data analysis section needs to address these questions and define any requirements for continuous calibration of digital equipment proposed for use. The equipment should be specified as completely as possible, such as, for example, an "XYZ Corp. Model 62 Dissolved Oxygen meter" and an operating and calibration manual for that equipment should be appended to the experiment design sheet when available.

Once the data have been collected and analyzed, there will be a set of outcomes from the experiment. With luck, those outcomes will match the expected outcomes although in reality they seldom do. It is important, therefore, to consider how the actual outcome data differ from the expected outcome data and to think through why there are variances. Variances can occur from a variety of causes, including poor experimental design, poor implementation, operator error using the analyzers, improper calibration of equipment, equipment failure, or an unrealistic expectation of anticipated outcomes. In any case, the actual data should be believed *unless and until* proven false. The vast majority of experimental data are real and correct for the experiment that was actually performed. Why they did not match the expected outcome is usually because the expectations were not correct or there were some interferences not anticipated. See Section 2.4 for further discussion of this issue.

The experiments in chapters 9 through 14 provide sample data sheets as models for experiment design, data collection, data analysis, and outcome interpretation. (Chapter 6 provides a template for a lab report.)

5.3   EXPERIMENT DESIGN FORMAT MODEL

TITLE OF EXPERIMENT

Date: _____

Principal Investigator:

      Name: _____

      Email: _____

      Phone: _____

Collaborators:

      Name: _____

      Email: _____

      Phone: _____

      Name: _____

      Email: _____

      Phone: _____

      Name: _____

      Email: _____

      Phone: _____

      Name: _____

      Email: _____

      Phone: _____

      Name: _____

      Email: _____

      Phone: _____

Objective or Question to Be Addressed:
(This section defines the intended outcome of the experiment. Experiments are done for a reason and that reason needs to be clearly defined in this section of the experiment and subsequent laboratory report.)

Theory Behind Experiment:
(The theoretical basis for any experiment informs the procedures to be used and the methods of data analysis to be used. This section of the experiment design and report

provides an outline of the theory behind the experiment and justifies the bases for the data collection, experiment procedures, and data analysis sections.)

Potential Interferences and Interference Management Plan:
(This section requires the experimenter to think through the procedures to be followed and to ensure that a minimum of potential interferences are unaccounted for, or that those not addressed are not likely to skew the outcomes significantly. It may be possible to allow certain interferences if their effects can be easily quantified and the outcome data can be appropriately corrected for the interferences.)

Data to Be Collected with an Explanation of How They Will Be Collected (Ex.: "Water Temperature Data for 3 Days Using a Continuous Data Logger")
(This section requires the experimenter to think through the intended procedures and to develop a plan for collecting useful data during the experiment. The quality of the data to be developed in the laboratory is directly related to the quality of the samples collected in the field. Therefore, where field sampling is part of the exercise, this section must completely outline the field collection procedures to be used to protect the quality of the samples collected.)

Tools, Equipment, and Supplies Required:
(This list should be sufficiently complete that an experimenter taking this list of equipment into an isolation chamber on the moon could conduct the experiment without leaving the chamber or having anything else delivered to it.)

Safety:
(This section describes the health and safety plans utilized for the collection, handling, and analysis of the samples and for the disposal of materials at the end of the experiment. Disposal procedures of the laboratory may be appended to the report to justify procedures used in this section.)

Planned Experimental Procedures and Steps, in Order:
(In this section, the procedures to be followed need to be very clearly described and defined. The steps should be sufficiently defined and ordered such that a complete novice, who did not read the theoretical section of the experiment outline, could conduct the experiment successfully, and generate the required data even if the experimenter had no idea what the collected data mean.)

Data Collection Format and Data Collection Sheets Tailored to Experiment:
(In this section, the experimenter will think through the most reasonable format and manner of collecting the data to facilitate analysis of the data at the conclusion of the work. A form should be prepared in advance on which all the collected data can be entered as it is developed without having to worry about where to find data points later.)

Anticipated Outcomes:
(It is useful to know what to expect from an experiment so that the actual data can be compared to some baseline expectation. These are not always what the actual outcomes are, but the expected outcomes should be described here.)

Data Analysis Plan:
(Here the experimenter will determine what is going to be done with the data that are collected. Questions such as what analytical processes will be used to verify the accuracy of the data, what statistical analyses are going to be performed, whether the data will be graphed in some format, and what that format would look like, and similar issues.)

6 Laboratory Report

6.1 CONVERSION OF THEORY TO EXPERIMENTAL OUTPUT DATA

The purpose of an experiment is to provide new information to investigators in the present and in the future. The design of the experiment is based on a theory, but the theory may not be fully correct. Most theories are based initially on a pragmatic review of unverified anecdotal observations or other forms of unproven assertions. The experiment is designed to determine the veracity of the theory based on the earlier observations and to modify the theory to the extent necessary to incorporate both the earlier observations and the experimental data.

To accomplish the goal of incorporating the new experimental data into the existing theory, it is first necessary to understand the existing theory. Indeed, the entire experimental design must be based on that understanding or there will be no relationship possible between the existing theory and the new data. Consequently, the first step is to examine existing literature to determine what the theory is and how a new experiment can be designed to verify or refute that theory. The existing theory should then be described in the experiment design so that a reader of the design can understand how and why the experiment was designed to relate to the theory.

The theoretical basis for experiments is usually found by examining online sources, first, to identify the basic theory. Then, the academic documents in which it may be described and in which its basis is defined can be identified. Those academic and research documents are then examined to see the finer details. Online sources, such as webpages, are good for finding rough data sources and identifying possible word searches in the academic literature. Academic literature may be found online but would not be considered a "webpage" source because they are formally published as a part of a peer-reviewed journal. Webpages (that are not online sources of published journals) do not provide defensible data, in most cases, and should not be relied upon as the source of information. Often these sources are not reviewed, or fact-checked. Only known academic sources should be relied upon for accurate information and data. Google, for example, provides an academic search engine (Google Scholar), and most libraries, certainly most university libraries, have good online academic resources available to researchers.

6.2 COMPARE AND CONTRAST EXPERIMENTAL OUTPUT DATA TO EXISTING LITERATURE

Scientific and engineering theories are devised from the output of various experiments. Some of those experiments may be serendipitous outcomes from unrelated research that ultimately tweaks an idea that requires further investigation. Other times the idea comes first, and some experimentation is done to verify or refute

DOI: 10.1201/9781003184249-6

the expected outcome or basis for the idea. It happens, however, that there are very few questions that have never been asked previously in science or engineering. Sometimes the truth has not yet been observed or recognized but provides an opportunity for innovative research. Other times it is recognized, but not proven and someone decides to better understand a specific phenomenon or observed effect. The key takeaway from all of that is that there is almost always *some* literature that relates to the new theory or practice to provide context to experimental work.

That is important. Reinventing wheels really is a waste of time. Modifying wheels for different purposes can be useful, but the concept of a wheel is well defined and accepted now and need not be further pursued. That means that it is not only useful but also necessary, to do some research on new ideas to see who else may have come up with a similar idea in the past and what they did about it. Research conducted by others also provides context and validity to new work. Often people start to investigate things, lose interest for a variety of reasons, and then do not pursue the end objective. The idea may have merit, however, if evaluated slightly differently. Knowing what the first person or first few people did who investigated the question will save a lot of time, eliminate failures, and lead to greater value in the final outcome.

It is also true that not all data are properly recognized or evaluated. Sometimes a literature review will uncover a failed experiment because the investigator was looking for the wrong outcome, or the outcome was not what was expected or desired. The new investigator may see the true meaning of the data and be able to expand the notions involved to a great advantage rather quickly.

Regardless of the reasons for the work described in the prior literature, anyone reviewing the new work will want to know about the prior work and how the new work expands on that prior work. The prior literature may also suggest some new ways of looking at a new experiment or provide updated methods for current experiments. Those who are familiar with the concepts being investigated will likely be familiar with at least the most important prior work and will discount any new work that does not at least consider the prior efforts and outcomes. Consequently, any report of new experimentation must include a section on how the new work relates to prior studies of the same and related topics.

6.3 SUGGESTED LABORATORY REPORT TEMPLATE

The following template follows the outline of the recommended experiment design process with the addition of sections for the presentation of actual data collected, interpretation of those data, conclusions, and recommendations. Be mindful that this is only a recommended format and others (your professors) may have different report format requirements. All data included in this template should be provided somewhere in the experiment laboratory report, however.

TITLE OF EXPERIMENT

Laboratory Report

Date: _____

Principal Investigator:

    Name: _____

    Email: _____

    Phone: _____

Collaborators:

    Name: _____

    Email: _____

    Phone: _____

    Name: _____

    Email: _____

    Phone: _____

    Name: _____

    Email: _____

    Phone: _____

    Name: _____

    Email: _____

    Phone: _____

    Name: _____

    Email: _____

    Phone: _____

Objective or Question to Be Addressed:
(This section defines the intended outcome of the experiment. Experiments are done for a reason and that reason needs to be clearly defined in this section of the laboratory report.)

Theory Behind Experiment:
(The theoretical basis for any experiment informs the procedures to be used and the methods of data analysis to be used. This section of the report provides an outline of the theory behind the experiment and justifies the bases for the data collection, experiment procedures, and data analysis sections.)

Potential Interferences and Interference Management Plan:
(This section is used to consider what might go wrong with the experimental procedure and to describe what the researcher did to minimize or otherwise avoid the effects of any potential interferences identified.)

Data to Be Collected with an Explanation of How They Will Be Collected (e.g.: "Water Temperature Data for 3 Days Using a Continuous Data Logger"):
(This section provides a detailed description of the data collection procedures used during the experiment. The quality of the data developed in the laboratory is directly related to the quality of the samples collected in the field. Therefore, where field sampling was part of the exercise, this section must completely outline the field collection procedures used to protect the quality of the samples collected.)

Tools, Equipment, and Supplies Required:
(This list of equipment actually used should be sufficiently complete that an experimenter taking this list of equipment into an isolation chamber on the moon could conduct the experiment without leaving the chamber or having anything else delivered to it.)

Safety:
(This section describes the health and safety plans utilized for the collection, handling and analysis of the samples and for the disposal of materials at the end of the experiment. Disposal procedures of the laboratory may be appended to the report to justify procedures used in this section.)

Planned Experimental Procedures and Steps, in Order:
(In this section, the procedures followed need to be very carefully and very clearly described and defined. The steps should be sufficiently defined and ordered such that a complete novice, who did not read the theoretical section of the experiment outline, could successfully conduct the experiment following the stated procedures exactly, and generate identical outcome data even if the experimenter had no idea what the collected data mean.

Data Collection Format and Data Collection Sheets Tailored to Experiment:
(In this section, the experimenter will provide a description of the data collection form used; the timing of data collection; the sample preparation requirements used, if any; and any other relevant consideration related to collection of the samples tested.)

Data Analysis Plan:
(Here, the experimenter will describe what was done with the data that were collected. Questions such as what analytical processes were used to verify the accuracy of the data, what statistical analyses were performed, whether the data were graphed and what that format looks like, and similar issues. Consider that data and results are different from one another. Data may include a multitude of quantitative information, while results come from the interpretation of the data. Experimenters should be mindful of various ways to show results without including all of their data.)

Actual Outcomes Observed with Discussion of Variances from Anticipated Outcomes:

(If the actual outcomes are not consistent with the expected outcomes, it will be necessary to determine why that is so. Any variation from the expected outcomes must be described and explained in this section with documentation of how and why the outcomes varied. This section should also include a discussion of prior work on the same and related topics that influenced the expected outcomes from the current experiments.)

Conclusions and Recommendations:

(Here the investigators will draw conclusions from the actual outcome data and any variations from the expected outcome data. Those conclusions will be described and documented. Any recommendations for further testing resulting from this experiment will be outlined and described here.)

Appendices (If Any):

(Appendices will include such things as the filled-in data collection sheets, special operating procedures for specific analytical equipment used, or descriptions of unusual or special statistical analyses used and detailed explanations, documentation, and justification for special data collection or analysis techniques utilized.)

7 Effective Presentation of the Data in Outcome Reports

One of the more important things that engineers are called upon to do as professionals is to present information of a technical nature to nontechnical audiences. The ability to communicate professionally can make or break a career. This is true for all professionals but particularly important for engineers due to the complexities of design.

On their face, those two concepts – technical data and nontechnical audiences – sound, at the same time, both onerous and ridiculous (but they are not). The ways that engineers interact with clients and the general public will show that they are both accurate in their clarity and substance. Engineers are the key to everything people do, from roads and bridges to clean drinking water including the equipment and the outcomes. Nothing lasting will be built or manufactured without quality engineering.

Engineers are called upon to assess problems to be solved, collect data during the analysis, analyze data accurately, present various interpretations of those data, discuss alternative interpretations of the data, and determine the recommended alternatives.

The audience to whom the engineer is presenting data and analyses may or may not be technically competent, or a mix of stakeholders may have various degrees of competence in the technical areas under discussion. The presentation needs to be tailored to meet the expectations and competence of the entire audience at hand. The technically competent audience does not generally need to hear about the theory behind the science; only an identification of the methodology used, the results of the analyses, and the recommendation. The nontechnical audience needs to understand the basic concepts behind the science used and the justification for the use of that specific analytical technique before they try to understand the results of the analyses. The mixed audience needs some understanding of the science, but not as much as a nontechnical audience. The key is to ensure understanding and keep everyone involved with the discussion at all times.

How the engineer presents the data at the outset can have a significant, and expensive, impact on the decision made by the client. This section describes some of the more common issues and errors made when presenting technical data, particularly to a nontechnical audience, and how to overcome those conceptual issues.

There are a variety of ways to present data. Tables are useful for organizing and presenting large sets of numerical data. An example of such a data set is the environmental data collected over long periods of time from the groundwater quality monitoring of a contaminated site. Typically, monitoring will occur at several monitoring

DOI: 10.1201/9781003184249-7

wells on a site as frequently as monthly for several years. A site with 14 or 15, or more, monitoring wells, monitored monthly for, say 5 years, with each sample being tested for 15–20 contaminants, will yield a data set of perhaps 10,000–15,000 data points. In addition, a column or row with the regulatory standard for each of the data points is needed that includes each of the contaminants for which tests were conducted at the site. A table presenting those data would typically be done on a spreadsheet of approximately 20–50 columns and several hundred rows. It is not realistic to consider printing a data set of that magnitude on a single sheet of paper, and if it were done, it would be totally indecipherable.

Moreover, if the data were presented on a series of sheets of paper, the number of data points that violate the standards, versus those that do not, would still be difficult to discern. If the engineer were to highlight the violations, they could be found on the spreadsheet more easily, but recognizing a pattern of improvement or degeneration over an extended time frame, or seeing the changes in the concentrations of degradation by-products or contaminant reduction over time, would become extremely difficult.

Presenting data, particularly large or very large data sets, on a timeline, as a visual, can be much more effective. The concept is to *present as much information as possible, in the smallest amount of space, with maximum clarity,*[1] for both the technical and nontechnical audiences. This is the difference between data and results. The presenter wants to aggregate all of the data into meaningful and presentable results.

A selection of the data would be better presented in a series of graphs that depict the changes in concentration of the various contaminants in a single monitoring well over time. Several contaminants could be shown on each of the charts to illustrate potential changes in by-products or the changes in several key contaminants at a single location. The lines shown would help the reader to understand the changing relationships most easily. Each line is typically done in a different color and line type to further enhance the ability of the reader to understand the data quickly.

The use of PowerPoint and similar programs for the presentation of data is a common practice, but one that is fraught with pitfalls. Very few slideshows end up wowing the audience. Presentations that do wow an audience present the material in a way that supports the discussion, but is not the main delivery tool. The engineer who writes out the entire presentation on slides and ends up basically reading the slides to the audience may indeed afflict the audience with "Death by PowerPoint".

The first common mistake made by presenters is a lack of preparation. The slides are there to keep the audience focused and to help guide the presenter through the topics. Anyone who thinks they can pick up a set of slides prepared by someone else and use them to make a cogent presentation is kidding themselves. The person who does not prepare the slides will have no idea why particular information is provided or how it relates to the topic at hand. They will also have no idea what the next slide is going to be or what information is provided later in the show. This will be painfully obvious to the audience and destroy the credibility of the presenter. It takes a lot of

[1] Tufte, E. R. (2001). *The Visual Display of Quantitative Information* (Second Edition) Cheshire, CT: Graphics Press.

practice to get it right, but the effort is always worth it. Every slide needs to be there to help the audience *focus* on the narrative, not to *tell* the narrative.

The second problem that often occurs is that the slides are too busy or complicated, overloaded with bullets and lists, lacking in focus, or filled with poor-quality images. Slides are a visual aide to help the presenter and the audience stay focused on the message; not an entertainment for the audience. Visual simplicity, a clear and meaningful message, and quality visuals are essential to achieving those objectives. A general 6/6 standard is recommended, meaning no more than six bullets on a slide with no more than six words for each bullet. Slides should use a minimum of words, set large enough for the hard of seeing to read from a distance (25–30 points minimum) to avoid having the audience try to read the words on the screen instead of hearing the presenter.

The third problem is using images that fail to convey the intended message. In fact, the audience should never actually notice the image, but immediately perceive the message when looking at the image. Clip art images do get attention but seldom convey the proper message, particularly in a professional setting. Professional, stock images generally work best for this purpose, although personally photographed images (not snapshots) have their place in specific presentations. It is true that, in general, simple graphics and diagrams illustrate or highlight information better than text.

A fourth problem has to do with the use of color on slides. Most presentation software has built-in color palettes that can be used to color the words, the background, or the graphics. Unfortunately, the colors that show up best on the computer screen are typically those that show up the worst on the projection screen. In general, colors tend to become washed out and faded when projected from the computer screen to the presentation screen. Yellows, light blues, pinks, and grays, for example, tend to disappear when projected. Yellows and pastels tend to fade the most because they are already so weak, even on the computer screen. It is also best (when possible) to practice the presentation using the presentation screen to observe how the colors actually appear during the presentation.

Even bright colors may appear faded and often difficult to see, particularly when the lighting in the presentation room is not adequately dimmed and the background color of the slide does not provide adequate contrast. Changing the background color can allow some otherwise weak colors to pop but will also cause other colors that are usually bright to fade. In general, black and red colors show up well on the presentation screen. Outlined letters and wide letters should be avoided unless used very sparingly to highlight specific comments. A deep blue or dark green color will show up well on both screens but beware of the fact that writing on a deep blue or dark green with black lettering will look great on the computer screen, but be unreadable on the presentation screen. Using white letters on the blue or green background, or other dark backgrounds, can work well.

A fifth issue is font size selection and font type. Selecting a font and size other than the defaults preprogrammed into the slideshow can accent a presentation if done carefully and judiciously. Font size is a matter of personal preference. However, if the presenter prefers to allow the audience the opportunity to read the slide, the font size needs to be large enough for that to happen. In general, a font size of at least 28 should be used for the main message on any slide, with 24, or even 20-point fonts for less important information. Anything smaller than 20 points should be avoided.

Transitions should be avoided, particularly those that are distracting, such as, cutesy fading, twirling, and snapping in and out. Sounds can be more distracting if used throughout the presentation. An occasional sound clip or short video can enhance presentations if they pertain clearly to the message. Otherwise, they should be avoided. If videos are used, they are often web-based links embedded into the slideshow. They only work where there is sufficient bandwidth and an internet connection available at the site of the presentation. Videos often do not work smoothly when presented. Positive verification of this availability and a trial run are important before adding videos.

8 Designing Research Experiment Projects

Experimenting and assessing data obtained from standard methods are important parts of engineering. To further the profession, the next steps for an engineer would be to innovate and research topics of interest. Research projects in environmental engineering generally involve more experimentation than interpretation and understanding of undergraduate engineering concepts. A colleague recently described the various level of academic research as:

- Bachelor's level experimentation looks at a question that has an answer, which is derived from standard experimental protocols.
- Master's level experimentation considers a question that may not have an answer that is fully resolved with a single experiment.
- Doctoral level experimentation involves the unknown, both in terms of the actual question to be asked and the answer to be obtained.

The following describes two areas of research which are used to demonstrate the idea of further exploring the concepts presented in the previous chapters. The research areas are examples of current unresolved questions. Both explore ways to challenge the accepted protocols for testing in order to accelerate the processes or otherwise improve the test outcomes.

8.1 RESEARCH TO ASSESS STANDARD SAMPLE DRYING PROTOCOLS

The first example considers the question of whether alternatives exist to the normal drying times during the analysis of water samples for total solids and the component portions of those solids. Currently, accepted protocols require drying filters and complete samples at 100°C (212°F) to remove water. This process takes up to 6 or 8 hours depending on the sample and sample size. The samples are then weighed and placed in a muffle furnace to oxidize, or burn off, the organic fractions. The careful measurement of weights is needed to ensure reliable results, and there is a potential for loss of fidelity in the outcome data.

Potentially, a better method may be determined to dry the sample and then to extract the organic fractions, with shorter turnaround times and less potential for loss of organics in the process, and this new protocol would assist in the management of water and wastewater treatment plants. An area to explore could be the equipment used for drying by assessing if an option, such as a microwave oven, to first dry the samples may work more efficiently than a standard drying oven, and to then use the

DOI: 10.1201/9781003184249-8

microwave oven to oxidize the organics more quickly than a standard muffle furnace procedure.

It is known that microwave ovens can heat materials much faster than ovens and could, hypothetically, dry the samples being tested for solids content much more quickly than an oven. There is limited evidence that drying the samples in this fashion either does or does not destroy any portion of the organic fractions during the drying period. It is also unclear what intensity setting on the microwave would yield the best results and over what time period the heating should be done for optimal efficiency and efficacy.

The frequency of the microwave used would need to be considered. Most consumer microwave ovens operate with a wavelength at or around a nominal 2.45 gigahertz (GHz), or about 12.2 cm (4.80 in) in the 2.4–2.5 GHz ISM band. The actual wavelength may be anywhere within that range of 2.4–2.5 GHz. Each oven usually includes a statement somewhere on a data panel indicating the actual wavelength for that oven. Commercial and industrial ovens often use 915 megahertz (MHz), or 32.8 cm (12.9 in).

The reason for the big difference is that the frequency at which consumer microwave ovens operate is determined by the need for those microwaves to cook food. 2.45 GHz is the approximate resonant frequency of the free water molecule. The higher the frequency, the less effectively the energy would penetrate, and at high frequencies, the food would tend to cook less evenly. Lower frequencies penetrate better, but they are generally absorbed so weakly by food that they would not cook well. Cooking food is the defined purpose for these ovens so the 2.4 – 2.5 GHz range is a good compromise that allows food to cook in a short time, but also cook through evenly.

Commercial microwave ovens are often used primarily to heat precooked food, but not to cook or recook food, so they can use a lower frequency (and therefore operate at a lower cost) without loss of effectiveness. Vending machines that sell hot food, for example, will heat the selected package for a specified length of time. Most ovens also include power options. The power options indicate the approximate percentage of the time that the oven is producing microwaves while it is operating. When the oven is set to "Low", it normally produces microwaves for about 30% of the time it is on, and it shuts off the microwave production for 70% of that time in equal-timed cycles. For example, an oven set to "Low" for 10 minutes would be expected to produce microwaves for 18 seconds, shut off the microwaves for 42 seconds, turn the microwaves on again for 18 seconds, and so forth for the full 10 minutes. During the periods when the microwaves are shut off, the materials inside the oven continue to heat through by convection within the materials, but not overheat.

At a power setting of "Medium", a microwave oven will normally produce microwaves for 50% of the time it is on, shutting off the microwaves for the remaining 50% in equal-timed cycles. At a setting of "High", microwaves are generated for 100% of the time that the oven is operating. Some ovens also include intermediary settings between these three, and researchers are encouraged to do additional testing at those power levels for a better understanding of the efficacy of this procedure.

An experiment to evaluate this question would require separating a well-mixed sample from a specific water or wastewater source into several aliquots. Each aliquot would then need to be tested by a different set of parameters with all of the micro-waved sample output data compared to the data from the standard protocol – and against the data from each of the test samples. With a microwave oven controlled by 5 power settings and samples tested at 3–5 time intervals for each power setting, plus at least two samples tested by the standard protocols for control purposes, the researcher will need to evaluate between 17 and 25 samples to generate a sufficient data set for appropriate evaluation. Once the data are generated, they could be plotted on graphs or charts to better visualize the optimum time and power setting for a spe-cific microwave oven. Several models of ovens would then be tested in a similar fash-ion to identify a standard operating protocol for solids analysis using a microwave oven for the drying and oxidizing steps. That protocol may need to include specific wavelengths, time intervals, and power settings to be universally applicable. It may also be determined that a power setting between those normally provided, or a wave-length different from those normally provided, is necessary for optimal performance with this use. A microwave oven modified to operate at those optimal settings could then be made, and the experiments run again to verify the assumptions.

It is noted, too, that the protocol for handling the samples during the microwave processing would need to be developed into a standard procedure. It may be neces-sary, therefore, to expand the research and evaluate the experimental series using different handling procedures to identify the optimal procedural processes.

8.2   RESEARCH TO ASSESS STANDARD INDICATOR ORGANISMS

A second example of this type of experimentation involves the use of indicator organ-isms for determining the presence or absence of fecal contamination, and an associ-ated presumption of the presence or absence of organisms considered or presumed to be pathogenic to humans. Indicator organism tests typically require 24 hours of incubation to determine presence or absence and may require additional time for the determination of actual counts. Standards currently rely on counts per 100 mL (3.4 oz) of water or wastewater as an indicator of pollutant concentrations and pathogenic organism presence. If a faster and equally reliable method could be found to identify the probability of pathogenic organism presence, the testing could be done more rapidly in times of sewage overflows near beaches, water treatment plant failures, pipe breakages, civil unrest, and other emergencies. If the new method were also less costly to run, its acceptance as a standard test protocol would be even more widely approved. In addition, the identification and later the simultaneous applica-tion of multiple water quality indicators with variable environmental persistence and fate could yield greater confidence in fecal pollution assessment and could properly inform remediation or other management decisions.

There are several promising options that have been investigated recently in this regard. They include testing for various chemical indicators that are closely associ-ated with specific pathogens, often total coliform and *E. coli*, for example, and the testing for genes associated with the key, accepted, indicator organisms of coliform and *E. coli*.

Researchers have determined that human-source fecal pollution was indicated by the *esp* gene and that chemical and gene-based indicators of fecal contamination may be present even when fecal indicator bacteria standards are met. Haack et al. (2009) reported that some of the chemical and gene-based indicators may indicate potential sources. The research concluded that "only the EC *eae*A gene was positively correlated with fecal indicator bacteria concentrations".

Researchers have also considered the use of chemical markers to indicate for fecal contamination, such as the use of caffeine. The water quality downstream of a waste discharge is significantly affected by the distance, time, and area through which the water body flows with respect to correlations between fecal indicator bacteria and chemical constituents. Peeler et al. (2006) found that "The presence of caffeine and elevated nitrate in streams was associated with anthropogenic inputs and population centers, whereas bacterial indicators did not correlate to these chemical indicators and appeared to have non-human sources. In contrast, caffeine in an urban coastal lagoon was generally linked to fecal coliform abundance."

As a research field, there are several opportunities for assessing specific chemicals common to water or wastewater treatment operations that are sufficiently and predictably persistent in the environment and continuously well-correlated with fecal indicator bacteria. Alternatively, the biological makeup of the bacteria load in the treatment plant discharge can be studied to identify additional bacteria that are equal to the traditional coliform and fecal coliform bacteria as fecal indicator organisms, and that correlate well with specific chemicals.

These examples demonstrate that there are several research topics involved when investigating the current methods for the assessment of the potential for pathogens within a water source. This will involve multiple experiments to determine appropriate indicators to trace, then a series of samplings in various weather conditions downstream of a discharge to adequately correlate specific chemicals to accepted fecal indicator bacteria.

8.3   RESEARCH RECOMMENDATIONS

Research questions the known and explores the unknown. The experiments to examine an unknown need to be modified from the basic concepts generally espoused in this book to provide an open-ended question and adjust the experiments to adapt to the outcomes developed from standard experimental protocols. It is generally recognized that experimental data are consistent only when the procedures are identical for identical aliquots of the same material or source. Ensuring good recordkeeping during the experiments is essential to later verification of the desired protocols. These steps will allow a researcher to expand upon known protocols and define methods to question standard industry procedures.

9 General Experiments

This chapter provides completed designs for example experiments which can be used to demonstrate specific engineering phenomena in a university laboratory or field collection site. They may be used as presented or modified by the user to adapt to other desired outcomes. Sections on actual outcomes and data interpretation are necessarily left blank in these examples. They should be completed by the investigators upon collection of the data.

The experiments in this chapter are:

9.1 Turbidity Meter Calibration
9.2 Calibration of Spectrophotometers
9.3 Jar Test Procedure
9.4 Duct Tape Permeability Test
9.5 Determination of Specific Heat Capacity
9.6 Determination of Insulation R-Values for Various Materials
9.7 Headspace Analysis for the Presence of Volatile Organic Compounds
9.8 Surface Runoff Rate Determination and Volume Calculation
9.9 Water Filtration Media Evaluation
9.10 Water Filtration Media Evaluation Remote Area Options

DOI: 10.1201/9781003184249-9

EXPERIMENT 9.1: TURBIDITY METER CALIBRATION

Date: _____

Principal Investigator:

    Name: _____

    Email: _____

    Phone: _____

Collaborators:

    Name: _____

    Email: _____

    Phone: _____

    Name: _____

    Email: _____

    Phone: _____

    Name: _____

    Email: _____

    Phone: _____

    Name: _____

    Email: _____

    Phone: _____

    Name: _____

    Email: _____

    Phone: _____

Objective or Question to Be Addressed:
The objective of this experiment is to practice the art of equipment calibration; in particular, the calibration of a turbidity meter.

Theory Behind Experiment:
Turbidity meters use the passage of light of specific wavelengths through a specific length of sample to determine the turbidity of the sample. The length of the sample is controlled by using a special, optically matched, glass compound in the manufacturing of the test tubes used in the meter for calibration and subsequent testing. Most meters come with, or may be provided with as an accessory, a set of calibration standards to be used to calibrate the machine. Note that those standards are made of

a fixed gel, *formazin*, that has been inserted into test tubes designed for that machine and tightly capped. They are there to record the total turbidity of a sample based on the turbidity of the standards in what are know as Nephelometric Turbidity Units (NTUs).

The concept of measuring light that passes through a sample as a means of defining the turbidity of that sample stems from the way people perceive the clarity of water in nature. A standard field measurement of natural water turbidity is a Secchi disk reading. A Secchi disk is an 8 inch (20 cm) diameter, weighted, plastic disk that is divided into four equal quadrants. The opposite quadrants are painted black and white. The disk is suspended on a cord of sufficient length and lowered slowly into the water. As the disk sinks, the white and black quadrants become less and less clear until they can no longer be seen by the surface observer. The depth at which the disk disappears from view is referred to as the Secchi depth. Note that this measurement reflects the clarity of the water, and it is not a direct measurement of turbidity. There are a lot of things that can affect water clarity including dissolved tannins, algae, and suspended solids in the water column, the strength and angle of the sun during observation of the disk, and so forth. A Secchi depth is a subjective measurement, whereas a turbidity meter reading is an objective measurement and directly reflects the suspended solids concentrations because color and other factors are able to be minimized by the size of the sample being tested.

Prior turbidity meters used a variety of different units for measuring turbidity. Those include Formazin Nephelometric Units (FNUs), Formazin Attenuation Units (FAUs), Formazin Turbidity Units (FTUs), and Jackson Turbidity Units (JTUs), but most laboratories in the United States now use NTU machines. The differences between these units are based on the way the light that passes through the standards, or the sample, is scattered and measured.

NTU units mean that the machine is measuring the scattering of light at a 90° angle from the incidence of the light source.

FNU units also mean that the machine is measuring the light scatter at a 90° angle to the incident light, but may use a different wavelength of light than an NTU instrument. This is an international standard commonly used as a uniform standard when doing ISO 7027 turbidity testing. FNU units are generally considered a European method not commonly used in the Unioted States outside the ISO certification process.

FAU units indicate that the scattered light is being measured at 180° to the incident light. This is the method often used in spectrophotometers or colorimeters due to the convenience of design, but it is often not considered a valid turbidity measurement by regulatory agencies.

FTU units were first introduced when formazin was selected as the universal standard material. The units are used in both 90° and 180° scatter measurement machine, however, and often do not indicate the method of scatter measurement being used by that machine.

JTUs are an historic unit of turbidity measurement developed when turbidity was measured visually by observing the change in light scatter using a Jackson Candle

Turbidity meter. These are judgmental units that are no longer used in any modern turbidity machines.

Note that all of the units, except the Jackson Turbidity Units, are based on the formazin standards. Therefore, all machines using these standards will show the same turbidity with the same standard. However, since the way the scattered light passing through the unit is measured is different in different machines, the results from testing samples will also be different, often by a lot. It is important, therefore, to know for sure what units are being used and how to interpret them.

Since the formazin standards are set, calibration of the turbidity meter for suspended solids becomes a matter of creating a calibration curve, then plotting the test sample NTU value against the curve. The standards are created using known suspended solids concentration, so determining the suspended solids concentration directly from a calibration curve is direct. For measuring the concentration of other things, a calibration curve based on that which is to be measured is required. The process is the same, except that the formazin standards have already been prepared.

Potential Interferences and Interference Management Plan:
In this experiment, standards will be created to measure the concentration of a known substance in water. The standards used will be based on otherwise clean water which is presumed to have no concentration of the target substance at the outset. That is not always a valid assumption in external environments. In addition, there may be other compounds present in natural sources that are not known about, but which could scatter some of the light passing through the sample, thereby skewing the output data.

Using source water to establish the standards for the target substance should eliminate most of those interferences unless the target substance reacts with one or more of the unknown substances in the water.

Data to be collected with an explanation of how they will be collected (e.g. "Water temperature data for three days using a continuous data logger")
Turbidity meter readings will be taken from known standards established in the laboratory. An unknown concentration of the same substance will then be measured and compared to the curve to determine the concentration of the known substance in the test sample.

Tools, Equipment, and Supplies Required:
    Turbidity meter measuring in NTU turbidity units
    An optically matched set of test tubes for calibrating the meter and measuring
        the sample concentration
    11 clean 150 mL glass beakers

Safety
This experiment uses samples of source water (tap water, in this case) and a known substance (dye, in this case). Neither is particularly dangerous; however, care is needed to avoid contact between the skin and the dye to avoid staining of the skin, and between the dye and eyes to avoid serious eye damage. Gloves, eye protection, and a lab coat are required for this experiment.

In the event of contact between the skin and the dye, immediately washing the affected area with warm water and soap will remove most of the dye. Any remaining stains will dissipate over time. In the event of contact between the dye and the eyes, immediate flushing with an eyewash for up to 15 minutes is required, along with immediate attention by medical personnel.

Planned Experimental Procedures and Steps, in Order:

1. Assemble the required equipment and supplies and put on the appropriate personal protective equipment (PPE).
2. Measure out 100 mL aliquots of source water in a graduated cylinder and add one aliquot to each of the 150 mL beakers.
3. Prepare calibration samples of the dye at specific concentrations by adding the following amounts of dye to the 150 mL glass beakers. Special care is needed when preparing these standards since a minor error here may lead to a large error in the determination of the unknown concentration later.

Beaker	Volume of Dye to Add	Resulting Concentration
1	0.0 mL (0.0 oz)	0 mL/L
2	0.10 mL (0.003 oz)	1 mL/L
3	0.30 mL (0.010 oz)	3 mL/L
4	0.50 mL (0.017 oz)	5 mL/L
5	1.00 mL (0.034 oz)	10 mL/L
6	1.50 mL (0.051 oz)	15 mL/L
7	3.00 mL (0.101 oz)	30 mL/L
8	4.50 mL (0.152 oz)	45 mL/L
9	6.00 mL (0.203 oz)	60 mL/L
10	7.50 mL (0.254 oz)	75 mL/L
11	10.0 mL (0.358 oz)	100 mL/L

4. Insert test tube number 1 into the instrument to calibrate the zero concentration value.
5. Insert test tube number 2 into the turbidity meter and record the NTU value for that concentration.
6. Repeat Step 5 for each of the other ten concentrations and record those data.
7. Plot a graph, on normal-normal graph paper, of the concentration of dye versus the NTU reading from the meter. Plot the NTU readings along the X-axis and the concentration of dye along the Y-axis.
8. Collect a test tube full of the same source water with an unknown concentration of the same dye and test that sample with the turbidity meter. Record that value.
9. Compare the value from the sample of unknown concentration to the curve of known concentrations to determine the concentration of dye in the unknown sample.

Data Collection Format and Data Collection Sheets Tailored to Experiment:
See attached data collection form.

Data Analysis Plan:
The analysis of the collected data from this experiment is straightforward. The recorded NTU values at each of the prepared concentrations are plotted on a single normal-normal graph, and a line of best fit is drawn through those 11 points. The NTU value of the unknown sample is plotted along that line, and the corresponding concentration of the dye is read from the Y-axis.

Expected Outcomes:
It is expected that the calibration curve will be a smooth curve with the variation in NTU values following a predictable variation per mL/L of dye added. If it does not do that, it is likely that an error was made in creating the standards, and the standards associated with the out-of-line NTU values should be redone and the curve recalculated for that concentration. If the calibration curve is a smooth line, the probability that the reading for the unknown concentration is accurate will become very high. Plotting a standard regression line of the data will smooth out any minor variations in the calibrated data.

Data Collection Sheet for Turbidity Meter Calibration				
Beaker	Volume of Source Liquid in Standard, mL	Volume of Dye Added, mL	Resulting Concentration, mL/L	NTU Value of Standard
1				
2				
3				
4				
5				
6				
7				
8				
10				
11				
Test Sample				

EXPERIMENT 9.2:   CALIBRATION OF SPECTROPHOTOMETERS

Date: _____

Principal Investigator:

    Name: _____

    Email: _____

    Phone: _____

Collaborators:

    Name: _____

    Email: _____

    Phone: _____

    Name: _____

    Email: _____

    Phone: _____

    Name: _____

    Email: _____

    Phone: _____

    Name: _____

    Email: _____

    Phone: _____

    Name: _____

    Email: _____

    Phone: _____

Objective or Question to Be Addressed:

The objective of this experiment is to practice the art of equipment calibration; specifically, the calibration of a spectrophotometer.

Theory Behind Experiment

Spectrophotometers use the refraction of light of specific wavelengths passing through a specific length of sample to determine the concentration of various compounds or chemicals in the sample. The length of the sample through which the light flows is controlled by using a glass compound in the manufacturing of special test tubes, usually square, called *cuvettes*, used in the meter for calibration and subsequent testing.

Most meters come with, or may be provided with as an accessory, a set of optically matched cuvettes to be used to calibrate the machine and test samples. These instruments typically measure light intensity as a function of wavelength. Depending on the type or manufacturer of the instrument, different wavelengths of light may be analyzed. What is measured is the amount of light at a specific wavelength that is absorbed by the sample by measuring the amount received at the receptor and subtracting that from the amount emitted at the light generator.

A spectrophotometer is comprised of two intimately connected instruments: a spectrometer and a photometer. The spectrometer produces light of any desired wavelength, while the photometer measures the intensity of that light after it passes through a sample. The sample is placed between the spectrometer and the photometer. The amount of light that passes through the sample is measured by the spectrometer and converted to a voltage signal to the display. As the intensity of the absorbed light changes, the voltage signal changes proportionally and the display shows the change in concentration of the target compound. Spectrophotometers come in a variety of shapes and sizes and have multipurpose uses.

There are many different types of spectrophotometers available which differ based on their application and desired functionality. The most common spectrophotometers are designated as 45 degrees, sphere and multi-angle spectrophotometers.

The physics of the instrument involve the following equations.

$$T = 1/l_o$$

$$A = -\log_{10} T$$

where:
  T = transmittance of the sample
  l = the intensity of the light after it passes through a sample, measured in photons per second
  l_o = the intensity of the light source measured in photons per second
  A = absorbance of the light by the sample

The transmittance and absorption relationship is characterized by:

$$(A) = -\log(T) = -\log(l_t/l_o)$$

The transmittance of an unknown sample can be calculated, therefore, by:

$$(T) = l_t / l_o$$

Here,
  T = transmittance of the sample
  l_t = Light intensity after passing through the cuvette
  l_o = Light intensity before passing through the cuvette

The intensity of the light is first measured as it passes through a blank sample, typically the solvent carrying the compound to be measured. Then the blank is replaced by a sample of the compound to be measured, and the light passing through it is calculated by the instrument to yield an output signal that is displayed as a concentration.

There is a large variety of spectrophotometers in use today. These include UV spectrometers, IR spectrophotometers, and atomic absorption spectrophotometers, among others. This experiment is designed for use on UV–visible light instruments.

Potential Interferences and Interference Management Plan
In this experiment, an instrument will be calibrated to measure the concentration of an unknown substance in water. The standards used will be clean water which is presumed to have no concentration of the target substance at the outset. That is not always a valid assumption in external environments. In addition, there may be other compounds present in natural sources that are not known about, but which could scatter some of the light passing through the sample, thereby skewing the output data.

Using source water to establish the standards for the target substance should eliminate most of those interferences unless the target substance reacts with one or more of the unknown substances in the water.

Data to be collected with an explanation of how they will be collected (e.g. "Water temperature data for three days using a continuous data logger")
Spectrophotometer readings will be taken from a blank sample of source water presumed to contain none of the target substance. An unknown concentration of the same substance will then be measured to determine the concentration of the unknown substance in the test sample. The readout will be in mg/L on most instruments.

Tools, Equipment, and Supplies Required:
Spectrophotometer
An optically matched set of cuvettes for calibrating the meter and measuring the sample concentration

Safety
This experiment uses samples of source water (tap water, in this case) and a known substance (various chemicals, in this case). The chemicals are dangerous to the health of individuals who may accidentally ingest or inhale the compounds or who may allow the chemicals to come in contact with skin or eyes. Most of the issues related to the use of these chemicals are related to staining of the skin when coming in contact with the liquid chemicals. Care is needed to avoid these events. Gloves, eye protection, and a lab coat are required for this experiment.

In the event of contact between the skin and any of the chemicals, immediately washing the affected area with warm water and soap will remove most of the dye. Any remaining stains will dissipate over time. In the event of contact between the chemicals and the eyes, immediate flushing with an eyewash for up to 15 minutes is required, along with immediate attention by medical personnel.

Planned Experimental Procedures and Steps, in Order:

1. Assemble the required equipment and supplies and put on the appropriate PPE.
2. Prepare a calibration sample of the source water (tap water in this case) by filling a clean cuvette designed for the machine. Care is necessary to ensure that the cuvette is not touched with bare hands as that may impart some skin oils to the outside of the glass and skew the readings by the machine.

3. Determine the correct wavelength to be used to identify the target compound. This is generally found either in the Owner's Manual that came with the instrument, in a built-in computer program on the spectrophotometer from which the target substance wavelength can be selected, or from an online version of the instrument Owner's Manual.
4. Turn the instrument on and warm it up for 30–45 minutes or until the instrument indicates that it is ready for use.
5. Set the machine to the desired wavelength using the appropriate dials or computerized setting controls.
6. Prepare a sample of the unknown concentration by filling a clean cuvette, optically matched to the cuvette used for the unknown sample, and insert it into the instrument.
7. Depending on the specific instrument, select "Read" or "Zero" and allow the instrument to calibrate to that blank.
8. Insert the NIST (National Institute of Calibrations Standards) calibration standard that came with the unit into the cuvette receptacle, select the read option, and record the concentration.
9. Verify that the reading from the standard is consistent with the reading from the standard certificate of calibration provided with the standard, within the limits of accuracy stated on the certificate.
10. If the reading is consistent with the certificate, the instrument is properly calibrated. If not, check the Owner's Manual for the photometric accuracy tolerance of the instrument. If this information is not in the manual, then call the spectrophotometer manufacturer to get that information and add this tolerance to the tolerance for the standard used to get the extended tolerance.
11. If the numbers still do not match, then either the spectrophotometer or the calibration standard is the problem. Clean the outside of the standard cuvette and retry to calibrate. If that does not work, try the standard on another spectrophotometer to see if it is working properly. In general, either the standard or the instrument is where the error lies.
12. If the calibration step is successful, a sample of the unknown solution can then be inserted into the instrument and the concentration of that sample read directly from the instrument display.
13. Multiple samples of the same compound in the same solvent can be measured sequentially without recalibration of the unit. It is, however, good practice to zero the machine after each sample is tested if the results are critical or do not seem to be as accurate as they should be.

Data Collection Format and Data Collection Sheets Tailored to Experiment:
The data to be collected will depend on the nature of the testing being done and a unique data collection form is needed for each testing event.

Data Analysis Plan:
The analysis of the collected data from this experiment will depend upon the nature of the study being conducted. This experiment design sets up the instrument but does not establish a protocol for any specific test.

Expected Outcomes:

As with the data collection and analysis steps, the expected outcomes from this experiment are going to depend upon the specific study being undertaken and should be established by modifying those three headings to accommodate those study objectives.

EXPERIMENT 9.3:   JAR TEST PROCEDURE

Date: _____

Principal Investigator:

      Name: _____

      Email: _____

      Phone: _____

Collaborators:

      Name: _____

      Email: _____

      Phone: _____

      Name: _____

      Email: _____

      Phone: _____

      Name: _____

      Email: _____

      Phone: _____

      Name: _____

      Email: _____

      Phone: _____

      Name: _____

      Email: _____

      Phone: _____

Objective or Question to Be Addressed:

Jar tests are pilot-scale assessments of chemical dosing and are used for a variety of reasons in environmental engineering. A common use is to determine the best reactant to use for a particular treatment goal or to determine the optimal dose of a reactant to achieve a specific objective. For example, a jar test may be used to determine which of two or more coagulants will work best to treat a given water source in terms of the removal of organic and inorganic constituents. A second test may then be conducted to determine the optimal concentration of the selected coagulant.

    This experiment demonstrates the use of a jar test to determine the optimal mix of coagulants for artificially prepared wastewater and select the optimal concentration of the selected mix of coagulants.

Theory Behind Experiment:
Large particles will settle out due to the physical transport mechanisms of gravity; however, small particles may not be impacted by the gravity forces. Chemical coagulants may be used to create particle bonds and form larger particles. Most organic compounds and many inorganic compounds may be coagulated and removed from wastewater with aluminum hydroxide, sodium hydroxide, ferric chloride, or ferrous chloride. These chemicals form insoluble precipitates in the water which collect other particles of organic and inorganic origin as the insoluble particles settle out of the treated water. The optimal chemical for organics or inorganics in a water source may depend on complicating factors such as water composition, the various concentrations, and the probability that any given contaminant may have as an affinity for a particular coagulant.

By applying a series of concentrations of coagulant to a sample of wastewater and observing the results, optimal mixes of the best available coagulants can be determined empirically. This process can be less time-consuming when compared to complicated calculations or extensive research. This can be helpful when water quality parameters are changing due to site-specific impacts such as seasonal changes.

Potential Interferences and Interference Management Plan
Some of the coagulants used may work for several of the contaminants with varying degrees of efficacy. For example, when one type of coagulant is added, one type of contaminant may be fully removed while another type of contaminant may not be impacted at all. Then, if a second coagulant is added, it is possible to undo some of the work of the first additive and put some of the contaminants back into solution while removing more of others. It is also possible that less of one coagulant, yielding less than ideal results with many contaminants, but excellent results for one (or more) specific contaminants if used in conjunction with slightly more of a less costly secondary coagulant, may yield far greater results for the contaminants treated poorly with the first coagulant. The ability of the coagulants to create the larger particles for settling is based on the electrical potential of the particles and balancing the charges can be complex.

These relationships may not be easily calculated, so conducting the empirical test is more feasible. To minimize these cross-purpose results, it is useful to do a separate jar test with each coagulant to determine which of the contaminants each coagulant is best at removing, then preparing a mix of coagulants based on the optimal concentration of each. The final jar test with the mix of contaminants will determine whether there are any interferences among the coagulants. If interferences do occur, planning to separate the precipitates after each addition will provide exceptional treatment of the target water.

Data to be collected with an explanation of how they will be collected (e.g. "Water temperature data for three days using a continuous data logger")
The data to be collected are the concentrations of various contaminants introduced into an artificial wastewater. Samples will be collected from the wastewater before treatment and after treatment at various coagulant concentrations. Testing will be done with a spectrophotometer (such as a Hach Company test kit, or equivalent), following the manufacturer's instructions. In most cases, a reactant (in a powder packet)

will be utilized in these tests, and the concentration is determined from a spectrophotometer programmed for the specific test and calibrated for each test in accordance with the manufacturer's instructions.

A separate jar test will be set up for each of the coagulants being tested, and the wastewater will be tested for concentrations of the target contaminants in each "jar" of each test for the concentration of each contaminant.

Tools, Equipment, and Supplies Required:

Programmable spectrophotometer, such as Hach, or equivalent

Phipps and Bird 6-paddle mixer, or equivalent

Six clean 2 L (0.53 gal) glass or plastic beakers, round or square, that fit the mixer

One clean 60 L (20 gal) glass or plastic container to mix the artificial wastewater

Clean spatulas to measure contaminants and coagulants

A supply of approximately 100 grams or more of each of the following chemicals:

- Calcium nitrate (CaN_2O_6)
- Ferrous carbonate ($FeCO_3$)
- Ferrous sulfate ($FeSO_4$)
- Manganese sulfate ($MnSO_4$)
- Aluminum hydroxide
- Ferric chloride ($FeCl_3$)

Several 25–50 mL pipettes with disposable tips for sampling the reactors during the test

Several sets of clean, optically matched, test tubes or sample jars for the spectrophotometer

Any other spectrophotometer supplies, such as sufficient powder pillows and other reagents, needed for the testing of 30 samples, as required by the spectrophotometer manufacturer

Safety

The chemicals used in this experiment are toxic and caustic. Ingestion, inhalation, and skin contact should be avoided. Drying and irritation of the skin, serious damage to vision, or illness may result from contact.

In the event of skin contact, wash immediately with warm water and soap. In the event of eye contact, wash immediately with an eye flush station for up to 15 minutes and seek immediate medical assistance. In the event of inhalation, seek medical assistance immediately.

Gloves, eye protection, an inhalation mask, and a lab coat are required for this experiment.

Planned Experimental Procedures and Steps, in Order:

1. Gather all materials and equipment together and put on the appropriate PPE.
2. Collect 55 L (15 gal) of tap water in a 60 L (20 gal) container and add the following chemicals in the amounts indicated and stir until all the materials

are completely dissolved. Note that the ferric carbonate may dissolve slowly. This will be the artificial wastewater.

Calcium nitrate (CaNO$_3$)$_2$	100 g (3.5274 oz)
Ferrous carbonate (FeCO$_3$)	2 g (0.0705 oz)
Ferrous sulfate (FeSO$_4$)	50 g (1.7637 oz)
Manganese sulfate (MnSO$_4$)	50 g (1.7637 oz)

3. Sample this container for total iron, total calcium, total nitrate, total nitrite, and total manganese and record those values.
4. Collect 2 L (0.5283 gal) of the artificial wastewater in each of six 2 L beakers and place them on the 6-paddle mixer.
5. Add the following amounts of aluminum hydroxide (alum) to the indicated beakers and record those amounts on the Data Sheet.

Beaker	Mass of Alum Added
1	200 mg (0.00705 oz)
2	400 mg (0.01411 oz)
3	600 mg (0.02116 oz)
4	800 mg (0.02822 oz)
5	1,000 mg (0.03527 oz)
6	1,200 mg (0.04233 oz)

6. Turn the mixer on at a moderate rate (approximately 150 rpm) until all of the chemicals are dissolved in all of the containers and then turn off the mixer. Allow the contents to settle, any floc to form, and the floc to settle. This should take about 30 minutes.
7. Sample the liquid above the floc and test for total iron, total calcium, total nitrate, total nitrite, and total manganese and record those values.
8. Plot the resulting concentrations of the recorded contaminants on normal-normal graph paper with the concentration of alum on the Y-axis and the percent removal of each tested contaminant on the X-axis.
9. Dispose of the contents of the six beakers in accordance with the hazardous waste disposal protocols of the laboratory.
10. Clean the six beakers and refill each with 2 L (0.5283 gal) of the artificial wastewater.
11. Place the six beakers on the mixer and add the following amounts of ferric chloride to the designated beakers.

Beaker	Mass of Ferric Chloride Added
1	200 mg (0.00705 oz)
2	400 mg (0.01411 oz)
3	600 mg (0.02116 oz)
4	800 mg (0.02822 oz)
5	1,000 mg (0.03527 oz)
6	1,200 mg (0.04233 oz)

12. Turn the mixer on at a moderate rate (approximately 150 rpm) until all of the chemicals are dissolved in all of the containers and then turn off the mixer. Allow the contents to settle, any floc to form, and the floc to settle. This should take about 30 minutes.
13. Sample the liquid above the floc and test for total iron, total calcium, total nitrate, total nitrite, and total manganese and record those values.
14. Dispose of the contents of the six beakers in accordance with the hazardous waste disposal protocols of the laboratory.
15. Plot the resulting concentrations of the recorded contaminants on normal-normal graph paper with the concentration of ferric chloride on the Y-axis and the percent removal of each tested contaminant on the X-axis.
16. Create a table with the total removal percentage of each contaminant versus the concentration of each coagulant (see the Data Analysis section below).
17. Select the concentration of each coagulant that optimizes the removal of the most contaminants.
18. Fill one clean 2 L beaker with artificial wastewater and place it on the mixer.
19. Add the calculated dose of each coagulant to the beaker, turn on the mixer until the coagulants are dissolved, then turn off the mixer, and allow the contents to settle. This could take up to 30 minutes or so.
20. Sample the water above the floc and test for total iron, total calcium, total nitrate, total nitrite, and total manganese and record those values.
21. Compare the resulting values to the predicted values from the 10 graphs and the chart, and discuss why there may be differences in the actual values versus the predicted values. Also determine whether a sediment removal step between the addition of the two coagulants might result in a better overall contaminant removal efficiency and justify that recommendation.

Data Collection Format and Data Collection Sheets Tailored to Experiment:
See attached Data Collection form.

Data Sheet for Jar Test Procedure						
Chemicals Added to Create Artificial Wastewater	Amount Added in mg/L	Resulting Concentrations in mg/L				
		Calcium	Iron	Nitrate	Nitrite	Manganese
Calcium nitrate $(CaNO_3)_2)$						
Ferrous carbonate $(FeCO_3)$						
Ferrous sulfate $(FeSO_4)$						
Manganese sulfate $(MnSO_4)$						
Coagulant added in the first test						
Aluminum hydroxide						
Coagulant added in the second test						
Ferric chloride						
		Percent Removal				
		Calcium	Iron	Nitrate	Nitrite	Manganese
Aluminum hydroxide						
Ferric chloride						
Aggregate						

Data Analysis Plan:

The data collected in this experiment will be plotted on graph paper, and the optimal concentrations for each are listed on a chart showing percent removal efficiencies versus coagulant concentrations. The table should look something like the following:

Contaminant (Total)	Percent Contaminant Removal		
	Alum	Ferric Chloride	Aggregate
Calcium			
Iron			
Nitrate			
Nitrite			
Manganese			

The optimal dosages will be those which together exhibit the most effective aggregate contaminant removal efficiency.

Expected Outcomes:

It is expected that neither coagulant will remove all of any of the contaminants, but that each will be better for some and less effective for others. The actual percent removal efficiencies to be expected could be calculated from the chemical equations, but the complexity of the mixture is such that some of the molecules could easily combine with more than one of the coagulants or byproducts and a calculated determination is more easily done after a more thorough chemical analysis of the resulting solution concentrations.

EXPERIMENT 9.4: DUCT TAPE PERMEABILITY TEST

Date: _____

Principal Investigator:

       Name: _____

       Email: _____

       Phone: _____

Collaborators:

       Name: _____

       Email: _____

       Phone: _____

       Name: _____

       Email: _____

       Phone: _____

       Name: _____

       Email: _____

       Phone: _____

       Name: _____

       Email: _____

       Phone: _____

       Name: _____

       Email: _____

       Phone: _____

Objective or Question to Be Addressed:

The purpose of this experiment is to assess standard duct tape and its ability to prevent the transmission of various chemical classes through the tape material. Duct tape is used to seal Tyvek suits that protect workers at hazardous waste sites. The effectiveness of the duct tape in preventing passage of the hazardous material through the tape material is a key element in the overall success of the personal protection suits. This experiment will evaluate a specific type of duct tape against a strong acid (concentrated nitric acid), a weak acid (1:100 concentrated nitric acid in tap water), and a strong base solution of sodium hydroxide in tap water. Tap water will be used as a control.

(Note that several brands or types of duct tape may be tested simultaneously with this methodology and a comparative chart of the outcomes prepared as part of the Data Analysis section.)

Theory Behind Experiment

The porosity of a material such as duct tape refers to the size and number of minute holes per unit of surface area that exist in the material as a function of their physical and chemical characteristics and their manufacturing. The larger the holes, or pores, and the greater the number of holes, the higher the porosity. It is noted that the thickness of the material will affect the ability of the pores to pass contaminants through the material. Pores in thicker material do not need to pass completely through the material to present a problem if they are able to communicate with other pores internal to the material.

The thickness and porosity of duct tape are specific to type and manufacturer. This experiment tests only the porosity of the tape of one or more types or manufacturers. The results are not universally applicable, although they can indicate general probabilities of exposure using other types and tapes from other manufacturers.

All flexible materials, and many nonflexible materials, are porous to one degree or another. The magnitude of that porosity can have profound effects on the efficacy of the material to prevent the passage of liquids, solids, or gases. Where more porous duct tape is being used to provide protection against the passage of hazardous materials from a contaminated environment to the skin or respiratory system of a potentially exposed individual, the magnitude of that porosity can be life-threatening.

First responders and those assigned to assess the risks associated with a release of hazardous materials must enter a contaminated zone. To protect themselves from the risks associated with the release, often a release of unknown chemical constituents, the responders wear high-level PPE. That PPE must be selected to prevent direct contact between the person and the contaminant.

In conditions of unknown risk, people conducting field testing wear completely enclosing suits of Tyvek, vinyl or rubber, or other material which provide protection from the elements. In addition to the suit, they wear booties, gloves, hoods (if not part of the basic suit), and a respirator of a suitable type. All of those components are then sealed together at their junctions using an appropriate sealant or tape. The most commonly used tape is duct tape. The porosity is the variable which determine the level of protection for the user. The individual is potentially exposed to the extent the tape permits the transmission of contaminants through the tape pores.

This experiment is designed to determine the porosity of duct tape as a function of time of exposure and as a function of the pH of the contaminant. This procedure can also be used to determine the porosity of Tyvek or other materials used in hazardous waste sampling and testing and in any other application in which the material porosity is relevant.

Data to be collected with an explanation of how they will be collected

A specific brand of duct tape will be subjected to concentrated acid, weak acid, and strong base solutions to determine whether the tape will prevent breakthrough of those chemical classes for a period of up to 12 hours. The time of applying the chemical to the tape and the time of breakthrough, if any, will be recorded for each of a strong acid, a weak acid, a strong base, and tap water (used as a control).

Potential Interferences and Interference Management Plan:

1. The adhesive on the tape could interfere with the penetration of the liquid or modify the concentration of the chemicals during penetration. This experiment is intended to determine whether a risk is present for hazardous waste workers using this brand of duct tape on their PPE. Consequently, any effect of the adhesive on the breakthrough speed or concentration of the chemicals during breakthrough would also occur during use and is acceptable during the experiment.
2. The liquids could evaporate prior to the end of the experiment. Maintaining a constant temperature and a minimum of airflow through the hood during the experiment will minimize this issue.
3. Vaporization of the acids in the wells of the tape could permeate the air inside the hood and cause a premature discoloration of the litmus paper, falsely indicating a breakthrough of the acid or base in that beaker. Suspending a couple of strips of litmus paper above the beakers will indicate any vaporization of the acids into the hood atmosphere and can be used to indicate whether the litmus paper beneath any strip of duct tape may have been compromised. This is not expected to happen, but if it does, redoing the experiment with the entire top of the beaker covered by the duct tape will prevent the atmospheric acid vapors from reaching the underside of the duct tape on the beakers. In this case, care needs to be taken to minimize the overlapping of duct tape strips in the area where the liquid is placed so that the liquid still has only one layer of tape to penetrate.

Safety

This experiment relies upon the use of a strong acid and a strong base. These compounds will cause significant chemical burns if in contact with human skin and can cause significant damage to other materials found in the laboratory, including countertops and equipment.

Care is required when handling strong acids and bases.

Investigators will wear rubber or neoprene gloves, eye goggles, and a lab coat when working with these materials. Appropriate mixing protocols will be followed when mixing the nitric acid and the aluminum hydroxide with water. Be sure to slowly pour the acid or base into the water and not conversely. Tools will be placed in appropriate containers prior to cleaning and clean-up will be performed in accordance with laboratory cleaning procedures.

In the event of skin contact, flushing with tap water immediately and copiously will minimize damage to the skin. Medical attention may be warranted if burning sensations continue.

Eye contact will require immediate flushing with an eyewash for up to 20 minutes or until emergency response personnel can be called and arrive. Medical attention is required as soon as possible following exposure to the eyes.

Inhalation of fumes from the chemicals must be prevented. Burning of the airways and lungs is possible from these vapors. In the event such burning sensations are experienced, or redness or burning of eyes is experienced, immediately move to fresh air and seek medical attention.

An emergency medical assistance calling device, such as a wall-mounted telephone, a cell phone, or a direct intercom system, must be available at all times in the laboratory while this experiment is being conducted.

Tools, Equipment, and Supplies Required:
Four 25 mL (0.82 oz) or 50 mL (1.64 oz) clean glass beakers
Roll of duct tape to be tested
1 mL (0.038 oz) of concentrated nitric acid
1 mL (0.038 oz) of 1:100 nitric acid in tap water
1 mL (0.038 oz) of 0.1 N Sodium Hydroxide solution (in tap water) (4 g/L = 0.1 N)
1 mL (0.038 oz) of tap water
6–8 strips of litmus paper, each approximately 10 cm (4 in) long
Fume hood with a positive fume exhaust system
PPE including latex, vinyl, or rubber gloves, eye goggles, and lab coat
Portable pH meter

Planned Experimental Procedures and Steps, in Order:

1. Four 25 mL (0.82 oz) or 50 mL (1.64 oz) beakers will be collected and cleaned with dish soap and water, then dried thoroughly.
2. A piece of the selected duct tape (specify here the manufacturer and brand used for this experiment) will be loosely inserted across the top of each beaker, adhesive side down, such that a small well is produced in the duct tape directly over the center of the beaker opening so that any liquid that penetrates the tape will be collected inside the beaker. The tape will be secured at each end to the outside of the beaker using the tape adhesive.
3. A small piece of litmus paper will be adhered to the underside of the tape by sticking it to the adhesive on the tape. This litmus paper will be placed directly under the well on the top side of the tape to indicate by a color change when, and if, a breakthrough has occurred.
4. 1 mL (0.038 oz) of tap water will be placed in the well of the tape on the first beaker, 1 mL (0.38 oz) of concentrated nitric acid will be placed in the well of the tape on the second beaker, 1 mL (0.038 oz) of 1:100 nitric acid in tap water will be placed in the well of the tape on the third beaker, and 1 mL (0.038 oz) of 0.1 N sodium hydroxide in tap water will be placed in the well of the tape on the fourth beaker. Record the time of chemical addition.
5. The probe of the pH meter will be inserted into each of the four liquids to determine the starting pH of each liquid and those data will be recorded.
6. All the beakers will be carefully placed inside a hood where they may remain undisturbed for an extended period of time. It is good practice to provide a sign on the face of the hood with contact information for the principal investigator and the names of the chemicals in the space, in case someone needs to disturb the experiment for any reason.

7. Every hour for a period of up to 12 hours, the color of the litmus paper will be examined to determine when, and if, penetration has occurred through the tape and what pH is indicated by the color of the litmus paper. Once penetration is observed, the date and time will be recorded and the beaker affected will be removed from the hood. All liquids will be tested again with a litmus paper to determine the ending pH and those data will be recorded. The contents of the well and the tape used on that beaker will be immediately disposed in accordance with laboratory procedures for disposing of liquid acid wastes and contaminated hazardous solid waste, and the beaker will be properly cleaned and returned to storage.

8. The experiment will end after 12 hours or after beakers 2–4 have all indicated a breakthrough of the acid or base.

9. At the end of the experiment, all remaining beakers will be cleaned in accordance with Step 7 and returned to storage.

Data Collection Format and Data Collection Sheets Tailored to Experiment:
The attached data collection sheet will be utilized for this experiment.

Anticipated Outcomes:
It is expected that the duct tape will not pass any of the experimental liquids. It is also expected that if the tape does pass any of the liquids, the strong acid will penetrate first, the weak acid will penetrate second, and the strong base will penetrate last. The tap water is not expected to penetrate the tape during the experiment. It is expected that the pH of any liquid penetrating the tape will not experience a significant change (greater than 0.1 pH units) as it passes through the tape.

Data Analysis Plan:
Once the data have been collected, a chart of the time for breakthrough of each liquid will be created and the actual time to breakthrough will be compared to the anticipated outcomes. Any variance from the expected outcomes will be noted in the notes section of the data collection sheet and discussed in the final laboratory report.

Data Collection Sheet Duct Tape Permeability Analysis				
Date Collected:				
Date Tested:				
Principal Investigator:				
Manufacturer Name and Model of Duct Tape Being Tested:				
Manufacturer Name and Model of Litmus Paper Being Used:				
Test	**Results**	**Expected Results**	**Variations Noted**	**Notes**
Initial pH Beaker 1 (Tap Water)		±7		
Initial pH Beaker 2 (Strong acid)		<2		
Initial pH Beaker 3 (Weak Acid)		<5		
Initial pH Beaker 4 (Strong base)		±13		
Observation hour 1		Change in color of litmus paper if breakthrough has occurred; otherwise, none.		
Observation hour 2		Change in color of litmus paper if breakthrough has occurred; otherwise, none.		
Observation hour 3		Change in color of litmus paper if breakthrough has occurred; otherwise, none.		
Observation hour 4		Change in color of litmus paper if breakthrough has occurred; otherwise, none.		
Observation hour 5		Change in color of litmus paper if breakthrough has occurred; otherwise, none.		
Observation hour 6		Change in color of litmus paper if breakthrough has occurred; otherwise, none.		
Observation hour 7		Change in color of litmus paper if breakthrough has occurred; otherwise, none.		

(*Continued*)

Experiment Design for Environmental Engineering

Data Collection Sheet Duct Tape Permeability Analysis (*Continued*)				
Test	Results	Expected Results	Variations Noted	Notes
Observation hour 8		Change in color of litmus paper if breakthrough has occurred; otherwise, none.		
Observation hour 9		Change in color of litmus paper if breakthrough has occurred; otherwise, none.		
Observation hour 10		Change in color of litmus paper if breakthrough has occurred; otherwise, none.		
Observation hour 11		Change in color of litmus paper if breakthrough has occurred; otherwise, none.		
Observation hour 12		Change in color of litmus paper if breakthrough has occurred; otherwise, none.		
Final pH Beaker 1 (Tap water)		±7		
Final pH Beaker 2 (Strong acid)		<2		
Final pH Beaker 3 (Weak acid)		<4		
Final pH Beaker 4 (Strong base)		>12		
Final pH of penetrated liquid in Beaker 1 (Tap water)		±7		
Final pH of penetrated liquid in Beaker 2 (Strong acid)		<4		
Final pH of penetrated liquid in Beaker 3 (Weak acid)		<7		
Final pH of penetrated liquid in Beaker 4 (Strong base)		>12		

EXPERIMENT 9.5: DETERMINATION OF SPECIFIC HEAT CAPACITY

Date: _____

Principal Investigator:

Name: _____

Email: _____

Phone: _____

Collaborators:

Name: _____

Email: _____

Phone: _____

Name: _____

Email: _____

Phone: _____

Name: _____

Email: _____

Phone: _____

Name: _____

Email: _____

Phone: _____

Name: _____

Email: _____

Phone: _____

Objective or Question to Be Addressed:

The objective of this experiment is to determine the specific heat capacity of various materials of interest.

Theory Behind Experiment:

Specific heat capacity is a characteristic of a material or substance. It is an indication of the energy required to heat or cool an object. These factors are important in assessing energy consumption and assessing climate change. The *specific heat capacity* of a substance used for this experiment, indicated by the symbol C, is the heat capacity of a sample of the substance divided by the mass of the sample. In essence, it is the amount of energy that must be added to one unit of mass of the material, generally in the form of heat, to cause an increase of one unit in its temperature, generally measured in °C or °K. Note that °C needs to be converted to °K for consistency with the definition of specific heat. Most thermometers do not measure directly in °K, however, so °C are usually used for measurement because a change of 1°C is equivalent to a change of 1°K and the actual temperature is not important; only the change in temperature is important in the experiment.

The SI units of specific heat are joules per kelvin per kilogram, J/°K/kg. The English units of specific heat are BTU/°F/lb. 1 BTU/°F/lb. = 4177.6 J/°K/kg. The English measurement units were originally defined such that the specific heat of water would be equal to 1 BTU/°F/lb.

Note that the specific heat often varies with temperature, however, and is different for each state of matter. For example, liquid water has a specific heat of about 4,182 J/°K/kg at 20°C; ice just below 0°C (32°F) has a specific heat of only 2,093 J/°K/kg. When a substance is undergoing a phase transition, such as melting or boiling, its specific heat is technically infinite, because the heat goes into changing its state rather than raising its temperature. When discussing *specific heat capacity* remember that the word specific denoted an intrinsic characteristic and in this case means that the property is not dependent on the mass of the substance, while the term *heat capacity* is an extensive property and varies with the amount of a substance.

Note, too, that the specific heat of some substances, especially gases, is often much higher when they are allowed to expand as the heating occurs (referred to as the specific heat *at constant pressure, c_p*) than when is heated in a closed vessel that prevents expansion (referred to as the specific heat *at constant volume, c_v*). The term heat capacity ratio is applied to the quotient of these two values and denoted by the symbol γ. Doing such an experiment under constant volume conditions requires extensive procedures to guarantee no change in volume. That also dramatically increases internal pressures that need to be controlled. That procedure being dangerous, the use of constant pressure calculations is most commonly done. If a constant volume value is needed, calculation of that value from the constant pressure value and the various physical properties of the material, such as its coefficient of heat expansion, can be done. The procedure described here is a constant pressure procedure.

There are other definitions of specific heat used in esoteric applications that can be identified if ever needed.

The specific heat capacity of each material is calculated from the formula:

$$C = \frac{Q}{m * T}$$

where:
   C = Specific heat capacity, Joules/(kg/°C)
   Q = Amount of heat added, – Joules
   M = Mass of material being heated, – kg
   T = Change in temperature of the material, – °C

The value of Q for this experiment design can be reasonably approximated by the formula:

$$Q = (\text{Temperature of the hotplate}) \times (\text{time of heating in minutes})$$

Table A.3 in the Appendix provides standard values of specific heat for a variety of materials suitable for testing by the experiment procedure. Results from this experiment should be evaluated by comparison with the standard values shown. Note that the reported values for some materials differ significantly based on different sources. That suggests that calculation of these values is not a precise science for many materials. Experimental results from this experiment should be within reasonable concurrence with the range of values shown.

Conversion between units of measurement is based on the following equations:

1 BTU/lb/°F = 1.8 BTU/lb/°C
1 BTU/lb/°F = 4177.6 J/kg/°K
1 J/kg/°K = 1000 J/g/°C

Data to be collected with an explanation of how they will be collected (e.g. "Water temperature data for three days using a continuous data logger")

1. The mass of material being tested will be determined by weighing on a scale to the nearest 0.01 g (0.035 oz).
2. The temperature of the hotplates will be measured using the preset temperature control guides on the units, verified by careful calibration of the units, to set them at 100°C ±0.1°C or 212°F ±0.25°F
3. The temperature of the mass will be measured initially and at the end of the test period using a thermometer inserted through a cork or rubber stopper on the top of the heating flask capable of reading to 0.01°C or 0.25°F.
4. The time of heating will be measured with a stopwatch, wristwatch, or other suitably accurate clock.

Potential Interferences and Interference Management Plan:
Interferences in this test procedure include impurities in the test samples, inaccuracies in the calibration of the hotplates and thermometers, improper calibration of scales used to mass the samples, inaccurate reading of heating times, and inaccurate calculation of results. To avoid these complications, care must be taken to calibrate the equipment properly and to check calculations carefully. Impurities are difficult to see in most samples, but it is unlikely that a pure substance will be available, suggesting that a variation, perhaps significant, from the stated values in the table may result from the experimental procedure.

Tools, Equipment, and Supplies Required:
1 hotplate capable of temperature control to within 0.1°C at 100°C (0.02°F at 212°F) for each sample to be tested
One 250 mL (8.5 oz) Erlenmeyer flask for each sample to be tested
1 cork or rubber stopper for each flask sufficient to cover the top of the flask and containing a hole for the insertion of the selected thermometer or temperature probe.

1 digital thermometer or electronic thermometer with a long enough probe to be inserted through the stopper of a 250 mL (8.5 oz) Erlenmeyer flask. The thermometer must be capable of being inserted into the test sample contained within the flask and extend far enough out of the flask to read the temperature of the sample before and after heating to within 0.01°C (0.02°F).

Safety

Wear lab coats, safety glasses, and use heat-resistant gloves. This experiment uses hotplates set at a temperature of 100°C (212°F), and glass flasks are placed on top of those hotplates to heat the flasks and their contents. Everything will be very hot, and care must be used to handle all equipment with heat-resistant gloves or tongs at all times. Burns are the biggest risk faced with this experiment.

In addition to physical burns to the skin, touching a hot surface generally elicits an uncontrolled reaction in people which can dislodge glassware and cause breakage, yielding flying glass shards and burning of other people, laboratory tables and floors, and other materials nearby. Cuts from hot glass are a risk in that scenario.

Depending on the material being tested, heating of the material may cause off-gassing of hazardous or dangerous gases. Being knowledgeable about the potential emissions from hot samples is important to safeguard experimenters. The use of a fume hood in which to conduct the heating of the flasks will minimize the risks of accidental breakage and off-gassing.

Heating of material is being done inside a covered Erlenmeyer flask. The cork or stopper is to be placed over the mouth of the flask, *but not inserted into the mouth of the flask, to avoid an increase in pressure inside the flask which could cause an explosion.* An increase in the internal pressure inside the flask would also change the constant pressure value of the calculated specific heat, rendering the experimental results inaccurate.

Planned Experimental Procedures and Steps, in Order:

1. Preheat all hot plates to 100°C (212°F) and put on appropriate personal protection equipment.
2. Arrange 250 mL (8.5 oz) Erlenmeyer flasks with a label to indicate the material to be tested in that beaker.
3. Place exactly 100 g (3.2 oz) of each material to be tested in separate beakers. (Any other mass is also acceptable provided the actual mass is recorded precisely.)
4. Place a cork or rubber stopper on the top of each beaker and insert a thermometer through the hole in the center of each cork or stopper so that the thermometer is inserted into the mass of material being tested. *Do not insert the cork or stopper into the mouth of the flask to avoid overpressure during heating.*
5. Record the initial temperature of each material.
6. Set each beaker on a separate hot plate sequentially at 2-minute intervals so that end results can be read without haste at approximate intervals of 2 minutes.

7. Allow the materials to heat for 10 minutes. Record the actual start time of heating.
8. At the end of the 10 minute heating time, record the temperature of the material from the thermometer.
9. Calculate the change in temperature of the material being tested.
10. Calculate the value of Q using the formula:

$$Q = (\text{Temperature of the hotplate}) \times (\text{time of heating in minutes})$$

11. Calculate the specific heat capacity of each material using the formula:

$$C = \left(\frac{Q}{M * T} \right)$$

where:
   C = Specific heat capacity, Joules/(kg °C)
   Q = Amount of heat added, Joules
   M = Mass of material being heated, kg
   T = Change in temperature of the material, °C

Data Collection Format and Data Collection Sheets Tailored to Experiment:
See attached Data Collection Sheet

Anticipated Outcomes:
The specific heat values calculated are very different for each material tested. The actual results will vary depending upon how accurately the hotplates are calibrated, how accurately they hold the set temperature, the starting and ending temperature of the samples tested, and the accuracy of the thermometer measuring the temperature of the test samples. Calculated values should be consistent with the values shown in Table A.3.

Data Analysis Plan:
A comparison will be made between the specific heat calculated for the test materials and the standard values for specific heat of that material as published elsewhere. In the event there is no identified standard value published for the material tested, a comparison will be made with similar materials demonstrating specific heat values slightly higher and slightly lower than that measured to determine whether the measured value is reasonable.

Data Collection Sheet for Determination of Specific Heat Capacities

Date Samples Collected:

Date Samples Tested:

Principal Investigator:

Material Being Tested	Sample 1	Sample 2	Sample 3	Sample 4	Sample 5
Mass of sample placed into beaker					
Initial temperature of sample, °C					
Actual time of heating, mins					
Temperature of sample after heating, °C					
Change in temperature during heating, °C					
Calculated value of Q					
Calculate specific heat of each sample					

EXPERIMENT 9.6: DETERMINATION OF INSULATION R-VALUES FOR VARIOUS MATERIALS

Date: _____

Principal Investigator:

    Name: _____

    Email: _____

    Phone: _____

Collaborators:

    Name: _____

    Email: _____

    Phone: _____

    Name: _____

    Email: _____

    Phone: _____

    Name: _____

    Email: _____

    Phone: _____

    Name: _____

    Email: _____

    Phone: _____

    Name: _____

    Email: _____

    Phone: _____

Objective or Question to Be Addressed:

Environmental sustainability concepts encompass many things. One of those is the conservation of energy, particularly heat energy. The conservation of heat energy is a function of several factors, one of which is the insulating value, or heat retention value, of the insulation in a structure and of the materials from which the structure is constructed.

This experiment is designed to provide some insight into the insulating value, or R-value, of various materials and thicknesses of those materials.

Theory Behind Experiment:

The R-value of a substance or material is a function of the material characteristics and the thickness of the material between the inside and the outside of a building or structure. The conservation of heat, and therefore the conservation of heat energy, requires an understanding of the R-value of various materials at various thicknesses.

Heat is generally transferred from one material to another by heat moving from the hotter substance to the cooler one (as opposed to "cool" moving to the hotter material). The substance could be heat from air moving through insulation to cooler air (and note that it is the *heat energy* that is moving, not the actual air in most cases), the movement of heat from air through wood or other building materials to cooler air, and so forth. This transfer of heat energy is related to the thermodynamic quantity referred to as entropy, which represents the amount of a system's thermal energy that is unavailable for conversion into mechanical work, often interpreted as the degree of disorder or randomness in the system, caused by losses as the energy travels through various media.

Note that the second law of thermodynamics says that entropy always increases with time. This reflects the concept that losses of heat energy are always occurring as energy passes through one medium and enters another.

Thermal conductivity, denoted by the symbol k, is the property of a material that indicates its ability to conduct heat. Heat is conducted if there exists a temperature gradient in the material. Conductive heat flow occurs in the direction of decreasing temperature in accordance with Fourier's Law which expresses conductive heat transfer mathematically as:

$$H = kA\left(T_2 - T_1\right)/x$$

or:

$$k = Hx/A\left(T_2 - T_1\right)$$

where:

H = the steady-state rate of heat transfer, W/m² K (Watts/m²/°Kelvin)
　　　or BTU/hr/(ft² ∗ °F) Note: $[(°\mathbf{F} - 32) \times 5/9] + 273.15 = °\mathbf{K}$
k = the thermal conductivity of the sample, W/m-K (Watts/meter/°K)
　　　or BTU/hr/(ft ∗ °F) Note: 1 w/m-K = 0.57818 BTU/hr-ft-°F
A = the cross-sectional area of the sample, square meters (10.7639 ft²/m²)
$(T_2 - T_1)$ = the temperature difference across the sample thickness, °K (°F)
x = the thickness of the sample, meters (3.28 feet/m)

This calculation assumes that the heat loss from the sides of the sample is negligible. To keep the loss from the sides small, the sample is typically made in the form of a thin disk with a large cross-sectional area compared to the area exposed at the edge. Keeping the area large and the thickness small produces a large rate of energy transfer across the sample. Keeping the thickness small also allows the system to achieve a desired steady-state condition, which is defined to mean when the values of the temperatures T_1 and T_2 are constant, more quickly than would occur with a greater sample thickness.

Thermal conductivity can be measured in a variety of ways; most are complicated and fraught with dangerous conditions. Each method is also suitable for a limited range of materials, such as those that have high heat conductivity or those that have a low heat conductivity. The most commonly used methods are Searle's method, for materials with high heat transfer potential (such as steel or copper, for example), and Lee's disc method, for materials with poor heat transfer potential (such as glass, for example).

This experiment describes a modified method to approximate the R-value of a material rather than the more rigorous methodology required of manufacturers of insulating materials. A detailed description of Searle's method may be found at:

https://www.schoolphysics.co.uk/age16-19/Thermal%20physics/Transfer%20 of%20heat/text/

Searle's bar/index.html

and a detailed description of Lee's method can be found at:

iiserprune.ac.in/~bhasbapat/phy221_files/Lee's%20method.pdf

Regardless of the method used, the R-value, also called the thermal conductivity coefficient, indicates how well a certain material retains heat; in essence, how well it insulates. The higher the R-value, the better the material insulates. The following formula is used to calculate the R-value:

R-value = thickness of the insulation / k

where:

R-value = thermal conductivity coefficient

x = thickness, m

k = thermal conductivity of the material W/m-K (Watts/meter/°K)

or BTU/hr/(ft * °F) Note: 1 w/m-K = 0.57818 BTU/hr-ft-°F

An example: a one square meter (10.7639 square feet) piece of insulating material, 10 cm (0.10 m or 0.3208 ft) thick, with a k of 0.05 W/mK (0.02891 BTU/hr – ft – °F)) results in an R-value of 2 m^2K/W or 11.10 BTU/hr/(ft^2 * °F)

The better the insulating material (the lower the k), the thinner the insulation needs to be to achieve the same result in terms of thermal insulation.

Every material has its own unique k-value and that is a variable depending on various characteristics of the material at the time. The following table provides some insights into this issue.

Factor	Effect on Thermal Conductivity
The physical or chemical phase of the material	A sharp change in heat conductivity may occur if the phase of a material changes, such as from a solid to a liquid or a liquid to a gas.
Thermal Anisotropy	Heat, magnetic forces, and other physical or chemical factors can cause some substances to exhibit different values of thermal conductivity along different crystal axes. This characteristic, called *thermal anisotropy*, implies that the direction in which the heat flows through the substance may not be the same as the normal temperature gradient direction, from hot to cold. This is not a significant issue with most common materials.
The electrical conductivity of the material	The relationship between electrical conductivity and thermal conductivity, only applicable to metals, can affect the k-value of certain metals. The heat conductivity of most nonmetals is relatively unaffected by their electrical conductivity.
Influence of magnetic fields	A change in the thermal conductivity of a conductor may occur when it is subjected to a magnetic field.
Purity of the material	The purity of the isotope being measured can have an effect on the heat conductivity of that material.

Adapted from: https://byjus.com/chemistry/thermal-conductivity/ accessed 12-21-20.

The value of k is usually reported at 25°C and that value is used interchangeably with the value for 25°K. It turns out that the difference in the value for °C and °K are not significantly different provided all the measurements are in the same units because the k-value depends on the differences in temperature rather than the specific value. Since °C and °K are always the same 273° apart, they will always yield the same difference when subtracted in either units. The results are still reported in W/m-K.

Table A.3 in the Appendix provides data on the specific heat of selected materials, and Table A.4 provides a list of the k-values of selected material reported by various sources, as noted. Figure A.1a–A.1c in the Appendix provides the design of an insulated box suitable for insertion into a drying oven or incubator to provide a controllable external heat source for this experiment.

Sometimes manufacturers or others will use a U-value, rather than an R-value. The U-value is the inverse of the R-value. Thus, an R-value of 4 would yield a U-value of ¼, or 0.25. Similarly, the U-value formula is:

$$U\text{-Value} = k / \text{thickness of the insulation}$$

where:
    k = thermal conductivity of the material

The current experiment is a less-than-precise method of estimating the approximate value of k for a material. This modified method is used for safety reasons and because the more difficult methods are not necessary to illustrate the phenomena described.

Here, the experimenter will take advantage of the following concepts:

$$\left(\frac{Q}{t}\right) = \frac{kA\left(T_{hot} - T_{cold}\right)}{x}$$

where:

(Q/t) = Heat transferred, Joules/second, or Watts
t = Time, seconds
k = Thermal conductivity, W/m-K
A = Area of the insulating material, m^2
T = Temperature, °K (or °C)
x = Thickness of the insulating material, m

Therefore:

$$k = \left(\frac{Q}{t}\right)\frac{x}{A\left(T_{hot} - T_{cold}\right)}$$

and:

$$\left(\frac{Q}{t}\right) = m\,c\left(T_{hot} - T_{cold}\right)$$

where:

m = Mass of the insulating material, kg
c = Specific heat of the insulating material, J/(kg-°K)
t = Time, seconds

The technique, then, is to measure the amount of heat (Q) that is transferred across a mass (m) of material in a given time frame (t). The specific heat of the material being tested is determined from published sources (See Table A.3 in the Appendix), and the value Q/t is calculated in Watts. Recall that 1 J/sec = 1 W.

The value of Q/t is then inserted into the equation for k, along with the thickness of the test material, the area of the test material exposed to heat transfer, the time duration of the test, and the change in temperature over that time frame.

The value of k thus determined is likely to be different from published data (See Table A.4 in the Appendix) due to the slight variation of k with the temperature of the material being tested. The value determined here should be reasonably close to that in the published data, however.

Once the k-value is determined, division of the material thickness by the k-value will determine the R-value of the material.

Data to be collected with an explanation of how they will be collected (e.g. "Water temperature data for three days using a continuous data logger")
The data to be generated are the thickness of the test material, the area of the test material exposed inside the test frame, the temperature inside an incubator or oven being used to test the material, time, and the temperature inside the test box.

A thermometer inserted into the test box will be used to record the temperature inside the box. The temperature indicator built into the incubator or oven will be used to measure the temperature inside the incubator or oven, a watch or clock will be used to measure time, and a ruler or tape measure will be used to measure the thickness of soft test material, while a caliper will be used to measure the thickness of a solid test material.

Any material of suitable size and thickness (no greater than 13 inches (0.33 m) square and 1 inch thick) will fit into the frame as designed. A thicker material may be used provided that the thickness where the frame clamps the test material sample may not be larger than 1 inch or the frame will not be able to be adequately clamped to the test material and losses will be experienced around the edge of the test material that will be very difficult to measure or estimate.

Potential Interferences and Interference Management Plan:
Interferences in this experiment will arise from losses through the material clamped in the frame of the test box. Those losses should be minimal since the area of the loss is principally the thickness of the edge of the test material if the material is properly clamped into the frame, and those edges will be insulated against loss by the test box material. Over a relatively short time frame of the test, those losses may reasonably be neglected for most materials. The thicker the test material, the greater those losses will become, however, and some attempt to account for them should be made if the test data and the published data are significantly different.

In addition, k-values and R-values are dependent upon the temperatures on both sides of the insulation. Higher temperatures on either side will negatively impact the k-values and R-values. Most published values assume a test temperature of approximately 25°C (77°F), or slightly above room temperature. At the elevated temperatures needed to generate useful data, the values may be somewhat different from the published values.

There will be losses associated with the hole through which the thermometer is inserted into the test box. The more tightly the thermometer fits into the hole, the lower the losses will be. Moreover, the glass from which the thermometer is made can conduct heat much more quickly into the interior of the test box than the insulation from which the box is made. Over a short time frame of 5–10 minutes, this increase should not be excessive. It may account for some variation in the value of k or R, however, relative to published data.

Tools, Equipment, and Supplies Required:
Incubator or oven capable of heating to 100°F (37.8°C), with a glass door through which the test box inside can be viewed.
Test box per Figure A.1 in the Appendix (or equivalent)
Suitable sample of one or more materials to be tested
Watch or clock to measure time
Ruler or caliper to measure the area and thickness of the samples

Safety
This experiment relies on the transfer of heat through a test sample. The test sample is secured inside a test box which, in turn, is placed inside an incubator or oven. The entire test assembly is then heated to a temperature of 100°F (37.8°C). That

temperature is sufficient to cause burns to the human skin. Heat-resistant gloves must be worn at all times during the conduct of the experiment.

Depending on the material to be tested, minute fibers may be inadvertently released into the surrounding atmosphere or adhere to clothing. When the material being tested has been shown to exhibit this behavior, respiratory and eye protection is required.

The melting point of the polyisocyanurate material from which the test box is to be built is between 200° and 250°F (93.3°C and 121.1°C). It is important to prevent the incubator or oven from heating above 150°F (65.5°C) to avoid burns or fires associated with melting of the polyisocyanurate. Should melting be observed, immediately turn off the oven or incubator, but *DO NOT OPEN THE DOOR* until after the material has cooled as the inrush of air could exacerbate any potential fire risk.

Planned Experimental Procedures and Steps, in Order:

1. Prepare an insulated box per Figures A.1a–A.1c in the Appendix.
2. Gather all materials and equipment ready for use and put on appropriate personal safety equipment.
3. Insert the test material sample into the frame of the test box and secure it firmly in place. Record the exposed area of the test sample inside the frame and the thickness of the sample in the opening of the frame. These are the values of A and x, respectively.
4. Place the box with the sample attached inside an incubator or oven with a glass door in such a position that the thermometer inserted into the top of the test box can be easily read from the exterior of the incubator or oven.
5. Record the internal temperature of the incubator or oven and the temperature inside the test box.
6. Turn on the incubator or oven and set the heat to 100°F (37.8°C).
7. Record the time at which the incubator or oven is turned on.
8. Watch the temperature in the incubator or oven and record the time at which it reaches the preset temperature. Record that time and simultaneously note the temperature inside the test box.
9. Record the time that the temperature inside the test box and the temperature outside the test box, but inside the incubator stabilize at the same value.
10. Calculate the change in the temperature inside the box per unit of time that the heating took place. This is Q/t.
11. Calculate the difference between the temperature inside the incubator or oven and the temperature inside the test box. These are the T_{hot} and T_{cold} temperatures.
12. Adjust the Q/t value for a Q per hour, adjust the A value to square meters, adjust the x value to meters, and adjust the T_{hot} and T_{cold} temperatures to °C, as necessary.
13. Calculate the k-value using the adjusted Q/t, A, x, and T_{hot} and T_{cold} temperatures values.
14. Calculate the R-value for the test sample from the calculated k-value.

Data Collection Format and Data Collection Sheets Tailored to Experiment:
See attached data collection sheet

Anticipated Outcomes:
It is expected that a rational value for the k-value and the R-value of the test material will be developed. A value within 5% of the average value shown in the literature will normally be accepted as rational. To the extent the values developed in this experiment are not within approximately 5% of the published values, a discussion of why they are outside that limit is warranted.

Data Analysis Plan:
The data generated by this experiment will be adjusted as specified, then used to calculate the k-value and the R-value of the test sample using the equations provided. The resulting values will then be compared to published data for the same material. Any differences will be discussed and justified.

Data Collection Sheet for Determination of Insulation R-Values for Various Materials

Material Being Tested:

Parameter	Value
Area of opening in test box, m² (A)	
Thickness of sample in frame opening, m (x)	
Internal temp of oven, °C or °F	
Initial temp inside test box, °C or °F	
Time oven is turned on	
Time at which oven reaches preset temp	
Length of time between turning on the oven and achieving the preset internal temperature (t)	
Verify temp inside oven, °C or °F (T_{Hot})	
Change in internal temp from time oven turned on to time internal temp reaches preset value, °C or °F (Q/t)	
Temperature inside the test box when the oven reaches the preset internal temperature (T_{cold})	
Adjusted Q/t value	
Adjusted A value	
Adjusted x value	
Adjusted $T_{Ho}t$ value	
Adjusted T_{cold} value	
Calculated k-value	
Calculated R-value	

EXPERIMENT 9.7: HEADSPACE ANALYSIS FOR THE PRESENCE OF VOLATILE ORGANIC COMPOUNDS

Date: _____

Principal Investigator:

    Name: _____

    Email: _____

    Phone: _____

Collaborators:

    Name: _____

    Email: _____

    Phone: _____

    Name: _____

    Email: _____

    Phone: _____

    Name: _____

    Email: _____

    Phone: _____

    Name: _____

    Email: _____

    Phone: _____

    Name: _____

    Email: _____

    Phone: _____

Objective or Question to Be Addressed:
When soil or groundwater sites are known to be contaminated, or suspected to be contaminated, with volatile organic compounds, it is useful to assess quickly whether the concentration of the contaminants exceeds the reportable concentrations under applicable local, state, or federal environmental protection agency Contingency Plans. A simple screening test, known as the *Headspace Test* or *Jar Headspace Test*, is frequently conducted on-site to assist with making that judgment. This experiment demonstrates that Headspace Test procedure.

Theory Behind Experiment

Volatile organic compounds (VOCs), including their break-down byproducts, can remain in water or soil for significant periods of time if they are not disturbed or moved through groundwater movement. When the water or soil containing these compounds is disturbed, they volatilize rapidly and escape from the sample. If the water or soil suspected of being contaminated is carefully placed inside a closed container, then allowed to be rapidly disturbed (shaken), the resulting volatilization of the VOCs will occur inside the closed container. If the concentration of those contaminants in the air above the disturbed sample can be measured, an estimate of the total contaminants in the sample can be made. By projecting the estimated sample concentration to the overall area of suspected contamination, a decision can be made regarding the need for further testing of the water or soil for actual concentrations present and whether further site remediation is required.

This test places a small sample of the suspect material into a mason-type jar, the jar is quickly covered and sealed, then the contents are shaken and heated to allow any volatiles to begin to volatilize. After a suitable waiting period, the air above the sample is rapidly tested with a photoionization detector (PID) or other suitable instrument. If the concentration of VOCs in the air above the sample is high enough, the area from which the sample was collected is further sampled, preserved for testing, and sent to a laboratory for detailed testing.

Potential Interferences and Interference Management Plan

Interferences are not likely with this test, but the issue of accuracy is likely. The VOC concentration in the air will be artificially reduced under the following conditions:

- Improper handling of the sample as it is being placed in the jar
- Leakage around the seal of the jar during the volatilization phase
- Improper heating of the sample during the VOC development phase
- Failure to plunge the test instrument wand directly through the seal
- Making an insertion hole that is larger than necessary
- Reading the maximum value too slowly or missing it altogether

Overstating of the VOC concentration is unlikely with this screening procedure. Consequently, most regulatory agencies look for low values from this test as a guide to conducting further testing.

Data to be collected with an explanation of how they will be collected (e.g. "Water temperature data for three days using a continuous data logger")

VOC concentrations in the air above the sample inside the closed jar will be made with a PID or other suitable instrument.

Tools, Equipment, and Supplies Required:

Two 8 oz or 16 oz (250–500 mL) Mason-type jar with separate inner cap seal
Aluminum foil or parafilm
PID or other suitable test instrument

Safety

VOCs are toxic to humans at low concentrations. Inhalation should be avoided. This test is typically done outdoors or inside a vented laboratory hood to minimize exposure to the VOC vapors. If exposure does occur, or if headaches, nausea, or vision blurring occurs, immediately move to a fresh air source, away from the exposure, and put on a respirator for further study of the area. Exposure at concentrations in air sufficient to cause odors to be noticed requires a respirator. Concentrations at those levels generally indicate high enough concentrations in the surrounding media that the Headspace Test will not be useful since the concentrations will already be known to exceed all applicable allowable concentrations.

Exposure directly to the eyes can be serious. Immediately wash with an eyewash and seek medical assistance. Exposure to the skin will cause drying of the skin and a rash if untreated. Wash immediately with soap and water and apply a hand cream in the event of exposure.

Planned Experimental Procedures and Steps, in Order:

1. PID field instruments should be operated and calibrated to yield "total organic vapors" in ppm (v/v) as benzene. PID instruments must be operated with a 10.0 ± eV lamp source. Operation, maintenance, and calibration should be performed in accordance with the manufacturer's specifications. For jar headspace analysis, instrument calibration should be checked/adjusted no less than once every 10 analyses, or daily, whichever is greater.
2. Half fill, approximately, two clean glass jars with the sample to be analyzed. Quickly cover each open top with one or two sheets of clean parafilm or aluminum foil and apply screw caps, without the inner cover plate, to tightly seal the jars. Sixteen ounce (500 ml) soil or "mason"-type jars are preferred; jars less than 8 oz. (9250 mL) should not be used.
3. Allow headspace development for at least 10 minutes. Vigorously shake jars for 15 seconds both at the beginning and end of the headspace development period. Where ambient temperatures are below 32°F (0°C), headspace development should be done within a heated vehicle or building.
4. Subsequent to headspace development, if the lid on the jar is not a mason-type jar, and there is no inner seal plate on the cap that has been left off, remove the screw lid carefully, without disturbing the aluminum foil or parafilm covering. This step is not done if the aluminum foil or parafilm seal is exposed. Quickly puncture the aluminum foil or parafilm seal with the PID sampling probe to a point about one-half of the headspace depth. Exercise care to avoid uptake of water droplets or soil particles.

    As an alternative, syringe withdrawal of a headspace sample with subsequent injection to the instrument probe or septum-fitted inlet is acceptable contingent upon verification of methodology accuracy using a test gas standard.
5. Following probe insertion through the seal and/or sample injection to the probe, record the highest meter response as the jar headspace concentration. Using a parafilm or foil seal/probe insertion method, *the maximum*

response should occur between 2 and 5 seconds after probe insertion. Erratic meter response may occur at high organic vapor concentrations or conditions of elevated headspace moisture, in which case headspace data should be discounted.

6. The headspace screening data from both jar samples should be recorded and compared; generally, replicate values should be consistent to plus or minus 20%.

7. Measure control samples, as required by regulatory agencies, including clean soil, ambient air, gasoline/air partition, water saturated with gasoline/ air partition are tested at the same time that the test samples are run to ensure consistency.

   Note that instrumentation with digital (LED/LCD) displays may not be able to discern maximum headspace response unless equipped with a "maximum hold" feature or strip-chart recorder.

8. Complete the following table using data generated during the experiment and using the equations that follow the table for each VOC of interest. These calculations assume that all the VOCs measured are the contaminant of interest. This tends to overstate the concentration of each contaminant.

Sample Locations	Benzene Jar Headspace Conc'n (ppmv/v) (Read out from PID)	Benzene Jar Headspace Conc'n (mg/m³) (See Equation 1)	Predicted Benzene Groundwater Conc'n (mg/L) (See Equation 2)
1			
2			
3			
4			
5			
6			

Equation 1: Use the following equations to convert from ppm v/v (read out on the PID) to find the concentration of the target compound in the headspace (C_a).

$$C_a = mg/m^3 = \frac{(ppm\ v/v) \times GMW \times 273.15\,K}{22.414 \times T(K)} \times \frac{P(atm)}{1\,atm}$$

where:

(ppm v/v) = maximum concentration measured in the headspace, ppm
GMW = gram molecular weight of the target compound, mg
T = temperature, Kelvin (K)
P = atmospheric pressure, atm

Equation 2: Assuming soil is in equilibrium with the groundwater, use Henry's law to predict the groundwater concentration of benzene.

where
H_c = Henry's constant for target compound, unitless
C_a = concentration in headspace air, mg/m^3
C_w = concentration in groundwater, mg/m^3

For benzene:

$$H_c = C_a / C_w = 5.29 \times 10^{-2}$$

Data Collection Format and Data Collection Sheets Tailored to Experiment:
The data from this experiment are collected instantaneously and recorded in a note book for reporting to regulatory agencies. No data collection sheet is required.

Data Analysis Plan:
The data collected are air concentration for the space above the sample in the test jar. They are then converted to assumed sample concentrations using the equations provided. The sample concentrations are then referred to applicable regulatory standards to determine the need for and degree of clean-up to be done.

Expected Outcomes: For Testing by the Students:
Outcome data will depend on the samples tested and the concentration of contaminants present. For educational purposes, it is useful for the instructor to prepare two or three samples of artificially contaminated soil or water using a known concentration of various VOCs. A comparison with the known concentrations and the derived concentrations using this procedure will be instructive.

EXPERIMENT 9.8:   SURFACE RUNOFF RATE DETERMINATION AND VOLUME CALCULATION

Date: _____

Principal Investigator:

      Name: _____

      Email: _____

      Phone: _____

Collaborators:

      Name: _____

      Email: _____

      Phone: _____

      Name: _____

      Email: _____

      Phone: _____

      Name: _____

      Email: _____

      Phone: _____

      Name: _____

      Email: _____

      Phone: _____

      Name: _____

      Email: _____

      Phone: _____

Objective or Question to Be Addressed:
In this experiment, the investigator will determine the average runoff rate for various surface materials and use those data to calculate the estimated runoff volume expected from a specific area resulting from a specific storm of defined intensity and duration. The values determined by this experiment are average expected values because no actual surface area is as smooth and shallow as the one used in the experiment, and significant variations may be encountered depending on the previous rainfall or drought conditions present and the actual porosity of the soil or other surface materials. Table A.9 in the Appendix provides Typical Surface Stormwater Runoff Coefficients for reference.

Theory Behind Experiment:
All surfaces are porous to some degree. Asphalt, concrete, and stone are certainly less porous than sand or other soil types, but all surface materials exhibit some porosity. Porosity provides a way for rain or snowmelt to seep into the surface, rather than continue to just run off into a storm drain or ditch. The amount, or percentage, of the water falling onto the surface that actually runs off depends on the surface material, the roughness of that material, the slope of the surface, the intensity and length of the rainfall, the time and air temperature during the rain event, the humidity during the rain event, and a lot of other miscellaneous factors.

The volume of water that will run off a specified area and collect at a specific point is calculated from the formula:

$$Q = Cia$$

where:

Q = the volume of water that runs off, ft³/sec (m³/sec)

C = the runoff coefficient for the surface over which the runoff will occur, unitless

i = the intensity of the rain event, ft/h (m/h)

a = the area over which the runoff is being estimated, ft² (m²)

This equation does not take into account the slope of the land directly but does include that value in the determination of C.

A device is described in Figures A.2a–A.2g in the Appendix by which the runoff from various surface types may be estimated. This device is designed for a known volume of water to be poured into the upper segment from which it is distributed across a section of preset materials through a v-notch weir. Water could also be sprayed onto the surface if a spray device with an accurate volume control mechanism can be found or created. The key is to know how much water runs off the surface (Q), how long the water volume took to enter the surface (i), the area of the surface being measured (a), and how long it takes for that volume of water to run off the surface.

Potential Interferences and Interference Management Plan
Surface slopes are not uniform over large areas. Therefore, the runoff at a given slope may need to be adjusted to the average slope of an area. That is done by interpolation between values for known slopes developed and plotted on a chart during this experiment. A poor estimate of the average slope will yield poor estimates of actual runoff volumes.

The materials being tested during this experiment are attached to a plexiglass surface. The thickness of the material is determined by the investigator but will be finite and shallow. Actual soil conditions may be significantly different in the field.

This experiment does not account for sediment transport during a storm event. It is assumed that the area under consideration will have been subjected to sufficient prior storm events that sediment transport will not be a significant factor in the outcome of the experiments.

Data to be collected with an explanation of how they will be collected (e.g. "Water temperature data for three days using a continuous data logger")
Runoff is measured in terms of volume per unit of time. The intensity, or the rate at which the water is allowed to run over the surface (volume per unit of area), is an important function to control. The volume of water leaving the area over a measured time frame is equally important and is measured at the outlet of the testing device. Note that the volume entering at the top of the device and the volume leaving at the bottom of the device may be different because of absorption by the surface materials or a change over time in the rate of runoff as saturation of the surface occurs.

During this experiment, the volume of water added to the device per unit of time (i), the volume of water leaving the device per unit of time (Q), the area of the surface subjected to runoff (a), and the time of the experiment will be measured. C will then be calculated from the measured data.

Tools, Equipment, and Supplies Required:
Adjustable flow box similar to that shown in drawings A.2a–A.2g in the Appendix
Suitable surface plates for the flow box, per the drawings
Tap water and a sink for drainage
Means of measuring the flow from the flow box
Timer or stopwatch

Safety
This experiment uses a device similar to that shown in the Appendix. It is adjustable relative to the slope of the box, and it may be fitted with a variety of flow surfaces for testing. The device is constructed of plexiglass panels which may have sharp edges if not properly sanded and smoothed during construction. In addition, the box will be heavy, particularly after being fitted with a surface panel. Pinching of fingers could occur during raising or lowering of the panels within the device or when assembling the panels inside the box. Note that the box is designed such that the panels are attached to support brackets, and then the assembled panel with brackets is inserted into the box and secured from the outside with T-nuts. Care is needed when inserting the panel into the box.

The materials being used are not inherently dangerous, but water may splash or spill. Eye protection and a lab coat are recommended for use during the experiment.

Planned Experimental Procedures and Steps, in Order:

1. Assemble all required tools, equipment, and surface panels and put on PPE.
2. Assemble the flow box with a selected surface panel. Set the box on a sink or other location from which drainage may occur unimpeded and measured. Set the box to the lowest (flat) orientation.
3. Pour enough clean tap water behind the v-notch weir to saturate the surface panel and allow to drain.
4. Pour a continuous flow of water behind the v-notch weir, at a constant, measured flow rate (approximately 1 inch (2.54 cm) per hour over the measured surface area being tested), until drainage begins to occur at the bottom end of the box. Record the flow rate of the water entering the device behind the

weir, the time that water starts to flow onto the surface, and the time that water starts to flow out, and measure the volume of water that leaves the device over a 5 minute period. A time other than 5 minutes is acceptable, but needs to be noted if used. Note that the surface area is approximately 1 square foot (0.093 m²). This yields a desired flow rate into the box of 0.0116 gal/min (0.044 L/min). This reduces to 0.046 cups/min (10.9 mL/min). These flow rates into the box will allow easy conversion of the output to expected runoff volumes from a 1 inch/h (2.54 cm/h) rainfall event.

5. At the end of the 5 minute test, stop the flow at the top and allow the unit to finish draining.
6. Reset the device to the first slope angle of 15° and repeat steps 1–5.
7. Reset step 6 as many times as desired, raising the slope angle each time.
8. Change the surface panel and repeat steps 1–7.
9. Repeat step 8 as many times as panels are available.

Data Collection Format and Data Collection Sheets Tailored to Experiment:
See attached data collection sheet

Data Analysis Plan:
The data developed from this experiment will show an increase in runoff flow rates as the angle of the box is increased. The flow rate at each angle will be a function of the surface parameters and will be different for each surface. If the inflow is measured properly, the runoff rate per hour for each inch of rainfall per hour will be easily calculated. The data for each surface type and slope angle will be noted. A series of area calculations, based on U.S. Geologic Survey (USGS) maps of a small watershed that is monitored by the USGS, can be used to calculate the average expected runoff based on the average surface type and average slope angle across the target area. Those results can then be compared to measured data available from the USGS.

Assess the runoff volumes for the experimental runoff flow rates for a proposed construction area of 10,000 ft² in an area where the design rainfall intensity is 2.0 in/h.

Expected Outcomes:
It is expected that the data will show significant differences in the rate of runoff from different surface types and that those values will be reasonably consistent with published data, such as that shown in Table A.9 in the Appendix. An adjustment factor may be needed to account for the shallow depth of the test surfaces relative to actual soil conditions and surface conditions within the watershed used for comparison.

Surface Runoff Rate Determination and Volume Calculation Data Sheet					
Date:					
Principal Investigator:					
Surface Being Tested	Flow Rate, in/hr (cm/hr)	Time Measurement of Flow Out Started	Time Measurement of Flow Out Stopped	Measured Flow Volume out	Calculated Runoff Rate, in/hr (cm/hr)

EXPERIMENT 9.9:   WATER FILTRATION MEDIA EVALUATION

Date: _____

Principal Investigator:

     Name: _____

     Email: _____

     Phone: _____

Collaborators:

     Name: _____

     Email: _____

     Phone: _____

     Name: _____

     Email: _____

     Phone: _____

     Name: _____

     Email: _____

     Phone: _____

     Name: _____

     Email: _____

     Phone: _____

     Name: _____

     Email: _____

     Phone: _____

Objective or Question to Be Addressed:

Water from lakes and rivers often has contaminants that make it unfit for drinking. The water may contain dirt, rocks, and other objects that can be easily identified. Water may also contain bacteria and other microscopic organisms that cannot be seen easily. For these reasons, water that is delivered to homes must go through a water treatment process. This is typically a five-part process that consists of aeration, coagulation, sedimentation, filtration, and disinfection. This exercise is only concerned with filtration, which removes most, but not all, of the impurities from the water. *Filtration alone does not render the water fit to drink, and the water resulting from this exercise will not be rendered safe to drink.*

In this exercise, students are challenged to design and build a water filtration device using commonly available materials. To meet this challenge, students use an iterative process as they build, test, and measure the performance of the filtration device; analyze the data collected; and use this information to work toward an improved filtration design.

Although students may work in teams, they are encouraged to think of their entire class as a single design team working cooperatively and learning from the efforts of all members in order to produce the best water filtration device. Students will measure the effectiveness of their filtration device using pH meters, DO meters, turbidimeters, and conductivity meters.

This activity can be guided by competition of the student teams. To make a qualitative assessment of the filtered water: hold a piece of white paper in back of the filtered water and examine for particulate matter and color. The winning team has the clearest water sample.

The student-built filtration device is to be made from two 2-liter water bottles with the bottoms cut off. The bottles will be stacked so as to allow the wastewater to filter through filter media in the top bottle and collect in the bottom bottle. The challenge is for students to determine which filter media they should use to get the purest filtered water.

Theory Behind Experiment:
Students should research the definition of pure water, as it is defined for safe human consumption.

Describe to students the filter media available and have them research any materials with which they are unfamiliar (usually zeolite and activated carbon, if using). Discuss the meaning of pH (acidity or alkalinity of the solution) and the recommended pH for drinking water.

If using conductivity testers, discuss their use at this time. A conductivity tester creates a circuit through the water in order to measure the conductivity of the water. Conductivity is a standard method used to measure the purity of water, specifically the quantity of inorganic contaminants. Completely pure water will not conduct electrical current. Thus, the smaller the amount of current that flows through the treated wastewater, the lower the concentration of inorganic contaminants.

Data to be collected with an explanation of how they will be collected (e.g. "Water temperature data for three days using a continuous data logger")
Assessment for this activity varies based on materials available and testing methods used. If filtered water is more pure than the simulated wastewater, then the student-built filtration device was somewhat effective. The degree to which purity is possibly attained is dependent on materials available, so, in most classes, encourage students to use data collected in the course of the water analysis to decide which filters are most effective.

Potential Interferences and Interference Management Plan:
Potential interferences in this experiment will depend on the media being tested. Some minerals may dissolve during the experiment causing changes in conductivity, for example, which could indicate a less effective treatment than is actually

occurring. Similarly, some minerals or inorganics in the treated water may adhere to media during the test at such a rate that rapid saturation occurs. Thus, even though the test results may indicate effective treatment, the media may be on the verge of a breakthrough after a relatively short filter run.

Tools, Equipment, and Supplies Required:

Digital balances (for weighing filter media)
Graduated cylinders -250 mL (for measuring simulated wastewater)
Empty 2 L plastic water bottles (2 per team), these should be precut horizontally at about one inch above the middle of the bottle
Filtration materials, such as:
  Coffee filters
  Cheesecloth
  Elastic bands
  Gravel (saturated and cleaned)
  Sand (saturated and cleaned)
  Cotton balls
  Uncooked macaroni
  Zeolite
  Activated carbon (rinse carbon with water and dry before using)
Paper or plastic cups (to use as scoops in loose filter media)
Simulated wastewater (For 1 gallon: combine 2 cups distilled vinegar, several drops yellow food coloring, dust, a half-cup topsoil or sand, and enough water to fill the gallon. Shake well.) (Other pollutants to add if available: dirt, litter (bits of plastic, small objects like paperclips, etc.), cooking oil, glitter, salt or other spices; use any of the above, or any other materials conveniently available)
Water quality testing instruments:
  Conductivity meter
  DO meter
  pH meter
  Turbidimeter

Preparation:

- Empty 2 L soda bottles, remove labels, and clean.
- Cut soda bottle in half horizontally about 1 inch above the mid-point.
- Be sure to use clean and saturated gravel and sand.
- Be sure to rinse and thoroughly dry activate carbon (if using). Unrinsed carbon will turn the water black.
- Provide a large container to collect used filter materials, and note that there will be a lot of liquid waste.

**Note: Water filtered in this experiment SHOULD NOT be consumed by humans.

Safety:

This experiment requires plastic bottles to be cut. Box cutters and sharp knives can cause serious injury if not handled properly. Activated carbon contains a lot of carbon dust when first delivered. This dust can be inhaled easily and cause significant respiratory problems later – sometimes many years later – if care is not taken when handling this material.

Eye protection, a respirator or dust mask, gloves, and a lab coat are required for this experiment.

In the event of a cut or puncture wound, apply pressure to the wound to help stem bleeding and seek medical assistance immediately. Even a minor cut or puncture in the laboratory may introduce potentially hazardous materials into the bloodstream.

In the event of eye exposure, wash the eyes at an eyewash station for up to 15 minutes. Seek medical assistance to remove any particulate remaining in the eye. These particulates will be hard, small, and dangerous to eye tissue if not removed promptly.

In the event of respiratory exposure, remove the exposed patient to fresh air and seek medical advice for long-term monitoring.

Planned Experimental Procedures and Steps, in Order:

1. Nest the two bottles. Place the top half of the soda bottle upside-down (like a funnel) inside the bottom half.
2. The top half will be the filter, and the bottom half will hold the filtered water.
3. Fill the top bottle to within 1.5 inches (3.75 cm) of its top with filter media of various types and layers.
4. Document the amounts and sequence of filter media used.
5. Measure and record the pH, DO, turbidity, and conductivity of the simulated wastewater.
6. Slowly pour 200 mL (6.75 oz) of simulated wastewater through each student-built water filtration device.
7. Measure and record the pH and conductivity of the filtered water.
8. Observe what the filtered water looks like.
9. Measure and record the pH, DO, turbidity, and conductivity of the filtered water.
10. Take the filters apart and look at each of the different layers. Try to identify and record how much of what contaminants each filter material filtered from the water.
11. Compare the results (color, odor, pH, conductivity) among student groups. Discuss the filter media used and results achieved.
12. Try it Again.
13. Allow each group to design and build a better filter, based on the class data.
14. Empty the bottle, throw out the filter materials, and wipe out the bottle.
15. See if you can make the filtered water even cleaner. Try putting materials in different layers or try using different amounts of each material.

Data Collection Format and Data Collection Sheets Tailored to Experiment:
See attached Data Collection Sheet

Anticipated Outcomes:
Which filter media were most effective at filtering the water?
   How might you further improve upon the water filter design?

Data Analysis Plan:
Filter Your Water and Make Observations:
   Write your observations of the filtered water here:

   Color: _____ Transparency: _____ Smell: _____

   Does this water seem like it could be drinkable? _____
   Were your predictions about the filter layers correct? If no, why not? Explain
below:
   Filter Layer 1:

   Filter Layer 2:

   Filter Layer 3:

   Filter Layer 4:

Data Collection Sheet Water Filtration Media Options	
Date Collected:	
Date Tested:	
Principal Investigator:	
Source Water:	

Test Water Quality (Students should include the units obtained from the instrumentation used.)

Sample	pH	Turbidity	Conductivity	Dissolved Oxygen
Contaminated Water				
Filtered Water				

EXPERIMENT 9.10:   WATER FILTRATION MEDIA EVALUATION REMOTE AREA OPTIONS

Date: _____

Principal Investigator:

    Name: _____

    Email: _____

    Phone: _____

Collaborators:

    Name: _____

    Email: _____

    Phone: _____

    Name: _____

    Email: _____

    Phone: _____

    Name: _____

    Email: _____

    Phone: _____

    Name: _____

    Email: _____

    Phone: _____

    Name: _____

    Email: _____

    Phone: _____

Objective or Question to Be Addressed:

Water from lakes, rivers streams, and springs often has contaminants that make it unfit for drinking. The water may contain dirt, rocks, and other objects that can be easily identified. Water from streams and springs may also contain bacteria and other microscopic organisms associated with animal wastes that cannot be seen easily. For these reasons, water that is collected from these sources and used without treatment for human consumption can present unacceptable risks to people living in remote areas or developing parts of the world where modern water treatment systems do not exist. Water treatment is typically a five-part process that consists of aeration, coagulation, sedimentation, filtration, and disinfection. Most of those steps will not exist in remote areas or a developing country. This experiment is only concerned with filtration, which removes most, but not all, of the impurities from the water, using various fibers and materials shown in various experiments over time to be effective, to varying degrees, at treating the water from those otherwise untreated sources.

In most cases, filtration will be the only treatment available; however, Experiment 9.9 in this series allows examination of some alternative filtration media options for remote areas, as well. Disinfection will work most effectively on prefiltered water, in most cases. See Experiments 12.4 and 12.5 in this series for disinfection options.

Filtration alone does not render the water fit to drink and the water resulting from this experiment will not be rendered safe to drink.

In this experiment, various media components of a potential remote area water filtration system are examined to help identify the uses and limitations of each. The experiment is designed as an iterative process to allow for testing and measurement of the performance of the various filtration media, analyze the data collected, and use this information to work toward an improved filtration design.

Theory Behind Experiment:
Water filtration occurs in a number of different ways inside a filtration system. The various types of media involved each provide specific beneficial filtering, but each in a different way and each filters out a different type of contaminant. For example, some media remove coarse particulate materials and some remove finer particulate materials. Some remove dissolved organic materials, while others remove dissolved inorganic materials. Design of a water filtration system needs to take into consideration the nature of the contaminants in the water to be treated and the removal efficiencies of the various media available.

Filter media types commonly available and commonly used in remote areas include Unified Soil Classification System (USCS) coarse sand (clean), USCS fine sand (clean),; mixed sand, activated carbon, and membranes of various proprietary types.

Coarse Sand

The Unified Soil Classification System (USCS) defines coarse sand as a mix of granular particles with dimensions between a No. 4 sieve and a No. 10 sieve. Fine sand is defined as soil with particle sizes between a No. 40 sieve size and a No. 200 sieve. In both cases, the particles are assumed to have been washed to remove dust and other finer particles. In remote areas, the selection of specific grain sizes is generally not a practical consideration. Sand is generally available, however, in mixed sand grain sizes. The current experiment utilizes a mixed sand of defined coarse to fine grain sizes (No. 4–200 sieve sizes) in order to provide a rational basis for data analysis. It should be recognized that the actual sand available to users in the field may be different from that in the laboratory and may provide different results as a consequence.

Fine Sand

The Unified Soil Classification System (USCS) defines fine sand as granular soil with particle sizes between a No. 40 sieve size and a No. 200 sieve.

A No. 40 sieve has an opening that is 0.425 mm (1/64 inch). A No. 200 sieve has an opening of 0.00295 mm (5/256 inch). The particles are assumed to have been washed to remove dust and other finer particles. Water will move through this sand at a very slow rate; hence, the term "slow sand filter" is applied to filters using primarily fine sand. The slow rate is a potential drawback, but it also foretells a good, suspended contaminant removal efficiency.

Mixed Sand

Where mixed sand types are used in the same filter layer, it is also useful to consider how well the sand particles will interact with each other. This consideration is defined by two parameters called the Uniformity Coefficient and the Effective Size.

The uniformity coefficient, C_u, is calculated by plotting the various grain sizes on a standard soil gradation curve chart and determining the diameter of the particles, typically in millimeters (this can be done equally as effectively in inches, but the numbers are very small fractions of an inch) at which 10% of the soil particles are finer (the D_{10} diameter) and the diameter of the particles at which 60% are finer (the D_{60} diameter). Dividing the D_{60} diameter by the D_{10} diameter yields the C_u. This is a unitless ratio of grain diameters. In general, a uniformity coefficient less than 7 is desirable in most mixed sand filter media.

The effective size of the sand particles is defined as the diameter at which less than 10% of the particles are finer; the same D_{10} diameter defined for the C_u. An effective size between 0.3 and 0.5 mm (0.012 and 0.20 inches) has been found to be the most effective for wastewater filtration.

Activated Carbon

Activated carbon is charcoal (or coal) that has been processed to create a large number of small pores and crevices in the particles, which in turn create a very large surface area per unit of volume. This allows the material to provide a much larger absorption capacity than would otherwise exist in the same volume of charcoal. Activated carbon is available in powdered form and in granular form. Granular forms are generally easier to handle and powdered forms tend to be difficult to remove from the treated wastewater once they are spent. In addition, granular forms are often renewable, depending on the nature of the contaminants they are used to remove.

Where available, a fine sand filter, generally also considered a *slow sand filter*, is the preferred option because it is often easier to backwash or clean and easy to discard and replace where fine sand is readily available.

A mixed sand is used in this experiment as a rough guide to the relative effectiveness of the alternative materials most commonly available in remote areas of the world. For purposes of this experiment, the mixed sand media should consist of uniformly graded sand containing particles from a No. 4 sieve through a No. 200 sieve, with an overall Uniformity Coefficient of less than 7 and an Effective Size between 0.3 mm and 0.5 mm (0.012 and 0.20 inches).

In this experiment, materials not normally associated with water filtration will be used. These will include coconut fibers, crushed clamshells, charcoal (nonactivated), zeolite, and muslin cloth. Three to five of these materials are suggested for use. The experiment is designed to use five of these materials. See Experiment 14.6 in this series for how to determine the suitability of granular materials for use in granular media filters.

Coconut Fiber

Coconut fiber is a natural fiber extracted from the husk of unripe coconuts. The coconut husk is usually boiled in hot seawater, and the fibers are removed from the shell by combing and crushing. Typical raw coconut fibers vary in length from about 15–35 cm (6–14 inch) and have a diameter between 50 and 300 μm (0.002–0.12 inch). They are flexible and can be bundled for transport and molded to fit tightly inside a container or filter.

Clamshells

Crushed clamshells are exactly what the name implies: clamshells that have been cleaned of remnants of the clams that once inhabited them, then crushed to small size particles in the range of approximately 1/8 inch (30 mm) or so. Note that the use of clamshells may introduce high concentrations of alkali into the treated water, and some form of recarbonation – such as using a crushed charcoal filter after the clamshells – may be necessary.

Unactivated Carbon

In remote areas, the process for treating the charcoal is difficult to create or operate, and most available charcoal is not "activated". It is readily available, however, and can be broken into small pieces for use in a filtration bucket or container. This experiment uses nonactivated charcoal to replicate that most readily available in remote areas of the world.

Muslin

Muslin is a soft, woven, 100-percent cotton, multilayer cloth popular for baby clothes and blankets because the fabric is gentle on the skin and highly absorbent. A clean cloth baby's diaper is suggested as a good source. This material should be folded over several times (record the number of layers used) and molded around the edges of the acrylic cylinder (See equipment list below) so that all the tested sample water passes through the cloth without significant short-circuiting.

The instruments used to determine the effectiveness or efficiency of the various media during these experiments will include a dissolved oxygen (DO) meter, a turbidity meter, a pH meter, and a conductivity tester, depending on what contaminants are being targeted by the individual media types. Note that this experiment does not deal with the disinfection of the filtered water. That is the topic in a separate experiment in this series.

Data to be collected with an explanation of how they will be collected (e.g. "Water temperature data for three days using a continuous data logger")

Five separate filter media are to be tested during this experiment, followed by a combined filter designed by the experimenter(s). Assessment of each is described in the procedures section, below. In general, the defined data will be collected from the instruments and recorded on an attached data collection sheet. Those data will include dissolved oxygen concentration, turbidity in NTU, pH in pH units, and conductivity in microsiemens (μS).

Potential Interferences and Interference Management Plan:
The expectations from this experiment include "normal" outcomes from filtering a manufactured contaminated water through each of the filter media. "Normal" outcomes are not well defined or guaranteed, however, and outcomes that differ from the norm can be anticipated. Not all sand is the same or consists of grain sizes consistent with the provided definition; not all coconut fibers, clamshells, charcoal, or cloth fibers work the same way; and not all contaminants react the same way to each type of media. Consequently, indefinable interferences may occur during the experiment that will vary the outcomes. Experimenters should recognize this possibility and use the data developed from their own experiments to design the final set of layers.

In addition, it is noted that some materials may require greater volumes than others to achieve successful cleansing of target contaminants. Thus, for example, a layer of mixed sand may need to be more shallow or deep than a layer of charcoal to achieve equivalent efficiency for all the targeted contaminants in a specific source water.

Note that in a commercial or industrial application, the filters need to be backwashed on a regular basis to clean the captured contaminants out. This is done by forcing water back up through the media from the bottom and floating the captured contaminants out of the filter bed. The bed is then allowed to resettle into its original configuration. However, if the media components are not of sufficiently different densities, they will not resettle into suitable layers, and if the densities are not such that the heaviest components are on the bottom, the layers will not resettle in the same order after backwashing.

The users of the products tested in this experiment are unlikely to have the ability to effectively backwash the filters and will need, instead, to dispose of the materials once they are so contaminated as to no longer serve their purpose. This will be an important consideration to evaluate for the final steps in this experiment, particularly if one or more of the tested media become unusable due to fouling much more quickly than others.

Tools, Equipment, and Supplies Required:
    Digital balances (for weighing filter media)
    Graduated cylinders -250 mL (for measuring simulated wastewater)
    10" high by 6" deep acrylic cylinder with a drain hole at the bottom, a drain nipple of convenient size threaded into the bottom outlet, and suitable tubing arranged to drain the cylinder into a flask or beaker
    3" square of standard window screen, or similar material, to cover opening in the drainage hole and prevent loss of filter media

Filtration materials, including three to five of the following materials, or similar materials available locally in remote areas:

    Mixed sand (saturated and cleaned) approximately 1.5 L (0.06 ft^3) per experimenter or group
    Fine sand (saturated and cleaned) approximately 1.5 L (0.06 ft^3) per experimenter or group

Mixed sands (50% or more of grain sizes, on a mass basis, smaller than No. 4 sieve and 50% or more of grain sizes, on a mass basis, greater than a No. 200 sieve) approximately 1.5 L (0.06 ft³) per experimenter or group

Charcoal (not briquettes – if only briquettes are available, they should be broken into peanut-sized pieces), rinsed with clean water before being used because the briquettes are compressed and the surface is too smooth for proper water penetration and unwashed charcoal will turn the test samples black; approximately 1.5 L (0.06 ft³) per experimenter or group will be needed.

Muslim, clean and dry when inserted into the test cylinder

Small scoops or spatulas (to use as scoops for loose filter media)

Simulated source water (for 1 gallon (3.8 L): combine 2 cups of distilled vinegar, 6–8 oz (175–250 mL) of brewed black tea, 100 g (3.5 oz) of silt (100% passing a No. 200 sieve), and enough water to fill the container. Note: any other artificial contaminants of choice may be substituted here, water from a potential surface water or groundwater source may be used instead of the artificial source water. Preparing 2 gallons (7.5 L) for each experimenter or group is suggested.

Water quality testing instruments:

Conductivity meter

DO meter

pH meter

Turbidimeter

Large container to hold waste material prior to disposal. There will be a lot of waste. This waste may be hazardous and will, in any event, be unsuitable for sewer discharge. Disposal in accordance with waste disposal protocols of the testing laboratory is important.

Safety

Neither an artificial source water nor an actual source water used in this experiment is safe for human consumption. Filtration alone should be considered insufficient to render any source water safe for human consumption. Care is needed to avoid accidental or deliberate ingestion. Safety gloves, eye protection, and a lab coat are recommended. Note that touching things with a gloved hand, and then using that same hand to touch the face or mouth, even if only to scratch an itch or brush away a hair, can cause accidental ingestion of the contaminants.

In the event of skin contact, wash immediately with warm water and soap. In the event of eye contact, wash immediately with an eyewash for up to 15 minutes and seek immediate medical advice. In the event of subcutaneous injection through a cut or puncture wound, wash the area immediately with warm water and a disinfectant designed for medical treatment, then seek medical advice.

In the event of ingestion, immediately rinse the mouth and seek medical assistance. Do not induce vomiting without medical direction.

**Note: Water filtered in this experiment *should not* be consumed by humans.

Planned Experimental Procedures and Steps, in Order:

1. Set the acrylic cylinder on a suitable stand so that the drainage system is unobstructed. Place the piece of screening over the drainage opening to contain the filter media.
2. Add 6 inches of the filter media of choice to the acrylic cylinder. Use only one media type at a time for each step of the experiment. Multiple media at the same time will obfuscate the results. Do not compact the media except for the coconut fiber which should be tightly molded into the filter. Wrap the muslin inside the entire interior of the cylinder wall.
3. Measure and record the mass, the volume, and the depth (or thickness) of the filter media used.
4. Measure and record the pH, DO, turbidity, and conductivity of the simulated wastewater.
5. Slowly pour 200 mL of simulated wastewater through the water filtration device, taking care to distribute the wastewater as evenly as possible across the surface of the filter media and avoiding cavitation of the media surface.
6. Measure and record the pH, DO, turbidity, and conductivity of the filtered water.
7. Record a visual observation of what the filtered water looks like in terms of clarity, color, suspended solids concentration, and any other parameter of note or interest.
8. Take the filters apart and examine the media particles. Identify and record each material filtered from the water by that media.
9. Clean the acrylic cylinder and verify that the drainage system is working properly, then reassemble the filter using a different filter media.
10. Repeat steps 4–9 for the second media type.
11. Repeat steps 4–9 for each of as many other filter media types as may be available.
12. Evaluate the data from each media experiment and determine the most effective *relative* mass and depth of each type of media tested to achieve the optimal contaminant removal efficiency for a mixed-media filter, based on the contaminants present in the wastewater tested. Note that the total depth of the final filter will need to fit inside the acrylic cylinder, so the *relative* masses and depths are important.
13. Design and build a mixed-media filter, based on the data generated for each individual media experiment. Estimate the water quality that will be generated by this mixed-media filter.
14. Repeat steps 4–9 for the mixed-media filter. Compare the actual results to the predicted results.
15. Clean the filter parts and rebuild the final filter with the media in a different order.
16. Repeat steps 4–9.
17. Evaluate the effects of changing the order of the layers.

Data Collection Format and Data Collection Sheets Tailored to Experiment:
See attached Data Collection Sheet

Anticipated Outcomes:
Each filter medium will remove different contaminants from the source water. There may be some overlap between media, but each should be more effective on some contaminants than on others. Evaluation of the test result data will indicate the best mix of layers and the best combination of mass and volume for each media to provide the optimal filter layering and size for the source water being tested.

Data Analysis Plan:
The data collected at each step of the procedure will be recorded on the attached data collection sheet. When all of the various media have been tested, an analysis of the accumulated data will be used to indicate the mass and volume of each media, on a relative basis, from which to construct a final filter. That filter will be tested and an adjustment made to the layering or masses for a revised final filter design.

Data Collection Sheet Water Filtration Media Remote Area Options

Date Collected:	
Date Tested:	
Principal Investigator:	
Source Water:	

Test Water Quality

Sample	Filter Media Used Type	Mass of Media Used, (mg)	Volume of Media Used, (mL)	pH	Turbidity, (NTU)	Conductivity, (µS)	Dissolved Oxygen, (mg/L)
Contaminated water	None	None	None				
Filtered water – Test 1							
Filtered water – Test 2							
Filtered water – Test 3							
Filtered water – Test 4							
Filtered water – Test 5							
Filtered water – Test 6							
Filtered water – Test 7							

10 Oil and Petroleum-Based Experiments

This chapter provides completed designs for example experiments which can be used to demonstrate specific engineering phenomena in a university laboratory or field collection site. They may be used as presented or modified by the user to adapt to other desired outcomes. Sections on actual outcomes and data interpretation are necessarily left blank in these examples. They should be completed by the investigators upon collection of the data.

The experiments in this chapter are:
10.1 Solubility of Oil in Water as a Function of Salinity
10.2 Gasoline Fingerprinting
10.3 Determination of Porosity and Void Ratio in Soils

DOI: 10.1201/9781003184249-10

EXPERIMENT 10.1: SOLUBILITY OF OIL IN WATER AS A FUNCTION OF SALINITY

Date: _____

Principal Investigator:

    Name: _____

    Email: _____

    Phone: _____

Collaborators:

    Name: _____

    Email: _____

    Phone: _____

    Name: _____

    Email: _____

    Phone: _____

    Name: _____

    Email: _____

    Phone: _____

    Name: _____

    Email: _____

    Phone: _____

Objective or Question to Be Addressed:

It is an accepted theory that oil and water do not mix. That turns out not to be entirely true, however, and there is an increasing knowledge base that oil releases to fresh and salt water result in significant increases in the concentration of dissolved constituents of the oil that spilled. This experiment looks at the change in the oil concentration as a function of the salinity of the affected water and the constituents of different types of oil.

Theory Behind Experiment

There is a growing body of evidence that suggests that freshwater will dissolve and sustain a higher concentration of oil components associated with an oil spill of a specific type and volume when compared to salt water. Oil is not generally able to dissolve in water because the water is not capable of breaking down the nonpolar structure of the oil. Various components of the oil, however, such as benzenes, hexanes, and various additives in processed oils, do provide polar functions in the water and allow various concentrations of oil, or its components, to dissolve in varying degrees.

The salinity of water is a function of many things in nature. Sodium chloride (common table salt) comprises a high percentage of salinity components in most saline waters. Salt is a compound with high polarity, and when the salinity is increased through the addition of the salt molecules, the polarity of the solution changes and significant amounts of the petroleum components are able to dissolve. The greater the salinity, the greater the affinity for dissolved petroleum components.

There are a lot of other things that affect the ability of oil and petroleum components to dissolve in water. The use of distilled water in this experiment will eliminate most of those competing agents. Temperature does affect the solubility, and maintaining a reasonably consistent temperature throughout this experiment will minimize those effects as well. This experiment will only address the solubility of the tested oils as a function of salinity, independent of any other compounding factor.

Other components are present at varying concentrations in different oils of the same type from different manufacturers and from different sources. Not all crude oil is the same, not all gasoline is the same, not all vegetable oils are the same, and so forth. Consequently, not all oils will dissolve equally in water and not all oils of the same generic type will dissolve equally in the same water. The process used here should be easily adaptable to other parameters that may affect the solubility of the same oils tested here as functions of those other parameters.

It is critical to know exactly what that salinity is when the concentrations are measured so that the concentration of petroleum components can be accurately graphed against the actual salinity. Salinity should be carefully measured at every stage immediately prior to the addition of the petroleum or oil product.

To adjust the salinity, it is useful to use some reasonable, consistent, changes. Note the following: NaCl (sodium chloride) has a maximum solubility at room temperature (20°C or 68°F) of approximately 36.1 g (1.273 oz) of NaCl in 100 g (3.527 oz) of pure water on a mass basis. This means that the maximum solubility would occur with 361 g of NaCl added to 1,000 g, or 1 L, of water based on an assumption that water has a mass of 1,000 g/L, which is a reasonable assumption at room temperature and distilled water. Table A.8 in the Appendix may be consulted for the actual density of water at various temperatures, and the mass of NaCl added may be adjusted accordingly for more precise outcomes. The differences in the mass of the water are in the fourth and fifth decimal place, however, and are unlikely to be significant.

For this experiment, the salinity will be changed several times and the resulting concentration of oil or petroleum hydrocarbons will be measured to determine the solubility of the oil or petroleum product as a function of the salinity of the water. The salinity of the sample may be measured indirectly by measuring the electrical conductivity (EC) of the sample. A more direct measure uses a hydrometer that floats at varying depths as a function of the water density, and the water density is a function of the added salt. Graduations on the hydrometer will indicate the salinity of the water based on the depth of submersion. Interestingly, salinity is usually reported on a mass/mass basis (parts per million, parts per billion, or parts per trillion). Chemists, however, prefer to use Molarity as the units of measure. The Molarity (M) of a solution is equal to the moles of solute/liter of solution and one M is equal to one gram molecular mass.

Data to be collected with an explanation of how they will be collected (Ex.: "Water temperature data for three days using a continuous data logger")
Salinity data for all water samples will be measured with a hydrometer (or salinity probe). The mass of oil or petroleum product to be added to each water sample will be measured with a graduated pipette or electronic scale. The time for stirring and dissolution of petroleum components will be recorded for each sample.

A gas chromatograph/mass spectrometer (GC/MS) will be used to determine the concentration of oil and petroleum, and their component parts, at various times during the experiment.

All data will be recorded on the data collection form.

Potential Interferences and Interference Management Plan
Salinity is determined in this experiment as a function of the concentration of sodium chloride. In most cases in nature, salinity is a function of many salts acting together. The effects of different salts on the solubility of oils may vary from those associated strictly with sodium chloride. The effects are expected to be marginal, however, and the absence of other salts will not change the basic educational outcomes from this experiment. They will be ignored.

Tools, Equipment, and Supplies Required:
    Glass hydrometer or Salinity probe for water
    Gas chromatograph/mass spectrophotometer (GC-MS) with columns to iden-
        tify the concentration of volatile and semivolatile petroleum hydrocarbons
        in the liquid sample
    Several 2 L (0.5284 gal) clean glass beakers. One for each type of oil or petro-
        leum product to be tested at each salinity concentration (3 products to be
        tested at 5 different salinities would require 15 beakers)
    One clean glass pipette for each beaker
    Samples of various petroleum and oil products to be tested (a vegetable-based
        cooking oil, gasoline, a 5 W lubricating oil, diesel (or home heating) oil, and
        a synthetic oil are suggested)
    5–10 L (1.3–2.6 gal) of distilled water at room temperature
    Phipps and Bird 6 paddle stirrer, or equivalent
    Sodium chloride
    Fume hood
    Appropriate personal protective equipment including gloves, goggles, and lab
        coat

Safety
This experiment requires the use of volatile petroleum products and other petroleum-based products with volatile components. None of those volatile components are good for human health and all are dangerous. Work within a fume hood with a positive fume removal system is required. Personal protective equipment required includes rubber, vinyl or latex gloves, eye goggles, and a lab coat.

Planned Experimental Procedures and Steps, in Order:

The following procedure assumes the testing of three products: a vegetable-based cooking oil, gasoline, and 5 W lubricating oil.

1. Put on the specified personal protective equipment, then collect and stage all necessary samples and testing equipment inside a fume hood.
2. Place exactly 1 L (0.02642 gal) of distilled water in each of five beakers
3. Add nothing to the first beaker, add 50 g (1.76 oz) of sodium chloride to the second beaker, 150 g of sodium chloride (5.29 oz) of sodium chloride to the third beaker, 225 g (7.94 oz) of sodium chloride to the fourth beaker, and 300 g (10.58 oz) of sodium chloride to the fifth beaker.
4. Carefully measure and record the salinity of each beaker.
5. Add 5 g (0.176 oz) of a vegetable-based cooking oil to each beaker
6. Place all five beakers on the stirrer and slowly stir for 5 minutes at approximately 25 rpm.
7. At the end of the stirring period, stop the stirrer and allow all beakers to rest for 5 minutes to allow undissolved components to float to the surface.
8. Collect a suitable sample from each beaker by selecting a location below any floating material and collecting a sample per the instructions for the GC-MS being used, and submit each one sequentially into the GC-MS. The sample with the lowest concentration of sodium chloride should be submitted first. Record the data from the GC-MS for each sample and record the total mass of dissolved components measured.
9. Repeat steps 2–8 for the gasoline and the 5 W lubricating oil and record those results.
10. Create a graph of salinity versus dissolved petroleum component concentration for each of the three samples tested. Note that if various separate components are identified by the GC-MS, each can be, and should be, separately graphed versus salinity, as well.
11. Compare the results and discuss the general nature of the results and what they may imply regarding releases of oil or petroleum products to the environment as a result of spills, accidents, or other causes.

Data Collection Format and Data Collection Sheets Tailored to Experiment:
See attached data collection sheets.

Data Analysis Plan:
The data from the salinity tests and the GC-MS analyses will be plotted on graphs of salinity versus petroleum component concentration. An opinion will be drawn from those data regarding the implications of those data for releases of the tested materials to the environment.

Expected Outcomes:
It is expected that the solubility of the components of the various oils tested will increase in the presence of increasing concentrations of sodium chloride, but that a peak may be reached indicating a maximum component solubility.

Data Collection Sheet Solubility of Oil in Water as a Function of Salinity

Beaker No.	Mass of Sodium Chloride Added to Beaker (mg)	Measured Salinity	Volume of Vegetable Oil Added (mL)	Mass of Petroleum Components in Water (mg/L)	Volume of Gasoline Added (mL)	Mass of Petroleum Components in Water (mg/L)	Volume of 5 W Lubricating Oil Added – (mL)	Mass of Petroleum Components in Water (mg/L)
1								
2								
3								
4								
5								
6								
7								
8								
9								
10								
11								
12								
13								
14								
15								

EXPERIMENT 10.2:   GASOLINE FINGERPRINTING

Date: _____

Principal Investigator:

      Name: _____

      Email: _____

      Phone: _____

Collaborators:

      Name: _____

      Email: _____

      Phone: _____

      Name: _____

      Email: _____

      Phone: _____

      Name: _____

      Email: _____

      Phone: _____

      Name: _____

      Email: _____

      Phone: _____

Objective or Question to Be Addressed:

Gasoline compositions (and other petroleum products) are not all the same. There are significant variations in the mass of various hydrocarbons that comprise the specific fuels and the mass of other additives included in those fuels. When a spill occurs, particularly a subsurface spill that may not become apparent for many months or years, it is often the role of the forensic scientist to determine the source of the gasoline or petroleum product.

This experiment is designed to identify the hydrocarbon fingerprint of various commercial types of gasoline and to compare an unknown gasoline to the experimental fingerprint results to determine the brand of gasoline represented by the unknown sample.

Theory Behind Experiment

Pure petroleum products are comprised of a mix of hydrocarbons. A hydrocarbon is an organic molecule that is a combination, exclusively, of hydrogen molecules and carbon molecules. These chemicals are generally divided into four categories:

alkanes, alkenes, alkynes, and aromatic hydrocarbons. The first three are referred to as aliphatic hydrocarbons, meaning that the carbon molecules form a straight line with the hydrogen molecules attached to the edges of that carbon chain. The fourth, the aromatic hydrocarbons, are comprised of a six-carbon ring, with the hydrogens attached to the outside of the ring.

Alkanes are a simple carbon chain where every carbon atom is bonded to two hydrogen atoms and two carbon atoms, except the carbons at the end of the chain which are bonded to a third hydrogen, instead of a second carbon. All the carbon bonds are single bonds. Alkanes include things such as methane, CH_4, which contains one carbon and four hydrogen molecules; ethane, C_2H_6, which contains two carbon and six hydrogen molecules; propane, C_3H_8, which contains three carbon and eight hydrogen molecules; and butane, C_4H_{10}, which contains four carbon and ten hydrogen molecules.

Alkenes are similar to alkanes except that alkenes contain a double bond between two carbon atoms, which reduces the number of hydrogen which can be bonded to the carbons present. The two simplest alkenes are ethene (C_2H_4) and propene (C_3H_6). Note that the double bond in ethene means that only four hydrogens can bond to the carbons, as opposed to the six that bond with the two carbons in ethane. Similarly, only six hydrogens can bond with three carbons in ethene, as opposed to the eight which can bond in ethane.

Alkynes are similar to alkanes except that alkynes contain a triple bond between two carbon atoms which further limits the number of hydrogen which can be bonded to the carbons. The three simplest alkynes are ethyne (C_2H_2), propyne (C_3H_4), and butyne (C_4H_6). Here it is seen, for example, that only two hydrogens can bond with two carbons in alkynes, as opposed to the six hydrogens in ethane and four in propene. Similarly, only four hydrogens can bond with three carbons in propyne, as opposed to eight with propane and six with propene, and only six hydrogens can bond with four carbons in butyne, as opposed to ten that can bond in butane and eight that can bond with butene.

An aromatic hydrocarbon consists of a ring of six carbon molecules in a ring formation, called an *arene*, with alternating single and double bonds between the carbon molecules. Six hydrogens attach to the outside of the ring, one to each carbon molecule, to form benzene, C_6H_6, the most common pure aromatic hydrocarbon. A variety of other things can form around a carbon ring, and nearly all are characterized by strong odor or fragrance (depending on the judgment of the observer), hence the term "aromatic" hydrocarbon.

The identification of the mix of the various types and examples of hydrocarbon in a sample of fuel can be diagnostic to the identification of the source of the material associated with a spill or other environmental release. A GC/MS can be used to identify the mix and concentrations of the various components in a sample fuel. Each brand has its own corporate mix of hydrocarbons and other compounds which can be identified with the GC/MS, and those profiles can then be compared to the profile of an unknown sample to determine its origin. It is important to note, however, that fuel degrades quickly in the environment, and aging changes the mix of hydrocarbons. Some hydrocarbons degrade to smaller carbon chains, for example, some degrade to elemental components, some remain as polyaromatic hydrocarbons, which are compounds containing more than one carbon ring attached to others and which are very persistent (and toxic) in the environment. In those cases, it is necessary to calculate the most likely original mix of pure hydrocarbons and other additives from historical degradation data and identifiable environmental conditions under which the original hydrocarbon has degraded. While these characteristics are important, that type of investigation is not a part of this experiment.

Potential Interferences and Interference Management Plan

Components of the tested fuels that are not hydrocarbons may still elute at temperatures close to or identical to target hydrocarbon components. Those will either make identification of the target components difficult or elute with the targets giving false values of concentration. This experiment is not sophisticated enough to differentiate those potential confounding components with sufficient accuracy to properly exclude them from the printouts. Consequently, for purposes of this experiment, they will be ignored unless they elute far enough away from target compounds to allow for accurate removal from the target compound values.

Data to be collected with an explanation of how they will be collected (Ex.: "Water temperature data for three days using a continuous data logger")

Hydrocarbon analysis of several commercially available brands of gasoline will be analyzed with a GC/MS, and the printouts from those analyses will be used to compare the readout from an unknown source. The components and their identified concentrations will be tabulated, along with those of the unknown source. The unknown source will then be identified from a comparison of those tabulated data.

Tools, Equipment, and Supplies Required:

Five 8-ounce (250 mL) jars with Teflon-lined caps in which samples of four specific brands of gasoline and one unidentified sample have been collected. Samples should not be mixed and samples with the same octane rating should be collected from each brand.

GC/MS

Safety

Gasoline is highly flammable and highly volatile. The vapors contain hazardous components that have been shown to cause cancer in humans. All sample collection activities need to be done outdoors. All testing activities need to be conducted inside a chemical hood with a positive exhaust rate to the outside of the building.

No flames, sparks, or heat sources may be used inside the hood while conducting the tests.

Gasoline dries the skin very quickly and can lead to dermal issues if allowed to accumulate on the skin. Contact with the skin should be avoided. In the event of contact, washing with warm water and strong soap is required as soon as possible. Application of a moisturizing hand cream immediately after washing is recommended.

Contact with the eyes will cause severe burning and a significant risk of permanent damage to the eye. Eye protection is required during the collection of the samples and during the conduct of the tests. In the event of eye exposure, immediate flushing at an eyewash station for up to 15 minutes is required and immediate medical attention is necessary.

Planned Experimental Procedures and Steps, in Order:

1. Collect all samples in sealed jars inside a vented hood and put on personal protective equipment.
2. Calibrate and prepare the GC/MS in accordance with manufacturer's instructions and verify that the correct column is inserted into the unit.
3. Sample the known brands of gasoline sequentially, as recommended by the GC/MS manufacturer, and run those tests through the machine. Some GC/MS analyzers include an automatic sequencing algorithm and that may be utilized to expedite the testing provided that the machine properly cleans itself between samples.
4. Collect the data sheets prepared by the GC/MS and tabulate the components and concentrations identified for each known brand sample and for the unknown sample.
5. Compare the data from the unknown sample to the data from the known sources to identify the source of the unknown sample.
6. Report the probable source of the unknown sample, noting any variations from the profile of the selected brand and discuss the cause of those variations.

Data Collection Format and Data Collection Sheets Tailored to Experiment:
See attached data collection sheets.

Data Analysis Plan:
Data collected from a GC/MS are graphical data showing peaks on a timeline. The location of a peak on the timeline indicates its evaporation temperature, and the height of the peak indicates the concentration of that compound present in the sample. Those data will be tabulated for each of the known brands and for the unknown sample. The data from the unknown sample will then be compared to those from the known samples to determine the most likely source of the unknown sample. The location of the peaks indicates the specific component eluting at that time and temperature. Standards associated with the specific GC/MS column being used can be reviewed to indicate the specific hydrocarbon being seen at each peak. Components other than hydrocarbons may also show up and should be noted since they may be associated with proprietary additives indicative of a specific brand of fuel.

Expected Outcomes:
It is expected that each of the known samples will exhibit different component profiles, along with different additives. It is further expected that the unknown sample, in this case selected by the instructor from one of the known sources, will match well, but not perfectly, with the profile from one of the known sources. If the unknown sample is collected from a source other than one of the four brand sources, it may not be possible to match the profile during this experiment. A larger library of known source profiles would be needed to identify a truly unknown source.

Data Collection Sheet for Gasoline Fingerprinting Experiment

Compound	Concentration (ppm)				
	Brand 1	Brand 2	Brand 3	Brand 4	Unknown Source

EXPERIMENT 10.3: DETERMINATION OF POROSITY AND VOID RATIO IN SOIL

Date: _____

Principal Investigator:

      Name: _____

      Email: _____

      Phone: _____

Collaborators:

      Name: _____

      Email: _____

      Phone: _____

      Name: _____

      Email: _____

      Phone: _____

      Name: _____

      Email: _____

      Phone: _____

      Name: _____

      Email: _____

      Phone: _____

Objective or Question to Be Addressed:

This experiment is designed to demonstrate the variation and magnitude of porosity and void ratio in various soil types and to allow comparison of those characteristics among the tested soil types.

Theory Behind Experiment

The characteristics associated with a specific soil type factor into the stability of the soil, the transport of water through the soil, and the ability of contamination to spread throughout the soil. Two of the soil characteristics are void ratio and porosity. The *void ratio* is the ratio of the volume of voids (open spaces, i.e., air and water) in a soil to the volume of solids. *Porosity* is the ratio of void volume to *total* volume.

Because it is a ratio between two components of a composite volume of material, the void ratio can be greater than 1. It can also be expressed as a fraction. The porosity is a ratio between a component of a given volume of material and the total volume of the composite material. Therefore, the porosity cannot be greater than 1, but it is expressed as a percentage or a fraction.

The void ratio and porosity are slightly different. The void ratio is the ratio of void volume to *solids volume*; porosity is the ratio of void volume to *total volume*. This creates a situation where the porosity can never be equal to or greater than 1.0, but the void ratio can, and does, exceed 1.0 in certain soil types in which the volume of the soil particles is less than the volume of the voids.

The generally accepted equation for the calculation of the void ratio is:

$$E = \frac{V_v}{V_s} = \frac{(V_a + V_w)}{V_s}$$

where:

E = Void ratio
V_v = Volume of voids (m^3 or ft^3)
V_s = Volume of solids (m^3 or ft^3)
V_a = Volume of air (m^3 or ft^3)
V_w = Volume of water (m^3 or ft^3)

The generally accepted equation for calculation of the porosity is:

$$\eta = \frac{V_v}{V_s}$$

where:

η = Porosity
V_v = Volume of voids (m^3 or ft^3)
V_s = Volume of total sample (m^3 or ft^3)

It is assumed that filling the voids in the soil with water will not cause an increase in the total volume of the saturated soil. It is also assumed that any void not filled with water will be filled with air. However, due to the inherent buoyancy of soil particles in water, it is possible for some swelling to occur as water is added. An adjustment needs to be made to the output data to account for any swelling that may occur. Hence, the test procedure requires a careful measurement of the volume of the soil prior to the addition of water and again at the end of the water addition phase.

Temperature can also affect the volume of the saturated soil. The water will expand in volume as the temperature rises. Therefore, it is important to ensure that the entire procedure is done as rapidly as possible and that all components remain at essentially the same room temperature throughout the procedure.

Data to be collected with an explanation of how they will be collected (Ex.: "Water temperature data for three days using a continuous data logger")

The information to be gathered in this experiment are those data required to properly calculate the void ratio and porosity of the various soil types being tested, the appropriate soil classification of the soil being tested by the USCS (Uniform Soil

Classification System), the volume of water used to fill the voids, and the total volume of soil and voids.

The soil volume is calculated in four ways:

- first from the volume of water required to fill the voids, subtracted from the total volume of saturated soil;
- second from the mass of the soil used multiplied by standard soil mass values found from standard references;
- third by subtracting the mass of water used to fill the voids, divided by the standard mass of water at the test temperature, from the total mass of saturated soil; and
- fourth by carefully measuring the volume used as indicated by the graduations on the side of each beaker

A reasonable average volume of soil is then calculated. The amount of compaction of the soil samples is important to these calculations. It is instructive, therefore, to test samples that are tamped lightly to represent "normal" soil conditions and to simultaneously test compacted samples to represent compacted conditions.

Potential Interferences and Interference Management Plan:
The accuracy of the results in this experiment is particularly important because small changes in the data can have a statistically significant influence on the results. The sensitivity of data to specific independent variable changes is not uniform. It is important to consider the issue of variable sensitivity when evaluating the dependent variable changes associated with multiple independent variable adjustments. See Section 2.6 for a discussion of variable sensitivity.

The masses of soil and water used are sufficiently small that minor changes in the measurements can generate significant errors in the final calculations. Therefore, it is important to weigh masses accurately, to measure volumes carefully, and to avoid disruption of the samples when adding water to the tamped soils.

The temperature of all the materials should be essentially the same ($\pm 1°C$ or $2°F$) at the start and conclusion of the experiment. Changes in temperature can change the volume of the water or soil by a minor amount, but that amount will become significant when extrapolated to a large area or volume of material. If additional water is needed beyond that previously set aside, it will be important to ensure that the temperature of the new water is essentially the same ($\pm 1°C$ or $2°F$) as the original water being used.

Tools, Equipment, and Supplies Required:
This experiment anticipates that soil from three different soil classifications will be tested. The materials and tools needed for more than three classifications or samples must be adjusted accordingly.
Approximately 2 kg (4.4 pounds) of each of three different soil types
Six 1 L (0.26 gal) clean, graduated, glass beakers
Three clean spatulas
Approximately 4 L (1.2 gal) of tap water

Safety
Safety issues with this experiment lie primarily in the potential for glass breakage, leading to cuts or puncture wounds and splashing of dirty water into eyes. Safety gloves, eye goggles, and a lab coat should be worn during the conduct of these experiments.

Planned Experimental Procedures and Steps, in Order:

1. Assemble all required tools and supplies in a convenient and handy location and put on the appropriate personal protection equipment.
2. Classify or verify prior classifications of all soil types to be tested.
3. Arrange and label all beakers for the type of soil and compaction status to be tested.
4. Weigh each beaker and record the weights.
5. Slowly scoop approximately 500 mL (0.13 gal) of the appropriate soil type into each labeled beaker.
6. Properly tamp the contents of each beaker either lightly or completely, as the particular beaker requires.
7. Weigh each beaker and record the mass of soil as the difference between the filled mass of the beaker and the empty mass of the beaker.
8. Measure and record the volume of soil in each beaker based on the graduations shown on the side of the beakers.
9. Record the temperature of the water to be used to saturate the soil and ensure that the soil samples are at normal room temperature (approximately 22°C or 72°F).
10. Slowly introduce tap water into each sample from a graduated cylinder or volumetric pipette. Care needs to be taken to avoid significant disruption of the tamped soil surface during addition of the water and to distribute the added water across the entire surface of the sample. Allow the soil to fully saturate as the water is added. Saturation has been attained when the water level in the beaker and the top of the soil in the beaker are identical and no further absorption is occurring.
11. Carefully record the volume of water added to each beaker.
12. Carefully weigh each beaker and record the masses.
13. Note any change in soil volume which has occurred, based on the graduations on the side of the beaker, as a result of water addition, leading to swelling of the soil, and record the changed total volume.
14. Calculate the volume of water used by subtracting the mass of dry soil from the mass of saturated soil and dividing by the unit weight of water at the measured temperature.
15. Calculate the volume of soil used by each of the four methods discussed in the experiment theory section and establish the volume to be used for the porosity and void ratio calculations.
16. Calculate the porosity and void ratios for each soil type using the equations provided in the experiment theory section.

Data Collection Format and Data Collection Sheets Tailored to Experiment:
See attached Data Collection Sheet

Anticipated Outcomes:
Soils classified by the USCS typically demonstrate void ratios and porosities as shown in Table A.5, in the Appendix. Density estimates for various soil types are provided in Table A.6 in the Appendix. Table A.8 provides the density of water at various temperatures. Intermediate temperatures may be interpolated linearly.

Data Analysis Plan:
Review of the measured and calculated data will determine the outcomes of this experiment. Since the experiment is designed to identify specific soil characteristics, reporting of those measured characteristics for each of the tested soils, being careful not to expand the data to soil classifications or types not measured, is the desired outcome of the experiment. Discussing any differences between the characteristics measured and the standard value provided will be instructive as an outcome of this experiment. Students may also consider the different characteristics and how they may impact engineering decisions such as structural design or contaminant treatment processes.

Data Collection Sheet for Soil Porosity and Void Ratio Determinations

Date Samples Collected:

Date Samples Tested:

Principal Investigator:

Soil Type and Compaction Status	Sample 1		Sample 2		Sample 3		Sample 4	
	Tamped	Compacted	Tamped	Compacted	Tamped	Compacted	Tamped	Compacted
Empty Beaker Weight (g)								
Filled Beaker weight (g)								
Weight of Sample in Beaker (g)								
Volume of Sample based on Beaker Markings (mL)								
Temperature of Water to be Added to Sample (°C)								
Volume of Water Added to Sample (mL)								
Weight of Saturated Sample and beaker (g)								
Volume of Saturated Sample Based on Beaker Markings (mL)								
Change in volume as a result of Saturation (mL)								
Calculated Volume of Water Used Based on Subtracting the mass of Dry Sample from the Mass of Saturated Sample and Dividing by the Unit Mass of Water at Test Temperature (mL)								

(*Continued*)

Data Collection Sheet for Soil Porosity and Void Ratio Determinations (*Continued*)

Soil Type and Compaction Status	Sample 1		Sample 2		Sample 3		Sample 4	
	Tamped	Compacted	Tamped	Compacted	Tamped	Compacted	Tamped	Compacted
Calculated Sample Volume Based on the Volume of Water Required to Fill the Voids, Subtracted from the Total Volume of Saturated Sample (mL)								
Calculated Sample Volume Based on the Mass of the Sample Used Multiplied by Standard Sample Mass Values Found from Standard References (mL)								
Calculated Sample Volume Based on Subtracting the Mass of Water used to fill the Voids, Divided by the Standard Density of Water at the Test Temperature, from the Total Mass of Saturated Sample (mL)								
Calculated Sample Volume Based on Carefully Measuring the Volume of Sample Used as Indicated by the Graduations on the side of Each Beaker (mL)								
Calculated Porosity of the Sample (%)								
Calculated Void Ratio of the Sample (%)								

11 Oxygen and BOD Experiments

This chapter provides completed designs for example experiments which can be used to demonstrate specific engineering phenomena in a university laboratory or field collection site. They may be used as presented or modified by the user to adapt to other desired outcomes. Sections on actual outcomes and data interpretation are necessarily left blank in these examples. They should be completed by the investigators upon collection of the data.

The experiments in this chapter are:
11.1 Calibration of DO Meter by Winkler Method
11.2 Oxygen Transfer Rate Determination
11.3 Maximum DO Concentration in Water as a Function of Temperature and Salinity
11.4 5-Day BOD Test with Determination of Exertion Rate, k

DOI: 10.1201/9781003184249-11

EXPERIMENT 11.1: CALIBRATION OF DO METER BY WINKLER METHOD

Based on methods published by APHA, 2017, 4500-O Oxygen Dissolved

Date: _____

Principal Investigator:

       Name: _____

       Email: _____

       Phone: _____

Collaborators:

       Name: _____

       Email: _____

       Phone: _____

       Name: _____

       Email: _____

       Phone: _____

       Name: _____

       Email: _____

       Phone: _____

       Name: _____

       Email: _____

       Phone: _____

Objective or Question to Be Addressed:
The determination of the dissolved oxygen concentration (DO) is an important parameter for water quality. It is key to many of the assessments, tests, and techniques common to water and wastewater treatment. Most DO tests are done using a calibrated DO Meter. Calibration of the meter is done using one of several techniques, but the most common is to calibrate the meter using the Winkler titration technique, as described in APHA (2017) Standard Methods. This experiment demonstrates the application of that technique.

Theory Behind Experiment
The Winkler titration technique uses titration to determine the quantity of dissolved oxygen in the water sample. A sample bottle is filled completely with water (no air is left to skew the results). The dissolved oxygen in the sample is then "fixed" by adding

a series of reagents ($MnSO_4$, an alkali-iodide-azide reagent, and sulfuric acid). The reagents form an acid compound that is then titrated with a neutralizing compound (0.0250 N sodium thiosulfate and a starch solution). The reaction results in a color change. The point of color change is called the "endpoint", which coincides with the dissolved oxygen concentration in the sample.

Potential Interferences and Interference Management Plan
The DO concentrations can be impacted by a mixture of potential chemical contaminants in the source waters and issues with sample collection. It is important not to introduce mixing during pumping or handling of the source water.

Data to be collected with an explanation of how they will be collected (Ex.: "Water temperature data for three days using a continuous data logger")
The data to be collected during this experiment are the number of drops and the volume of sodium thiosulfate titrant added at the end of the procedure.

Tools, Equipment, and Supplies Required:
Three 300 mL BOD bottles
4 Burettes or one burette with replaceable tip
Reagents are as follows:
1 L Aerated, distilled, dilution water
2 mL Manganese sulfate ($MnSO_4$) – Dissolve 480 g of hydrated manganese sulfate ($MnSO_4$)· H_2O in reagent water. Filter and dilute to 1 L with reagent water
2 mL Alkali-iodide-azide reagent – Dissolve 500 g sodium hydroxide (NaOH) and 135 g sodium iodide (NaI) in reagent water. Dilute to 1 L. Add 10 g sodium nitrite (NaN_3) dissolved in 40 mL reagent water. *This reagent should not give a color with starch solution when diluted and acidified*
30 mL Standard sodium thiosulfate titrant, 0.0250 N (purchase commercially)
5 mL Starch solution – Prepare an emulsion of 5 g soluble starch in a mortar or beaker with a small amount of distilled water. Pour this emulsion into 1 L of boiling water, allow to boil a few minutes, and let settle overnight. Use the clear supernate. This solution may be preserved by the addition of 1.25 g salicylic acid/L and storage at 4°C.

Safety
The reagents used in this experiment are toxic to humans. Avoid ingestion, contact with the eyes, or subcutaneous infection through cuts or abrasions. Use of eye protection, gloves, and a lab coat is required for this experiment.

In the event of exposure, wash the affected areas with copious volumes of water. In the event of eye exposure or ingestion, contact medical assistance for advice.

Planned Experimental Procedures and Steps, in Order:

1. Slowly siphon three portions of aerated dilution water into three separate BOD bottles. Avoid adding atmospheric O_2 to dilution water. Fill one bottle completely and stopper.
2. Add 200 mL of dilution water to each of the other two BOD bottles, then add 1 mL $MnSO_4$ solution, followed by 1 mL alkali-iodide-azide reagent to

each bottle. Submerge pipette tips in the sample when adding reagents to avoid introducing air with the reagent. Replace or rinse tips well between uses.

3. Stopper carefully to exclude air bubbles; mix by *gently* inverting the bottle several times.

4. When the precipitate has settled to about half the bottle volume, carefully remove the stopper and add 1.0 mL concentrated sulfuric acid. Re-stopper and mix by gentle inversion until the iodine is uniformly distributed throughout the bottle.

5. Titrate each bottle contents with 0.0250 N sodium thiosulfate to a pale straw color *counting the drops added*. Add 1–2 mL of starch solution and continue to titrate with the sodium thiosulfate to first disappearance of the blue color, carefully continuing to count the drops added. (200 mL of dilution water is equal to 203 mL of dilution water plus reagents.)

As this experiment reaches the endpoint, it will take only one more drop of the titrant to eliminate the blue color. Be especially careful that each drop is fully mixed into the sample before adding the next. It is sometimes helpful to hold the BOD bottle up to a white sheet of paper to check for absence of the blue color.

The concentration of dissolved oxygen in the sample is equivalent to the number of drops of sodium thiosulfate titrant used. Each drop of sodium thiosulfate added equals 1 mg/L dissolved oxygen.

To confirm your results, titrate both of the 200 mL bottles. Results should be within 0.1 mg/L if using a burette with increments of 0.05 mL. Calibrate the DO probe with the third bottle which should be equal in DO concentration to the two titrated bottles.

Data Collection Format and Data Collection Sheets Tailored to Experiment:

Calibration of DO Meter by Winkler Method Data Collection Sheet		
Date:		
Principal Investigator:		
Source:		
Bottle #	Sodium Thiosulfate Used, mL	Dissolved Oxygen Concentration, mg/L

Data Analysis Plan:

The data developed during this experiment are direct counts of the drops of sodium thiosulfate (and the total volume) titrated into the solution at the end of the procedure. Each drop represents 1 mg/L of DO in the sample. Two samples are titrated simultaneously to verify the results. A third bottle is then tested with the DO meter to calibrate the DO meter to the titrated DO concentration.

Expected Outcomes:

It is expected that the results of titrating the first two bottles will be consistent indicators of the DO in the sample. The meter can then be calibrated accordingly. If that does not occur, the titration portion of the experiment will need to be redone.

EXPERIMENT 11.2:   OXYGEN TRANSFER RATE DETERMINATION

Based on methods published by APHA 2017, 4500-O Oxygen Dissolved

Date: _____

Principal Investigator:

Name: _____

Email: _____

Phone: _____

Collaborators:

Name: _____

Email: _____

Phone: _____

Name: _____

Email: _____

Phone: _____

Name: _____

Email: _____

Phone: _____

Name: _____

Email: _____

Phone: _____

Objective or Question to Be Addressed:
The objective of this set of experiments is to examine the effects of various initial
conditions on the transfer rate of oxygen from air to water by conducting oxygen
transfer tests on water under three separate starting conditions.

Theory Behind Experiment
The first set of conditions is a 20-L (5.3 gal) sample of water that has been boiled,
then cooled in a closed container to room temperature to minimize the opportunity
for re-entrainment of oxygen from the air above the water while it cools. This sample
needs to be handled very gently to minimize the impact of agitation on oxygen transfer. The idea is to start with a very low dissolved oxygen concentration and to then
measure the change in oxygen transfer associated solely with deliberate reoxygen-
ation over time. Note that a hot, closed, container will generate a negative internal
pressure as it cools and that there will be a vacuum created in this vessel during the

experiment unless a loose cover, such as a watch glass, is used to seal the top of the container as it cools.

The second set of conditions involves a 20-L (5.3 gal) sample of water that has been collected from the effluent of a secondary clarifier at an activated sludge wastewater treatment plant. This sample is also likely to have a low concentration of dissolved oxygen. It also needs to be handled gently to minimize surface water reaeration that could interfere with proper data generation.

The third set of starting conditions involves a 20-L (5.3 gal) sample of water that has been collected from the cold water tap in the laboratory. This will be municipal drinking water that is expected to contain a dissolved oxygen concentration near saturation. Less concern needs to be shown when handling this sample, but minimal agitation is recommended in any case.

Oxygen transfer rates are controlled by several factors. These include the aeration rate, the volume of the liquid, the exposed surface area to volume ratio, the temperature of the liquid, the temperature of the air, the presence of organisms to utilize some of the oxygen present, and the momentary concentration of oxygen in the water. The general equation is the following.

$$OTR = k_L a (C^* - C_L)$$

where:
OTR = oxygen transfer rate, mg O_2 / L / h
k_L = oxygen transfer coefficient, cm/h
a = gas-liquid interfacial area per unit volume, cm^2/cm^3
$k_L a$ = volumetric oxygen transfer coefficient, h^{-1}
C^* = saturated DO concentration, mg/L
C_L = DO concentration in the reactor, mg/L

Note that the units of $k_L a$ are chemically indicated as mmol of O_2/mL. These units are generally used when determining the value of $k_L a$ in the presence of organisms in wastewater treatment reactors. For this current experiment, the simpler units in the provided equation will be more functional.

A simplified equation is available for determination of the oxygen transfer rate in clean water.

$$e^{-(k_L a)t} = \frac{C_S - C_t}{C_S - C_o}$$

where:
$k_L a$ = transfer rate desired, mg/hr
C_s = DO saturation concentration at water temperature, mg/L
C_t = DO concentration at any time t, mg/L
C_o = DO concentration at the start of the test, mg/L
t = The time after the start of the air pump at which the DO measurement is made, min

Alternatively, the data can be plotted with the value of time in minutes plotted along the X-axis and the value of $C_S - C_t$ in mg/L plotted on the Y-axis on semi-log paper. The equation above is then rewritten in linear form as:

$$\log(C_S - C_t) = \log(C_S - C_o) - (k_L a/2.303)t$$

Then:

$$k_L a = 2.303 \frac{(\log C_{t1} - \log C_{t2})}{t_2 - t_1}(60)$$

where:
   $k_L a$ = desired transfer rate, mg/hr
   2.303 is a conversion factor for e
   60 = conversion factor for time in minutes to time in hours
   t_1 and t_2 = are selected from the graph to determine the slope of the line by the
      selection of corresponding C_t values

Transfer rates are usually reported for water temperature at 20°C (68°F). If the water temperature is significantly different from those values, a correction can be made using a standard temperature correction equation.

$$K_L a_{(T)} = K_L a_{(20°C)} \theta^{(T-20)}$$

where:
   $K_L a_{(T)}$ = the calculated transfer rate at the measured temperature, mg/hr
   $K_L a_{(20°C)}$ = the transfer rate at 20°C, mg/hr
   θ = temperature coefficient
   T = temperature of the tested water, °C

Values of θ vary depending on the test conditions, but the value generally fluctuates between 1.015 and 1.040. A value of 1.024 is typical for clean water tests such as these.

Data to be collected with an explanation of how they will be collected (Ex.: "Water temperature data for three days using a continuous data logger")

A separate oxygen transfer rate is to be determined for each of the three starting conditions. The transfer rate is determined by first measuring the dissolved oxygen concentration (DO) under the starting conditions, and then initiating oxygen transfer by bubbling air through the test sample using a fine bubble diffuser (typically an air stone commonly used for aerating small fish tanks and aquariums). The airflow rate on the air pump must be recorded and care must be taken to ensure that the airflow rate remains constant or that any variations are duly noted and recorded during the time of the test. It will be necessary to know the average flow rate over the course of the test to calculate the transfer rate. It will also be necessary to calculate the average temperature of the air being applied to the water throughout the test period because the oxygen concentration in the air is slightly temperature dependent. Finally, it will be necessary to track and record the average temperature of the sample being tested throughout the test period because the maximum attainable oxygen concentration in the water is temperature dependent.

The DO, water temperature, and air temperature are recorded at the beginning of each test. The airflow is then started, and the initial flow rate is recorded. Every 30 seconds thereafter the DO, water temperature, air temperature, and airflow rate are measured and recorded until the change in DO is negligible, indicating that saturation conditions have been achieved. This is done for each of the three samples separately yielding three separate data sets. The most important parameters are the initial DO, the DO at each time interval, and the saturation DO based on the temperature of the water found in standard tables such as Table A.7 in the Appendix to this book. If the temperature of the water and air do not change substantially (by more than 1°C or 2°F) during the test period, the effects of temperature may be ignored. If there is a temperature differential, use of the average temperatures should minimize the inaccuracy of the test data.

Note that this experiment uses a fine bubble diffuser. A coarse bubble diffuser could also be used, but the results should indicate a longer time frame before saturation DO is achieved. This is because coarse bubbles need to breakdown into fine bubbles before efficient oxygen transfer to the water can occur. Coarse bubbles have a very short time frame in which to disintegrate and transfer their oxygen before they rise to the surface of the water and dissipate. Therefore, many more bubbles are needed to transfer the same volume of oxygen to the water. Conducting a parallel test using coarse bubble diffusers would be instructive in this regard.

Potential Interferences and Interference Management Plan
There are several things that could go wrong with this experiment. The first has to do with the temperature of the water being tested. The maximum dissolved oxygen content of any water is very much temperature dependent. It will be necessary to test the samples quickly to minimize the change in temperature during the testing procedure. Measuring the temperature at the start and end of the test on each sample would provide a guide as to whether the temperature change is sufficiently significant to warrant a retesting of that sample.

Anything in the water that is prone to slow oxidation will utilize some of the dissolved oxygen in the sample and dilute the concentrations being read during the test. Using distilled and deionized water would drastically reduce this possibility, but the rate at which that oxidation is likely to occur is expected to be sufficiently slow, in most cases, that further concern about this issue is not warranted.

Undue agitation of the samples prior to initiation of the reaeration step (turning on the air pump) will reintroduce oxygen that has escaped during the pretest steady-state equalization of the sample. Avoid unnecessary movement or agitation of the samples, other than that provided by the air stone activation, to minimize this effect.

Tools, Equipment, and Supplies Required:
    3 clean 20-L (5.3 gal) beakers or containers
    One small air stone

Air pump with flow rate controller (calibrated in advance)
Thermometers for the water and for the airflow
DO meter for continuous DO measurement of the water

Safety

This experiment has a lot of moving parts and the need for rapid measurement of several parameters at once. It is recommended that a team of investigators is assigned to conduct these experiments so that each person will have a specific parameter to monitor and record. It is important, to minimize the potential for personnel interferences and disruption of the test equipment, that the air flow pump monitor, the thermometers, and the DO meter be placed so that they can all be seen and read by designated individuals at the same moment in time..

Boiling the first sample involves placing the beaker on a hot plate and increasing the temperature until the water boils. This will result in the possibility of serious burns due to carelessness. Heat-resistant gloves are required for handling the beaker on the hotplate, sealing it, and removing it to a cooling location.

Wastewater collected from the secondary clarifier at a wastewater treatment plant will contain many varieties of bacteria, viruses, and chemical components that are extremely hazardous to human health. Ingestion, skin contact, inhalation, and eye contact must all be avoided. Use of eye protection, skin protection, and respiratory protection during the collection of this sample and the handling of this sample are required.

Planned Experimental Procedures and Steps, in Order:

1. Gather all required equipment and supplies and put on personal protective equipment.
2. Place one 20-L beaker of water on a hot plate and start the hotplate to boil the water. Once a rapid boil has been achieved, boil the water for 3 minutes, then remove the beaker from the hotplate, cover it with a glass watch cover or other loose cover, and allow it to cool, undisturbed, to room temperature.
3. While the first sample is boiling and cooling, place the second sample in a convenient location and slowly insert the air stone into the beaker with the stone resting on the bottom, near the center of the beaker. Connect the air stone to the air pump through the airflow monitoring and control device. Set up a thermometer at the intake to the air pump if there is no definitive way to measure the air coming out of the air pump to the flow controller. Insert a thermometer and a DO meter into the beaker.
4. Record the temperature of the water, the temperature of the air, and the DO concentration in the sample.
5. Turn on the air pump to the precalibrated flow rate desired. The flow rate should be sufficient to cause roiling and mixing of the sample, but not so vigorously as to spatter water out of the beaker. A flow rate of approximately 1 L (0.035 ft^3) per minute is suggested. Record the time that the air pump is turned on and the actual flow rate used.
6. One minute from the time the air pump is turned on, measure and record the water temperature, the air temperature, the airflow rate, and the DO

concentration in the beaker. Note that the water quality measurements should be outside the rising column of air bubbles from the air stone.

7. At 5 minutes after starting the air pump and every 5 minutes thereafter, for a total time of up to 1 hour, record the airflow rate, the water temperature, the air temperature, and the DO.

8. When the DO concentration has stabilized, stop the experiment, turn off the air pump, and disassemble the experiment components. The water may be discharged as nonhazardous lab waste.

9. Begin the experiment with the third sample by repeating steps 3–7, recording the data for this sample. At step 8, the secondary wastewater sample should be disposed in accordance with laboratory hazardous waste disposal protocols.

10. When the temperature of the first sample has cooled to room temperature, test this sample in the same manner as the other two by repeating steps 3–8 for this sample.

Data Collection Format and Data Collection Sheets Tailored to Experiment:
See attached data collection sheet.

Data Analysis Plan:
Once all the data are collected, they will be tabulated, per the data collection sheet, and then plotted with the value of time in minutes plotted along the X-axis and the value of $C_S - C_t$ in mg/L plotted along the Y-axis on semilog paper. The equation previously provided is then used to calculate the $k_L a$ rate for each sample.

$$\log(C_S - C_t) = \log(C_S - C_o) - (k_L a/2.303)t$$

Then:

$$k_L a = 2.303 \frac{(\log C_{t1} - \log C_{t2})}{t_2 - t_1}(60)$$

where:
  $k_L a$ = desired transfer rate, mg/hr
  2.303 is a conversion factor for e
  60 = conversion factor for time in minutes to time in hours
  t_1 and t_2 = are selected from the graph to determine the slope of the line by the selection of corresponding C_t values

Expected Outcomes:
It is expected that the oxygen transfer rate will be significantly different for the boiled water and the cold tap water due to a large, expected, variation in the initial DO. Both samples should stabilize at or near the same asymptote as the concentrations approach saturation. The oxygen transfer rate for the secondary wastewater and the boiled water are expected to be approximately the same, but the components of the wastewater sample may interfere with the transfer of the oxygen, causing a slower transfer rate there than in the boiled water.

Data Collection Sheet for Oxygen Transfer Rate Determination

Beaker	1	2	3		1	2	3
Start time of experiment							
Initial water temperature °C							
Initial air temperature °C							
Initial DO mg/L							
Initial air flow rate cfm							
At 1 minute							
Water temperature							
Air temperature							
DO							
Airflow rate							
At 5 minutes							
Water temperature							
Air temperature							
DO							
Airflow rate							
At 10 minutes							
Water temperature							
Air temperature							
DO							
Airflow rate							
At 30 minutes							
Water temperature							
Air Temperature							
DO							
Airflow rate							
At 35 Minutes							
Water temperature							
Air temperature							
DO							
Airflow rate							
At 40 minutes							
Water temperature							
Air temperature							
DO							
Airflow rate							
At 45 minutes							
Water temperature							
Air temperature							
DO							
Airflow rate							

(Continued)

Data Collection Sheet for Oxygen Transfer Rate Determination (*Continued*)

At 15 minutes	
Water temperature	
Air temperature	
DO	
Airflow rate	
At 20 minutes	
Water temperature	
Air temperature	
DO	
Airflow rate	
At 25 minutes	
Water temperature	
Air temperature	
DO	
Airflow rate	

At 50 minutes	
Water temperature	
Air temperature	
DO	
Airflow rate	
At 55 minutes	
Water temperature	
Air temperature	
DO	
Airflow rate	
At 60 minutes	
Water temperature	
Air temperature	
DO	
Airflow rate	

EXPERIMENT 11.3:   MAXIMUM DO CONCENTRATION IN WATER AS A FUNCTION OF TEMPERATURE AND SALINITY

Based on methods published by APHA, 2017, 4500-O Oxygen Dissolved

Date: _____

Principal Investigator:

Name: _____

Email: _____

Phone: _____

Collaborators:

Name: _____

Email: _____

Phone: _____

Name: _____

Email: _____

Phone: _____

Name: _____

Email: _____

Phone: _____

Name: _____

Email: _____

Phone: _____

Objective or Question to Be Addressed:

The concentration of dissolved oxygen is a key ingredient to the successful continuation of aquatic life. Plants and animals require oxygen to live and the concentration of available oxygen in the water is critical to sustaining those lives.

This experiment examines the maximum concentration of oxygen realistically possible in water as a function of the salinity of that water (measured as a function of the sodium chloride concentration) and the water temperature.

Theory Behind Experiment

It is generally accepted that water will be able to hold a lower concentration of dissolved oxygen (DO) at higher temperatures when compared to lower temperatures. There are a lot of tables available to suggest the maximum DO concentration attainable at various temperatures. See Table A.7 in the Appendix as an example. Tables to indicate the equivalent maximum DO concentrations available in saline brines are less commonly found. In general, however, the concentration of oxygen in water will decrease as the temperature rises and also decrease as the salinity rises.

At the standard measurement of 4°C (39.2°F), 100% air-saturated freshwater will hold about 10.9 mg/L (0.000364 oz/qt) of dissolved oxygen. At a room temperature of 21°C (69.8°F), the maximum concentration drops to about 8.7 mg/L (0.000291 oz/qt). Seawater generally holds about 20% less dissolved oxygen than fresh water at the same temperature.

The dissolved oxygen concentration is also affected by atmospheric pressure. In the current experiment, the air pressure is assumed constant over the time frame of the experiment and that it is sufficiently close to standard pressure that the results obtained will be sufficiently accurate for the academic purposes of the work. In addition, this experiment assumes 100% air saturation. In the event that the air is less than 100% saturated, the DO of the water at the actual air saturation percentage can be calculated from Henry's Law if the salinity and barometric pressures are known. There are also oxygen solubility charts available to cross-reference the 100% DO concentration from the known actual air saturation percentage, the water salinity, and the water temperature. These charts rely on an assumption that the measured DO in the water is equivalent to the percent oxygen saturation in the air. Thus, atmospheric air at 70% oxygen concentration will yield water at 70% of its maximum oxygen concentration. Note that these tables refer to fresh water and that they could indicate a less than 100% saturation of the air if the measured data from this experiment are significantly less than published saturation values.

Seawater is the most common brine people encounter. Seawater typically has an average salinity of about 3.4%–3.9%, although the actual values are highly variable around the world and from place to place in the same ocean. Actual values can exist significantly higher than that range, such as in the:

- Great Salt Lake in Utah, which has a highly variable salinity depending on the depth of water in the lake, but which ranges from about 5% to about 27%.
- Dead Sea in Israel has a salinity of around 33.7%.
- Gaet'ale Pond in Ethiopia is reported to have a salinity of around 43.3%.

Data to be collected with an explanation of how they will be collected (Ex.: "Water temperature data for three days using a continuous data logger")
The data to be collected will include water temperatures, using standard thermometers; water DO, using a DO probe; and water salinity, using a salinity probe. Probes are also available to report both temperature and salinity at the same time.

Potential Interferences and Interference Management Plan
Salinity of water in this experiment is a function of the concentration of sodium chloride. In nature, salinity is a function of the concentration of many different salts. The presence of the other salts may affect the outcomes slightly, but those effects are not

expected to be significant. The use of distilled water for this experiment will mitigate the effects of other salts.

Tools, Equipment, and Supplies Required:
    6 clean 2 L glass beakers
    6 clean glass mixing rods
    6 thermometers (if probes do not also report the temperature)
    DO probe
    Salinity probe
    Refrigerator that can chill water to approximately 4°C (39.2°F)
    6 hot plates to heat the beakers to approximately 50°C (122°F)
    12 L of distilled water

Safety
Heaters do get hot and cause burns to those who are careless around them. The beakers are glass, and they will be the same temperature as the contents. Handling hot glassware without proper tools or heat-resistant gloves will result in burns.

Salt, sodium chloride, is not inherently dangerous, but if it comes in contact with skin, it can cause drying of the skin and if contact with the eyes should occur, severe burning and eye damage can result. In the event of skin contact, wash with warm water immediately. In the event of eye contact, flush with an eyewash station immediately and continue for up to 15 minutes. Seek medical attention immediately.

Safety gloves, eye protection, and a lab coat are required for this experiment.

Planned Experimental Procedures and Steps, in Order:

1. Gather all necessary labware and supplies together and put on personal protective equipment.
2. Fill each of the six beakers with 2 L of distilled water.
3. Add the following amounts of sodium chloride to the indicated beakers and stir with a glass rod until all of the sodium chloride is dissolved.

Beaker	mg (oz) of NaCl to Add
1	2 (0.00007)
2	10 (0.00035)
3	20 (0.00071)
4	30 (0.00106)
5	40 (0.00141)
6	50 (0.00176)

4. Place all six beakers into the refrigerator until they have stabilized at a temperature of 4°C (39.2°F).
5. Remove the beakers from the refrigerator and immediately measure and record the actual water temperature, salinity, and DO of the water in each beaker.
6. Place each of the beakers on a hot plate and begin heating the beakers, carefully monitoring the temperatures.

7. When the temperatures reach approximately 10°C (50°F), record the actual temperature, salinity, and DO of each beaker.
8. Continue to monitor the heating of the beakers and record the actual temperature, salinity, and DO at the approximate temperatures of 20°C (68°F), 30°C (86°F), 40°C (104°F), and 50°C (122°F), recording the actual temperatures at which the readings are taken.
9. Turn off the heaters, allow the beakers to cool, and dispose of the contents in accordance with the waste disposal protocols of the laboratory.
10. Plot the DO as a function of temperature and as a function of salinity. Both curves should be on the same chart for comparison. Compare the results to published DO solubility data and discuss the cause of any differences. Note any changes in the salinity of any beaker and discuss the reason for those changes. Note the differences between measured data and published fresh water (zero salinity) data and discuss the cause of those differences, particularly to the extent they are not linear with respect to the measured salinity values.

Data Collection Format and Data Collection Sheets Tailored to Experiment:
See attached data collection sheets.

Data Analysis Plan:
The data generated by this experiment will be graphed with the water temperature increasing along the x-axis and the DO concentration along the y-axis.

Note: Table A.7 in the Appendix provides the maximum concentration of DO in *fresh* water at various temperatures for comparison.

Expected Outcomes:
It is expected that the DO concentrations will decline as the salinity increases and as the temperature increases. The decline is expected to be greater in the saline water than in the fresh water at the same temperatures.

Data Sheet for Maximum Do Concentration as a Function of Temperature and Salinity

Beaker	1			2			3		
Approx. Temp. °C (°F)	Actual Temperature	Actual Salinity	DO (mg/L)	Actual Temperature	Actual Salinity	DO (mg/L)	Actual Temperature	Actual Salinity	DO (mg/L)
4 (40)									
10 (50)									
20 (68)									
30 (86)									
40 (104)									
50 (122)									

Beaker	4			5			6		
Approx. Temp. – °C (°F)	Actual Temperature	Actual Salinity	DO (mg/L)	Actual Temperature	Actual Salinity	DO (mg/L)	Actual Temperature	Actual Salinity	DO (mg/L)
4 (40)									
10 (50)									
20 (68)									
30 (86)									
40 (104)									
50 (122)									

EXPERIMENT 11.4:   5-DAY BOD TEST WITH DETERMINATION
OF EXERTION RATE K

Based on methods published by APHA, 2017, 5210 Biochemical Oxygen Demand (BOD)

Date: _____

Principal Investigator:

      Name: _____

      Email: _____

      Phone: _____

Collaborators:

      Name: _____

      Email: _____

      Phone: _____

      Name: _____

      Email: _____

      Phone: _____

      Name: _____

      Email: _____

      Phone: _____

      Name: _____

      Email: _____

      Phone: _____

Objective or Question to Be Addressed:

The objective of this test procedure, adapted from APHA (2017) Standard Methods test 5210, is to determine the 5-day Biological Oxygen Demand (BOD) of a sample of water or wastewater. The term "wastewater" is used throughout this experiment because a 5-day BOD test is most commonly used to determine the relative strength of a wastewater. The "strength" relates to the need for oxygen to decompose the biological content of the waste. The procedure is suitable for any water or wastewater sample in which aerobic biological activity is utilizing organic contaminants as a food source.

Theory Behind Experiment

The 5-day BOD test measures the amount of oxygen needed by bacteria and other organisms in a wastewater sample to completely oxidize the organic waste present in that sample. This is a 5-day test because after about 5 days, any nitrate present in the sample starts to utilize the oxygen present which will start to skew the data. When the measured DO data are plotted over a longer time, a second bump in the curve will appear at about the 5-day mark indicating the start of nitrogenous BOD demand.

Aerobic organisms utilize dissolved oxygen in wastewater to fuel their own metabolism through the oxidation of organic matter in the wastewater. The number of organisms and the nature of those organisms are complex in nature and constantly changing. The precise mix of organisms treating the wastewater does not matter in the overall treatment process. Providing a sufficient dissolved oxygen supply to the wastewater to maintain a healthy biological growth curve accelerates the decomposition of the organic wastes and provides the highest possible biological treatment. Consequently, it is important to know how much oxygen is going to be needed to completely oxidize the organic matter present.

Measuring the mass of organic matter present and then calculating the equivalent mass of oxygen needed is a plausible option. That is not an easy test, however, and is fraught with interferences and difficulties. Measuring the actual oxygen demand by the organisms present is a much more straightforward approach and directly measures the parameter of interest.

The procedure that follows measures the amount of oxygen in a standard sample size, typically 300 mL (10.1 oz), of well-mixed wastewater placed in a sealed BOD bottle to prevent the introduction of extraneous sources of oxygen. BOD bottles of this size are manufactured specifically to conduct this test. Five identical samples are prepared simultaneously, the dissolved oxygen (DO) of each bottle is measured with a DO meter (each bottle should have essentially the same concentration of DO), and the five bottles are incubated together over a 5-day period. At the end of each day of incubation, the DO concentration in *one* of the five bottles is recorded with a DO meter and compared to the initial DO concentration in the sample. The difference in the readings is the amount of oxygen used by the volume of wastewater in the closed jar over that time frame. Those data are then plotted on a graph to provide a curve from which the oxygen utilization rate and ultimate oxygen demand can be directly calculated. Five bottles are used to prevent the introduction of additional oxygen to the sample during the daily testing. After each bottle is tested, the contents are disposed.

Wastewater samples are prepared for this test to account for pH variance, to provide adequate nutrients for the organisms to grow unimpeded, and to eliminate any potential growth interferences such as chlorine residuals. These procedures standardize the results for consistent comparison among samples from different sources and from different places within the same treatment plant.

Note that some BOD tests are run on samples of 60 mL (2.0 oz). Whether 60 mL or 300 mL bottles are used, a standard BOD bottle, which has a glass stopper that can be sealed with a water seal around the rim, is utilized for best results. The larger sample generally provides more reliable data, but the smaller sample may be used with acceptable results where incubation space is limited.

The rate at which the organisms in the wastewater exert the oxygen demand is called the k-rate; often defined as k_1. There are several basic equations relating BOD exerted at any given time, t, the BOD remaining at time, t, and the initial and ultimate BOD (which are necessarily equal). Those equations are the following:

$$BOD_t = L - y$$
$$L = BOD_t + y$$
$$y = L - BOD_t$$

where:
  BOD_t = BOD exerted in time t
  L = initial BOD (also equal to the ultimate BOD)
  y = BOD remaining at time t

In addition:

$$BOD_t = L\left(1 - e^{-kt}\right)$$
$$y = Le^{-kt}$$

where:
  k_1 = BOD exertion rate (base e)

For reference, the base 10 k_1 rate, K_1 is calculated as:

$$K_1 = k_1 / 2.303$$

The base e rate is the rate most commonly referred to when discussing BOD exertion rates.

The 5-day BOD determined from this experiment may be used to calculate the value of k. Note that the units of k are day^{-1}. The value represents a percentage of the remaining BOD that will be consumed per day. Since this is a function of the remaining BOD, not the initial or ultimate BOD, the amount of BOD it represents constantly changes and will only approach zero. The 5-day BOD generally represents about 60%–70% of the ultimate BOD.

Potential Interferences and Interference Management Plan

A common issue has to do with the preparation of the bottles. The wastewater used must be completely mixed at the time the bottles are filled, and the samples in each bottle must be as uniform as possible. Samples which are not well mixed or which have significantly different initial concentrations of DO yield poor results. Care in mixing the sample and rapidly filling all five bottles at the same time will minimize this risk.

Another problem associated with this procedure is the inadvertent opening of bottles before they have been fully incubated. Carefully numbering the bottles as they are prepared and ensuring that only one bottle is opened each day of the test will minimize this risk.

A third issue has to do with the preparation of the samples to minimize interferences. Chlorine, pH, and other growth inhibitors in the sample, even if the sample is well-mixed, will result in skewed and unusable data. Care taken during the sample preparation steps will minimize this risk.

The standard BOD bottle includes a glass stopper that fits tightly into the opening of the bottle. The neck of the bottle is designed to provide a space around the rim of the stopper to add a water seal after the stopper is placed in the neck. This minimizes the potential for extraneous oxygen entering the bottle during the incubation period. This seal must be checked daily for all bottles continuing the incubation process and must be removed from the well before the bottle is opened for DO testing.

Data to be collected with an explanation of how they will be collected (Ex.: "Water temperature data for three days using a continuous data logger")
The data to be collected during this experiment include the dissolved oxygen concentration of multiple samples using a calibrated DO meter.

Tools, Equipment, and Supplies Required:

5 clean 300 mL (10.1 oz) BOD bottles for each sample and each replicate being tested (approximately 10 per sample being tested)
3–5 L (0.8–1.5 gal) glass bottle with siphon. *Avoid using detergents to clean this bottle. Periodically clean with bleach water and rinse well.*
20°C ± 1°C (68°F) incubator
DO meter (See Experiment 11.1 for a procedure to calibrate the DO meter)
Pipettes
Nutrient solutions as specified below
Diluted wastewater sample – See chart below for dilution directions
Dechlorinate sample if final effluent from a treatment plant is being tested – See directions below for dichlorination procedure.

Nutrient Solutions:

1. **Phosphate buffer**: Dissolve 8.5 g KH_2PO_4, 21.75 g K_2HPO_4, 33.4 g $Na_2HPO_4 \cdot 7H_2O$, and 1.7 g NH_4Cl in approx. 500 mL reagent water. Dilute to 1 L. The pH should be 7.2. Store in 4°C (39 °F) refrigerator. Check before each use for contamination (if there is any indication of biological/microbial growth, discard remaining reagent and prepare fresh).
2. **Magnesium sulfate solution**: Dissolve 22.5 g $MgSO_4 \cdot 7H_2O$ in reagent water. Diluted to 1 L.
3. **Calcium chloride solution**: Dissolve 27.5 g $CaCl_2$ in reagent water. Dilute to 1 L.
4. **Ferric chloride solution**: Dissolve 0.25 g $FeCl_3 \cdot 6H_2O$ in reagent water. Dilute to 1 L

Pretreatment of Chlorinated BOD Samples Reagents:

1. **Acetic acid solution, 1+1**: Add 500 mL of concentrated acetic acid to 500 mL of distilled water.
2. **Potassium Iodide Solution**: Dissolve 10 grams KI in a 100 mL volumetric flask. Bring to volume with distilled water.

3. **Sodium Sulfite Solution, 0.0250 N**: Dissolve 1.575 grams anhydrous Na_2SO_3 in a 1,000 mL volumetric flask. Bring to volume with distilled water.

   NOTE: This solution is not stable and must be prepared daily.

4. **Starch Indicator Solution (For Analysis with Iodine)**: Prepare an emulsion of 5 g soluble starch in a mortar or beaker with a small amount of distilled water. Pour this emulsion into 1 L of boiling water, allow to boil a few minutes, and let settle overnight. Use the clear supernate. This solution may be preserved by the addition of 1.25 g salicylic acid/L and storage at 4°C.

Safety

Wastewater is inherently dangerous to humans when ingested or when it comes in contact with eyes or open wounds. Care must be used when sampling and handling untreated sewage. Gloves and eye protection are required for these procedures.

The incubation of samples in this experiment is done at 20°C. This is essentially room temperature and the temperature of the bottles and incubator should not pose a health risk.

The various additives described in the experiment are generally toxic to humans if ingested. Care in the handling and storage of these materials is needed. Gloves, eye protection, and a lab coat are required during this experiment.

The residuals from this experiment are hazardous to human health and must be disposed in accordance with laboratory protocols for hazardous waste disposal.

In the event of exposure from any product to the eyes, wash at an eye station immediately for up to 15 minutes and contact medical assistance for further advice.

In the event of ingestion, seek medical advice immediately.

In the event of exposure via puncture wounds, open cuts or other cutaneous abrasions, wash with disinfectant, and seek medical attention at once. There is no such thing as a "minor" exposure to these materials.

Safety glasses, gloves, and lab coats are always required for these experiments.

Planned Experimental Procedures and Steps, in Order:

1. Collect all required equipment and supplies and put on appropriate personal protective equipment.
2. Conduct a chlorine residual analysis on a portion of the sample collected. *Potassium iodide/starch paper can be used as a quick qualitative test for residual chlorine.* If no residual is found, proceed with the BOD analysis utilizing seeded dilution water. If a residual is found, proceed with the following steps before initiating the BOD test.
3. Determination of Appropriate Volume of Sodium Sulfite
   a. Obtain a 200 mL portion of the sample to be tested.
   b. Add 10 mL of 1+1 acetic acid solution
   c. Add 10 mL of potassium iodine solution
   d. Add 2 mL starch

    e. Titrate with 0.0250 N sodium sulfite. The end point has been reached when a clear color persists after complete mixing.

    f. Measure volume of 0.0250 N sodium sulfite used.

4. Sample Pretreatment

    a. Obtain another 200 mL portion of the same sample used in Step 2.

    b. Add to the sample the same volume of 0.0250 N sodium sulfite solution that was determined in Step 3.e and mix.

    c. Retest for residual chlorine after allowing the sample to stand for 10- - 20 minutes.

    d. If no residual chlorine is present, proceed with the BOD analysis. Samples which have been chlorinated must be seeded.

Dilution Technique:

1. Estimate the BOD of the sample and select suitable dilutions from the following tables:

Estimated BOD$_5$ (mg/L)	Suggested Sample Volumes (mL)	Estimated BOD$_5$ (mg/L)	Suggested Sample Volumes (mL)
< 5	200, 250, 300	90–150	5, 10, 15
< 10	100, 150, 200	150–300	3, 5, 10
10–30	25, 50, 100	300–700	1, 3, 5[a]
30–60	15, 25, 50	700–1500	0.5, 1, 3[a]
60–90	10, 15, 25	1500–2500	0.25, 0.5, 1[a]

[a] Standard Methods provide additional guidance as follows: use less than 3 mL for strong industrial wastes, 3–15 mL for raw and settled wastewater, and 15–75 mL for biologically treated effluent.

When preparing replicate samples for quality control purposes, prepare the replicate at exactly the same dilutions as the original sample.

2. Using a large-tipped, volumetric pipette (for samples less than 50 mL) or a graduated cylinder for larger sample volumes, measure the proper amount of *well-mixed* sample into thoroughly cleaned and rinsed 300 mL BOD bottles. Dilutions under 3 mL must be made by diluting the waste in a graduated cylinder before pipetting.

3. Dilution water may be prepared immediately before use, or, *except for the addition of the phosphate buffer*, days or weeks ahead of time. Add 1 mL of each nutrient solution per liter of dilution water. The phosphate buffer is the critical nutrient in stimulating contaminating growths so it must be added the day the water is to be used. Distilled water should be allowed to equilibrate in the incubator or with outside air for at least 24 hours at 20°C before use. To avoid dust or dirt contamination while allowing oxygenation, use a paper towel, cotton plug, or sponge to cover the bottle opening.

Care must be taken to ensure that dilution water is oxygen saturated. The use of aerator stones for this purpose should be discouraged as there

*is a tendency to develop growths on the stones which can prevent dilu-
tion water BOD criteria from being met. The best technique is to use compressed air which is passed through glass wool or a filter of some type to
prevent the introduction of contaminants.*

4. Each BOD bottle is filled by slowly adding sufficient dilution water so
   that the stopper can be inserted without leaving an air bubble but not so
   much that there is overflow. The siphon hose must be made of surgical gum
   (latex rubber), polypropylene, or polyethylene to avoid introducing BOD
   into the dilution water. Tygon and black rubber can add oxygen demand to
   the water.

   When volumes of sample used exceed 150 mL, an additional 0.1 mL of
   nutrients must be added for each 50 mL of sample used in excess of 150
   mL. For example, if the sample size is 200 mL, an additional 0.2 mL is
   required.

5. Completely fill two bottles with dilution water to be incubated as blanks.
6. Label each bottle carefully as to sample and volume used and record on the
   data collection form.

BOD Seeding Procedure
Preparation of Seed:

1. Collect a raw influent grab sample the day before performing the test. If the
   influent contains significant industrial loading, settled mixed liquor may
   provide a better seed than raw influent. If used for seed, settled mixed liquor
   does not need to be incubated at 20°C overnight. Seed can also be commercially obtained. There are at least two products widely in use: BioSeed™,
   and PolySeed™.
2. Place sample in an incubator at 20°C (68°F) overnight.

Preparation of Seed Controls:
BOD Seed Dilution Guidelines

Estimated BOD of Seed	Dilutions for Seed Control	# mL Seed per BOD bottle	# mL Diluted Seed (10 mL Seed + 90 mL Water)
30	15, 25, 50	6–10	NA
50	15, 25, 50	4–6	NA
100	5, 10, 15	2–3	NA
150	5, 10, 15	1–2	NA
250	3, 5, 10	1	6–10
500	1, 3, 5	0.5	5

If the BOD of the seed is 150 mg/L or less, the seed may be added directly to the
BOD samples without dilution. If dilution is necessary, use volumes noted in column
(4). Set up the seed control dilutions as shown in column (2). Prepare seed controls
with seed at full strength.

1. Take the incubated raw influent sample out of the incubator – DO NOT MIX.
2. Pipette 3, 5, and 7 mL of the clear supernatant into three BOD bottles marked respectively. Use other volumes of supernatant based on the strength of the system. At least two different dilutions must be used.
3. Fill these three bottles with BOD dilution water.
4. Determine the initial dissolved oxygen (L) in each of the three bottles and seal them.

Preparation of Seeded BOD Samples:

1. Fill the bottles approximately 1/3 –1/2 with dilution water.
2. Pipette 2 mL of the supernatant into each of the BOD sample bottles that will require seeding.
3. Add the appropriate amount of sample to each of the bottles.
4. Complete the filling of the BOD bottles with dilution water.
5. Determine the initial dissolved oxygen (L) in each of the bottles.

Calculation of BOD in sample:

$$BOD_5 = BOD\,mg/L = \left[(L - DO_5) - \text{seed correction}\right] \times \text{dilution factor}$$

where:

$\quad$ dilution factor = 300/sample size, mL

Example Calculation of Seed Correction

Seed Control Bottle	L (DO$_i$)	DO$_5$	Depletion	# mL Seed in Bottle	mg DO/mL Seed
A	8.5	0.3	8.2	30	-.--
B	8.4	1.6	6.8	20	0.34
C	8.4	4.3	4.1	10	0.41

Note: Bottle A is not used due to the insufficient final DO. There must be a residual DO of at least 1.0 mg/L after 5 days.

Here:

The average mg of DO/mL of SEED = $(0.34 + 0.41)/2 = 0.375$ mg DO/mL seed

If 2 mL undiluted seed were added to each sample bottle, the seed correction would be:

$$(0.375 \text{ mg DO/mL seed})(2 \text{ mL seed}) = 0.75 \text{ mg DO}$$

Calculation of BOD Exertion Rate, k_1

The value of k_1 is determined from the graph of BOD exerted over time. Once the curve of BOD exerted over time has been verified, any lag in the start of the BOD exertion is noted. This is determined by drawing a tangent to the rising leg of the BOD curve at the point where the curve begins to break back to the right and the rate of increase starts to decline (See Figure 9.1). The lag, in days, is determined from the point on the x-axis that the tangent line intersects with that axis.

All the BOD time data are then adjusted by the value of the lag. This is an important step in the accuracy of the k-rate calculated from those data because ignoring it lets the lag time extend the time for the reactions to occur and that causes a decrease in the k-rate value below the true value.

A new plot of the BOD exertion curve using the new time data, if there is a lag, and the original BOD exerted data is then drawn. This curve plots the following expression on the y-axis against the adjusted time on the x-axis in days. If there is no lag, the unadjusted data are plotted using the same equation.

$$Y = \left[\text{New time, days} / \text{BOD Exerted, mg/L} \right]^{-1/3}$$

This plot should yield data points through which a reasonably straight line of best fit can be drawn, as shown in Figure 11.2. The value of k is then determined by the following equation.

If there is no lag in the BOD curve, then the curve shown above uses the (Actual Time / BOD)$^{1/3}$ over time to determine the k-rate. That value is calculated by:

$$k = 2.61(B/A)$$

where:
    A = the y-axis intercept of the line of best fit
    B = the slope of the line of best fit

If there is a lag in the BOD curve, a more complicated solution is required, as shown by Example Problem, below. The values used are taken from Figures 11.1 and 11.2, as appropriate.

Example Problem

Given the following measured values for BOD from a specific wastewater over time, determine the ultimate BOD concentration (L) and the k-rate value for this waste.
    Time, days 0.5 1.0 2.0 3.0 4.0 5.0 7.0 10.0
    BOD, mg/L 4 16 72 128 160 176 190 200

Solution:

First, the data need to be plotted in a standard BOD curve, as has been done in Figure 11.1. Then a table needs to be constructed showing the time, the corrected time, based on the lag time determined from Figure 11.1; that is 1.3 days in this example, as shown in Figure 11.1, the original BOD values, and the value of (Time/BOD)$^{1/3}$. That table is shown below, and the (Corrected Time / BOD)$^{1/3}$ is plotted, as in Figure 11.2.

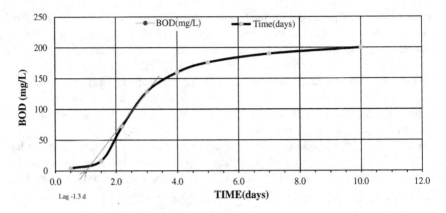

FIGURE 11.1 Typical BOD curve. (Hopcroft, F. J. (2015). *Wastewater Treatment Concepts and Practices*, Momentum Press.)

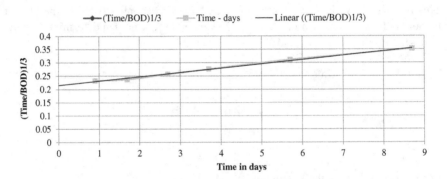

FIGURE 11.2 Log-normal plot of BOD data from Figure 11.1. (Hopcroft, F. J. (2015). *Wastewater Treatment Concepts and Practices*, Momentum Press.)

Table of Corrected Data Based on Lag Time

Time (days)	Corrected Time (days)	BOD (mg/L)	(Time/BOD)$^{1/3}$
0.5	–	4	–
1.0	–	16	–
2.0	0.9	72	0.2324
3.0	1.7	128	0.2372
4.0	2.7	160	0.2568
5.0	3.7	176	0.2763
7.0	5.7	190	0.3111
10.0	8.7	200	0.3521
From: Hopcroft, Francis J., Wastewater Treatment Concepts and Practices, Momentum Press, 2015.			

   The next step is to establish several equations that can be solved simultaneously to determine the value of k. These equations are empirical in nature, as follows.

   The y-intercept of the trend line on Figure 11.2 is equal to the value $(k*L)^{-1/3}$, Where:

k = reaction rate constant being sought
L = ultimate (or initial) carbonaceous BOD concentration

In this case,

$$(k*L)^{-1/3} = 0.21$$

$$(k*L) = (0.21)^{-3} = 107.98$$

$$L = 107.98/k$$

The second equation is the equation of the slope of the trend line in Figure 11.2. The vertical dimension of that slope at any point is equal to $k^{2/3}$. The horizontal dimension at the same location is equal to $6*L^{1/3}$. Thus, the slope of the line at any point is equal to:

$$\text{Slope} = k^{2/3} / 6 * L^{1/3}$$

By examination of the graph or the table above, it can be seen that the vertical component of the slope of the line between 2.7 and 3.7 days (a convenient horizontal distance of L) is $0.2568 - 0.2372 = 0.0196$. Thus, the slope of the line $= 0.0196 / L = 0.0196$.

   Therefore:

$k^{2/3} / 6*L^{1/3} = 0.0196$
$k^{2/3} = (6) (0.0196) L^{1/3} = 0.1176 \, L^{1/3}$
$k = (0.1176)^{3/2} (L)^{1/2}$
$k^2 = (0.1176)^3 L = 0.00163 \, L$
$k^2 = (0.00163) (107.98 /k)$
$k^3 = 0.1760$
$k = (0.1760)^{1/3}$
$k = 0.561 / \text{day}$
$L = 107.98 / 0.561 = 192.5 \text{ mg/L}$

Using the equation for a non-lag curve on these data would yield a value of $k = 0.2436$. Thus, it is important to know whether there is or is not a lag in the BOD data.

Data Collection Format and Data Collection Sheets Tailored to Experiment:
See attached Data Collection Sheet

Data Analysis Plan:
The data collected during the experiment will be used to calculate the BOD of the sample at the end of each day. The BOD value calculated will be plotted on a graph

of time (days) on the x-axis and BOD (mg/L) on the y-axis. This will yield a classic BOD curve if the experiment is successful. If the test is conducted for 7 days instead of only 5, there should be a secondary bump in the BOD curve around day 5 indicating the exertion of a nitrogenous BOD, in addition to a biological one.

Expected Outcomes:
Communication with staff and operators at the source of the sample will indicate a probable BOD outcome range. Those estimates will be essential for estimating the volume of dilution required and the amount of seed required, if any. If there is no wastewater plant involved, or the source water is a river or stream, the expected BOD value will need to be estimated by the experimenter prior to initiation of the experiment. Should the calculated BOD not plot on a curve reasonably close to the classic curve shape, or should the calculated values vary significantly from the estimated values. Redoing the experiment using the calculated BOD as the estimated value should be considered for verification of the data.

5-Day BOD Test Data Collection Sheet

Principal Investigator:

Sample Source

Date Sample Collected:

Preservation Techniques Utilized:

Date Sample Testing begun:

Bottle #	Sample (mL)	Initial DO (mg/L)	Final DO (mg/L)	Depletion (mg/L)	Comments
Blank					Depletion must be less than 0.2 mg/L
Seeded Blank					

Sample	Bottle #	Sample mL A	Seed mL added	Initial DO B	Final DO C	DO depletion $D = B - C$	Seed Control Factor E	Dilution factor $F = 300/A$	BOD$_5$ mg/L $F \times (D - E)$	Average BOD$_5$
Raw										
Final										
Replicate of ___										

12 Environmental Microbiology Experiments

This chapter provides completed designs for example experiments which can be used to demonstrate specific engineering phenomena in a university laboratory or field collection site. They may be used as presented or modified by the user to adapt to other desired outcomes. Sections on actual outcomes and data interpretation are necessarily left blank in these examples. They should be completed by the investigators upon collection of the data.

The experiments in this chapter are:

12.1 Total Coliforms and *E. coli* by IDEXX Quanitrays® and Colilert® Most Probable Number Methodologies

12.2 Field Testing and Quantification of Total Coliforms and *E. coli* by Colilert® and Petrifilm® Methodologies

12.3 Viral Indicators: Coliphage Quantification Based on EasyPhage® Method

12.4 Comparison of Disinfection Methods

12.5 Comparison of Water Disinfection Methods: Remote Area Options

DOI: 10.1201/9781003184249-12

EXPERIMENT 12.1: TOTAL COLIFORMS AND *E. COLI* BY IDEXX QUANTITRAYS® AND COLILERT® MOST PROBABLE NUMBER METHODOLOGIES

Date: _____

Principal Investigator:

      Name: _____

      Email: _____

      Phone: _____

Collaborators:

      Name: _____

      Email: _____

      Phone: _____

      Name: _____

      Email: _____

      Phone: _____

      Name: _____

      Email: _____

      Phone: _____

      Name: _____

      Email: _____

      Phone: _____

Objective or Question to Be Addressed:

A pathogen is a microorganism capable of causing a disease in a host. Pathogens are excreted in the feces of infected humans and animals and may directly or indirectly contaminate water intended for human consumption. Hundreds of different enteric microorganisms are known to infect humans. Pathogens capable of causing waterborne illness include viruses, bacteria, and protozoa. The impact of waterborne pathogens in humans is often acute gastrointestinal disease.

While testing for all enteric pathogens in drinking waters would be ideal, it is not practical because of time and financial constraints. Therefore, indicator organisms are used to assess the potential presence of pathogenic microorganisms. This experiment provides a method for quantifying the most probable number (MPN) of *E. coli* present in a wastewater sample.

Theory Behind Experiment:

Indicator organisms are used to establish potential risk from fecal contamination in drinking waters. Bacterial groups, such as total coliforms, are commonly used to indicate the microbiological quality of water, and their detection is a component of drinking water regulations. Total coliforms and *E. coli* are used as indicators of fecal contamination in regulations by the United States Environmental Protection Agency (EPA), the Council of European Communities (CEC), and the World Health Organization (WHO). However, waterborne viral outbreaks have occurred in treated drinking water systems where the systems were in compliance with regulations. Thus, coliform measurement is an imperfect indicator of public health risk from viruses.

There are many different indicator organisms, and not one single indicator is appropriate for every type of water system. Factors including detection methodology and survival rates influence the validity of an indicator system. The most important attribute of an indicator is a strong quantitative relationship between indicator concentration and the degree of public health risk; therefore, a strong correlation between the indicator concentration and pathogen levels is vital.

Indicators can be utilized for many different reasons. These include detection of fecal contamination, detection of wastewater contamination, determination of potential pathogenic organism presence, treatment system efficiency, and subsurface transport. The choice of an indicator is critical for assessment of the specific situation for its use. There is no single indicator that is appropriate for all situations, and there is not one single method for analysis. Although there is no perfect indicator organism, research is ongoing to determine a rapid, relatively inexpensive, and accurate method of assessing the microbial quality of water.

Various bacterial groups have been commonly used to indicate the microbiological quality of water. These indicators provide a method for identifying the potential presence of pathogens. Public health regulations provide specific requirements and methods to analyze risk. This is particularly important because the reuse of wastewater effluent as a drinking water source and agricultural irrigation are becoming more of a necessity in areas in which water is scarce.

The United States (U.S.) has been using bacteria as indicators for water quality since 1914. Currently, the U.S. Environmental Protection Agency (EPA) requires drinking water suppliers to monitor for total coliforms on a routine basis; the frequency of testing is dependent upon system size. If the total coliform results are positive, then the suppliers are required to conduct repeat samplings for total coliforms and also to test both for fecal coliforms and for *Escherichia coli*. Using coliforms as an indicator of contamination has several benefits based on their long history of use and standardized methods for detection. The coliform group has been used as an indicator of water quality for over 100 years; this history provides a depth of research knowledge that new methods cannot provide. These data allow researchers to compare data on past water quality. In addition, total coliforms are used worldwide, allowing for detailed comparisons of water quality around the world. The long history of use also provided the standardization of detection methodologies. There have also been recent advances in field tests for coliforms, making these tests appropriate for water quality monitoring in remote locations where challenges to conducting laboratory tests may exist.

IDEXX Quantitrays® and Colilert® utilize two active substrates, o-nitrophenyl-p-D-galactopyranoside (ONPG) and 4-methylumbelliferyl-p-D-glucuronide (MUG), which are combined to simultaneously detect total coliforms and *E. coli*. Total coliforms produce the enzyme β-galactosidase, which hydrolyzes ONPG and thereby releases o-nitrophenol, which produces a yellow color. *E. coli* produces the enzyme β-glucuronidase, which hydrolyzes MUG to form a fluorescent compound.

Data to be collected with an explanation of how they will be collected (Ex.: "Water temperature data for three days using a continuous data logger")

Data to be collected will include counts of positive indicators of coliform and *E. coli* bacteria in incubated trays prepared in accordance with the procedures provided. This is done by simple observation for total coliform and with a UV lamp for *E. coli*

Potential Interferences and Interference Management Plan:

In an experiment that involves the culturing of bacteria or other organisms, cross-contamination during the experiment can significantly skew the resulting data. Care is needed to ensure the minimal opportunity for cross-contamination. That includes using laminar flow hoods, autoclaved tools, and dilution water, and taking extreme care to avoid contact between the tools, the culture materials, or the body with the samples being cultured and the cultures being incubated. It is unlikely any cross-contamination that does occur will be obvious to the experimenter due to the large numbers of bacteria expected to be encountered.

Tools, Equipment, and Supplies Required:

    Autoclave
    Laminar flow hood
    Incubator
    UV lamp producing "Black Light"
    15 bottles (6 bottles of wastewater sample per test × 2 tests) + 2 negative control + 1 extra
    (15) 99 mL autoclaved buffered dilution water (PBS) bottles

Dilution Water – Phage Phosphate Buffered Saline (PBS) – Label Phage Only
- Add 8.0 g NaCl to a sterile 1000 ml bottle
- Add 0.2 g KH_2PO_4
- Add 0.12 g KCl
- Add 0.91 g anhydrous Na_2HPO_4 (or 2.9 g $Na_2HPO_4 \cdot 12H_2O$)
- Bring up to 1 L with Epure water
- Adjust pH to 7.2–7.4 (with 1 N HCl or NaOH)
- Autoclave, store refrigerated for 1 year

  5 Extra autoclaved dilution bottles
    (2) 50 mL Tryptic soy broth (TSB) shaker flasks – autoclaved
    35 autoclaved 1 mL pipette tips

15 IDEXX Quantitrays

Quantitray sealing machine

IDEXX Standard Quantitray for Total Coliforms and *E. coli* and IDEXX cross-reference sheets for MPN determinations

15 IDEXX Colilert Packets

Frozen *E. coli* stock (such as stock cultures of *E. coli* ATCC #11775)

Freezing E. coli stock samples in glycerol (for positive controls):
- When a bacterial strain is purchased, a small portion of the powder is transferred with a sterile pipette tip or inoculating loop to 50 mL TBS medium and incubated at 37°C for 2–8 hours on a shaker plate
- Autoclave 50% glycerol and cool to room temperature
- Add appropriate volume of 50% sterile glycerol (based on desired quantity of stock, 50% v/v) to a suspension of log-phase bacteria
- Vortex to dissociate the cells and ensure even mixing of the bacteria with the glycerol
- Transfer aliquots of the suspension into cryogenic screw-cap vials
- Snap-freeze the vials by immersing the tubes in either ethanol-dry ice or liquid nitrogen and then store in freezers (−20°C to −80°C)

Safety

The wastewater samples being tested are presumed to be contaminated with *E. coli* and total coliform bacteria. Ingestion of these organisms or infection through open wounds or abrasions will likely lead to intestinal upset and infections which could rapidly become serious. Care must be taken to avoid exposure through accidental ingestion, contact with the eyes, or contact with open wounds or skin abrasions.

In the event of ingestion or contact through open wounds, puncture wounds, or skin abrasions, seek medical advice immediately. In the event of contact with the eyes, immediately flush with an eyewash for up to 20 minutes and seek immediate medical attention.

Sterile gloves, eye protection, and lab coats are required during this experiment.

Safe disposal of the wastewater and the bacterial cultures developed are important for student and community safety. Untreated wastewater may be disposed into a normal wastewater sewer. Treated wastewater should be considered hazardous waste (infectious) and disposed in accordance with laboratory protocols for disposal of infectious materials. In general, killing the bacteria prior to disposal is necessary. That can be done in an autoclave or by other laboratory-approved methods.

The bacterial cultures developed during this experiment are also infectious and must be inactivated prior to disposal. That is normally done through autoclaving, but may also be done by other methods, such as the following, based on laboratory infectious waste disposal protocols.

Hypochlorite (bleach) solution can be used. Add 1–2 mL of hypochlorite (bleach) solution to each test container. If a container has a lid, do not close it tightly. Put the container in the microwave at 70°C - 80°C (158°F - 176°F) for 50 seconds. Wait 10 - 15 minutes. Pour the liquid down the drain.

Kill the cultured bacteria with autoclave pressure. Put the used test containers in a contaminated items bag or biohazard bag to prevent leaks. Do not seal the bag. Put the bag in the autoclave at 121°C (250°F) for 30 minutes at 15 lb of pressure. When the bag is cool, seal it and put it into a garbage bag. Make sure to tie the garbage bag tightly.

Planned Experimental Procedures and Steps, in Order:
Total coliforms and *E. coli* will be enumerated using APHA (2017) Standard Methods 9223 with Colilert® (IDEXX, Westbrook, ME) in the multiple well format (Quantitray®, IDEXX, Westbrook, ME) and equated to an MPN of the target organisms per 100 mL.

A. Prepare log-phase *E. coli* for positive control
   Make two cultures in a laminar flow hood sprayed with 50% ethanol or ethyl alcohol. Flame (or use previously sterilized) tubes, tops, caps, and loop before each use and in between each use. For each culture,
   1. Add 50 mL Tryptic Soy Broth (TSB) to a labeled flask
   2. Autoclave
   3. Add one loopful of frozen *E. coli* stock
   4. Incubate at 35°C at 100 rpm for 16–18 hours
B. Prepare workstation
   1. Turn on microbial hood blower
   2. Sterilize microbial hood and workstation with 50% ethanol solution
   3. Light alcohol burner in hood
C. Prepare wastewater samples
   1. Run cap and bottleneck under flame before and after wastewater is transferred, for sterilization purposes
   2. Remove first wastewater sample from refrigerator
   3. Invert bottle a few times to mix contents
   4. Pour 100 mL of wastewater into dilution bottle labeled 10-1A. Repeat for 10-1B
   5. Prepare dilutions:
      a. Pipette 1 mL of undiluted wastewater into a dilution bottle labeled 10-2A and add enough dilution water to bring the contents of each dilution to 100 mL
      b. Repeat for "B" series. Cap and invert dilution bottles twice
      c. Dispose used pipette tip as infectious waste
      d. Repeat this dilution series down to 10-4 and 10-6 for both series A & B adding two mL of wastewater to the second set, 3 mL of wastewater to the third set, and so forth until the sixth set receives 6 mL of wastewater and 94 mL of dilution water

Prepare Quantitrays:

   1. Add one Colilert packet to each dilution bottle
   2. After adding Colilert, recap bottle, and shake until no Colilert particles are left in suspension. Allow bottle to sit for 1–2 minutes for Colilert to dissolve

3. Label all Quantitrays as the individual dilution bottles are labeled
4. Slowly invert dilution bottle being careful not to create bubbles, then uncap dilution bottle
5. Slowly pour contents into Quantitray being careful not to create bubbles or turbulence
6. Place Quanitray onto Quantitray holder and run through Quantitray sealer machine
7. Record the time on the Quantitray and place the tray in an incubator at 35°C

Reading Quantitrays:

1. After 24 hours, remove Quantitrays from incubator and place under the hood before opening or reading
2. Count and record the number of yellow large and small wells (total coliform)
3. Turn off lights and using a UV light count, quantify and record the number of wells that fluoresce (*E. coli*)
4. Use the standard tray (from IDEXX) as a comparison
5. Use IDEXX cross reference sheet to quantify bacteria content (MPN) after adjusting for dilutions

Data Collection Format and Data Collection Sheets Tailored to Experiment:
See attached Data Collection Sheet

Anticipated Outcomes:
Wastewater is expected to contain various forms of coliform bacteria, specifically including *E. coli* bacteria. The intent of this experiment is to demonstrate a methodology for determining the MPN of total coliform and the MPN of *E. coli* bacteria present in each 100 mL of the tested wastewater. Those values will vary widely from source to source. It is expected, however, that significant numbers of both categories of bacteria will be found in the wastewater tested.

The microbiological populations should decrease by an order of magnitude based on the serial dilutions.

Data Analysis Plan:
The data collected will be analyzed in accordance with the procedures developed by IDEXX for use of its proprietary Quantitray and Colilert technologies. The MPNs found will be compared to standards provided by IDEXX to evaluate the quality of the wastewater samples tested.

Data collection sheet total coliforms and *E. coli* by IDEXX Quantitrays® and Colilert® MPN methodologies

Date Collected:					
Date Tested:					
Principal Investigator:					
Source Water:					

Test	Results		Expected Results	Variations Noted	Notes
	Total Coliform (MPN/100 mL)	*E. coli* (MPN/100 mL)			
Tray A (Negative Control)		—			
Tray B (Negative Control)	—				
Tray 1A		—			
Tray 1B	—				
Tray 2A		—			
Tray 2B	—				
Tray 3A		—			
Tray 3B	—				
Tray 4A		—			
Tray 4B	—				
Tray 5A		—			
Tray 5B	—				
Tray 6A		—			
Tray 6B	—				

EXPERIMENT 12.2: FIELD TESTING AND QUANTIFICATION OF TOTAL COLIFORMS AND *E. COLI* BY COLILERT AND PETRIFILM METHODOLOGIES

Date: _____

Principal Investigator:

    Name: _____

    Email: _____

    Phone: _____

Collaborators:

    Name: _____

    Email: _____

    Phone: _____

    Name: _____

    Email: _____

    Phone: _____

    Name: _____

    Email: _____

    Phone: _____

    Name: _____

    Email: _____

    Phone: _____

Objective or Question to Be Addressed:

It is important for communities to know if their drinking water sources are safe or contaminated because people can get sick if they drink water contaminated with disease-causing microbes, such as bacteria and viruses. Diseases such as typhoid, cholera, and dysentery are caused when these microbes infect the intestinal tract and are shed by billions in feces from sick people. When these microbes get into drinking water, they can infect other people and cause more disease. Until a few years ago, methods to test for microbial contamination in water required a well-equipped laboratory with electricity, incubators, and sterilization equipment.

This experiment is based on proprietary test equipment manufactured by IDEXX Corp. identified as the IDEXX Colilert Presence/Absence test method and on a proprietary 3M Corp. product called the Petrifilm *E. coli.*/Coliform Count Plate test method.

Theory Behind Experiment:
An indicator organism needs to be able to correlate to health risk and infectious pathogens, be cost effective, have minimal risk to the analyst, be measurable in a time and
cost-efficient manner, transport similarly to pathogens in treatment and the environment, and be specific to the source of origin. The American Water Works Association
(AWWA) recommends that the selection of appropriate indicators of fecal contamination and waterborne pathogens should be based on their survivability in water, suscep-
tibility to water disinfectants, and capability to detect increased health risks.

This experiment incorporates field-tested equipment that provides the charac-
teristics cited for useful indicator organisms. The steps include sample collection,
IDEXX Colilert® Presence/Absence test, and the 3M Petrifilm® *E. coli*/Coliform
Count Plate test.

The Colilert test is performed in a 120 mL plastic bottle that contains a dried
nutrient powder for *E. coli*. growth. The test indicates the dual presence/absence
of coliform and *E. coli* bacteria in a 100 mL water sample. The Petrifilm is used to
enumerate individual *E. coli* and coliform bacteria in 1 mL of water.

The Colilert simultaneously detects total coliforms and *E. coli* in water. It is based
on an IDEXX proprietary Defined Substrate Technology. When total coliforms
metabolize the Colilert DST nutrient-indicator (ONPG), the sample turns yellow.
When *E. coli* metabolize Colilert's DST nutrient-indicator (MUG), the sample also
fluoresces. Colilert can simultaneously detect these bacteria at concentrations as low
as 1 colony-forming unit (cfu) /100 mL within 24 hours.

The Colilert and Petrifilm tests correlate with the relative risk of disease from
drinking water according to the WHO Guidelines for Drinking Water, 2nd Edition. If
the Colilert test does not fluoresce when a UV light shines on it and there are no blue
colonies with gas bubbles on the Petrifilm, the risk of disease is low. If the Colilert
test fluoresces and the Petrifilm remains clear, the risk is moderate. If the Colilert test
fluoresces and between 1 and 10 blue colonies with gas appear on the Petrifilm, the
risk is high. Finally, if the Colilert test fluoresces and Petrifilm contains more than
10 blue colonies with gas, the risk is very high.

Colilert Presence/Absence Test:

1. ONPG (Ortho-nitro-phenol-beta D-galactopyranoside). Coliform bacteria can be induced to produce the beta-galactosidase enzyme, which
   breaks the bond between the indicator part, ONP, and the sugar, G
   (galactopyranoside) ONPG is colorless. ONP, however, has a bright yellow color. The identification of the bright yellow color identifies the presence of coliform bacteria.
2. MUG (4-methyl-umbelliferone-beta-D-glucuronide). Among the coliform bacteria, only *E. coli* produces the constitutive enzyme betagluc-
   uronidase, which hydrolyzes the bond between the indicator part, MU
   (methylumbelliferone), and the sugar, G (glucuronide). The glucuronide is
   metabolized to enable the growth of *E. coli*. MUG is colorless, but it fluoresces blue under a long-wave UV light (340 nm).

Petrifilm:

Petrifilm utilizes a prepared medium system for enumerating *E. coli* and coliforms. It is regularly used in the food industry to sample meat, seafood, and poultry. Petrifilm contains violet red bile nutrients, which include lactose. The salts and crystal violet in the medium inhibit Gram-positive bacteria. Fecal coliform bacteria ferment lactose to produce gas bubbles. The bubbles are trapped around the coliform colony and each of those units will be colony forming units (CFU) per 100 mL. This will distinguish coliform bacteria from other Gram-negative bacteria which do not produce gas bubbles from lactose. In addition, glucuronidase, produced by most *E. coli*, will hydrolyze the glucuronide from BCIG (5-bromo-4-chloro-3-indolyl-β-D-glucuronide). The BCI (β-glucuronidase, which is specific to *E. coli*) produces a blue precipitate around the colony allowing visual identification of *E. coli*, distinguishing it from non *E. coli* coliform colonies which are red with gas bubbles.

Both of these tests involve the use of autoclaved equipment and incubation at 35°C (95°F). Neither of those procedures is routinely done in the field, and this experiment is designed for use in remote areas and at remote field sites. Consequently, alternative methods of equipment sterilization and sample incubation are required.

Sterilization options:

The point of autoclaving is to sterilize the equipment so as to eliminate any bacteria or other organisms from the equipment being used. This ensures that the end results of the experiment can be clearly and unambiguously assigned to the water sample being tested. Bacteria are killed in an autoclave by subjecting the equipment or sample to saturated steam under a pressure of approximately 15 pounds per square inch to achieve a chamber temperature of at least 121°C (250°F) for 30–60 minutes. If an autoclave is not available, placing the equipment in boiling water for a period of 15–20 minutes will generally be sufficient to inactivate coliform and *E. coli*. This may not inactivate all bacteria or harmful organisms in the sample, but since the test being conducted is specific to Coliform and *E. coli* bacteria, the lack of inactivation of other organisms should not adversely affect the outcomes. In the event there is interference, it will be to produce a false positive or a higher than actual positive count. A false negative is highly unlikely.

UV light is also a good sterilizer. Most portable UV sterilization equipment operates at a wavelength of 260–280 nm. Normally an exposure to those light sources for 3 minutes will inactivate most organisms. The wavelength needed to identify *E. coli* in this experiment is 340 nm. Therefore, if this method is to be used, two separate lamps will be needed for the UV unit; one that emits light at 260–280 nm and one that emits light at 340 nm. Note that portable sterilizers also operate at various voltage inputs, and the lamps need to be compatible with the voltage of the unit being used.

Incubation is designed to provide the bacteria of interest, if any exist in the sample, the best opportunity to grow quickly so that their presence can be rapidly determined. The ideal temperature for coliform bacteria is 35°C (95°F). Maintenance of those precise temperatures in a remote field setting is tenuous, at best. There are several ways to try to maintain those temperatures for the normal 24 hour incubation periods.

One method of field incubation involves recognizing that the human body is generally operating at a temperature of around 36°C–37°C (98°F–99°F). That will vary a bit depending on the person and by the surrounding air temperature and level of activity of the individual person. A sample placed into an inside pocket of clothing being worn by a person, after the gel has set, can be expected to maintain a temperature reasonably close to the ideal temperature. Note that when the external air temperature is in the ideal range, leaving the sample in an enclosed (out of direct sunlight) but open to airflow, container during the day is also adequate for most samples. Care is needed to make sure the samples are removed to an alternative source from the ambient air as night approaches to be sure they do not cool below the ideal.

A second incubation option involves the use of an electric light bulb inside an enclosed box with a thermometer inserted to monitor the internal temperature. The box should be closed until the correct temperature is achieved, then slowly opened over a period of several minutes until the temperature stabilizes. The samples need to be protected from the direct rays from the lamp, as the bacteria prefer darkness to grow best.

A third incubation option involves using the exhaust heat from the top of a motor or generator to maintain the temperature in an enclosed box. In this case, the temperature needs to be carefully monitored to avoid overheating with aeration of the box provided to keep the temperature stable. The motor or generator used in this option would generally need to be running continuously for the temperature to be stabilized properly. Using this method in conjunction with daytime ambient temperatures may also be prudent and feasible.

Data to be collected with an explanation of how they will be collected (Ex.: "Water temperature data for three days using a continuous data logger")
The data to be collected during this experiment include the methodology used for sterilization, the methodology used for incubation, and the results of the tests. Any variations of sterilization or incubation temperatures encountered also need to be noted.

Potential Interferences and Interference Management Plan
Interferences are unlikely when this experimental procedure is carried out carefully. Field sterilization of equipment may not inactivate all organisms in or on the equipment being used but should inactivate all bacteria of interest. In the event of interference, a false positive or a higher than actual positive will result.

Tools, Equipment, and Supplies Required
Field operable autoclave or substitute equipment sterilization methodology; 150 mL (5 oz) autoclavable bottle with cap (more if dilution of the source water is determined to be necessary); 150 mL (5 oz) of sample (more if dilution of the source water is determined to be necessary); IDEXX Colilert test kit (more if dilution of the source water is determined to be necessary); 1 3M Petrifilm kit (more if dilution of the source water is determined to be necessary); incubator, or suitable option cooler with ice or refrigerator: UV light source ("Black light" source operating at a wavelength of approximately 340 nm); 2 autoclavable 1 mL (0.3 oz) pipettes (more if dilution of the source water is determined to be necessary)

Safety

Samples being tested for the presence of coliform, and *E. coli* bacteria are presumed to be contaminated with bacteria and other organisms that are detrimental to human health. The wrong kind in the right concentration can be lethal. Care is needed to prevent ingestion of these organisms or infection through open wounds, puncture wounds, or skin abrasions.

Safety equipment required to conduct this experiment includes gloves, eye protection, and a lab coat. Apply an antibiotic cream, if available, and contact medical personnel for further advice.

In the event of exposure through ingestion, immediately contact medical personnel for advice.

In the event of contact with the eyes, flush at an eyewash station for up to 15 minutes and contact medical personnel immediately for advice.

In the event of infection or possible infection through an open wound, a puncture wound, or skin abrasion, wash the affected area with mild soap and water immediately.

Note that this experiment requires the field collection of a sample of water to test. Since the source is expected to be contaminated, care during sampling is required to prevent falling into a stream, water body, or well.

Sterilization equipment and sterilized tools will be very hot. Care needs to be taken to use sterilized clamps or tongs to handle the hot glassware.

Planned Experimental Procedures and Steps, in Order:

Step 1: Sample Collection

1. Label bottles to be autoclaved or sterilized and mark with autoclave tape. Bottles sterilized by field methods may require post-sterilization marking, but autoclave tape should be suitable for all sterilization methods.
2. Close the caps loosely on the bottles; do not close them tightly.
3. Autoclave or sterilize the bottles.
4. Wearing gloves and working in an aseptic environment, where possible, carefully remove the caps from the autoclaved bottles and place them on a sterile paper.
5. The inside of the bottle is sterile, and care must be taken not to contaminate it by touching it with fingers or other tools or equipment.
6. Collect a water sample by using a set of sterilized clamps to submerge the bottle into the water source.
7. Fill the bottle completely, leaving a small meniscus on top of the water before capping. See Chapter 3.1 for sampling guidance.
8. Once the sample has been collected, cap the bottle tightly and wipe the outside dry.
9. Place the bottle in a cooler with ice or in a refrigerator until ready to process.
10. Process the sample within 6 hours.

Step 2: Presence/Absence – Colilert
1. Measure 100 mL (3.4 oz) of the water sample and add to a previously sterilized and cooled bottle.
2. Add the contents of one Colilert package.
3. Replace the cap. Mix the contents of the bottle by inverting the bottle several times, to dissolve the nutrients.
4. Incubate the bottle at 35°C (95°F).
5. Examine the bottles after incubation for at least 12 hours and up to 24 hours.
6. If the contents of the bottle turn yellow, the sample contains total coliforms.
7. Shine a UV light on the sample to indicate the presence of *E. coli.*

Step 3: Quantification of Colony-Forming Units
1. Place the *E. coli.* Count Petrifilm on a flat surface.
2. On the white part of the film, write the location, date, and time the sample is tested and record the same data on the Data Collection Sheet.
3. Carefully lift the top film and dispense 1 mL of sample onto the center of the red, dried nutrients using a sterilized pipette
4. Do not touch the surface of the Petrifilm beneath the cover film or on the underside of the cover film.
5. Slowly roll the cover film down onto the sample to prevent the entrapment of air bubbles.
6. Distribute the sample evenly within the circular area using a gentle downward pressure of a large beaker (press gently and do not slide).
7. Leave the Petrifilm undisturbed for 1 minute to allow the gel to solidify.
8. Incubate with the clear side up at 35°C for 24 hours.

Data Collection Format and Data Collection Sheets Tailored to Experiment:
See attached Data Collection Sheet.

Anticipated Outcomes:
Anticipated Outcomes from Step 2 – Presence/Absence

1. If the tube is clear, no coliforms are present.
2. If the tube is yellow, but there is no fluorescence under long-wave UV light, coliform bacteria other than *E. coli* are present. These are likely to have come from the environment and do not have public health significance.
3. If the tube is yellow and fluoresces blue when a long-wave UV light shines on it, *E. coli* was present in the water sample, and the water poses a substantial health risk.

Anticipated Outcomes from Step 3

1. *E. coli* colonies will appear blue with gas bubbles. One or more *E. coli.* colonies signifies heavily contaminated water, which should be treated before drinking.
2. Non *E. coli.* coliform colonies will be red with a gas bubble.

3. Non-coliform Gram-negative bacteria form red colonies without a gas bubble.
4. If there are too many colonies to distinguish a count, this means that the sample needed log 10 dilutions to quantify the bacteria.

Data Analysis Plan:
Data from this test come in two parts. The first part is a presence-absence test. This test indicates whether coliform or *E. coli* are present. If the presence of the target bacteria is indicated, then the second part of the experiment is done to indicate the concentration of target organisms. The count is recorded as the colony-forming units (cfu) per 100 mL of water.

Field Testing and Quantification of Total Coliforms and *E. coli* by Colilert and Petrifilm Methodologies

Date Collected:

Date Tested:

Principal Investigator:

Source Water:

Sample Bottle	Disinfection Method	Time of Sample Collection	Sample Preservation Method Used	Time of Sample Testing	Presence (P) or Absence (A)	Time of Confirmation Test	Count per 100 mL (cfu/100mL)

UN (2010) A Practical Method for Rapid Assessment of the Bacterial Quality of Water.

EXPERIMENT 12.3: VIRAL INDICATORS COLIPHAGE QUANTIFICATION BASED ON EASYPHAGE METHOD

Date: _____

Principal Investigator:

    Name: _____

    Email: _____

    Phone: _____

Collaborators:

    Name: _____

    Email: _____

    Phone: _____

    Name: _____

    Email: _____

    Phone: _____

    Name: _____

    Email: _____

    Phone: _____

    Name: _____

    Email: _____

    Phone: _____

Objective or Question to Be Addressed:

As a result of pathogen outbreaks in drinking water, despite compliance with current drinking water regulations, a new indicator may be necessary to better characterize water quality, particularly in terms of potential viral contamination. An effective indicator needs to be relatively inexpensive, reliable to monitor, safe to work with in the laboratory, and detected when pathogens are present. Identifying a new indicator requires the development of a standard assay, monitoring of the incidences of the indicator, and quantification of the indicator in several different environments or eco-systems. Once a standard method and quantification of the indicator are complete, a potential indicator should be evaluated for the presence in drinking water sources and assessed throughout the unit processes of drinking water treatment. Finally, the usefulness of an indicator is dependent on the occurrence of the indicator only when pathogens are present.

While bacteria are commonly used indicators of drinking water quality, disease-causing pathogens in developed countries are more often not bacteria but rather viruses or protozoa. In addition, outbreaks in the United States may occur more frequently than recorded, owing to the limited ability of *E. coli* to represent viral presence. Until recently, it was both difficult and time consuming to test for viruses. In addition, viruses and bacterial indicators do not colocate exclusively with infectious viruses, because coliforms respond differently to environmental stressors and engineered treatment processes than do protozoan and viral pathogens. Given these limitations, alternative indicators, such as bacteriophages, for viral pathogen risk are necessary.

This experiment provides experience conducting a coliphage testing procedure for the indication of pathogenic viral organisms.

Theory Behind Experiment

Bacteriophages have been studied as possible indicators of viral pathogens since the 1970s. Bacteriophages, specifically coliphages (viruses that infect coliforms), have potential as indicators of human enteric viruses because they resemble viruses in their physical structure and morphology. The detection of coliphages is achieved by a simple plaque assay, and coliphages are more easily and rapidly detected than enteric viruses. In addition, they are found in higher numbers than enteric viruses in wastewater and other environments.

Male-specific coliphages are a group of icosahedral phages that are morphologically similar to several human enteric virus groups; on account of this similarity, they have been proposed as enteric virus models. Male-specific coliphages infect *E. coli* that contains the male-specific plasmid, which codes for the sex pilus for the phage to attach. They are also known as F, F+, and F_{RNA} coliphages; MS2 is a type of male-specific coliphage. Male-specific coliphages resemble human viruses, in morphology, including their inability to multiply in water environments. Male-specific coliphages are considered indicators because of their high population counts in wastewaters.

F and F+ coliphages are amplified in host cells prior to introduction to a suspect water to magnify the results if *E. coli* or other target organisms are present. When amplified, the cells are called F_{amp} or F_{amp} host cells. They are prepared in 1 day in advance of testing to ensure reliable results.

Data to be collected with an explanation of how they will be collected (Ex.: "Water temperature data for three days using a continuous data logger")

Coliphage counts will be made from the prepared and incubated petri dishes.

Plaques appear as empty spots or "holes" in the colored medium on the petri dishes. Each plaque indicates a place where one virus infected a single bacterium. This virus then replicated and released hundreds or thousands of new viral particles to infect new bacterial cells. This leaves an empty spot.

Potential Interferences and Interference Management Plan:

Contamination of any of the bottles or equipment used in this procedure can dramatically skew the results. *E. coli* are ubiquitous in the environment and can be present on desks, tabletops, hands, or gloves. Care is needed to avoid touching sterile surfaces inside EasyPhage bottles, sterile transfer equipment, or petri dishes.

Bacteria, viruses, and other organisms grow best within very narrow temperature ranges. Incubating the prepared petri dishes at temperatures that vary from the prescribed range will likely provide false data. Careful monitoring of the incubator temperature throughout the procedure is necessary to ensure reliable data.

The EasyPhage product is a proprietary product containing specific chemical and biological components in predetermined quantities and ratios. Using other growth media to prepare the petri dishes will likely lead to unreliable results, or no data at all.

Tools, Equipment, and Supplies Required
Tryptic Soy Broth: sterile 1X TSB from manufacturer

Log-phase *E. coli* F_{amp} host cells should be prepared 1 day before use. Use an inoculation loop or other sterile transfer instrument to inoculate 10 mL (0.34 oz) of TSB with the *E. coli* F_{amp} and incubate for 18–24 hours at $36°C \pm 1°C$ ($97°F \pm 1°F$).

Lab strain male-specific coliphage such as MS2 should be used to serve as a positive control. (MS2 male-specific coliphage is provided as a positive control in the kit.) Approximately 70–100 MS2 plaque-forming unit (PFU) will be used in the positive control plate.

Sterile reagent water

Sterile medium EasyPhage EP-10 (Provided in kit, 10 mL (0.34 oz) per bottle)

Medium may settle, showing two layers during storage at 4°C. Mix the medium by gently swirling the bottle to avoid creating bubbles. Warm up the medium to room temperature or 35°C before use. Medium can be used when it is cold but will take longer to solidify.

Bacterial stain, sterile (provided in EasyPhage kit) 70 μL bacterial stain is needed per plate

Sterile pretreated petri dish (provided in EasyPhage kit)

Only pretreated petri dishes should be used with EasyPhage medium (regular petri dishes will NOT work)

Safety
Students should wear appropriate personal protection equipment, such as a lab coat, gloves, and safety goggles.Students should wear appropriate personal protection equipment, such as a lab coat, gloves, and safety goggles.

All the plates, bacterial culture, and coliphage stock should go into Biohazard bags to be autoclaved before discarding. *E. coli* F_{amp} host cells and MS2 coliphage are not considered as pathogens, but still need to be autoclaved prior to discard because of the high number of bacteria present after culturing.

Exposure to the materials used in this procedure may be deleterious to human health. In the event of skin exposure, wash thoroughly with hot water and soap. In the event of exposure through open wounds or punctures, wash the area immediately and seek medical advice. In the event of eye contact, flush immediately with an eyewash for up to 20 minutes and seek medical advice. In the event of ingestion, seek medical assistance immediately.

Planned Experimental Procedures and Steps, in Order:

1. Warm-up EasyPhage to room temperature.
2. In a bottle containing 10 mL (0.34 oz) of EasyPhage provided in the kit, add water sample or sample concentrate, and sterile reagent water to achieve a total volume of 18–20 mL (0.6–0.7 oz) (see table below). Add 70 μL (0.002 oz) of bacterial stain, and 0.3 mL (0.01 oz) log-phase *E. coli* F_{amp}, previously prepared.
3. Mix the solution by swirling the bottle 10 times (do not vortex to avoid creating bubbles) and pour the mixture into the pretreated petri dish.
4. Gently swirl the petri dish a few times to make sure of even liquid distribution.
5. Swirl the dish gently several times to settle the bubbles on the edge of the dish.
6. Let the medium mixture solidify on a horizontal bench for about 1 hour.
7. An alternative way is to let the medium solidify inside the incubator, which has been checked for shelf horizontal level. After pouring the plate, stack up the dishes in an upright position, a maximum of 4 in a stack, and carefully move them to the incubator. Plates can be incubated in an upright position.
8. Negative control plate: Add 8 mL (0.27 oz) of sterile reagent water, 70 μL (0.002 oz) of bacterial stain, and 0.3 mL (0.01 oz) of *E. coli* F_{amp} to the 10 mL (0.34 oz) bottle of EasyPhage.
9. Mix well, per steps 3 and 4, and pour into a pretreated petri dish.
10. Positive control plate: Add 8 mL (0.27 oz) of sterile reagent water, 70 μL (0.002 oz) of bacterial stain, 0.1 mL (0.003 oz) of MS2 or volume equivalent to 70–100 pfu, and 0.3 mL (0.10 oz) of *E. coli* F_{amp} to the 10 mL (0.34 oz) bottle of EasyPhage.
11. Mix well, per steps 3 and 4, and pour into a pretreated petri dish.
12. Incubate plates upright at 35°C (95°F) for 24 hours.
13. Count the plaques on the background of colored bacterial lawn. Plaques may show up in different sizes and shapes, and all of them should be counted for calculation of the coliphage concentration present in the original water sample. Students should be able to see "holes" in the colored medium on the petri dishes. These empty spots are called plaques. Each plaque indicates a place where one virus infected a single bacterium. This virus then replicated and released hundreds or thousands of new viral particles to infect new bacterial cells. This leaves an empty spot.
14. Place all the plates, bacterial culture, and coliphage stock into a Biohazard bag to be autoclaved before discarding. *E. coli* F_{amp} host cells and MS2 coliphage are not considered as pathogens, but still need to be autoclaved prior to discarding because of the high number of bacteria likely to be present after culturing.

Data Collection Format and Data Collection Sheets Tailored to Experiment:
See attached Data Collection Sheet

Anticipated Outcomes:

If all procedures have been followed correctly, a sufficient number of plaques should be observable in the petri dishes prepared from contaminated water. Using a water known to be, or very likely to be, contaminated, for purposes of understanding the procedure, is strongly recommended. A parallel test for *E. coli* based on other methods as an indication of the relative accuracy of the EasyPhage test is suggested.

Data Analysis Plan:

The petri dish will be placed on top of a light box with the bottom facing up (if a light box is not available, the plate will be upright against a light source or window), a sharpie will be used to mark the dots while counting.

It is expected that all the plaques should be very countable. For small or tiny plaques, the surface of the plaques and bacterial lawn will be observed with a light source shining on the surface of the bacterial lawn.

Read results within 24 hours. The plates must not stay in the incubator longer than 24 hours. *E. coli* and phage will continue to grow if the plates incubate longer. This will cause plaques to enlarge until they overlap and are no longer distinct. The indicator dye will also fade over time.

Sample Volume (mL)	Sterile Water (mL)	EasyPhage (mL)	Bacterial Stain (µL)	*E. coil* (mL)
0 (Controls)	8	10	70	0.3
1	7	10	70	0.3
2	6	10	70	0.3
3	5	10	70	0.3
4	4	10	70	0.3
5	3	10	70	0.3
6	2	10	70	0.3
7	1	10	70	0.3
8	0	10	70	0.3
9	0	10	70	0.3
10	0	10	70	0.3

(Multiply the mL volumes shown by 0.033814 to yield the equivalent volume in fluid ounces. Microliters shown need to be multiplied by 0.000033814 to yield the equivalent volume in fluid ounces.)

Data Collection Sheet Viral Indicators Coliphage Quantification Based on EasyPhage Method

Date Collected:
Date Tested:
Principal Investigator:
Source Water:

Test	Results (PFU/100mL)	Expected Results (PFU/100mL)	Variations Noted	Notes

EXPERIMENT 12.4: COMPARISON OF DISINFECTION METHODS

Date: _____

Principal Investigator:

      Name: _____

      Email: _____

      Phone: _____

Collaborators:

      Name: _____

      Email: _____

      Phone: _____

      Name: _____

      Email: _____

      Phone: _____

      Name: _____

      Email: _____

      Phone: _____

      Name: _____

      Email: _____

      Phone: _____

Objective or Question to Be Addressed

Contamination in drinking water systems can occur in systems with surface water and groundwater sources. The contamination may be a result of lack of treatment or inadequate treatment. The factors contributing to contaminant outbreaks include fecal or wastewater contamination, inadequate knowledge of source waters, inadequate disinfection, extreme weather events, filtration failures, distribution failures, and operation and maintenance failures.

Disinfection refers to the process of inactivating microbiological contaminants. Several methods of disinfection exist, including free chlorine, ozone, chlorine dioxide, iodine, heat (pasteurization), and UV light. Chlorine disinfection has the advantages that it is simple and that residual disinfection capacity remains after water is treated. Unfortunately, the taste and odor of treated water with residual chlorine may actually discourage users from drinking the water.

The US EPA Surface Water Treatment Rule (SWTR) requires treatment plants receive log10 credits for disinfection. A disinfection credit is the number of credits assigned to a specific treatment process (e.g., chlorine disinfection, UV oxidation, etc.), expressed in log units, for the inactivation of a specific microorganism or a group of microorganisms. A reduction of 90% corresponds to one log of credit reduction. Log10 credit for disinfection is based on disinfectant concentration (C) and exposure time (T) needed to inactivate specific pathogens. The required C*T value is dependent upon the disinfectant used, the pathogen measured, and water quality parameters. Lastly, the SWTR also requires a minimum concentration of residual disinfectant to be maintained in the distribution system.

The C*T is used to determine the expected inactivation of pathogens by disinfection using a logarithmic scale, thus it is referred to as "log inactivation". Log inactivation is the order of magnitude for the inactivation of microorganisms. For example, a 2-log inactivation corresponds to a 99% inactivation and a 3-log inactivation corresponds to a 99.9% inactivation.

This experiment compares the inactivation rates of three disinfection options: chlorine, UV light, and heat (pasteurization).

Theory Behind Experiment
Disinfection by chlorine occurs in two ways: primary disinfection, which involves the inactivation of bacterial pollution; and secondary disinfection, which results from residual chlorine that remains in the treated water. Chlorine demand refers to the amount of chlorine required for primary disinfection. Once all the bacterial pollutants are destroyed after primary disinfection, excess chlorine remains as residual chlorine. Disinfection requires a free residual chlorine concentration of more than 0.2 mg/L (0.2 ppm) for more than 30 minutes. The WHO guideline for chlorine is 0.2–0.5 mg/L (0.5 ppm) which means the WHO considers concentrations above 0.2 mg/L and below 0.5 mg/L to be safe. The optimal dose is between 0.4 and 0.5 mg/L. The quantity of residual chlorine needs to be high enough to ensure proper disinfection, but low enough to not cause negative taste or health effects due to too much chlorine.

Residual chlorine provides capacity to deactivate pathogens due to contamination of drinking water, for example, contamination that occurs between the source water and consumption. The best results for chlorine disinfection are for water with a pH below 8.0 and a turbidity less than 20 NTU. Household bleach (sodium hypochlorite) contains between 1% and 18% chlorine. Sodium hypochlorite is a chemical compound with the formula $NaOCl$ formed from a sodium cation (Na^+) and a hypochlorite anion (OCl^-).

Hypochlorous acid and hypochlorite ions together are often referred to as free chlorine. Both of these chemical species are active disinfecting agents. The equilibrium constant is:

$$HOCl \rightarrow H^+ + OCl^-$$

Free chlorine refers to the sum of the $HOCl + OCl^-$ ions formed from the hydrogen in the water and the hypochlorite ions released from the dissociation of the sodium hypochlorite.

At a pH of 7.5, there are equal amounts of $HOCl$ and OCl^- present in the treated water. $HOCl$ is the predominant chemical species at a pH less than 7.5. Chlorination is more effective in water with pH less than 7.5. Natural water has a pH in the range of 6.5–8.5.

Ultraviolet (UV) rays are part of the light spectrum from the sun. Lower wavelengths of light disinfect water by inactivating the DNA of bacteria, viruses, and other pathogens. Note that UV treatment inactivates microorganisms but does not remove them. The effectiveness of this process is related to exposure time and lamp intensity, as well as general water quality parameters. This experiment does not utilize sunlight as a UV source because UV lamps are readily available and produce a more focused and reliable energy wavelength.

A UV lamp, similar to a fluorescent lamp, provides light of wavelengths around 254 nm, an appropriate range for the destruction of target organisms. In addition to the effects of direct absorption of the radiation by the bacteria, light radiation also produces reactive forms of oxygen that kill microorganisms. This experiment utilizes a UV lamp to produce UV disinfection.

Pasteurization utilizes heat to disinfect because most microorganisms are killed by high temperatures. The water must be maintained at a temperature of 65°C (150°F) for 6 minutes to effectively inactivate pathogens. A Water Pasteurization Indicator (WAPI) is a simple indicator that shows water has reached pasteurization temperature and is safe to drink. The WAPI is a polycarbonate tube which contains a wax that melts when the water is pasteurized. A WAPI may be used in this experiment at the discretion of the instructor, but maintaining the temperatures indicated for the time indicated will also be effective.

Data to be collected with an explanation of how they will be collected (Ex.: "Water temperature data for three days using a continuous data logger")

The data to be collected during this experiment are coliform counts. Coliforms are pathogenic indicator organisms, and they are assumed to be present in the surface water being tested. The presence of coliform organisms indicates the likely presence of pathogenic organisms. Care must be taken to avoid accidental ingestion of samples while testing for coliform.

Procedures for testing the samples for the presence of coliform organisms are provided in Experiments 12.1, 12.2, and 12.3.

Potential Interferences and Interference Management Plan

Chlorine is a particularly aggressive chemical which can react with many things in water besides bacteria. Chlorine which has reacted with other chemicals and compounds in the water will not be available for disinfection. Consequently, the actual concentration of free chlorine in the water after addition of the designated masses of sodium chloride may be lower than the indicated concentrations. If the reduction in concentration is significant, additional sodium chloride may need to be added to yield a free chlorine concentration suitable for disinfection.

Tools, Equipment, and Supplies Required

17 L each of laboratory water (distilled and deionized) and a surface water (river/lake source)

Eight 1.5 L nonmetallic containers

Six 500 mL glass bottles with caps

Six 600 mL glass beakers

Spectrophotometer

Free chlorine reagent powder pillows as required by the spectrophotometer manufacturer

Supplies for microbiological testing (see Experiments 12.1, 12.2, and 12.3 in this series)

UV lamp (wavelength of 240 – 280 nm, with a peak at approximately 265 nm)

6 WAPI or 6 thermometers

6 Heated stir plates

Safety:

The laboratory water used in this experiment is expected to be pure and uncontaminated. The surface water sample is assumed to be impure and contaminated. Care should be taken to avoid ingestion of any liquids in any laboratory. Coliforms are indicator organisms indicating the possible presence of pathogenic organisms. Ingestion of pathogenic organisms can lead to serious health-related symptoms and conditions. The following safety equipment is required for this experiment:

- Gloves
- Lab coats
- Safety glasses
- Heat-resistant gloves

In the event of skin exposure, washing with warm water and soap is recommended. In the event of accidental ingestion, contact a medical professional immediately for appropriate advice. In the event of eye exposure, wash with an eyewash for up to 15 minutes and immediately contact medical specialists for advice.

Planned Experimental Procedures and Steps, in Order:

Test laboratory water (as a control test) and surface (river/lake) water in each of three separate ways, as defined and described below.

Chlorine:

1. Collect 10 L samples of laboratory water (distilled and deionized) and surface (river/lake) water
2. Test each sample for total coliforms per the instructions in Experiments 12.1, 12.2, and 12.3 in this chapter or by other equivalent means.
3. Place 1 L of laboratory water and 1 L of the surface water in a 1.25 L, or larger, nonmetallic containers for each water type to yield:
   - four 1 L samples of laboratory water
   - four 1 L samples of surface (river/lake) water
4. Add the following amounts of NaCl (table salt) to the containers: 1.647 mg in the first container, 2.471 mg in the second container, 3.294 mg in the third container, and 8.235 mg in the fourth container. This should yield

chlorine concentrations of 1, 1.5, 2.0, and 5 mg/L in the respective containers.

5. Wait for 30 minutes and then measure the residual free chlorine concentration in each container.

6. Free chorine can be measured with a spectrophotometer and the US EPA DPD Method 8021 for quantities in the range of 0.02–2.00 mg/L Cl_2. Chlorine concentrations above 2.00 mg/L indicate a dose that is too high and is therefore not relevant to this experiment. The precise procedure for this step will depend on the manufacturer of the spectrophotometer being used. Read the procedure manual in advance so that all necessary steps are carried out in the correct order.

7. The procedure for a HACH UV-Vis DR 2800 spectrophotometer follows:

   a. Start program 80 chlorine F&T PP.
   b. Prepare the blank: Fill the sample cell with 10 mL of sample.
   c. Clean the prepared sample cell.
   d. Insert the blank into the cell holder.
   e. Push ZERO. The display shows 0.00 mg/L.
   f. Prepare the sample: Fill a second sample cell with 10 mL of sample.
   g. Add the contents of one powder pillow (DPD free chlorine reagent powder pillows, 10-mL) to the sample cell.
   h. Swirl the sample cell for 20 seconds to mix. A pink color will develop if chlorine is present. Proceed to the next step immediately.
   i. Clean the prepared sample cell. Within 60 seconds of the reagent addition, insert the prepared sample into the cell holder.
   j. Read. Push READ. Results show in mg/L Cl_2.

8. The container of surface water with a residual chlorine concentration of 0.4–0.5 mg/L has the appropriate dosage. There should be no loss of chlorine concentration in the laboratory water. Any loss that does occur will be related to nonbiological contaminants present unless the laboratory water has been contaminated from some unintentional source (which should be carefully investigated and eliminated).

9. Test the sample with the most appropriate dosage for total coliforms and record the inactivation rate when comparing the original coliform count to the treated water coliform count.

UV Disinfection:

1. Collect 5 L samples of laboratory water (distilled and deionized) and surface (river/lake) water.

2. Test each sample for total coliforms following the procedures included with Experiments 12.1, 12.2, and 12.3 in this series or equivalent.

3. Collect six clear sample bottles (such as 500 mL Nalgene Media Bottles). Two (one each of laboratory water and surface (river/lake) water) will be placed in a closed closet or drawer in the laboratory, two will be placed under a UV light in the laboratory, and two will be placed outdoors in

natural sunlight (be sure to note meteorological conditions to minimize the risk of freezing and conditions of sunlight availability).

4. Fill each bottle 75% full of either laboratory water or surface water, cover it, and shake it for 20 seconds to aerate the water and increase the dissolved oxygen. Higher oxygen may result in greater disinfection efficiency due to oxygen free radicals and hydrogen peroxides that are produced by the sunlight in water. On the other hand, air bubbles may also reduce disinfection so only shake the bottles at the beginning of the experiment.
5. Finish filling each bottle fully and replace the cover.
6. Place one bottle of laboratory water and one bottle of surface water under a laboratory UV light-emitting light at a wavelength between 240 and 280 nm, with a peak at approximately 265 nm for 15 minutes.
7. Test both UV-treated samples for total coliform and record the inactivation rate by comparing the coliform count in the untreated water to the coliform count in the treated water.
8. Place one bottle of laboratory water and one bottle of surface water in a safe location, in full sunlight for a minimum of 6 hours.
9. Test both sunlight-treated samples for total coliforms and record the inactivation rate by comparing the coliform count in the untreated water to the coliform count in the treated water.
10. Place one bottle of laboratory water and one bottle of surface water in a dark space for a minimum of 6 hours.
11. Test the treated samples for total coliforms and record the inactivation rate by comparing the coliform count in the original untreated water to the coliform count in the final treated water.

Pasteurization:

1. Collect 2 L samples of laboratory water and surface (river/lake) water.
2. Test each sample for total coliforms following the procedures included with Experiments 12.1, 12.2, and 12.3 in this series or equivalent.
3. Collect six 600 mL beakers and fill each with 500 mL of one of the samples (laboratory water and surface (river/lake) water).
4. Place a WAPI in each of the beakers and heat with a heated stir plate until the wax in the WAPI melts. Alternatively, heat each container to a temperature of 65°C (150°F) and maintain that temperature for 6 minutes.
5. Allow the water to cool to room temperature and retest for total coliforms.
6. Determine and record the inactivation log rate by comparing the coliform count in the original untreated water to the coliform count in the final treated water.

Comparison of Results:

1. Compare the inactivation rates of the three disinfection methods to each other to determine the most effective disinfection option for the surface water being tested. Note any discrepancies between the results from the

laboratory water and the surface water tested. Investigate and report on the causes of significant discrepancies noted.

Data Collection Format and Data Collection Sheets Tailored to Experiment:
See attached Data Collection Sheet

Anticipated Outcomes:
It is expected that the laboratory water samples will show no coliform counts before and after the treatment processes used. There should, in fact, be no coliform present in any of the laboratory water samples at any time. Should any of the laboratory water samples contain significant coliform counts, the source will need to be investigated and eliminated and a determination made as to whether the counts found in the laboratory water need to be subtracted from the counts found in the treated surface water or whether the entire experiment has been compromised and needs to be repeated.

Data Analysis Plan:
The data will be collected on the data collection sheet and the results of the coliform counts recorded in terms of coliform reduction rates. The coliform reduction rate is calculated as the final coliform count divided by the original coliform count in each container. That value is converted to a percentage and then to a log inactivation value per the theory section of this experiment design.

Data Collection Sheet Comparison of Disinfection Methods

Date Collected:				
Date Tested:				
Principal Investigator:				
Surface Water Source:				
Chlorine Disinfection Experiment				
Beaker	**Concentration (mg/Cl)**	**Results Coliform (CFU/100 mL)**	**Log Inactivation Achieved**	**Notes**
Untreated sample	0.0			
Lab water 1	1.0			
Lab water 2	1.5			
Lab water 3	2.0			
Lab water 4	5.0			
Untreated sample	0.0			
Surface water 1	1.0			
Surface water 2	1.5			
Surface water 3	2.0			
Surface water 4	5.0			
UV Light Disinfection Experiment				
Bottle	**Exposure Time**	**Results Coliform (CFU /100 mL)**	**Log Inactivation Achieved**	**Notes**
Lab water 1				
Lab water 2				
Lab water 3				
Surface water 1				
Surface water 2				
Surface water 3				
Heat Disinfection Experiment				
Bottle	**Time for WAPI to melt or Time at Temperature**	**Results Coliform (CFU /100 mL)**	**Log Inactivation Achieved**	**Notes**
Lab water 1				
Lab water 2				
Lab water 3				
Surface water 1				
Surface water 2				
Surface water 3				

EXPERIMENT 12.5: COMPARISON OF DISINFECTION METHODS: REMOTE AREA OPTIONS

Date: _____

Principal Investigator:

    Name: _____

    Email: _____

    Phone: _____

Collaborators:

    Name: _____

    Email: _____

    Phone: _____

    Name: _____

    Email: _____

    Phone: _____

    Name: _____

    Email: _____

    Phone: _____

    Name: _____

    Email: _____

    Phone: _____

Objective or Question to Be Addressed

Contaminated drinking water can occur in systems with surface water and groundwater sources. The contamination may be a result of lack of treatment or inadequate treatment. The factors contributing to contaminant outbreaks include fecal or wastewater contamination, animal waste contamination, inadequate knowledge of source waters, inadequate disinfection, extreme weather events, filtration failures, distribution failures, and operation and maintenance failures, among others.

Disinfection refers to the process of inactivating microbiological contaminants. Several methods of disinfection exist, including free chlorine, ozone, chlorine dioxide, iodine, heat (pasteurization), and UV light. Chlorine disinfection has advantages that it is simple and that residual disinfection capacity remains after water is treated. Unfortunately, the taste and odor of treated water with residual chlorine may discourage users from drinking the water.

Unfortunately, people living in remote areas and some developing countries do not have access to any of those normal disinfection options. Those people need to utilize materials and systems readily available to them at a very low cost in order to generate useful disinfection of drinking water, regardless of the source water.

The US EPA Surface Water Treatment Rule (SWTR) requires treatment plants receive log10 credits for disinfection. A disinfection credit is the number of credits assigned to a specific treatment process, expressed in log units, for the inactivation of a specific microorganism or a group of microorganisms. A reduction of 90% corresponds to one log of credit reduction. Inactivation of pathogens by disinfection is assessed using a logarithmic scale, thus it is referred to as "log inactivation". Log inactivation is the order of magnitude for the inactivation of microorganisms. For example, a 2-log inactivation corresponds to a 99% inactivation, and a 3-log inactivation corresponds to a 99.9% inactivation.

This experiment compares the inactivation rates of three disinfection options: moringa seeds, sunlight radiation, and boiling.

Theory Behind Experiment

The *Moringa oleifera* tree grows abundantly throughout many tropical and subtropical regions of the world. It reaches fruition in only 6 months, and the seeds of this tree contain a protein called the *Moringa oleifera* Cationic Protein (MOCP). MOCP has the ability to kill bacteria and clarify water. In fact, women in ancient Egypt reportedly rubbed Moringa seeds on their clay water pots, and dried powder from crushed seeds has been used as a handwash for many years.

Importantly, organic dried seed powder that remains in the water can provide a food source for any bacteria that have not been killed. As a result, water treated with this seed should not be stored for long periods unless adequate filtration has occurred following the disinfection stage, and disinfection shortly before use is recommended.

It also happens that not all Moringa seeds are equally as potent at water treatment. The extracted protein of mature dried seeds collected in the rainy season is most effective, followed by mature dried seeds collected in the dry season. The Moringa seeds promote coagulation and flocculation of turbid water and remove microorganisms through settling.

Ultraviolet (UV) rays are part of the light spectrum that comes from the sun. Lower wavelengths of light disinfect water by inactivating the DNA of bacteria, viruses, and other pathogens. Note that UV treatment inactivates microorganisms but does not remove them. The effectiveness of this process is related to exposure time and lamp intensity as well as general water quality parameters. This experiment utilizes the UV in sunlight as a disinfection agent.

A UV lamp, similar to a fluorescent lamp, provides light of wavelengths around 254 nm, an appropriate range for the destruction of target organisms. In addition to the effects of direct absorption of the radiation by the bacteria, light radiation also produces reactive forms of oxygen that kill microorganisms. The treatment of water in remote locations involves placing clear bottles of water to be treated in direct sunlight for a determined amount of time. Plastic bottles are lightweight and less breakable polyethylene terephthalate (PET) or polyvinyl chloride (PVC), but the PET bottles contain fewer terephthalates than the PVC bottles and so are chemically more stable. A UV lamp is not used in this experiment because those devices are seldom available in remote areas.

Pasteurization utilizes heat to disinfect because most microorganisms are killed by high temperatures. The water must be maintained at a temperature of 65°C (150°F) for 6 minutes to effectively inactivate pathogens. Since thermometers are not readily available in most remote locations, boiling the water for 6 minutes can provide suitable disinfection.

Data to be collected with an explanation of how they will be collected (Ex.: "Water temperature data for three days using a continuous data logger")
The data to be collected during this experiment are coliform counts. Coliforms are indicators of potential pathogenic organisms, and they are assumed to be present in the surface water being tested. Care must be taken to avoid accidental ingestion of samples.

The procedure for testing the samples for the quantifying presence of coliform organisms is provided in the laboratory experiment design for biological testing of water samples included in this series, Experiments 12.1, 12.2, and 12.3 or equivalent.

Potential Interferences and Interference Management Plan
The disinfection options used in this experiment are not subject to significant interferences since they are based on simple procedures. However, where disinfection by UV light is used, discoloration of the bottles can be a problem with UV light transmission. Verification of the cleanliness and clarity of the plastic bottles used is important for elimination of this interference.

Tools, Equipment, and Supplies Required

   17L each of laboratory water (distilled and deionized) and a surface water (river/lake source)
   Eight 1.5L nonmetallic containers, six 500mL glass bottles with caps, six 600mL glass beakers
   Spectrophotometer and necessary supplies, such as:
   Free Chlorine Reagent Powder Pillows as required by the manufacturer
   Supplies for microbiological testing (see Experiments 12.1, 12.2, and 12.3 in this series)
   6 WAPI or 6 thermometers
   6 Heated stir plates

Safety:
The laboratory water used in this experiment is expected to be pure and uncontaminated. The surface water sample is assumed to be impure and definitely contaminated. Care should be taken to avoid ingestion of any liquids in any laboratory. Coliforms are indicator organisms indicating the potential presence of pathogenic organisms. Ingestion of pathogenic organisms can lead to serious health-related symptoms and conditions. The following safety equipment is required for this experiment.

- Gloves
- Lab coats

- Safety glasses
- Heat-resistant gloves

In the event of skin exposure, washing with warm water and soap is recommended. In the event of accidental ingestion, contact a medical professional immediately for appropriate advice. In the event of eye exposure, wash with an eyewash for up to 15 minutes and immediately contact medical specialists for advice.

Planned Experimental Procedures and Steps, in Order:
Test laboratory water (as a control test) and surface (river/lake) water in each of three separate ways, as defined and described below.

Moringa Seeds:

1. Collect approximately 500 g (1.1 lb) of suitable moringa seeds and remove the whitish kernels from the husks.
2. Crush the Moringa seeds, but not the seed husks, using a mortar and pestle, to a coarse powder, such as uncooked cream of wheat, for example. A total of approximately 220 g (0.5 lb) of powder are needed for the experiment.
3. Collect 10 L (2.5 gal) samples each of laboratory water (distilled and deionized) and surface (river/lake) water.
4. Test each sample for total coliforms per the procedures in Experiments 12.1, 12.2, and 12.3 in this series or equivalent.
5. Place 0.5 L (1 pint) of laboratory water and 0.5 L (1 pint) of the surface water in 8 separate, 1.25 L (1 qt), or larger, containers to yield four 0.5 L samples of laboratory water and four 0.5 L samples of surface (river/lake) water.
6. Add the following amounts of Moringa seed powder to the containers of each type of water: 10 g (0.35 oz) in each first container, 20 g (0.7 oz) in each second container, 30 g (1.1 oz) in each third container, and 50 g (1.8 oz) in each fourth container.
7. Slowly stir each container every few minutes for 30 minutes.
8. Stop stirring and allow the water to settle for approximately 60 minutes.
9. Test each container for coliform bacteria and record the removal efficiency as a log inactivation rate based on a comparison with the original coliform counts from step 4.

UV Disinfection:

1. Collect 5 L (1.3 gal) samples of laboratory water (distilled and deionized) and surface (river/lake) water.
2. Test each sample for total coliforms per the procedures in Experiments 12.1, 12.2, and 12.3 in this series or equivalent.
3. Collect 2 clear plastic 2 L (1 gal) soda bottles or similar plastic containers with caps. PET bottles are preferred.

4. One each of laboratory water and surface (river/lake) water will be placed in a closed closet or drawer in the laboratory, and the other will be placed outdoors in natural sunlight (be sure to note meteorological conditions to minimize the risk of freezing and conditions of sunlight availability).

5. Fill each bottle 75% full of either laboratory water or surface water, cap it, and shake it for 20 seconds to aerate the water and increase the dissolved oxygen. Higher oxygen may result in greater disinfection efficiency due to oxygen-free radicals and hydrogen peroxides that are produced by the sunlight in water. On the other hand, air bubbles may also reduce disinfection so only shake at the beginning.

6. Finish filling each bottle fully and replace the cap.

7. Place one bottle of laboratory water and one bottle of surface water in a safe location, in full sunlight for a minimum of 6 hours.

8. Test both sunlight-treated samples for total coliforms and record the inactivation rate by comparing the coliform count in the untreated water to the coliform count in the treated water.

9. Place one bottle of laboratory water and one bottle of surface water in a dark space in the laboratory for a minimum of 6 hours (the actual storage time for the bottles in the sunlight and the bottles in the laboratory should be essentially the same).

10. Test both treated samples for total coliforms and record the inactivation rate by comparing the coliform count in the original untreated water to the coliform count in the final treated water.

Pasteurization:

1. Collect 1 L (0.5 gal) samples of laboratory water and surface (river/lake) water and test each sample for total coliforms per the procedures in Experiments 12.1, 12.2, and 12.3 in this series or equivalent.

2. Collect two 600 mL (1.3 pint) beakers and fill each with 500 mL (0.5 qt) of one of the samples (laboratory water and surface (river/lake) water).

3. Heat each container until the water has reached a rapid boil and maintain that condition for 6 minutes.

4. Allow the water to cool to room temperature and retest for total coliforms.

5. Determine the inactivation log rate based on a comparison of the final coliform counts to the original coliform counts.

Comparison of Results

Compare the inactivation rates of the three disinfection methods to each other to determine the most effective disinfection option for the surface water being tested. Note any discrepancies between the results from the laboratory water and the surface water tested. Investigate and report on the causes of significant discrepancies noted.

Data Collection Format and Data Collection Sheets Tailored to Experiment:
See attached Data Collection Sheet

Anticipated Outcomes:
It is expected that the laboratory water samples will show no significant coliform counts as a result of the treatment processes used. There should, in fact, be no coliform present in any of the laboratory water samples at any time. Should any of the laboratory water samples contain significant coliform counts, the source will need to be investigated and eliminated and a determination made as to whether the counts found in the laboratory water need to be subtracted from the counts found in the treated surface water or whether the entire experiment has been compromised and needs to be repeated.

Inactivation log rates anticipated from each of the three disinfection options are expected to be variable. The Moringa seeds are expected to produce suitable results if the seed mass used is adequate. The adequacy of the seed mass used will be determined by the final coliform counts. If the final counts are not acceptable, higher masses of Moringa seed powder will be indicated and should be estimated based on the log rates resulting from the masses used. Boiling should yield total inactivation of the coliform in the surface water samples. The UV light may result in suitable log inactivation. If not, the necessary exposure time needed to achieve suitable log inactivation rates should be estimated from the log rate achieved.

Data Analysis Plan:
The data will be collected on the data collection sheet and the results of the coliform counts recorded in terms of coliform reduction rates. The coliform reduction rate is calculated as the final coliform count divided by the original coliform count in each container. That value is converted to a percentage and then to a log inactivation value per the theory section of this experiment design.

Data Collection Sheet Comparison of Disinfection Methods Remote Area Options

Date Collected:				
Date Tested:				
Principal Investigator:				
Surface Water Source				
Moringa Seed Disinfection Experiment				

Beaker	Concentration (g seed/L)	Results Coliform (CFU /100 mL)	Log Inactivation Achieved	Notes
Lab water 1	20			
Lab water 2	40			
Lab water 3	60			
Lab water 4	100			
Surface water 1	20			
Surface water 2	40			
Surface water 3	60			
Surface water 4	100			
UV Light Disinfection Experiment				

Bottle	Exposure Time (min)	Results Coliform (CFU /100 mL)	Log Inactivation Achieved	Notes
Lab water				
Surface water				
Heat Disinfection Experiment				

Bottle	Time for WAPI to melt or Time at Temperature (min)	Results Coliform (CFU/100 mL)	Log Inactivation Achieved	Notes
Lab water				
Surface water				

13 Water Quality Experiments

This chapter provides completed designs for example experiments which can be used to demonstrate specific engineering phenomena in a university laboratory or field collection site. They may be used as presented or modified by the user to adapt to other desired outcomes. Sections on actual outcomes and data interpretation are necessarily left blank in these examples. They should be completed by the investigators upon collection of the data.

The experiments in this chapter are:
13.1   Introduction to Water Quality Parameters
13.2   pH as a Function of Acid/Base Concentration with pH Neutralization Calculations
13.3   Determination of Mean Cell Residence Time in a Dispersed Plug Flow Reactor
13.4   Determination of Surface Water Evaporation Rate
13.5   Characterization of Pond, Lake, or Stream Foam

DOI: 10.1201/9781003184249-13

EXPERIMENT 13.1:   INTRODUCTION TO WATER QUALITY PARAMETERS

Date: _____

Principal Investigator:

    Name: _____

    Email: _____

    Phone: _____

Collaborators:

    Name: _____

    Email: _____

    Phone: _____

    Name: _____

    Email: _____

    Phone: _____

    Name: _____

    Email: _____

    Phone: _____

    Name: _____

    Email: _____

    Phone: _____

    Name: _____

    Email: _____

    Phone: _____

Objective or Question to Be Addressed:
One of the most important factors in an environmental system is water. The parameters surrounding water tend to fall into two categories: quantity and quality. This lab seeks to introduce quality parameters. The lab includes the quality of tap water, lab water, and surface water (lake/pond/river). Students will compare their results to quality parameters most ideal for fish habitats and determine if they can "Keep Your Fish Alive". The assessment will be conducted for a freshwater fish that prefers cool water, such as pike, walleye, and perch. This lab details the importance of water quality impacts on ecosystems for plants and animals. For example, they may need to receive oxygen from the water, so there must be a

minimum concentration of dissolved oxygen. While parameters will be measured individually, students should understand that water quality factors influence and interact with each other.

Instructors can also use this lab to discuss sampling plans, in general. An ideal sampling program would be valid and representation of the system. The collection of samples would be randomly selected usually based on access to a water source. An investigator needs to ensure a sample is representative of the water system and exhibits the same physicochemical characteristics with the sampled water at the time and site of sampling. Additional factors include frequency of sample collection, total number of samples, size of each sample, sites of sample collection, method of sample collection, data to be collected with each sample, and transportation and care of samples (as discussed previously in Section 3.1).

Theory Behind Experiment:

Parameters Measured in This Experiment Include:

- Temperature
- pH
- Conductivity
- Dissolved oxygen
- Turbidity

Water temperature is important to fish welfare because it can affect their behavior, feeding, growth, and reproduction. Metabolic rates in fish double for each 10°C (18°F) rise in temperature. The temperature of a water system also controls the reaction rate of chemicals, influences the solubility of gases in water, and influences the toxicity of ammonia and therapeutants; average temperature ranges for the optimal growth of fish vary depending on whether the fish is cold water, cool water, or warm water.

The pH is a measure of the quantity of hydrogen ions (H+) in water and determines if it is an acid or a base. The scale for measuring the degree of acidity is called the pH scale, which ranges from 1 to 14. A value of 7 is considered neutral, neither acidic or basic; values below 7 are considered acidic; above 7, basic. The acceptable pH range for fish culture is normally between pH 6.5 and 9.0.

Conductivity is the ability of water to conduct an electrical current, and the dissolved ions are the conductors. Conductivity is reciprocal to resistance and is measured in the amount of conductance, typically electrical conductance, but occasionally things like heat conductance are also measured, over a certain distance. Salts that are found in nature in a dissolved form break into positively and negatively charged ions when dissolved in water. These conductive ions come from dissolved salts and inorganic materials. Common charged ions are sodium, (Na^+), calcium (Ca^{+2}), potassium (K^+), magnesium (Mg^{+2}), chloride (Cl^-), sulfate $\left(SO_4{}^{-2}\right)$, carbonate $\left(CO_3{}^{-2}\right)$, and bicarbonate ($HCO_3{}^-$). The more ions that are present, the higher the conductivity of the water. The conductivity unit has been called "mho" because it is the inverse of "ohm", the resistance unit. The basic unit is "mho/cm", otherwise known as 1 Siemen. Conductivity is usually measured in microsiemens or millisiemens per centimeter (µS/cm or mS/cm). Microsiemens per centimeter is the standard unit for freshwater measurements. (Multiply the result by 0.393 to convert to inches from centimeters.)

The dissolved oxygen concentration of water (DO) impacts solubility, which decreases with increasing temperature and elevation; respiratory rate, which increases with increasing temperature; and fish activity and feeding. Surface water with dissolved oxygen concentrations that are too low is responsible for more fish kills, either directly or indirectly, than all other problems combined. The amount of oxygen consumed by the fish is a function of its size, feeding rate, activity level, and temperature. Recommended DO concentrations are a saturation of at least 5 ppm.

Turbidity is a measure of light penetration into the water; the degree to which the water loses its transparency due to the presence of suspended particulates. The lack of transparency is a measure of suspended particles which can diffuse sunlight and absorb heat. This can increase temperature and reduce light available for algal blooms. A turbidity measurement could be used to provide an estimation of the TSS (total suspended solids) and also correlates to the probability of microbiological contaminants. Turbidity is typically measured using a Secchi disk (in lakes or bays) or a turbidimeter (in a lab). There are various parameters influencing turbidity including phytoplankton, sediments from erosion, resuspended sediments, waste discharge, algae growth, and urban runoff.

Data to be collected with an explanation of how they will be collected (Ex.: "Water temperature data for three days using a continuous data logger")
Each student or group will have access to three types of water: tap water, lab water (distilled/deionized water), and surface water (river water). Each student in the group will measure DO, pH, turbidity, and conductivity four times and find the average values of each of these parameters for their waters. Finally, the students will compare their results to published ecosystem standards to see if their fish would survive.

Potential Interferences and Interference Management Plan:
The water quality parameters can be impacted by a mixture of natural and anthropogenic impacts. If this happens, the results of the observations in this experiment will be unclear, at best. Samples should be collected and tested in the field or immediately after collection.

Tools, Equipment, and Supplies Required

> Electrode probe capable of measuring temperature, pH, and conductivity
> DO probe
> Turbidimeter
> Approximately 300 mL (10 oz) each of tap water, lab water (distilled and deionized), and surface water for each student or group involved in the experiments

Safety:
Students should wear appropriate personal protection equipment, such as a lab coat, gloves, and safety goggles

The water and materials used in this experiment are not inherently dangerous. Avoidance of ingesting any of the water or samples is recommended. This experiment, as written, does not involve the collection of natural waters from streams, lakes, or ponds. However, if that is included, care must be taken near the shores of such water bodies to ensure safety during sampling. Chapter 3 in this manual includes further guidance on sampling surface water.

Planned Experimental Procedures and Steps, in Order:
Prepare 50 mL (1.7 oz) aliquots of the water samples.

1. Temperature
   a. Temperature is measured with an electrode probe thermometer (the same probe usually is capable of measuring temperature, pH, and conductivity).
   b. Rinse the electrode thoroughly with distilled water.
   c. Dry the electrode by gently blotting with a soft tissue paper.
   d. Ensure that the probe is set correctly to record temperature in the °C or °F, as desired or required.
   e. Place the probe in the sample.
   f. Determine and record the temperature of the sample.
2. pH
   a. pH is determined by measurement of the electromotive force with an electrode probe immersed in the test solution.
   b. Rinse the electrode thoroughly with distilled water.
   c. Dry the electrode by gently blotting with a soft tissue paper.
   d. Ensure that the probe is set correctly to record pH.
   e. Place the probe in the sample.
   f. Determine and record the pH of the sample.
3. Conductivity
   a. Conductivity is measured by an electrode probe, which applies a voltage between two electrodes (change in voltage is used to measure the resistance of the water, which is then converted to conductivity).
   b. Rinse the electrode thoroughly with distilled water.
   c. Dry the electrode by gently blotting with a soft tissue paper.
   d. Ensure that the probe is set correctly to record conductivity.
   e. Place the probe in the sample.
   f. Determine and record the conductivity of the sample.
4. Dissolved oxygen
   A DO membrane electrode is composed of two solid metal electrodes in contact with supporting electrolytes separated from the test solution by a gas-permeable membrane. Oxygen dissolved in the sample diffuses through the membrane on the DO probe and is chemically reduced (accepts electrons) producing an electrical current between the anode and cathode in the probe. The amount of current is proportional to the concentration of DO.
   a. Rinse the electrode thoroughly with distilled water.
   b. Dry the electrode by gently blotting with a soft tissue paper.

c. Place the probe in the sample.
d. Determine and record the DO of the sample.
5. Turbidity

Turbidity is measured in NTU (Nephelometric Turbidity Units). The instrument used for measuring it is called nephelometer, colorimeter, or turbidimeter, which measures the intensity of light scattered at 90° as a beam of light passes through a water sample.

a. Collect a representative sample in a clean container (the container must be a standard cuvette designed for the test instrument and optically matched to a second cuvette which is used as a control device).
b. Fill a sample cell to the line (about 15 mL or 0.5 oz) (take care to handle the sample cell by the top, as fingerprints or other contaminants on the glass will alter the readings significantly).
c. Cap the cell.
d. Wipe the cell with a soft, lint-free cloth to remove water spots and fingerprints.
e. Place the instrument on a flat, sturdy surface.
f. Push the Power key to turn the meter on.
g. Gently invert and then insert the sample cell in the instrument cell compartment so the diamond or orientation mark aligns with the raised orientation mark in front of the cell compartment.
h. Close the lid.
i. Push Read.
j. When the display stabilizes read the turbidity in NTU.

Data Collection Format and Data Collection Sheets Tailored to Experiment:
See attached Data Collection Sheet

Anticipated Outcomes:

Parameter	Allowable range for your ecosystem
Temperature	15°C–27°C (59°F–81°F)
pH	7–8
Dissolved Oxygen	> 5 mg/L (0.00002 oz/qt)
Turbidity	< 80 NTU
Conductivity	< 50 mS

Data Analysis Plan:
Data will be collected as indicated and recorded on the data collection sheet as read from the instruments. The collected data will then be compared to the standards provided for the various parameters and a judgment made regarding the suitability of the tested water samples for survival of cool water fish.

Data Collection Sheet Water Quality Parameters

Date Collected:

Date Tested:

Principal Investigator:

Source Water:

Test	Results	Expected Results	Variations Noted	Notes

EXPERIMENT 13.2: pH AS A FUNCTION OF ACID/ BASE CONCENTRATION WITH pH NEUTRALIZATION CALCULATIONS

Date: _____

Principal Investigator:

    Name: _____

    Email: _____

    Phone: _____

Collaborators:

    Name: _____

    Email: _____

    Phone: _____

    Name: _____

    Email: _____

    Phone: _____

    Name: _____

    Email: _____

    Phone: _____

    Name: _____

    Email: _____

    Phone: _____

    Name: _____

    Email: _____

    Phone: _____

Objective or Question to Be Addressed:

The objective of this experiment is to evaluate the change in pH of water as a function of the concentration of a strong acid or a strong base and to then calculate the amount of acid or base needed to neutralize the extremes of pH created during the exercise.

Theory Behind Experiment

The measure of how acidic or basic a sample of water is, is quantified by pH. It is defined mathematically as the negative log of the hydrogen ion concentration.

Measuring the pH is generally done most easily and accurately with a pH meter. Litmus paper, which changes color depending on the pH of the solution to which it is exposed, is usually reliable, but not overly accurate.

When acid is added to pure water, the water becomes more acidic and the pH declines. When a base is added to pure water, the pH increases as the water becomes more basic.

Normal water has a pH of around 7.0, defined as neutral pH. When the pH is caused to vary from neutral by more than 1–1.5 points, it is often necessary to correct the pH by adding an acid to a basic water or a base to an acidic water.

This experiment will examine the rate at which the pH changes with the addition of an acid or a base. Those values will be used to determine how much acid to add back to the basic solution and how much base to add back to the acidic solution to neutralize them.

The calculation of how much acid or base to add back is based on the chemistry of the specific acid and base. In this experiment, nitric acid (HNO_3) will be used to create the acidic solution. Sodium hydroxide ($NaOH$) will be used for the base.

When these two compounds are mixed together, they react in the following way.

$$HNO_3 + NaOH \Rightarrow NaNO_3 + H_2O$$

In essence, the reaction product is a salt ($NaNO_3$) and water. In this reaction, the two substances to the left are completely used up. Therefore, one mole of this acid should exactly neutralize one mole of this base. To determine the amount of acid needed to neutralize the basic solution created in this experiment, it will be necessary to calculate the molar mass of base added to the solution. An identical molar mass of the acid is needed to neutralize the molar mass of the base. The reverse is true for neutralizing the acid with the base.

The molar mass of a compound is calculated by adding together the molar weights of the individual components. The components in question for this experiment, and their molar weights, are shown in the following table.

Element	Molar Weight (g)
Hydrogen	1.008
Nitrogen	28.014
Oxygen	15.999
Sodium	22.990

Therefore, the molar weight of the acid, the base, and the reaction byproducts are the following.

Compound	Molar Weight (g)
HNO_3	$1.008 + 28.014 + 3(15.999) = 77.019$
$NaOH$	$22.990 + 15.999 + 1.008 = 39.997$
$NaNO_3$	$22.990 + 28.014 + 3(15.999) = 99.001$
H_2O	$2(1.008) + 15.999 = 18.015$

The experiment will determine the molar mass of base added to create the basic solution and add back the molar weight of acid to neutralize it. Similarly, the molar mass of acid in the acid solution created will require an identical molar mass of base to neutralize it. Careful and precise measurement of the acid and base added during this experiment are important to a quality outcome.

Potential Interferences and Interference Management Plan

This experiment uses distilled and deionized water as the solvent to create the acid and the base solutions. That should eliminate anything that could react with the additives other than each other. In nature that is unlikely to happen and a precise measurement of the neutralizing compound may not be as easily calculated there as in the laboratory. Careful attention to what is in the water to be neutralized in nature is important to properly calculate the masses of additives.

Data to be collected with an explanation of how they will be collected (Ex.: "Water temperature data for three days using a continuous data logger")

In this experiment, the pH of water and the pH of two solutions will be measured with a calibrated pH meter. In addition, the volume (and mass) of a liquid acid (nitric acid) and a dry base (sodium hydroxide) will be measured with an analytical scale capable of reading to 0.001 g.

Tools, Equipment, and Supplies Required:

Analytical scale capable of reading to 0.001 g
Clean pipettes for adding the acid
Clean spatula for the base
Two 2 L clean glass beakers
Two clean glass stirring rods
pH meter calibrated for pH between 2.0 and 12.0
4 L of distilled and deionized water
Supply of nitric acid
Supply of sodium hydroxide
Acid spill kit in case of emergency
Clean 500 mL graduated glass cylinder

Safety

A strong acid is being used in this experiment. It is highly caustic and will cause immediate destruction of skin tissue if contacted. It will also destroy clothing and cause damage to other materials with which it may come into contact. Gloves, eye protection, a face mask, and a lab coat are required when working with this chemical.

This experiment also uses a strong base. In its dry form, the base is mildly caustic and will cause serious skin irritation and slow destruction of skin tissue if not immediately washed off. In its liquid form, this base is highly caustic and will cause rapid burning of skin tissues and damage to clothing with which it comes in contact.

In the event of an acid spill, a spill kit should be kept at the site of the experiment for rapid deployment over the spill.

In the event of exposure to the acid, wash the area with running water and soap as quickly as possible and seek immediate medical assistance. If the skin is broken, wash with plain water, only and seek medical assistance.

In the event of exposure to the dry base, immediately wash the area with water and soap. In the event of contact with the liquid base, immediately wash with warm water and soap and seek medical attention if the skin remains red or broken.

In the event of exposure to the eyes with either material, or either of the solutions, immediately flush at an eye station for up to 15 minutes while seeking emergency medical assistance.

Planned Experimental Procedures and Steps, in Order:

1. Gather all required equipment and supplies and put on appropriate personal protective equipment.
2. Fill the two 2 L glass beakers with exactly 2 L of distilled and deionized water using a graduated cylinder for that purpose.
3. Measure and record the pH of the first beaker.
4. Add 0.05 mL (0.0017 oz) of concentrated nitric acid to the first beaker, stir the contents thoroughly, and then measure and record the pH.
5. Repeat Step 4 until the pH of the solution reaches 2.0 or less, or 5 mL (0.169 oz) of acid have been added, whichever occurs first.
6. Carefully set the first beaker aside.
7. Measure and record the pH of the second beaker.
8. Add 5 mg (0.00017 oz) of sodium hydroxide to this beaker stirring thoroughly and until all of the sodium hydroxide has dissolved, then measure and record the pH of this solution.
9. Repeat Step 8 until the pH of this solution reaches 12.0 or higher or 50 mg (0.0017 oz) of base have been added, whichever occurs first.
10. Plot the pH of the acid solution along the Y-axis and the molar mass of acid added along the X-axis of normal-normal graph paper.
11. Plot the pH on the Y-axis and the molar mass of base added along the X-axis of a second piece of normal-normal graph paper.
12. Based on the final pH of the acid solution, calculate the mass of sodium hydroxide required to exactly neutralize the acid solution.
13. Based on the final pH of the base solution, calculate the molar mass of acid needed to exactly neutralize the base solution.
14. Calculate the volume of base needed to provide exactly the molar mass of the base calculated in Step 12 as necessary to neutralize the acid solution, add that mass to the acid solution, and stir thoroughly. Measure and record the resulting pH.
15. Calculate the volume or mass of the acid needed to provide exactly the molar mass of the acid calculated in Step 13 as necessary to neutralize the base solution, add that mass to the base solution, and stir thoroughly. Measure and record the resulting pH.
16. Using an available technique, such as a spectrophotometer (with HACH powder pillow method or similar system), determine the concentration of

sodium nitrate in both neutralized solutions and conduct a mass balance to determine the amount of sodium hydroxide and nitric acid still in solution in the two original beakers.

17. Discuss why the final pH of each solution is or is not exactly 7.0 and why the mass balances do or do not show total removal of the acid or base in either beaker after neutralization.

Data Collection Format and Data Collection Sheets Tailored to Experiment:
See attached data collection sheet.

Data Analysis Plan:
The data generated by this experiment include pH values and acid or base concentrations. Those concentrations need to be converted to molar masses. The calculated molar masses are then used to determine the amount of an anti-acid or anti-base necessary to neutralize the amounts of acids and base added to the solution during the experiment.

Expected Outcomes:
It is expected that careful conduct of the experiment, including careful measurement of the initial volumes of distilled and deionized water, the careful weighing and measuring of the volume of acid and base used during the experiment to develop the pH curves, followed by careful calculation of the mass needed to neutralize the two solutions and careful measurement of those masses will yield two solutions that are essentially pH neutral, but containing a predictable concentration of residual sodium nitrate salt and a potentially measurable volume of additional water created during the chemical reactions of neutralization.

Data Collection Sheet for pH as a Function of Acid/Base Concentration and pH Neutralization Calculations

Parameter	Value	Parameter	Value
BEAKER #1		BEAKER #2	
Initial pH		Initial pH	
Mass of acid added, mL		Mass of base added, mg/L	
Mass of acid added, gmolar weight		Mass of base added, gmolar weight	
New pH		New pH	
Mass of acid added, mL		Mass of base added, mg/L	
Mass of acid added, g molar weight		Mass of base added, gmolar weight	
New pH		New pH	
Mass of acid added, mL		Mass of base added, mg/L	
Mass of acid added, g molar weight		Mass of base added, g molar weight	
New pH		New pH	
Mass of acid added, mL		Mass of base added, mg/L	
Mass of acid added, g molar weight		Mass of base added, g molar weight	
New pH		New pH	
Mass of acid added, mL		Mass of base added, mg/L	
Mass of acid added, g molar weight		Mass of base added, g molar weight	
New pH		New pH	
Mass of acid added, mL		Mass of base added, mg/L	

(*Continued*)

Data Collection Sheet for pH as a Function of Acid/Base Concentration and pH Neutralization Calculations (*Continued*)

Parameter	Value	Parameter	Value
Mass of acid added, g molar weight		Mass of base added, g molar weight	
New pH		New pH	
Mass of acid added, mL		Mass of base added, mg/L	
Mass of acid added, g molar weight		Mass of base added, gmolar weight	
New pH		New pH	
Mass of acid added, mL		Mass of base added, mg/L	
Mass of acid added, g molar weight		Mass of base added, g molar weight	
New pH		New pH	
Mass of acid added, mL		Mass of base added, mg/L	
Mass of acid added, g molar weight		Mass of base added, g molar weight	
New pH		New pH	
Mass of acid added, mL		Mass of base added, mg/L	
Mass of acid added, g molar weight		Mass of base added, g molar weight	
New pH		New pH	
Total mass of acid added, mg/L		Total mass of base added, mg/L	
Total mass of base needed to neutralize, mg/L		Total mass of acid needed to neutralize, mL	
Mass of sodium nitrate in original acid solution, mg/L		Mass of sodium nitrate in original base solution, mg/L	

EXPERIMENT 13.3: DETERMINATION OF MEAN CELL RESIDENCE TIME IN A DISPERSED PLUG FLOW REACTOR

Date: _____

Principal Investigator:

       Name: _____

       Email: _____

       Phone: _____

Collaborators:

       Name: _____

       Email: _____

       Phone: _____

       Name: _____

       Email: _____

       Phone: _____

       Name: _____

       Email: _____

       Phone: _____

       Name: _____

       Email: _____

       Phone: _____

       Name: _____

       Email: _____

       Phone: _____

Objective or Question to Be Addressed:

The objective of this experiment is to determine the mean cell residence time in a bench-scale, dispersed plug flow reactor by using a pulse tracer study and by so doing to experiment with the methodology for finding the mean cell residence time in a similar full-scale reactor.

Theory Behind Experiment

Flow through a tank operating in a plug flow mode does not strictly follow the rules of ideal plug flow reactors. The ideal reactor is visualized as a garden hose.

The flow is introduced in one end, travels through the reactor to the other end, and discharges without measurable mixing during its passage through the reactor. Chemical and biological reactions are expected to occur during that passage, but mixing does not.

Reality seldom follows idealistic visualizations. In a full-scale plug flow reactor, axial intermixing and backmixing occur regularly due to the turbulence resulting from the nonideal flow through the reactor. The nonideal flow is caused by the need to introduce the flow at one location and discharge it at a different location that is not close to the inlet. The turbulent mixing that occurs in this situation is somewhere between the turbulence of a completely mixed reactor and the nonturbulence of the ideal plug flow reactor. The concept of a dispersed plug flow reactor tries to account for these turbulent inter-mixings, but note that it does not account for stagnant pockets that may develop in certain reactors, particularly square or rectangular reactors with square corners, or for short-circuiting of flow directly to the outlet.

In a tracer study, a substance for which the concentration over time can be easily measured at very low concentrations, but which is nonreactive with the reactor contents, is introduced at the inlet of a reactor, and the concentration in the reactor is measured over a reasonable period of time, typically the time it takes for three volumes of the reactor to flow through the system. An inert dye of some kind is typically used for this purpose, and the concentration at any time is determined from a previously calibrated spectrophotometric analysis of a sample of the reactor contents at the outlet.

Two ways of introducing the tracer are commonly found. The first involves injecting a known quantity of tracer into the flow stream and mixing it very quickly into the flow so that it closely mimics a slug of tracer introduced all at once. The outlet concentration is then measured normally to yield a bell curve of outlet tracer concentration, called a *C-curve* for concentration versus time. The second method is to continuously introduce the tracer in a step input fashion until the outlet concentration matches the input concentration. At that point, the input is stopped, and the outlet concentration is monitored over time to yield a decreasing, somewhat s-shaped, outlet concentration curve, called an *F-curve*, for fraction remaining versus time.

This experiment design uses the simpler slug flow introduction of the dye, and the analysis of the output data should result in a bell curve when the tracer concentration at the outlet is plotted on the Y-axis against time on the X-axis. Note that with this type of analysis, the magnitude of the bell curve and the narrowness of the space between the vertical legs of the curve are an indication of the degree of short-circuiting that is occurring inside the reactor. A tall, narrow curve indicates that the tracer has reached the outlet suddenly and passed through quickly. The peak of this curve should be essentially identical to the theoretical retention time for the reactor. If the curve is slightly lower, and the peak has displaced to the left of the theoretical detention time, a modest amount of short-circuiting is indicated. If the curve is low and displaced significantly to the left, perhaps to as much as ½ the theoretical detention time, significant short-circuiting is indicated. The mean cell residence time (MCRT) is determined from the time after injection of the tracer at which the peak of the bell curve occurs.

Potential Interferences and Interference Management Plan

A lot of things can go wrong with this experiment. The first has to do with the introduction of the tracer. The tracer needs to be introduced at the inlet as close to a single mass as possible and in the shortest possible time frame, consistent with not creating undue mixing or turbulence in the flow. Practice makes perfect in this regard.

The second thing that can go wrong is that the spectrophotometer is not properly calibrated for the concentration of the tracer being used. This will result in an inaccurate reading of the tracer concentration at the outlet and a false output curve. See the experiment in this book related to the calibration of a spectrophotometer for a specific tracer to ensure proper calibration of the spectrophotometer.

The output curve from which the mean cell residence time is to be determined is time dependent. It is important to collect samples at the reactor outlet at carefully selected times in order to ensure that the actual peak of the curve is not missed. Should a specific reading not be taken at the appropriate time, careful attention to exactly when the sample was collected becomes important so that the concentration point can be properly plotted against the timeline on the graph.

The actual concentration of the tracer at the outset is not critical, but it is critical to know exactly what that concentration is. Without that knowledge, it will be difficult to ascertain when the peak has arrived and the distribution curve is starting to fall or at what time the concentration at the outlet has reached essentially zero again.

Flow through the reactor must be constant in order to be able to calculate a theoretical detention time. To ensure this, a hose is attached to the outlet at the bottom of the reactor and then attached to the outside of the reactor such that the outlet from the hose is at the same elevation as the inlet to the reactor. The flow rate can then be established at a reasonable value that can be measured. A flow meter should be inserted into the inlet line to allow constant monitoring of the flow rate and the setting of a suitable rate that will allow for easier calculation of the theoretical detention time.

Data to be collected with an explanation of how they will be collected (Ex.: "Water temperature data for three days using a continuous data logger")

The data to be collected in this experiment are the concentration of a specific tracer at the outlet of the bench-scale reactor over time. The data will be determined from a small aliquot of outlet flow collected in a selected collection tube suitable for the spectrophotometer being used. The collection tube will be inserted into a previously calibrated spectrophotometer to determine the concentration based on the calibration curve for the instrument.

Tools, Equipment, and Supplies Required:

  Spectrophotometer precalibrated for the tracer to be used

  30 clean, 25 mL beakers for collecting outlet samples

  20 L (5.3 gal) flow through reactor with the inlet at the top and the outlet at the bottom and a hose connected to the outlet, taped to the side of the reactor such that the discharge from the hose is at the inlet elevation of the reactor contents

  Stopwatch to measure time

Safety

Tracers can be toxic to humans if ingested in significant quantities. Care must be taken to avoid accidental ingestion. The tracer planned for this experiment is a dye. Dyes have the habit of staining the hands and clothes of the users who are not careful. The use of gloves and lab coats is recommended to avoid this.

Eye protection is always recommended when using liquids and contaminants such as the dyes used in this experiment.

In the event of skin contact, rapid flushing and washing with warm water and soap may reduce the amount of staining. Stains will dissipate over time and should not be inherently dangerous to health.

In the event of eye contact, flush immediately with an eyewash for at least 15 minutes and seek medical attention as soon as possible.

Planned Experimental Procedures and Steps, in Order:

1. Gather all necessary equipment and supplies and put on appropriate personal protective equipment.
2. Establish a spectrophotometer calibration curve for the tracer to be used by following the manufacturer's instructions or by following the Spectrophotometer Calibration Curve experiment in this book.
3. Set up a 20 L (5.3 gal) reactor with an inlet at the top of the reactor and an outlet at the bottom. Attach a hose from the outlet up the outside of the reactor such that the invert of the discharge hose is at the same elevation as the top of the inlet hose to the reactor. This will minimize flow rate variation through the reactor and simplify standardization of that flow rate for better control of the theoretical detention time. Insert a flow meter into the inlet hose to monitor the flow rate so that the flow rate can be stabilized, and the theoretical detention time can be properly and accurately determined.
4. Set up all 30 of the 25 mL collection beakers and collection tubes for sampling the outlet. Mark each one as to the time of sampling since sampling events will be happening too quickly to mark them as the testing proceeds.
5. Set the reactor up in a location where the outlet can discharge directly to a sink or drain and where collection of an outlet sample for tracer concentration testing can be easily accessed regularly throughout the experiment.
6. Start the flow of water into the reactor and allow it to fill to the elevation of the discharge outlet. Adjust the flow rate such that the inlet and outlet flow rates are equal, and the reactor is not continuing to fill or drain. This will establish a steady-state flow rate through the reactor. Record that flow rate.
7. Calculate the theoretical detention time in the reactor based on the flow rate and the volume of water inside the reactor.
8. Calculate the volume of tracer required to provide an input slug of 10 mg/L of tracer based on the actual volume of water in the reactor under steady-state flow conditions.
9. Insert the tracer into the inlet flow downstream of the flow meter and as far upstream of the reactor inlet as possible. This will minimize turbulent mixing as the tracer is introduced to the reactor.

10. Collect the first sample of outlet 10 seconds after the tracer first begins to enter the reactor, collect the second sample at 20 seconds after the tracer first begins to enter the reactor, and continue to collect samples every 20 seconds thereafter for a period of at least 5 minutes or for the time it will take for three volumes of the reactor to flow through the reactor, whichever is longer. At a flow rate of 2 gallons per minute, for example, and a volume of 5.3 gallons in the reactor, it should take 2.65 minutes for 1 volume to flow through the reactor, yielding a theoretical detention time of 2.65 minutes. Three volumes would require 8 minutes of sampling every 20 seconds, for a total of 24 sampling beakers required.
11. Once the required samples have been collected, shut off the water and break down the reactor set-up.
12. Test each of the collected samples with the spectrophotometer to determine the tracer concentration at each time interval.
13. Plot the tracer concentrations over time with time on the X-axis and concentration on the Y-axis.
14. Plot the theoretical detention time on the curve and the theoretical maximum tracer concentration, which will be less than the initial concentration because of the mixing that occurs, changing the actual detention time to a somewhat longer detention time.
15. Determine the reactor detention time as the time at which the mean value of the tracer concentration occurred at the outlet.
16. Compare the mean residence time determined from the tracer study to the theoretical detention time and opine as to the occurrence of short-circuiting in this reactor.

Data Collection Format and Data Collection Sheets Tailored to Experiment:
See attached Data Collection Sheet

Data Analysis Plan:
The data collected will be plotted on a graph of tracer concentration versus time. The mean value of the outlet tracer concentration will be calculated and plotted on the same curve to determine the time at which that mean value occurred. That time will be considered the actual mean cell residence time for this reactor.

Expected Outcomes:
It is expected that the curve resulting from this experiment will not be a perfect bell curve peaking at exactly the theoretical detention time. There may, in fact, be significant short-circuiting in this reactor yielding a flat outlet concentration curve with a very early peak.

Data Collection Sheet Determination of Mean Cell Residence Time in a Dispersed Plug Flow Reactor

Measurement	Time After Start Seconds	Outlet Tracer Concentration (mg/L)	Measurement	Time After Start Seconds	Outlet Tracer Concentration (mg/L)	Measurement	Time After Start Seconds	Outlet Tracer Concentration (mg/L)
Total volume of water in reactor (L)			Sample collection time (t_{130})			Sample collection time (t_{310})		
Mass of tracer needed to yield 10 mg/L concentration			Sample collection time (t_{150})			Sample collection time (t_{330})		
Flow rate through reactor								
Experiment start time (t_0)			Sample collection time (t_{170})			Sample collection time (t_{370})		
Sample collection time (t_{10})			Sample collection time (t_{190})			Sample collection time (t_{390})		
Sample collection time (t_{20})			Sample collection time (t_{210})			Sample collection time (t_{410})		
Sample collection time (t_{50})			Sample collection time (t_{230})			Sample collection time (t_{430})		
Sample collection time (t_{70})			Sample collection time (t_{250})			Sample collection time (t_{470})		
Sample collection time (t_{90})			Sample collection time (t_{270})			Sample collection time (t_{490})		
Sample collection time (t_{110})			Sample collection time (t_{290})			Sample collection time (t_{510})		
			Sample collection time (t_{310})					

EXPERIMENT 13.4: DETERMINATION OF SURFACE WATER EVAPORATION RATE

Date: _____

Principal Investigator:

      Name: _____

      Email: _____

      Phone: _____

Collaborators:

      Name: _____

      Email: _____

      Phone: _____

      Name: _____

      Email: _____

      Phone: _____

      Name: _____

      Email: _____

      Phone: _____

      Name: _____

      Email: _____

      Phone: _____

      Name: _____

      Email: _____

      Phone: _____

Objective or Question to Be Addressed:

This experiment is designed to determine the evaporation rate of surface waters as a function of water temperature, air temperature, wind speed at the water surface, and atmospheric pressure.

Theory Behind the Experiment

Water evaporates from the surface of ponds, streams, lakes, lagoons (including sludge drying beds), and other surface water sources on a continuous basis. The rate at which that evaporation occurs is a function of many things. The most influential factors are the water temperature, the air temperature, the air speed over the water surface, and the atmospheric pressure. These parameters are site specific and are not necessarily linear. This experiment is designed to determine the values of those determinants over a reasonable time frame to help estimate the long term evaporation rate of a given surface water source.

Water and air temperatures are important functions because lower temperatures, slow the evaporation rate. Evaporation occurs because the molecules of the water are constantly in motion and have sufficient energy to escape the surface tension of the water source; thus, the colder the water becomes, the slower the molecules move and the lower the evaporation rate becomes.

Air temperature is important because it directly affects the surface molecules of the water source. When the air temperature is significantly higher than the water temperature, the surface molecules on the water source are energized to a higher degree than the general water temperature would indicate. The water molecules at the surface will move more rapidly, and with that artificial energy boost, these molecules will evaporate into the atmosphere more easily than would be expected from the water temperature alone. Similarly, when the air temperature is significantly lower than the water temperature, the surface molecules are artificially slowed at the air/water interface and the evaporation rate is slowed. These effects are not expected to be linear.

Atmospheric pressure is a key indicator of the evaporation rate because an increase in atmospheric pressure requires the water molecules to exert a higher energy than otherwise needed to escape the surface tension based solely on temperature and simultaneously overcome the atmospheric pressure holding them down. Similarly, a decrease in atmospheric pressure allows the water molecules to escape more easily from the water surface than they would under the sole effects of temperature.

Air speed becomes an important parameter after the effects of all other factors are considered. A dead calm air mass will absorb the evaporating water molecules at a constant rate following stabilization of that rate as the air mass movement decreases to zero. Once the air mass stabilizes, the air/water interface will become saturated quickly and the rate of evaporation will stabilize at a rate below that expected based on temperature and pressure alone. As the air mass begins to move, the water molecules at the air/water interface thin out and the rate of evaporation increases. The greater the air movement, the faster the evaporation will occur, but only up to a maximum rate determined by the other factors.

To estimate the long-term or short-term evaporation rates of a water source, it is necessary to measure the four parameters cited and to then insert those values into an empirical equation to calculate the rate. This experiment develops the equation for the water body being tested and calibrates the equation from real-time data. The equation is developed by including a term for each of the four parameters. Calibration of the equation is done by observing actual evaporation rates over time while measuring the four parameters in real time, then comparing the calculated evaporation rate to the actual evaporation rate.

Note that evaporation rates are not static. Air temperature, water temperature, atmospheric pressure, and wind speed are seldom constant over small time frames and certainly not over longer ones. Any estimate of evaporation rate is going to be an average value determined over the length of time the data are monitored. As seasons change and the various parameter values change, the effects predicted are also likely to change. To determine long-term effects, it would be necessary to monitor the data continuously for several years, perhaps even a decade or more. The values determined by long-term studies would relate to long-term evaporation, while rates determined from short-term studies would determine short-term rates relative to the weather and water conditions at the time of measurement, only.

Data to be collected with an explanation of how they will be collected (Ex.: "Water temperature data for three days using a continuous data logger")
Data to be collected are the actual measurements of water temperature, air temperature, air speed, and atmospheric pressure at the study site over a 5 day period. Those data are to be collected using an automated set of probes located at the study site and connected to a data logger.

In addition, the actual loss of water from a carefully designed bowl of water set at the site will provide actual rates of evaporation over the study period by measurement of the depth of water in the bowl with a continuous depth probe.

The time that the probes and data loggers are activated at the study site and the date and time they are stopped will be recorded. Any time periods during which any probe or data logger malfunctions will be identified and recorded as carefully as possible.

Potential Interferences and Interference Management Plan:
Malfunction of one or more probes during the study period may significantly impact the outcome of the experiment. Care taken during the installation and calibration of the probes and data loggers will be important to minimizing this risk.

Water being inadvertently added to, or deleted from, the calibration box will adversely affect the calibration of the equation developed from the probes and data loggers. Setting the edges of the box high enough above the surface of the lake or pond surface to minimize the potential for wave action to affect the water volume inside the box and using a screen over the top of the box to minimize access by water fowl which could cause spillage should minimize these risks.

Rainfall during the period of the study will adversely affect the evaporation rate from the calibration box disproportionally to that of the overall water body. This will occur because the water body as a whole will dissipate the added rainfall over the larger area resulting in a minimal temperature change and depth change in the water source. The rain falling directly into the calibration box will fill the box adversely and affect the water temperature in the box directly. Using a temperature probe inside the calibration box to monitor the water temperature inside the box relative to that outside the box will allow adjustment of the water temperature and the calculation of the evaporation rate from the calibration box. A significant storm event during the study period should be considered grounds for re-starting the experiment. If a short term event occurs during the study period, particularly near the end of the study, use of the data before and after the event may be possible. A judgment will need to be made regarding the value of the data collected outside the storm event in order to complete the data analysis. For educational purposes, the effects will be seen and noted and education will occur. For professional application, the effects of the storm event on the collected data need to be more carefully considered.

This experiment is based on the design of a floating evaporation box that allows the evaporation from the box to mimic, as closely as possible, the evaporation rate from the larger pond or lake. Class A Evaporation Pans may also be utilized for this experiment. Note that an evaporation pan of this type is set on land, typically adjacent to the pond or lake, but not in the pond or lake. There will be a difference between the evaporation rate from the pan and the evaporation rate from the pond, referred to as the evaporation pan coefficient. The typical coefficient value is generally around 1.3 for the pan indicating that the evaporation rate from the pan is around 30% greater than from the adjacent pond due to excessive heat build-up in the pan from sunlight and warm air adjacent to the metal sides. The pan described in this experiment is constructed of plexiglass to minimize heat transfer through the box walls and then set in the water for the same reason. The coefficient for this box should be very close to 1.0, or identical to the evaporation rate from the pond it is sitting in.

Tools, Equipment, and Supplies Required:
   Temperature probe for water temperature inside the calibration box
   Temperature probe for water temperature of the source water
   Temperature probe for air temperature outside the calibration box and above
       the source water
   Air speed monitor to be installed close to, but above, the source water
   Air pressure probe to monitor air pressure close to, but above, the source water
   Data logger for each probe that can record data for up to seven continuous days
   Power source for each data logger
   Calibration box of known internal dimensions: a cube, with sealed seams,
       created from ½ inch (12.7 mm) thick plexiglass that is exactly 12 inches
       (304.8 mm) *inside* in all three directions, should float with approximately 5
       inches (127 mm) of external freeboard when filled with 4 inches (101.6 mm)
       of water, and will be easy to use when calculating water losses over time
       because the surface area from which evaporation will take place will be
       exactly one square foot (0.093 m^2)

Safety
Water measurements at natural locations necessarily involve access to the natural water source. Water bodies typically embody significant depths of detritus and muds on the bottom such that wading into a test site can pose risks of slipping, falling, and drowning.

All of the probes and data loggers require a power source. That will normally be either a solar array or a battery pack for each unit. Stray electrical currents, even at the low voltages produced by these sources, can cause negative impacts on fish, plants, and people. Care is needed to protect connections and power sources in the wet environment of the study area.

Planned Experimental Procedures and Steps, in Order:

   1. Collect all necessary equipment and supplies, test equipment for performance, and assemble the data loggers, probes, and calibration box at the study site.

2. Set the calibration box firmly in place and fill it to a depth of 4 inches (101.6 mm) with surface water from the source. The exact depth of source water inside the box is not critical, but a precise measurement of that depth *is* critical. Record that precise depth.

3. Set the probes firmly in place within the calibration box, within the source water and within the atmosphere adjacent to the calibration box. Probes are needed to measure water temperature in the source water, water temperature inside the calibration box, air temperature, atmospheric pressure, and air speed, and to continuously log those data.

4. Activate all probes and all power sources and verify that they are working properly. Record the date and time that the probes and data loggers are activated.

5. Check the study site daily for 7 days, without adjusting or moving any of the probes that appear to be working properly and without adding or deleting water from the calibration box. Reset probes that are not working properly and record the time they have been working improperly or off, if possible. If the calibration box is close to becoming empty, refill the box, noting and recording the date and time at which this is done and the exact depth of water in the box just before and just after refilling.

6. At the end of the study period, turn off all probes and data loggers simultaneously and record the time the study is stopped. Measure and record the precise depth of water in the calibration box.

7. Download all the data and evaluate in accordance with the data analysis plan.

Data Collection Format and Data Collection Sheets Tailored to Experiment:
See attached Data Collection Sheet

Anticipated Outcomes:
It is expected that the evaporation rate determined from the equation developed from the probes and data loggers will compare favorably to the rate determined from the calibration box and that those rates will be consistent with published evaporation rates for the time of year of the study in the study area, if any.

Data Analysis Plan:
The data loggers will provide a timeline of the data collected. Those data should be plotted against the timeline and the equation of the resulting data curve determined. A separate graph for each of the four parameters measured outside the calibration box will be required. The four resulting curve equations will then need to be standardized to a unitary evaporation rate in $cm/m^2/day$ (in/acre/day or acre-feet/day) or in $L/m^2/day$ (gal/acre/day) integrated into a singular mathematical model of the evaporation rate developed through linear regression techniques or multiple linear regression techniques using the measured evaporation from the calibration box to calibrate the linear regression equations.

Adjustments may be made to the empirical equation or to the calibration box data based on identified variations in the data collection system, such as malfunctions of equipment, missing data, storm events, and similar anomalies. All adjustments and calculations will be carefully explained and justified in the laboratory report.

Linear regression and multiple linear regression models are used to describe relationships between variables by fitting a line on a graph to the observed data. Regression analysis allows the experimenter to estimate how one variable of interest, typically referred to as the dependent variable because the value of that variable depends on the value of the independent, or measured variables, changes as the independent variables change. In this experiment, the dependent variable is the evaporation rate, while the independent variables are the air temperature, the water temperature, the wind speed, and the atmospheric pressure. The rate at which the water evaporates from the surface of the water body is dependent upon the values of the independent variables.

Linear regression analysis is generally used when there is only one dependent variable and one independent variable. Multiple linear regression is generally used when there are more than one independent variable acting simultaneously on the dependent variable.

Regression analysis assumes the following things to be true with respect to all the variables.

First, it is assumed that the data are sufficiently consistent that the size of any errors in the predictions made from the measured data does not change significantly across the entire range of the data of interest. For example, the error margins are slight from negative air temperatures to higher than normal air temperatures and the evaporation rate associated with air temperature is constant across that entire range of temperatures. This is called *Homogeneity of Variance* in mathematical terms.

Second, there is assumed to be independence in the sampling of the independent variables. This implies that the measured values in the data sets from which the equation is developed were collected using statistically valid methods and that there are no unknown connections between the variables. This is called *Independence of Observations* in mathematical terms. Note that in this experiment, the air temperature and the water temperature are not totally independent, but that the dependence between them is likely so marginal as to be safely ignored in the analyses of those data.

The above statement notwithstanding, with multiple linear regression, it is possible that some of the independent variables are actually correlated with one another, so it is important to check these before developing the regression model. If two independent variables are too highly correlated ($r^2 > \sim0.6$), then only one of them should be used in the regression model. It is not expected that any of the variables in this experiment will fit that criterion.

Third, it is assumed that the measured data could be plotted on a frequency diagram and that they would form a normal distribution curve. This is called *Normality* in mathematical terms.

This form of data analysis is called *Linear* because it is assumed that the data are, in fact, linearly related. That implies that the line of best fit, the regression line, is a straight line, rather than a curve or other line form. This is called *Linearity* in mathematical terms.

For this experiment, a simple linear regression line for each of the four independent variables, each plotted against the measured values of the evaporation rate from the calibration box, will yield four graphs from which an evaporation rate can be determined. Those four rates can then be averaged to get an approximate evaporation rate over time for the site. For a more accurate value, or if the experimenter wants to develop a continuous evaporation rate analog with constant input from remote data loggers, multiple regression analysis is required.

A simple form of multiple linear regression analysis uses the equations from each of the four independent variable linear regression graphs. The four equations are added together using the measured values for each of the four variables and the sum is then divided by 4. This can be set up in an Excel spreadsheet, or similar data management computer program, to automatically calculate the expected evaporation rate for any set of input variables. This will yield a more precise value for the evaporation rate than a visual readout of the four graphs, but note that the calibration data are not going to include numbers of more than 2 decimal places, so generating an evaporation rate from a calculation to more than 2 decimal places is not valid.

The formula for a multiple linear regression, should the experimenter choose to use it, is:

$$y = \beta_0 + \beta_1 + \beta_1 X_1 + \cdots + \beta_n X_n + \varepsilon$$

where:

y = predicted value of the evaporation rate (the dependent variable)

β_0 = y-intercept (value of y when all other parameters are set to 0 – this will be the sum of the constants when the four linear regression line equations are added together)

$\beta_1 X_1$ = regression coefficient (β_1) of the first independent variable (X_1) (the effect that increasing the value of the independent variable has on the predicted y value)

$\cdots +$ = regression coefficient (β_x) of each of the other independent variables (X_x)

$\beta_n X_n$ = regression coefficient of the last independent variable

ε = model error (how much variation there is in the estimate of y)

To find the best-fit line for each independent variable, multiple linear regression calculates three things:

The regression coefficients that lead to the smallest overall model error.

The t-statistic of the overall model (the coefficient divided by its standard error. The standard error is an estimate of the standard deviation of the coefficient, the amount it varies across cases. It is a measure of the precision with which the regression coefficient is measured).

The associated p-value (how likely it is that the t-statistic would have occurred by chance if the assumption of no relationship between the independent and dependent variables was true).

The model then calculates the t-statistic and p-value for each regression coefficient in the model.

Regardless of which model is used, the value for evaporation rate determined is an instantaneous rate because the data are all instantaneous. To determine a rate over time, multiple calculations are needed over the desired time frame and the sums integrated over that time frame. There are very few absolutes in nature, so being overly precise with the calculation of an approximate value serves no useful end.

Data Collection Sheet Determination of Surface Water Evaporation Rate

Principle Investigator:

Dates of Data Collection:

Date of Analysis: | Page:

Source Water Data

Date/ Time	Water Temperature of Source Water, °C or °F	Average Daily Air Temperature, °C or °F	Average Daily Air Speed, mph or kph	Average Daily Barometric Pressure, Hg or bars

Data Collection Sheet Determination of Surface Water Evaporation Rate

Principal Investigator:	
Dates of Data Collection:	
Date of Analysis:	Page:

Calibration Box Data

Date/ Time	Average Daily Water Temperature, °C or °F	Measured Water Depth, in or mm	Surface Area, ft² or m²	Evaporation Rate Since Start of Study, in/d or m/d

EXPERIMENT 13.5: CHARACTERIZATION OF POND, LAKE, OR STREAM FOAM

Date: _____

Principal Investigator:

    Name: _____

    Email: _____

    Phone: _____

Collaborators:

    Name: _____

    Email: _____

    Phone: _____

    Name: _____

    Email: _____

    Phone: _____

    Name: _____

    Email: _____

    Phone: _____

    Name: _____

    Email: _____

    Phone: _____

    Name: _____

    Email: _____

    Phone: _____

Objective or Question to Be Addressed:
Lakes, ponds, and streams are subject to significant detritus deposition and that debris eventually degrades and decomposes. This organic material is a component of foam that can form over open bodies of water during periods of strong winds or other disturbances. This foam tends to form along shorelines in downwind areas. It can also mimic detergent foam caused by contamination from discharged surfactants. It is often useful to do a physical analysis of the foam to determine the cause, particularly where contamination is suspected or likely. This experiment is designed to determine whether the foam at a specific location is organic protein foam or a detergent foam

from surfactant contaminants. Once that determination is made, a surfactant foam would need to be much more rigorously analyzed for foam components since there are dozens, if not hundreds of different compounds that can cause surfactant foam.

Theory Behind Experiment

Naturally occurring, or organic foams, are usually caused by the die-off and decay of small organic organisms, such as algae or dead leaves and detritus in the water. The decay of those materials releases various organic proteins that can act to break the surface tension of the water, particularly when agitated by currents or winds, and result in a foamy accumulation along shores and banks. Silt and mud in the water can also cause foaming, but that foam is usually a dark or muddy color, as opposed to the whiter (but seldom pure white) color of the detritus foam.

Note that this type of foam is common at wastewater treatment plants, particularly in the aeration basins. It causes some issues with operations if not properly controlled. There the control is to spray the foam with cold water which is usually very effective at destroying the foam bubbles. Wastewater treatment plant foam is usually assumed to be an organic foam rather than a detergent foam unless there is evidence to suggest otherwise.

The following indicators can be used to differentiate a natural foam from a foam due to anthropological impacts. This experiment relies on direct observation of the suspect material, rather than a chemical analysis. Prior to conducting the experiment, students should consider the differences between a quantitative and qualitative experiment.

Characteristics of Foam in Water Bodies

Natural Foam	Anthropological Foam
Natural foams cannot create large bubbles easily, so they tend to have small bubbles that are more uniform in size	Bubbles in surfactant foams often are large and of variable size
Earthy or fishy odor	Perfumed, fragrant, or soapy odor
Light tan or brown color (but may be white or off-white) Tends to begin to turn brown within hours of being formed due to biodegradation of the organic content	Usually retain a bright white color regardless of the color or clarity of the water due to the brighteners used to formulate the surfactant
Light feel; bubbles break down when squeezed between the finger tips Residue does not feel slimy to the touch	Bubbles break down easily Residue feels slimy between squeezed finger tips
Breaks down quickly when not agitated	Persists in the environment, perhaps for days, even when not agitated
Found in an agitated water body in which decay is occurring from dead vegetation or animal matter; typically below rapids, near flow pinch points, at downwind end of long ponds or lakes, or other sources of water agitation	Found downstream of contaminant sources such as paper mills, oil refining facilities, manufacturing facilities, and firefighting activities
Natural foams do not disperse well and tend to stay where they become lodged	Surfactant foams are able to disperse easily, so they often spread out from their source quickly

Data to be collected with an explanation of how they will be collected (Ex.: "Water temperature data for three days using a continuous data logger")
For this experiment, it will be necessary to collect and examine a sample of foam from the location in question. Use of a field microscope or strong hand lens to examine the sample at the point of collection is necessary.

Testing will entail a physical examination and evaluation of the foam for various physical characteristics, consistent with the table of characteristics provided.

Potential Interferences and Interference Management Plan:

A mixture of natural and anthropogenic foams could occur. If this happens, the results of the observations in this experiment will be unclear, at best. Where there is no clear evidence of one form or the other, it will be assumed that there is a mix of foams and an investigation will be considered to determine the source of the anthropologic components.

Tools, Equipment, and Supplies Required:

Field microscope or strong hand lens
6 clean, stainless steel or plastic spatulas
Microscope examination slides

Safety

There are several potential risks associated with this experiment. The first is that shorelines where foam collects tend to be steep, muddy, rocky, and slippery. Slips and falls can occur, and care needs to be taken to avoid those physical hazards during sample collection.

It is not expected that the foam or the source water will be hazardous, but prudence indicates that nitrile or latex gloves be worn during sampling and field testing to minimize risk to the samplers and to minimize potential organic contamination of the samples.

Planned Experimental Procedures and Steps, in Order:

1. Select the site to be sampled and stage the specified equipment for transport to the site. This is a field experiment since the materials may not survive a trip back to the lab.
2. Using a clean spatula, collect a small sample of foam and place it on an examination slide. Examine the sample under the field microscope or hand lens and record the shape, bubble size and other notable characteristics, if any, such as dirt particles or debris trapped inside the foam.
3. Using a clean spatula, collect a second sample and record the nature of the odor, if necessary, waft the sample but do not put directly under your nose.
4. Observe the color of the sample and record this observation. Several samples should be selected from the foam mass to determine the "average" color of the mass.
5. Place a small sample of the bubbles between gloved thumb and first finger and squeeze the sample gently, moving the fingers around a bit to feel the consistency of the material. Record the observations regarding the feel of the material.

6. Observe the location of the foam relative to rapids, flow pinch points, or other sources of agitation and record these observations.
7. Observe the location of the foam relative to potential contaminant sources, such as paper mills, manufacturing plants, restaurants, oil refineries, and similar potential contaminant sources. Record these observations.
8. Observe the behavior of the foam where it intersects with moving water; whether it remains intact or dissipates quickly. Record these observations.

Data Collection Format and Data Collection Sheets Tailored to Experiment:
See attached Data Collection Sheet

Anticipated Outcomes:
Most foam samples found in routine investigations will be organic protein foams. In certain locations, however, it is certainly possible for contamination sources to create detergent foams where none are expected.

It is anticipated that the results will show consistency with the natural foam characteristics described in the table. Absolute consistency is not normal since nature is not that precise in its make-up. There should, however, be an abundance of evidence pointing to a natural form of foam or to an anthropological form.

Data Analysis Plan:
All data will be collected on the Data Collection Sheet as they are developed. Upon completion of the experiment, a review of the data relative to the expected outcomes will be made visually by the investigator(s) to determine the nature of the foam sampled.

Data Collection Sheet Characterization of Pond, Lake, or Stream Foam

Date Collected:

Date Tested:

Principal Investigator:

Source Water:

Test	Results	Expected Results	Variations Noted	Notes
Microscopic analysis		Small bubbles of uniform size		
Sniff test		Slightly earthy or fishy odor		
Color observations		Tan, brown, or off-white color		
Feel of sample when squeezed between the fingertips		Smooth, but not slimy		
Location relative to agitation source		Downstream location		
Location relative to contaminant sources		None		
Dispersal of foam in open-source water		Slow dispersal		

14 Contaminant Removal Experiments

This chapter provides completed designs for example experiments which can be used to demonstrate specific engineering phenomena in a university laboratory or field collection site. They may be used as presented or modified by the user to adapt to other desired outcomes. Sections on actual outcomes and data interpretation are necessarily left blank in these examples. They should be completed by the investigators upon collection of the data.

The experiments in this chapter are:

14.1 Determination of Contaminant Removal Rate
14.2 Technique for Metal Ion Precipitation from Water
14.3 Separation of Liquid Phase Components Through a Distillation Process
14.4 Technique for Potable Water Softening
14.5 Coagulation, Flocculation, and Sedimentation for the Removal of Organic and Inorganic Water Contaminants
14.6 Determination of Granular Media Suitability for Use in Granular Media Filters
14.7 Analysis of Suspended Solids in Water
14.8 Analysis of Total Solids in Water

DOI: 10.1201/9781003184249-14

EXPERIMENT 14.1:   DETERMINATION OF CONTAMINANT REMOVAL RATE

Date: _____

Principal Investigator:

      Name: _____

      Email: _____

      Phone: _____

Collaborators:

      Name: _____

      Email: _____

      Phone: _____

      Name: _____

      Email: _____

      Phone: _____

      Name: _____

      Email: _____

      Phone: _____

      Name: _____

      Email: _____

      Phone: _____

Objective or Question to Be Addressed:

The objective of this experiment is to practice a procedure for determining the reaction rate, k, for the removal of contaminants from water. In this case, a specific coagulant is used to remove hexavalent chromium from water. The concentrations will be quantified using atomic absorption spectrometry (AAS). This experiment is designed to determine the rate at which the contaminant and the coagulant react and settle the target contaminant out of the water.

This experiment is conducted in two distinct phases.

Theory Behind Experiment

Contaminants in water may be removed in a variety of different ways. One of the simplest ways is to add a coagulant, mix the coagulant rapidly into the water, then wait while the coagulant reacts with the target contaminant to form an insoluble compound which settles to the bottom of the reactor. The top layer, or *supernatant*, is drawn off containing a far lower concentration of the target contaminant. The actual final concentration of the contaminant will depend on the nature of the contaminant, coagulant used, water temperature, and reaction rate. The reaction rate, k, is the rate at which the selected coagulant reacts with and coagulates the target contaminant.

Removal of the contaminant by precipitation requires a suitable coagulant. There are many commercially available coagulants that could be tested, but sodium hydroxide should work well for hexavalent and total chromium removal.

The contaminant concentration is determined by AAS. The concept behind AAS is that each element, such as hexavalent chromium in this case, can be made to emit a specific and unique wavelength of detectable light. The amount of light emitted at that wavelength determines the concentration in the sample.

Functionally, the sample is atomized inside the AAS instrument and the characteristic wavelengths of its components are emitted and recorded. They are then excited to cause the electrons of the atoms to move to a higher energy level. The electrons are then allowed to return to their original energy levels and emit light at the characteristic wavelength. The emitted light has a distinct wavelength unique to that element. The presence of that wavelength of light and the intensity of it are used internally by the AAS instrument to determine the presence and concentration of the target contaminant.

Potential Interferences and Interference Management Plan
The water temperature can be an important factor in the reaction rate. This experiment is conducted at room temperature for convenience, but it could also be conducted on water that has been raised in temperature, or lowered in temperature, to get a feel for the effects of temperature on the value of the reaction rate, k.

The coagulant used, sodium hydroxide, is a standard coagulant that can also react with other contaminants besides the chromium. Since the source water is being spiked with chromium at the outset, and because the source water is tap water, it will be assumed that during this experiment the majority of the coagulation reactions will be with the target contaminant, chromium. This assumption may not be valid for a natural source water.

Careful measurement of the actual contaminant concentration over time and careful accounting of the time of measurement are both very important to an accurate calculation of k.

Data to be collected with an explanation of how they will be collected (Ex.: "Water temperature data for three days using a continuous data logger")
Measurements of the concentration of the target contaminant over time will be made using an AAS instrument. The mass of material used to create the standards for calibrating the AAS must be carefully measured and recorded, and the reading of the concentrations during the testing phase must be done quickly since they will continue to change over time. Sampling will be done with a pipette slowly inserted into the reactor so as to minimize the introduction of turbulence during sampling. The testing of that sample must be done rapidly after extraction and the actual time of testing must be carefully noted and recorded. Time will be measured with a stopwatch or clock.

Tools, Equipment, and Supplies Required:
Atomic absorption spectrophotometer

Supply of potassium dichromate
Supply of sodium hydroxide
2 clean 2 L glass beakers
8 clean pipettes each capable of drawing up to 200 mL (6.76 oz)
Stopwatch or smartphone
Magnetic stirrer (or paddle mixer) that can handle a 2 L (1.9 gal) glass beaker

Safety

Hexavalent chromium is a known carcinogen in humans. Ingestion is the primary route of exposure in this experiment. Care must be taken to avoid contact with the mouth during the experiment.

Potassium dichromate and sodium hydroxide are hazardous to human health if ingested or inhaled. Care must be taken to avoid creating dust clouds when collecting potassium dichromate or sodium hydroxide for insertion into the beakers and when handling liquid containing these chemicals.

In the event of accidental ingestion of any quantity, seek medical attention immediately.

In the event of skin contact, rapid washing with warm water and soap is indicated. In the event of eye contact, immediate washing with an eyewash for up to 15 minutes and immediate medical assistance is required.

Use of gloves, face masks, eye protection, and a lab coat are strongly recommended for personal protection.

Planned Experimental Procedures and Steps, in Order:

This experiment includes two parts. The first part is done to verify that the selected coagulant will be effective against the target contaminant. The second phase is to determine the reaction rate of the selected coagulant against the target contaminant.

Phase 1: Verification of Coagulant Efficacy

1. Collect all required equipment and supplies and put on appropriate personal protective equipment.
2. Fill a 2 L glass beaker with distilled water. Add 5 grams (0.1764 oz) potassium dichromate to the beaker and stir with the magnetic stirrer until all of the potassium dichromate is dissolved. This will yield a concentration of slightly less than 1,000 mg/L of hexavalent chromium.
3. Test a sample of the solution in the AAS instrument to determine the actual concentration.
4. Add 200 mg (0.00705 oz) of sodium hydroxide to the solution in the beaker to yield a concentration of approximately 100 mg/L (0.0133 oz/gal). Mix at high speed (300 rpm ±) on the magnetic mixer for 30 seconds and then at slow speed (20 rpm ±) for 15 minutes to allow the coagulant to interact with the chromium.
5. At the end of the mixing phase, turn off the mixer and allow the contents of the beaker to settle for 15 minutes. Collect a sample from the supernatant and test for chromium using the AAS.
6. Determine the efficacy of the selected coagulant based on the reduction in chromium found in the treated sample relative to the original,

untreated, concentration. If the selected coagulant is effective, the concentration after treatment should be significantly lower than the untreated concentration.

Phase 2: Reaction Rate Determination

1. Collect all required equipment and supplies and put on the appropriate personal safety equipment.
2. Prepare a clean 2 L beaker, fill the beaker with 2 L of distilled water measured using a graduated cylinder for accuracy, and then add 5.6574 g (0.19954 oz) of potassium dichromate. Stir on the magnetic stirrer until all of the chemical is dissolved. This should yield a solution with a concentration of 1,000 mg/L of hexavalent chromium. Test a sample of this solution with the AAS to verify the actual concentration.
3. Add 100 mg (0.0035 oz) of sodium hydroxide to the beaker and stir rapidly (300 rpm ±) for 15 seconds, then stir slowly (20 rpm ±) for the remainder of the experiment.
4. Collect samples from the beaker with a clean pipette at the following time intervals, avoiding suspended solids to the maximum extent possible, and test immediately with the AAS to determine the concentration of hexavalent chromium in each sample. Record those concentrations as they are developed and the actual time of sampling.
    Immediately after adding the sodium hydroxide
    1 minute after the rapid mix is stopped
    2 minutes after the rapid mix is stopped
    5 minutes after the rapid mix is stopped
    10 minutes after the rapid mix is stopped
    15 minutes after the rapid mix is stopped
    20 minutes after the rapid mix is stopped
    30 minutes after the rapid mix is stopped
5. Plot the concentration of each sample on the Y-axis and the time of sampling on the X- axis of normal-normal graph paper. Calculate the slope of the curve of best fit for the points plotted. The slope of that line will equal the desired reaction rate, k. If the line of best fit has a distinct curve to it, replot the data with the concentration on a log scale and time on a normal scale to straighten out the line.
6. Dispose of the treated water in accordance with the hazardous waste disposal protocols of the laboratory.

Data Collection Format and Data Collection Sheets Tailored to Experiment:
See attached Data Collection Sheet

Data Analysis Plan:
The data developed in this experiment are concentration data correlated with time data. The time and concentration data are plotted on a normal-normal curve to yield a straight line of best fit. The slope of that line is equal to the reaction rate, k.

Expected Outcomes:

It is expected that the concentration of hexavalent chromium will decline sharply over time and that the reaction rate curve will reflect that. A concentration of 100 mg/L of sodium hydroxide should produce an approximately 80% reduction in the concentration of hexavalent chromium during Phase 1.

Data Collection Sheet for Determination of Contaminant Removal Rate		
		Data
Verification phase		
	Initial Cr(VI) concentration, mg/L	
	Added sodium hydroxide, mg/L	
	Final Cr(VI) concentration, mg/L	
Rate determination phase		
	Initial Cr(VI) concentration, mg/L	
	Conc. after 1 minute	
	Conc. after 2 minutes	
	Conc. after 5 minutes	
	Conc. after 10 minutes	
	Conc. after 15 minutes	
	Conc. after 20 minutes	
	Conc. after 30 minutes	
Calculation of slope of line and reaction rate		

EXPERIMENT 14.2:   TECHNIQUE FOR METAL ION PRECIPITATION FROM WATER

Date: _____

Principal Investigator:

        Name: _____

        Email: _____

        Phone: _____

Collaborators:

        Name: _____

        Email: _____

        Phone: _____

        Name: _____

        Email: _____

        Phone: _____

        Name: _____

        Email: _____

        Phone: _____

        Name: _____

        Email: _____

        Phone: _____

Objective or Question to Be Addressed:

Industrial and manufacturing operations can produce a variety of wastewaters which may contain contaminants, such as dissolved metals. The treatment of those wastewaters often includes the reduction of the dissolved metal content prior to discharge. A convenient way to do that is often through the use of pH control. By increasing (and occasionally decreasing) the pH of the wastewater, specific metal ions can be made to drop out as part of a concentrated sludge. If the wastewater is treated at appropriate locations throughout the manufacturing or industrial process, high-cost metals can be recovered and reused after appropriate reconcentration and purification.

For example, in the metal plating and printed circuit board industries, it is often necessary to dissolve specific metal ions in an aqueous solution of a carrier fluid and the desired metal ions. By then introducing this solution to the material to be plated or printed on, and changing one characteristic of the solution, the metal ions will plate out of solution and coat the target material. This dissolution of the metal ions is usually pH dependent, and adjustment of the pH of the solution can raise or lower the rate of deposition of the ions onto the target material.

The objective of this experiment is to examine the ways in which modification of pH affects the ability of certain inorganic materials to dissolve or precipitate into or out of an aqueous solution.

Theory Behind Experiment

The metals of common interest in industrial wastewater treatment include copper, zinc, aluminum, calcium, manganese, iron, chromium, and lead. These metals are ionic when in solution, and they can usually be precipitated by adding a counter ion to the solution which also changes the pH. Typically, the higher the pH goes, the greater the concentration reduction in the target ion, although this is not universally true with some of the precipitates of certain metals and specific counter ions.

Normally, sodium hydroxide is used to raise the pH and to form an insoluble metal hydroxide with the target metals. For ions that do not respond well or sufficiently to sodium hydroxide, other chemicals, such as sulfides, may be used. However, metal hydroxides tend to be amphoteric, which means that their solubility increases at both low and high pH values in the solution. The optimum pH for precipitation, which is also the pH of minimum solubility, occurs at a different pH value for every metal. Thus, at the pH at which one metal hydroxide concentration may be minimized, the concentration of another may be relatively high. In addition, sequestering agents, bath additives, cleaners, and electrolysis formulations can interfere with the hydroxide precipitation. Changing the pH slightly may change the rate at which various metal hydroxides precipitate, and the treatment plant operator could spend a lot of time chasing ions unless the process is batched so that the hydroxides that precipitate first are removed before the pH is adjusted again.

Sometimes, the target metals form chelates within the solution. A chelate is a compound which contains a ligand (typically organic) bonded to a central metal atom at two or more points. They tend to be insoluble over a very large pH range and are difficult to precipitate. Various other things known as sequestering agents can be present which chelate one or more of the target metal ions and form a stable complex that does not decompose over a prolonged processing time period. Various chemical supply firms have developed proprietary "Chelate-Breakers" that will separate the chelated compounds and allow precipitation of the target metals. These are often sulfide-based compounds.

The process of pH precipitation follows standard chemical reaction kinetics, such as the following generalized formula.

$$Me_n + Ca(OH)_2 \Leftrightarrow Me(OH)_n \downarrow + Ca_2^+$$

where:

Me_n = target metal
$Ca(OH)_2$ = added chemical to adjust the pH
$Me(OH)_n$ = metal precipitate
Ca_2^+ = left over calcium ion in the solution

Down arrow indicates the precipitate falling out of solution

Sulfide precipitation is an alternative for the removal of certain metals. The removal efficiency of sulfide precipitation is often superior to the hydroxide method. A disadvantage of using sulfide is control of the optimal dosage. Unlike with hydroxide precipitation, which uses simple pH control, the optimization of sulfide addition in the field can be difficult when the concentration of the target metal varies significantly or frequently. Insufficient sulfide can lead to high target metal concentrations in the effluent, while too much sulfide can result in excessive residual sulfide and a hydrogen sulfide odor problem. Sulfide precipitation is generally carried out at a neutral pH in order to minimize this problem.

When sulfide precipitation is used, the formula has the following look.

$$Me_n^+ + S_{2-} \Leftrightarrow Me_nS$$

where:
   Me_n = target metal
   S_2^- = added sulfide
   Me_{nS} = precipitate

Carbonate precipitation can be an effective treatment alternative to hydroxide precipitation for specific metals. Carbonate precipitation uses sodium carbonate (soda ash) or calcium carbonate as the precipitating agent which forms basic carbonates as the precipitate, in accordance with the following generalized equations.

$$Me^{n+} + nNaCO_3 = nMeCO_3 + nNa^+$$

$$nMeCO_3 + H_2O = CO_2 \uparrow + (MeOH)_n CO_3$$

where:
   Me_n = target metal
   $nNaCO_3$ = sodium carbonate added
   $nMeCO_3$ = first stage metal carbonate formation
   nNa^+ = amount of sodium released from the sodium carbonate
   H_2O = water added or present
   CO_2 = released carbon dioxide gas
   $(MeOH)_nCO_3$ = metal carbonate that is converted to a hydroxide combined
        with additional carbonate to precipitate

The carbon dioxide released can cause gas bubbles to attach to the precipitate particles and float them to the surface in the sedimentation tanks.

Sodium hydroxide is also used to precipitate other inorganic compounds from wastewater. For example, hardness, which is a measure of the iron and manganese concentrations, is reduced by adding lime (sodium hydroxide) to the water. The precipitates create increased sludge volumes, which can be difficult to dewater, but they also do reduce the hardness considerably.

Ferric compounds, such as ferric chloride, are generally used to reduce organic compounds in water through a similar process of precipitation.

Note that with all of these processes, a very fine floc (*pin floc*) is created as the dissolved targets become insoluble particles. There is then a time lag of up to 30–60 minutes of slow stirring needed to coagulate the pin floc into a large enough floc to actually settle out and then a period of an hour or more of quiescent settling is needed to properly settle the larger floc before treatment is complete.

Data to be collected with an explanation of how they will be collected (Ex.: "Water temperature data for three days using a continuous data logger")
This experiment demonstrates the change in concentration of copper in a copper sulfate solution, resulting from the precipitation of copper from the copper sulfate solution by changing the pH of the solution. Data to be collected and recorded are the following.

> pH of distilled and deionized water being used to create the initial copper sulfate solution
> pH of sulfuric acid solution
> pH of sodium hydroxide solution
> pH of five separate treated copper sulfate solution aliquots
> Cu concentration of initial copper sulfate solution
> Cu concentration of each of five treated and filtered copper sulfate solution aliquots

Potential Interferences and Interference Management Plan:
The use of distilled and deionized water as a base for this experiment is intended to minimize the potential for interferences in the results. The temperature of the solutions is expected to be essentially equal and at room temperature during the experiment. Changes in the temperature of the solutions can affect the rate of precipitation of the metal, but a few degrees one way or the other around room temperature are not expected to significantly alter the results of this experiment. If a precise mass of copper needs to be precipitated, both the pH and the temperature of the metal solution would be carefully controlled.

Tools, Equipment, and Supplies Required:
> 2 L (0.52 gal) distilled and deionized water
> 5 N sulfuric acid, laboratory grade
> Sodium hydroxide, laboratory grade
> Copper sulfate, laboratory grade
> 2 clean 10 mL (0.34 oz) pipettes
> Analytical balance
> Weighing boats for the balance
> Two clean stainless steel or plastic spatulas
> Three 2 L (0.52 gal) clean glass beakers
> Five 250 mL (8.5 oz) clean glass beakers

Five 250 mL (8.5 oz) clean glass filtering flasks

Five filter cones with stoppers sized for the mouth of the 250 mL (8.5 oz) glass
   filtering flasks

Filter paper sized for the filter cones

200 mL (6.8 oz) graduated cylinder

Atomic absorption spectrophotometer (AAS)

Fume hood with a positive fume exhaust system

Stirring plate with speed adjustment controls set at a low speed

pH meter with clean probe

Vacuum pump to fit the filtering flasks, with appropriate hoses

Safety

This experiment utilizes concentrated sulfuric acid and concentrated sodium hydroxide solutions. Both are highly caustic. Rubber or latex gloves, eye goggles, and a lab
coat are required when handling these materials. There is also a slight chance of
vaporization of the acid during addition to the distilled and deionized water. This procedure must be conducted inside a fume hood with an operating fume exhaust system.

All solutions are considered hazardous waste at the conclusion of the experiment,
and all liquids must be disposed in accordance with laboratory hazardous waste disposal protocols.

In the event of contact by acids or bases with the skin, immediately wash the area
with warm water and soap. If redness or pain persists, or in the event of open skin
wounds caused by the exposure, medical attention is warranted. In the event of contact with the eyes, immediately wash for up to 20 minutes in an eye wash station or
until medical help can be summoned. Medical attention is required for eye contact
with these materials.

Planned Experimental Procedures and Steps, in Order:

1. Assemble all equipment and supplies for easy access and put on appropriate
   personal protection equipment.
2. Carefully measure out exactly 1 L (0.26 gal) of distilled and deionized water
   and place it into a clean, 2 L (0.52 gal) glass beaker and place the beaker
   inside the fume hood on top of a stirring mixer set at slow speed.
3. Measure and record the pH of the distilled and deionized water.
4. Slowly and carefully, using a clean pipette, add 5 N sulfuric acid (drop by
   drop) to the water in the beaker. Add acid while constantly monitoring the
   pH of the solution until the pH meter indicates that the solution has reached
   a pH of 2.0.
5. In a separate, clean, 2 L (0.52 gal) glass beaker, dissolve exactly 1 g (0.035
   oz) of copper sulfate in exactly 1 L (0.26 gal) of distilled and deionized
   water to yield a 1,000 mg/L (1.35 oz/gal) copper sulfate solution.
6. Measure and record the pH of this solution.
7. Analyze this solution for copper concentration using the AAS following the
   directions of the spectrometer manufacturer and record this concentration.

8. In a separate 2 L (0.52 gal) glass beaker, dissolve 1 g (0.035 oz) of sodium hydroxide in 1 L (0.26 gal) of distilled and deionized water to yield a 1,000 mg/L (1.35 oz/gal) sodium hydroxide solution.

9. Measure and record the pH of this solution.

10. Using a graduated cylinder, divide the 1 L (0.26 gal) of copper sulfate solution into five separate 200 mL (6.8 oz) samples with each sample placed into a separate, clean, 250 mL (8.5 oz) glass flask.

11. Label the first flask as "pH 2, Cu" and set it aside.

12. Slowly and carefully add sodium hydroxide solution to the second 250 mL (8.5 oz) flask, constantly monitoring the pH of the solution with the pH meter, until the pH reaches 6.0. Label this flask as "pH 6.0, Cu" and set it aside.

13. Slowly and carefully add sodium hydroxide solution to the third 250 mL (8.5 oz) flask, constantly monitoring the pH of the solution with the pH meter, until the pH reaches 8.0. Label this flask as "pH 8.0, Cu" and set it aside.

14. Slowly and carefully add sodium hydroxide solution to the fourth 250 mL (8.5 oz) flask, constantly monitoring the pH of the solution with the pH meter, until the pH reaches 10.0. Label this flask as "pH 10.0, Cu" and set it aside.

15. Slowly and carefully add sodium hydroxide solution to the fifth 250 mL (8.5 oz) flask, constantly monitoring the pH of the solution with the pH meter, until the pH reaches 12.0. Label this flask as "pH 12.0, Cu" and set it aside.

16. Insert a filter paper into each of five filter cones and set a cone securely into the top of each 250 mL (8.5 oz) clean glass filtering flask.

17. Filter each of the 200 mL (6.8 oz) samples previously created and labeled through a separate, clean, filter into a separate clean 250 mL (8.5 oz) glass flask.

18. Analyze each of the five filtered samples for Cu concentration using the AAS following the procedure specified by the spectrophotometer manufacturer and record each value found.

19. Compare the results of the concentration of copper resulting from the change in pH of the samples and prepare a graph showing the expected results from variable pH values.

20. Dispose of all solids and liquids generated from this experiment as hazardous waste in accordance with laboratory hazardous waste disposal protocols.

Data Collection Format and Data Collection Sheets Tailored to Experiment:
See attached Data Collection Sheet

Anticipated Outcomes:
It is expected that the copper concentration will be the highest in the sample labeled "pH 2.0, Cu". The actual concentration, as measured by the spectrophotometer, should be verified with a calculation of the expected concentration based on the mass

of copper sulfate added to the distilled and deionized water. Thereafter, the concentration of copper should decrease with increasing pH. This decrease is not expected to be linear because the rate of precipitation is often a function of the concentration and a linear increase in the pH is not likely to yield an equivalent linearity in the Cu concentration.

Data Analysis Plan:
The data from this experiment will yield a curve of Cu concentration versus pH of the solution. A review of a graph of these outputs will yield an understanding of the role of pH in the precipitation of inorganic compounds from water. This concept is not directly transferrable to precipitation by other chemical adjustment techniques but does suggest ways to cause the precipitation of things such as iron and magnesium from hard water samples to reduce the hardness of a water supply, for example. The optimal concentration of copper reduction as a function of pH should be researched and compared to the results obtained from this experiment.

Data Collection Sheet for Technique for Metal Ion Precipitation from Water

Date Samples Collected:

Date Samples Tested:

Principal Investigator:

Material Being Tested	Distilled and Deionized Water	Copper Sulfate Solution	Sodium Hydroxide Solution	pH 2.0, Cu	pH 6.0, Cu	pH 8.0, Cu	pH 10.0, Cu	pH 12.0, Cu
pH of prepared solution								
Cu concentration of prepared solution								
Cu concentration of filtered solution								

EXPERIMENT 14.3:   SEPARATION OF LIQUID PHASE COMPONENTS THROUGH A DISTILLATION PROCESS

Date: _____

Principal Investigator:

Name: _____

Email: _____

Phone: _____

Collaborators:

Name: _____

Email: _____

Phone: _____

Name: _____

Email: _____

Phone: _____

Name: _____

Email: _____

Phone: _____

Name: _____

Email: _____

Phone: _____

Objective or Question to Be Addressed:
The objective of this experiment is to demonstrate the concept of liquid/liquid separation using a distillation process. Mixed liquids may be fractionally separated on the basis of the volatility of the various components. Once vaporized, the independent liquid fractions can be condensed back into a more pure liquid form. Multiple sequential distillation steps can often be used to purify a sample to a very high degree of purity. This experiment does not get to the very pure distillate fractions.

Theory Behind Experiment
Distillation is a widely used process in industrial and manufacturing facilities to separate liquids with different boiling points. When the boiling points are very close

to each other, or a very high degree of purity is required in the distillate, a fractionating process is used, rather than simple distillation.

Functionally, the mixed liquids are heated slowly to a very precise temperature at which the first of the desired components begins to boil. In some cases, the "boiling" can be achieved by reducing the pressure in the liquid vessel, or by doing both heating and pressure reduction. "Boiling" occurs when the vapor pressure of the target liquid exceeds the surface tension of the mixed liquid and vaporizes into the air space above the mixed liquid. The more volatile components of the mixed liquids will volatilize at lower temperatures or pressures than less volatile ones. By carefully controlling the temperature of the mixed liquid at exactly the vaporization temperature of each component in order, from the most volatile to the least, separation of the various components can be achieved. The vapors generated are captured in a condenser, rapidly cooled to below the vaporization temperature, and collected as condensed liquids in a relatively pure form. If more than one component is desired, it is theoretically possible to continue to heat the liquid after the first component has boiled off, redirect the condensate to a second or third receiving vessel, and continue to separate various components from each other.

In the simplest demonstration of this phenomenon, the separation of a single volatile fraction, acetone for example, from a solution of the acetone in water, can recover a significant fraction of the acetone from the solution, leaving the nearly pure water behind. The greater the temperature difference between the vaporization temperatures, the greater the percentage of acetone capture will be and the purer both the recovered acetone and resulting water will be.

In the simple distillation process, a single distillation vessel is heated. The vapors resulting from the heating are captured in a condenser, and the condensed vapors are collected in a collection vessel. The purity of both products depends on the control of the temperatures in the distillation vessel and the condenser. When more than one component is desired, or it is desirable for the process to continue for extended periods of time, a fractionating column is used to cool the vapors in stages allowing a continuous operation of the system with multiple distillates being condensed into separate collection vessels.

Data to be collected with an explanation of how they will be collected (Ex.: "Water temperature data for three days using a continuous data logger")

The following measurements are to be made and recorded.

Weight of the empty distillation and receiving flasks used during the experiment

Weight of the distillation flask with distilled water added

Weight of the distillation flask with distilled water and acetone added

Weight of the distillation and receiving flasks after distillation of the acetone

Temperature of the mixed liquid at multiple times during the experiment using a thermometer inserted into the top of the distillation column

Mass of water in the distillation flask, the mass of acetone added to the distillation flask, the mass of acetone collected in the receiving flask, and the mass of water and remaining acetone in the distillation flask at the end of distillation

Percent recovery of the acetone from the distillation flask by this process

Potential Interferences and Interference Management Plan:
The water used in this experiment is designated as distilled, but it is not necessarily deionized. Any inorganic ions in the water could react with the acetone to delay or accelerate the distillation of the acetone through the column. If the temperature of the mixed liquid stabilizes at approximately 58°C (137°F), it will be assumed that there are no interfering compounds in the distilled water. If the stabilization temperature varies significantly from this value, it will be assumed that some interference has occurred and a repeat of the experiment using distilled and deionized water is recommended, although the educational value of the technique demonstration will not be diminished by such an event.

In spite of the fact that the water does not boil below 212°F (100°C), some water will vaporize at the boiling temperature of acetone and may condense out along with the acetone into the receiving flask. This contamination is not expected to be significant, but the mass of the water and remaining acetone in the distillation flask added to the mass of the acetone collected in the receiving flask should equal the original mass of water and acetone in the distillation flask prior to heating. Moreover, the mass remaining in the distillation flask should be no less than the mass of water originally placed in the distillation flask. If the sum of the masses do not add up properly, or if the mass of liquid remaining in the distillation flask after the heat rises above 58°C (137°F), some losses may have occurred and adjustments to the percent recovery may need to be made.

Tools, Equipment, and Supplies Required:
  Distillation column
  Distillation condenser
  1,000 mL (0.26 gal) clean distillation flask
  1,000 mL (0.26 gal) clean receiving flask
  Scale large enough to hold the 1,000 mL flasks and to record weights in milligrams (0.0005 lb)
  Hot plate of sufficient size to hold the 1,000 mL (0.26 gal) distillation flask and to support the distillation column above it and capable of heating to 80°C (176°F)
  Associated clean glass or plastic tubing for transport of the vapors of water and acetone from the heating flask to the distillation column and through the condenser to a collection flask
  Ring stand of sufficient size to hold the distillation column
  Ring stand of sufficient size to hold the condenser above the collection flask
  Constant supply of cold running water to cool the condenser during the experiment
  Fume hood of sufficient size to accommodate the experimental set-up with an active fume collection and removal system

Safety
This experiment utilizes heat to raise the temperature of a mixture of distilled water and acetone to a temperature greater than 58°C (137°F). A distillation column is suspended above the distillation flask and is connected to a condenser through which

cold water is circulated. A 1,000 mL (0.26 gal) receiving flask is situated to collect the condensed liquid that forms in the condenser.

The hot plate, all the glassware, and any connecting tubing will become very hot during the conduct of this experiment. All components should be handled only with heat-resistant gloves once the hot plate has been turned on. Note that the equipment will not cool quickly after the hot plate is turned off and that all components should be considered very hot until proven otherwise.

Acetone vapors can be hazardous to human health and should not be breathed in. Accordingly, this experiment must be conducted inside a fume hood with an active fume collection and exhaust system operating during the experiment.

Planned Experimental Procedures and Steps, in Order:

1. Carefully calibrate the thermometer to be used by placing it in an ice bath of distilled water. Once the thermometer has reached equilibrium, record the actual temperature and then move the thermometer to a beaker of boiling distilled water. When the thermometer has reached equilibrium again, record the actual temperature. If the high temperature and low temperature are both within 2°F (1°C) of the expected temperature, the thermometer should work well for the experiment. If this is not the case, a different thermometer is recommended.

2. Carefully weigh the two flasks and record the weights to the nearest mg (0.0005 lb).

3. Measure 500 mL (0.13 gal) of distilled water into the 1,000 mL (0.26 gal) distillation flask.

4. Weigh the flask with the water and record the mass of the filled flask, then calculate the mass of water added, by subtracting the mass of the flask, and record that value.

5. Add 50 mL (1.7 oz) of acetone to the water in the distillation flask, weigh the flask with the water and acetone, and record that value, then calculate the mass of acetone in the water by subtracting the mass of the flask and water and record that value.

6. Place the 1,000 mL (0.26 gal) distillation flask with the water and acetone on the hot plate; connect the condenser column to the mouth of the flask, the collection flask to the end of the condenser, and a water supply to the inlet and outlet of the condenser; and insert the thermometer into the top of the distillation flask.

7. Turn on the hot plate to high and record the time that event occurs.

8. Immediately turn on the water supply to the condenser.

9. Monitor the temperature in the column until it reaches 58°C (137°F) and record the time at which that occurs.

10. When the temperature in the column starts to rise above 58°C (137°F), immediately turn off the hot plate, and carefully remove the column from the mouth of the distillation flask. *The column and the flask will be very hot.* Record the time this occurs.

11. Turn off the water supply to the condenser and disassemble the condenser from the receiving flask.

12. Weigh and record the weight of the 1,000 mL (0.26 gal) distillation flask with the remaining liquid and the 1,000 mL (0.26 gal) receiving flask with the recovered acetone.

13. Calculate the mass of the recovered acetone in the receiving flask and the mass of the water remaining with any remaining acetone in the distillation flask and record those values.

14. Calculate and record the effectiveness of the distillation process in separating the acetone from the water based on the mass of residual acetone in the water remaining in the distillation flask and the mass of acetone collected in the receiving flask.

15. Dispose of the heated water, after allowing it to cool appropriately, and the collected acetone as hazardous liquid waste in accordance with the hazardous waste disposal protocols of the laboratory.

Data Collection Format and Data Collection Sheets Tailored to Experiment:
See attached Data Collection Sheet

Anticipated Outcomes:
Pure acetone boils and vaporizes at 58°C (137°F) under standard temperature and pressure conditions. It is expected that this experiment will approximate those conditions in the laboratory. Consequently, it is expected that the temperature of the vapors will rise from room temperature to approximately 58°C (137°F) and stabilize at that temperature for several minutes. As soon as the acetone is boiled off, the temperature will begin to rise again until it reaches 100°C (212°F), the boiling temperature of the water. Ideally, a 100% recovery of the acetone will occur. The ideal is unlikely, but a recovery close to that value is expected.

Data Analysis Plan:
The data collected should provide sufficient information to determine the boiling temperature of the mixture being distilled and the percentage recovery of the acetone from the mixture.

Data Collection Sheet for Evaluation of Separation of Liquid Phase Components through a Distillation Process

Date Samples Collected:

Date Samples Tested:

Principal Investigator:

Component or Characteristic	Value	Component or Characteristic	Value
Weight of 1,000 mL distillation flask, empty (g)		Time when mixture reaches 58°C	
Weight of 1,000 mL collection flask, empty (g)		Time when temperature starts to rise above 58°C	
Weight of 1000 mL distillation flask with water added (g)		Weight of 1,000 mL distillation flask after distillation (g)	
Calculated mass of water added (g)		Mass of water remaining in distillation flask after distillation (g)	
Weight of 1,000 mL distillation flask with water and acetone added (kg)		Weight of 1,000 mL collection flask with acetone after distillation (g)	
Calculated mass of acetone added (g)		Mass of acetone collected in collection flask (g)	
Initial temperature of mixture (°C)		Percent recovery of acetone through this process (%)	
Time that heating pad is turned on			

EXPERIMENT 14.4: TECHNIQUE FOR POTABLE WATER SOFTENING

Date: _____

Principal Investigator:

>   Name: _____

>   Email: _____

>   Phone: _____

Collaborators:

>   Name: _____

>   Email: _____

>   Phone: _____

>   Name: _____

>   Email: _____

>   Phone: _____

>   Name: _____

>   Email: _____

>   Phone: _____

>   Name: _____

>   Email: _____

>   Phone: _____

>   Name: _____

>   Email: _____

>   Phone: _____

Objective or Question to Be Addressed:
This experiment is designed to observe the effects of adding chemicals to hard water to soften the water for public use.

Theory Behind Experiment
Hard water is generally considered to be water that is naturally high in metallic ions, most commonly calcium and magnesium, and sometimes iron. These contaminants, at high concentrations, can cause discoloration of laundry, cause deposition of rust or black colored rings around toilet bowls and bath tubs, and present unpleasant tastes to humans using that water for domestic purposes, along with various industrial process problems associated with scaling. Softening of the water removes the

objectionable ions to a sufficient degree as to eliminate the negative consequences of the water uses. Hardness in water is generally defined as the concentration of multi-valent cations, which are metal ions with an electrical charge greater than 1+ (mainly 2+). These cations include Ca^{2+} and Mg^{2+} among others at lesser concentrations, such as iron in the form of Fe^{2+}, and it is the presence of these ions in the water that make it difficult for products with other positively charged ions, such as laundry detergents and cleaners, to dissolve in the water.

Hardness can be in the form of *carbonate hardness*, which is the most common and includes generally CO_2, $Ca(HCO_3)_2$, $Mg(HCO_3)_2$, and $MgCO_3$ or *noncarbonate hardness*, typically in the form of $CaSO_4$ and $MgSO_4$.

Water softening is the process of removing the ions of calcium and magnesium by precipitation with an ion exchange compound. The ion exchange process is done through the addition of a chemical to the hard water, typically lime $(Ca(OH)_2)$ and soda ash (Na_2CO_3), designed to form insoluble compounds with the objectionable ions and then settle the insoluble compounds out of the solution as a precipitate. pH adjustment may be needed after removal of the precipitate to avoid negative taste and other consequences of the bonding agent. Lime will do most of the work, but when the magnesium is in the form of a magnesium sulfate $(MgSO_4)$, instead of a magnesium carbonate $(MgCO_3)$, soda ash will be needed to effectively remove the magnesium ions.

Lime $(Ca(OH)_2)$ is an inorganic mineral composed primarily of oxides, and hydroxide, usually calcium oxide, calcium hydroxide, or both. Various other oxides and hydroxides may be present in varying concentrations depending on the source of the lime. Lime is generally derived from limestone and primarily consists of calcium carbonate. The raw ore is burned in a lime kiln, a process known as *calcination*, which converts the ore into calcium oxide, a caustic material known as *burnt lime, unslaked lime, or quick-lime*. The subsequent addition of water converts the calcium oxide into the less caustic calcium hydroxide form known as *slaked lime* or *hydrated lime* $(Ca(OH)_2)$. Slaked lime is far less caustic than unslaked lime but is still sufficiently alkaline to serve its purpose in water softening, which is essential for the removal of carbonate hardness from the water. Soda ash is sodium carbonate (Na_2CO_3) and its various hydrates. All forms are white, water-soluble salts that yield moderately alkaline solutions in water.

The chemical equations for lime addition for carbonate hardness removal are as follows.

$$CO_2 + Ca(OH)_2 => CaCO_3 + H_2O$$
$$Ca(HCO_3)_2 + Ca(OH)_2 => 2CaCO_3 + 2H_2O$$
$$Mg(HCO_3)_2 + Ca(OH)_2 => CaCO_3 + MgCO_3 + 2H_2O$$
$$MgCO_3 + Ca(OH)_2 => CaCO_3 + Mg(OH)_2$$

where:
 CO_2 = carbon dioxide
 $Ca(OH)_2$ = calcium hydroxide or hydrated lime
 $CaCO_3$ = calcium carbonate
 $Ca(HCO_3)_2$ = calcium bicarbonate

$Mg(HCO_3)_2$ = magnesium bicarbonate
$MgCO_3$ = magnesium carbonate
$Mg(OH)_2$ = magnesium hydroxide
H_2O = water

The CO_2 does not actually contribute to the hardness, but it does react with the lime and therefore uses up some lime before the lime can start removing the hardness.

The chemical reactions associated with noncarbonate hardness removal with soda ash are the following.

$$MgSO_4 + Ca(OH)_2 => Mg(OH)_2 + CaSO_4$$
$$CaSO_4 + Na_2CO_3 => CaCO_3 + Na_2SO_4$$

where:
Ca(OH)$_2$ = calcium hydroxide or hydrated lime
CaCO$_3$ = calcium carbonate
Mg(OH)$_2$ = magnesium hydroxide
MgSO$_4$ = magnesium sulfate
CaSO$_4$ = calcium sulfate
Na$_2$SO$_4$ = sodium sulfate
Na$_2$CO$_3$ = sodium carbonate or soda ash

For the purpose of water treatment, hardness is measured in milligrams per liter (mg/L) or the equivalent designation of parts per million (ppm). Occasionally, grains per gallon (gpg) is used. Grains per gallon is defined as one grain (64.8 mg) of calcium carbonate ($CaCO_3$) per gallon (3.785 l) of water (equivalent to 17.1 mg/L). Parts per million is defined as one milligram of calcium carbonate ($CaCO_3$) per liter of water. 1 gpg = 17.1 ppm = 1 mg/L.

One mole of calcium carbonate hardness is removed by one mole of added lime. One mole of magnesium carbonate hardness is removed by two moles of added lime. One mole of non-carbonate calcium hardness or one mole of non-carbonate magnesium hardness is removed by one mole of added soda ash.

When water has minimal magnesium hardness and only calcium needs to be removed, sufficient lime and soda ash are added to the water to raise the pH to between 10.3 and 10.6. When magnesium hardness exceeds about 40 mg/L as $CaCO_3$, magnesium hydroxide scale deposits become problematic. In that case, additional lime is added to raise the pH above 10.6 to precipitate the magnesium hydroxide.

Water containing high amounts of magnesium hardness is often treated with a split treatment concept. With this approach, approximately 80% of the water is treated with excess lime to raise the pH above 11. Then the treated portion is blended with 20% of the untreated source water. Split treatment tends to reduce the amount of carbon dioxide required to recarbonate the water as well as reduce the amount of lime required. The treated water will contain excess lime, and the magnesium is almost completely removed from this treated portion. When this water is mixed with the untreated source water, the carbon dioxide and bicarbonate in that water recarbonate the final blend.

There are two methods for calculating lime and soda ash dosages that are generally recognized. The first is the conversion factor method which is simpler, quicker, and more practical for daily operations. The second is referred to as the conventional dosage method. This method takes considerably longer to conduct but can be much more helpful in understanding the chemical and mathematical relationships involved in the softening process. Regardless of the method used, lime and soda ash dosages depend on the relative magnitudes of the carbonate and noncarbonate hardness in the water.

As noted at the beginning of this experiment design, lime is used to remove carbonate harness, and both lime and soda ash are used to remove non-carbonate hardness. If total hardness is less than or equal to total alkalinity, there is no non-carbonate hardness (only carbonate hardness). If total hardness is greater than total alkalinity, non-carbonate hardness equals the difference between total hardness and total alkalinity (and carbonate hardness equals total alkalinity).

If total hardness is equal to or less than total alkalinity, then the lime dosage is based on the concentrations of the various components, as follows.

$$\text{Lime Dosage} = CO_2 + \text{Total Hardness} + Mg + \text{Excess}$$

where:
Lime dosage = required amount of lime, mg/L (lb/million gallons)
CO_2 = carbon dioxide concentration, mg/L (lb/million gallons)
Total hardness = sum of metallic ion concentrations as determined by a total hardness test, mg/L (lb/million gallons)
Mg = concentration of magnesium in the water, mg/L (lb/million gallons)
Excess = amount determined by the user that is to be added in addition to the calculated amount to ensure complete removal of the hardness, mg/L (lb/million gallons)

Note: 1 mg/L = 8.3454 lb/million gallons

If soda ash is required due to the presence of non-carbonate hardness, the amount of soda ash to add is calculated as follows.

$$\text{Soda ash dosage} = CaCO_3 \times 1.06$$

where:
Soda ash dosage = amount of Na_2CO_3 to be added, mg/L (lb/million gallons)
$CaCO_3$ = non-carbonate hardness concentration equivalent as $CaCO_3$, mg/L (lb/million gallons)
1.06 = conversion factor to convert moles of soda ash to moles of non-carbonate hardness to be removed

Note that hardness removal generally leaves the treated water at a pH of around 10. To return the pH to an acceptable range (between 6.5 and 8.0, generally), carbon dioxide is added to create a carbonic acid in the water that will neutralize the alkalinity causing the high pH.

The amount of CO_2 to add back is estimated as follows.

$$CO_2 = \left[Ca(OH)_2 \times 0.59 \right] + \left[Mg(OH)_2 \times 0.75 \right]$$

where:
    CO_2 = amount of CO_2 to be added, mg/L (lb/million gallons)
    $Ca(OH)_2$ = concentration of $Ca(OH)_2$, mg/L (lb/million gallons)
    $Mg(OH)_2$ = concentration of $Mg(OH)_2$, mg/L (lb/million gallons)
    0.59 and 0.75 = constants to convert moles of CO_2 to moles of alkalinity

Data to be collected with an explanation of how they will be collected (Ex.: "Water temperature data for three days using a continuous data logger")
The concentration of calcium carbonate ($CaCO_3$), calcium bicarbonate ($Ca(HCO_3)_2$), carbon dioxide (CO_2), magnesium carbonate ($MgCO_3$), magnesium sulfate ($MgSO_4$), sodium carbonate (Na_2CO_3), sodium sulfate (Na_2SO_4), total hardness, total alkalinity, and pH will be measured at the start of the procedure to establish a baseline. The values can be calculated from mass balance calculations, if desired, but direct measurement is simpler and more commonly used. Those same values will be measured after treatment of the water per the instructions to determine end values. A graph of results showing the hardness reduction as a function of lime dosage, and lime and soda ash dosage will then be made to determine the optimum dosages for this water. Calculations will then be made to determine the carbon dioxide dose needed at the optimum lime and soda ash dosages to restore the pH of the water after treatment.

Tools, Equipment, and Supplies Required:
    6 L of distilled and deionized water
    6 clean 2L beakers
    Direct read probes or necessary test equipment and materials to test the water
        for the concentration of:

- Calcium carbonate ($CaCO_3$)
- Calcium bicarbonate ($Ca(HCO_3)_2$)
- Carbon dioxide (CO_2)
- Magnesium carbonate ($MgCO_3$)
- Magnesium sulfate ($MgSO_4$)
- Sodium carbonate (Na_2CO_3)
- Sodium sulfate (Na_2SO_4)
- Total hardness
- Total alkalinity
- pH

Safety
Chemicals used to test the water for the various components listed are toxic. Gloves should be worn when handling these materials, and care should be taken to avoid accidental ingestion. Eye protection is required to avoid contacting the eyes with

chemical dust or residuals. A lab coat is required to avoid stains or contamination of personal clothing.

In the event of exposure to skin, immediately washing with warm water is recommended. For contact with eyes, immediate flushing at an eye wash station for 15 minutes and immediate medical attention are recommended.

Planned Experimental Procedures and Steps, in Order:

1. Gather all materials and supplies and put on personal protective equipment.
2. Add 1 L (1.057 qt) of distilled and deionized water to each of the six beakers.
3. Add 20 mg (0.00071 oz) of calcium bicarbonate ($Ca(HCO_3)_2$), 20 mg (0.00071 oz) of magnesium bicarbonate ($Mg(HCO_3)_2$), and 20 mg (0.00071 oz) of magnesium sulfate ($MgSO_4$) to each beaker.
4. Place all beakers on a paddle mixer and stir at slow speed until all the added compounds have dissolved.
5. When all added compounds have been dissolved, stop the mixer.
6. Test the water in each beaker and record the concentration of calcium carbonate ($CaCO_3$), calcium bicarbonate ($Ca(HCO_3)_2$), carbon dioxide (CO_2), magnesium carbonate ($MgCO_3$), magnesium sulfate ($MgSO_4$), sodium carbonate (Na_2CO_3), sodium sulfate (Na_2SO_4), total hardness, total alkalinity, and pH.
7. Add 5 mg (0.000176 oz) of slaked lime ($Ca(OH)_2$) to the first beaker.
8. Add 5 mg (0.000176 oz) of slaked lime ($Ca(OH)_2$) and 5 mg (0.000176 oz) of soda ash (Na_2CO_3) to the second beaker.
9. Add 10 mg (0.000353 oz) of slaked lime ($Ca(OH)_2$) to the third beaker.
10. Add 10 mg (0.000353 oz) of slaked lime ($Ca(OH)_2$) and 10 mg (0.000353 oz) of soda ash (Na_2CO_3) to the fourth beaker.
11. Add 15 mg (0.000529 oz) of slaked lime ($Ca(OH)_2$) to the fifth beaker.
12. Add 15 mg (0.000529 oz) of slaked lime ($Ca(OH)_2$) and 15 mg (0.000529 oz) of soda ash (Na_2CO_3) to the sixth beaker.
13. Restart the mixer and mix all the beakers at slow speed (15–20 rpm) until all added components have dissolved.
14. When all the added components have dissolved, stop the mixer.
15. Retest the water in each beaker and record the concentration of calcium carbonate ($CaCO_3$), calcium bicarbonate ($Ca(HCO_3)_2$), carbon dioxide (CO_2), magnesium carbonate ($MgCO_3$), magnesium sulfate ($MgSO_4$), sodium carbonate (Na_2CO_3), sodium sulfate (Na_2SO_4), total hardness, total alkalinity, and pH.
16. Graph the hardness reductions as a function of the lime dosage and the lime and soda ash dosages added and establish the optimum dosages to reduce the hardness in this water. Then calculate the required CO_2 dosage to restore the pH to an optimum value.

Data Collection Format and Data Collection Sheets Tailored to Experiment:
See attached Data Collection Sheet

Anticipated Outcomes:

It is expected that the addition of the slaked lime will significantly reduce the hardness in the test samples and that increasing the lime dosage will reduce the hardness by a greater amount. The lime should reduce the carbonate hardness, while the soda ash should reduce the non-carbonate hardness.

Potential Interferences and Interference Management Plan:
Slaked lime and soda ash will react with other things in water besides hardness components. By using distilled and deionized water as the solvent for the experiments, it should be possible to reduce to insignificance or eliminate those interferences. When conducting the experiment for the purpose of establishing a proper dosage of lime or soda ash at a water treatment or reclamation facility, it will be necessary to do a series of jar tests, such as those done here, to determine the average or normal hardness, plus interferences, that will utilize the lime or soda ash. The dosage will normally be higher in those circumstances than the results of this experiment would indicate.

Data Analysis Plan:
The specified data will be collected as shown on the attached data collection sheet and the appropriate calculations made per the equations provided. Total carbonate and total non-carbonate hardness will be reported and calculations will determine the estimated dosages of slaked lime and soda ash needed to treat this water to a suitable hardness and pH.

Data Collection Sheet Technique For Potable Water Softening Experiment

Beaker — Materials Added – , mg/L

Beaker	Slaked Lime	Na_2CO_3					
1							
2							
3							
4							
6							

Beaker — Initial Concentrations, mg/L

Beaker	$CaCO_3$	$(Ca(HCO_3)_2$	CO_2	$MgCO_3$	$MgSO_4$	Na_2CO_3	Na_2SO_4	Total Hardness	Total Alkalinity	pH
1										
2										
3										
4										
5										
6										

Beaker — Post-treatment Concentrations, mg/L

Beaker										
1										
2										
3										
4										
5										
6										

**EXPERIMENT 14.5:   COAGULATION, FLOCCULATION, AND
SEDIMENTATION FOR THE REMOVAL
OF ORGANIC AND INORGANIC
WATER CONTAMINANTS**

Date: _____

Principal Investigator:

      Name: _____

      Email: _____

      Phone: _____

Collaborators:

      Name: _____

      Email: _____

      Phone: _____

      Name: _____

      Email: _____

      Phone: _____

      Name: _____

      Email: _____

      Phone: _____

      Name: _____

      Email: _____

      Phone: _____

Objective or Question to Be Addressed:

The removal of dissolved contaminants from water is as much an art as a science. The science has been well developed over time, but the application requires some patience and careful attention to the concentration of contaminants in the water. Organic contaminants and inorganic contaminants can be removed in essentially the same way, but the chemicals used are quite different.

This experiment will examine the general nature of the three separate steps to remove dissolved solids from water or wastewater.

Theory Behind Experiment

The general process for removal of dissolved solids is to convert the dissolved solids to fine solid particles, called *pin floc*, in a process called *coagulation*, to then combine the fine pin floc particles together, in a process called *flocculation*, into large enough particles to settle out, and to then let the large particles settle out of the water through a process of *sedimentation*.

The process of coagulation requires the changing of the surface electric charge of the dissolved particles so that they can detach from the water molecules and coalesce together into fine pin floc particles; in essence converting the dissolved solids to suspended solids. This is done through the addition of a *coagulant*, a chemical selected for that purpose. The objective of the coagulant is to neutralize the negative electrical charge of the dissolved solid by combining with those solids using the positive charge of the coagulant. Once that occurs, the dissolved solids can combine with each other to form the pin floc.

The selection of the coagulant depends on the nature of the contaminant. A coagulant which works well for organic contaminants, generally will not work as well for inorganic contaminants. The opposite is also true. The coagulant most commonly used at water treatment plants in the United States is aluminum sulfate, also called alum, for organic contaminants, and ferric sulfate, ferric chloride, or a commercial polymer for inorganic contaminants.

In the second step, the water containing the pin floc is slowly stirred to allow the fine particles to contact each other and stick together, without being so agitated as to break the floc up as soon as it forms. This is the process of flocculation. Note that sometimes the concepts of coagulation and flocculation are combined in discussion and referred to as either coagulation or flocculation. We believe they are two separate steps and can best be understood if viewed in that fashion.

The final step of the process is removal of the large floc from the treated water. Historically, this has been done using sedimentation principles. It can also be done effectively using filtration principles, generally with a sand filter or some form of microfiltration or ultrafiltration. The use of microfilters or ultrafiltration reduces the amount of time needed to form the larger floc and to allow those larger floc to settle out. The filters tend to clog faster, however, and require greater operating maintenance. A sand filter following sedimentation is recommended in most cases, in any event, and that is often seen as the justification for going straight to filtration from flocculation.

In a water treatment facility, the coagulant is added to the water and it is rapidly mixed so that the coagulant is circulated throughout the water. This step is often done with an inline mixer and is confined to about 15–30 seconds of mixing. The treated water is then discharged to a second reactor where it is slowly stirred for a period of 30 minutes to 1 hour. If sedimentation is used following the flocculation step, a third reactor is used to allow the water 1–4 hours to settle out. If filtration is used, the time to filter is based on the overflow rate of the filter media.

This experiment uses the sedimentation process and does not delve into the filtration process.

Data to be collected with an explanation of how they will be collected (Ex.: "Water temperature data for three days using a continuous data logger")
During this test, visual observations will be made and recorded every 5 minutes of the color, size, and volume of floc being developed during the stirring phase. During

the settling phase, measurements using the markings on the side of the beakers will be made every 5 minutes of the depth and color of sediments collecting at the bottom of the beaker.

Potential Interferences and Interference Management Plan

The processes described in this experiment are as much an art as a science. Unless there is absolute knowledge regarding the constituents of the water being treated, it is unlikely that an ideal concentration of any coagulant will be selected at any given moment. Indeed, the constituent concentrations are often a constantly moving target and any jar test data developed will be obsolete before they can even begin. Therefore, it should not be taken as a failure if lower than expected or desired results occur during this experiment. In addition, not all organic contaminants respond the same way to alum and not all inorganics respond equally to ferric coagulants. Consequently, there is likely to be some variation in the effectiveness of any coagulant with any specific water or wastewater.

Dealing with these variations in performance is a trial and error process based on historic changes at the treatment location. For the purposes of this experiment, they will be ignored and the data will be assumed correct for the contaminants present.

Tools, Equipment, and Supplies Required:

    6-paddle Phipps and Bird mixer, or equivalent.
    6 clean 2 L beakers that will fit the mixer and which have volumetric markings
        on the side of the beaker
    Approximately 3,500 mg (0.1235 oz) of aluminum sulfate
    Approximately 3,500 mg (0.1235 oz) of ferric sulfate
    Approximately 25 g of fine organic silt
    Approximately 25 g of fine inorganic clay
    Testing equipment and supplies sufficient to test the settled water for the con-
        centration of aluminum sulfate and ferric sulfate

Safety

The chemicals used in this experiment are toxic to human health if ingested or if placed in contact with eyes. Safety gloves, eye protections, and a lab coat are recommended for personal protection.

In the event of skin exposure, washing with warm water and soap is recommended. In the event of eye contact, flush with an eye wash for 15 minutes and seek medical attention immediately.

Planned Experimental Procedures and Steps, in Order:

1. Gather all required equipment and materials and put on appropriate personal protective equipment.
2. Fill six 2 L (2.11 qt) beakers with tap water to the 2 L mark on the beakers.
3. Add 3 g (0.109 oz) of fine inorganic clay particles and 3 g (0.109 oz) of fine organic silt to each beaker.
4. Place the six beakers on the 6-paddle mixer and set the bottom of the paddle blades at approximately the 0.5 L mark on the beakers for stirring.

5. Set the mixer to stir the six beakers at a high speed (approximately 100–150 rpm) and turn the mixer on. Let the mixer stir the samples for 5 minutes, then turn the mixer off.
6. After turning off the mixer, let the samples rest for 5 additional minutes.
7. At the end of the rest period, note and record the depth of silt and clay which has settled, if any.
8. Add aluminum sulfate (alum) and ferric sulfate to each of the beakers in the following concentrations. Note that the beakers contain 2 L of water and the concentrations shown are in mg/L. If alum or ferric sulfate is not added at exactly these concentrations, report the concentrations actually used.

Beaker 1	50 mg/L (0.00167 oz/qt) of each chemical
Beaker 2	100 mg/L (0.00334 oz/qt) of each chemical
Beaker 3	200 mg/L (0.00668 oz/qt) of each chemical
Beaker 4	300 mg/L (0.0100 oz/qt) of each chemical
Beaker 5	400 mg/L (0.0134 oz/qt) of each chemical
Beaker 6	500 mg/L (0.0167 oz/qt) of each chemical

9. Turn the mixer on for 15 seconds at very high speed – approximately 250–300 rpm – to simulate the rapid mix phase of water treatment.
10. At the end of the 15 second rapid mix phase, immediately turn the mixer speed down to a slow stirring rate of approximately 7–10 rpm for 30 minutes to simulate the stirring phase of water treatment. Every 5 minutes during the stirring period, note and record observations regarding the development of floc, including color, size, and number. Note that these parameters are observed as anecdotal observations, rather than precise measurements.
11. At the end of the 30 minute stirring period, turn off the mixer and let the beakers settle for 30 additional minutes. Every 5 minutes during this settling period, note and record observations regarding the depth and color of accumulated floc in each beaker. Note that these parameters are based on the volume markers on the side of the beakers. The settlements may not be uniform, and it may be necessary to estimate an average depth of sediment in specific beakers. The accuracy of these measurements is important for data analysis.
12. At the end of the settling period, test the settled water in each beaker for the concentration of aluminum sulfate and ferric sulfate and record those values.
13. Calculate and record the amount of aluminum sulfate and the amount of ferric sulfate used by the creation of the floc in each beaker during this test in mg/L.
14. Plot the concentration of aluminum sulfate used in each beaker against the depth of settled sediments in that beaker and the concentration of ferric sulfate used in each beaker against the depth of sediments in that beaker. Both lines should be graphed on the same chart for easy comparison. Determine

and report the optimum concentrations of aluminum sulfate and ferric sulfate needed to adequately treat these samples.
15. Dispose of the contents of all beakers in accordance with laboratory waste disposal practices.

Data Collection Format and Data Collection Sheets Tailored to Experiment:
See attached Data Collection Form

Data Analysis Plan:
The observations specified will be made during the conduct of the experiment. The amount of each chemical used will be converted to mg/L and plotted against the volume of sediment generated in each beaker. Based on the two lines on the chart, the optimal concentration of aluminum sulfate and ferric sulfate will be determined and reported.

Expected Outcomes:
It is expected that a fine pin floc will rapidly develop as soon as the stirring phase begins and that the larger floc will develop rapidly thereafter. Settling of the large floc will occur rapidly, and the accumulations of sediments will stabilize in each beaker quickly. The volume of sediment in each beaker is expected to increase based on the amount of each chemical utilized. It is expected that essentially all of the chemicals will be used in the first two or three beakers and that only a portion of the chemicals will be utilized in the other three beakers. The two graph lines should flatten out as the optimal concentration of each chemical is achieved.

Data Collection form Coagulation, Flocculation, Sedimentation Experiment

Beaker	Mass of Al$_2$(SO$_4$)$_3$ Added (mg)	Mass of Fe$_2$(SO$_4$)$_3$ Added (mg)	Final Mass of Al$_2$(SO$_4$)$_3$ In Settled Water (mg)	Final Mass of Fe$_2$(SO$_4$)$_3$ In Settled Water (mg)	Mass of Al$_2$(SO$_4$)$_3$ Utilized During Experiment (mg)	Mass of Fe$_2$(SO$_4$)$_3$ Utilized During Experiment (mg)
1						
2						
3						
4						
5						
6						

Observation of Floc During Stirring Phase

Observations of Floc Color

Beaker	1	2	3	4	5	6
Time (min)						
5						
10						
15						
20						
25						
30						

Observation of Floc During Settling Phase

Observations of Floc Color

Beaker	1	2	3	4	5	6
Time (min)						
5						
10						
15						
20						
25						
30						

(Continued)

Data Collection form Coagulation, Flocculation, Sedimentation Experiment (Continued)

Beaker	Mass of Al$_2$(SO$_4$)$_3$ Added (mg)	Mass of Fe$_2$(SO$_4$)$_3$ Added (mg)	Final Mass of Al$_2$(SO$_4$)$_3$ In Settled Water (mg)	Final Mass of Fe$_2$(SO$_4$)$_3$ In Settled Water (mg)	Mass of Al$_2$(SO$_4$)$_3$ Utilized During Experiment (mg)	Mass of Fe$_2$(SO$_4$)$_3$ Utilized During Experiment (mg)

Observations of Floc Size

Beaker	1	2	3	4	5	6
Time (min)						
5						
10						
15						
20						
25						
30						

Observations of Floc Volume (mL)

Beaker	1	2	3	4	5	6

Observations of Floc Density

Beaker	1	2	3	4	5	6
Time (min)						
5						
10						
15						
20						
25						
30						

EXPERIMENT 14.6: DETERMINATION OF GRANULAR MEDIA SUITABILITY FOR USE IN GRANULAR MEDIA FILTERS

Date: _____

Principal Investigator:

    Name: _____

    Email: _____

    Phone: _____

Collaborators:

    Name: _____

    Email: _____

    Phone: _____

    Name: _____

    Email: _____

    Phone: _____

    Name: _____

    Email: _____

    Phone: _____

    Name: _____

    Email: _____

    Phone: _____

Objective or Question to Be Addressed:

Sand filters are a very old technology that has proved highly successful over centuries of use. The most suitable characteristics of the sand or other granular media used in a sand filter have evolved over time to a standard set of characteristics that can be measured.

    This experiment measures the relevant characteristics of a sand sample to determine whether the source of that material is suitable for use in a sand filter.

Theory Behind Experiment

The technology of sand filtration has evolved over time based on several distinct characteristics of the sand. The particles of sand, or other granular media, need to be large enough that the pore spaces between the particles will pass the water to be treated, but small enough that the particles of contaminants in the water will be intercepted and removed without clogging the filter. The ideal characteristics are based on the grain size distribution of the media particles. They include the actual particle size, the ratio of the d_{10} *particle diameter*, and the d_{60} *particle diameter*. The d_{10} diameter is the diameter of the particles at which 10% of the mass of particles is smaller. The d_{60} diameter is the diameter at which 60% of the mass of the particles is smaller.

The d_{10} diameter is referred to as the *effective size* of the particles. The ratio of the d_{60} diameter divided by the d_{10} diameter is referred to as the *uniformity coefficient*.

The ideal values of the granular media for a filter depend upon the intended use of that filter. They may be used in water or wastewater treatment operations and are designed slightly differently depending upon which use is intended.

There are, however, some operating and design principles common to every type of granular media filter system. First, wastewater must be pretreated to remove solids and scum before being subjected to filtration to avoid clogging of the filter media. Water treatment filters seldom require this solids removal pretreatment step.

After the coarse solids have been removed, the filter is dosed in timed intervals or when the pretreatment tank becomes full. Dosing allows the filter media to drain between doses. This helps ensure that oxygen, important for the biological and chemical treatment processes that take place inside the filter, is introduced with every dose of water or wastewater. It is also important that the water or wastewater be applied evenly across the filter surface by flooding the surface completely with a thin layer or spraying the water evenly over the filter surface.

Most treatment occurs in the first 6–12 inches of the filter surface in wastewater filters, but the first 1–2 inches in water treatment filters, due to the lower concentration of solids in the water filter, unless coagulation and flocculation have been done and the flocculated water has not been allowed to settle before being applied to the filter.

Solids removal occurs in several ways inside the filter media. Some particles stick to individual grains of the media or get caught in the interstitial spaces between the grains. Biological slimes will build up on the surfaces of the grains as nutrients and bacteria intermix in those spaces. As the slime *biomat*, or *Schmutzdecke*, grows, it does an increasingly better job of removing additional bacteria and small organic particles. The bacteria in this layer consume particles in the wastewater. Protozoa feed on the bacteria and help prevent the biomat from becoming so dense that it clogs the filter. Some inorganic particles may also react chemically with the media particles and attach firmly to the media. This balance between various biological processes and the physical and chemical processes results in a very efficient wastewater treatment system requiring minimal operation and maintenance.

Eventually, the biomat will become clogged, and the top layer of sand needs to be raked or removed as part of regular filter maintenance. Alternatively, the entire depth of media is backwashed to scour all the particles and reset the system. The media are installed with deliberately designed layers of increasing density to allow the backwashed filter media to resettle in the original configuration after backwashing.

Sand is not the only media used in sand filters. Sometimes activated charcoal can be used, crushed slag can be used, or other reasonably hard materials can be used. A quartz-based sand generally works best for most applications, but activated charcoal is much better at removing organic components and odors that may be present. Using a mixed media filter with charcoal for odor control and sand for filtration is also a recognized technology.

The current experiment looks at verification of the media characteristics useful for efficient and effective filtration. This is done by conducting a soil grain analysis of the selected source material, plotting the grain sizes on a standard grain size distribution chart, calculating the d_{10} and d_{60} grain sizes, and comparing those values to the standard values found over the centuries to be most effective.

Sand filters may be operated in several modes. The most common mode for wastewater is the slow sand filter mode in which wastewater is dosed to the filter over a long time period. This is because the mass of solids in the wastewater will tend to clog the filter too quickly if a more rapid flow rate is used. Water treatment typically uses a rapid sand filter because the mass of solids is generally low enough to prevent rapid clogging. The difference between the slow and fast filtration modes relates to the overflow rate, or the volume of water fed to the surface per unit of time, and the organic loading rate in kg of BOD per square meter per day (pounds of BOD per square foot per day). The following table shows the range of overflow rates, effective grain size, and normal uniformity coefficient for each type of filter. A recirculating sand filter has been found to be effective at odor control when approximately 50% of the filter discharge is recirculated through the filter.

Granular Media Filter Characteristics

Type of Filter	Grain Size Range, mm (in)	Effective Grain Size, mm (in)	Uniformity Coefficient	Hydraulic Loading Rate, L/day/m² (gal/day/ft²)	Organic Loading Rate, kg/day/m² (lb/day/ft²)
Slow[a]	0.3–1.0 (0.012–0.039)		<4.0	1.36–3.40 (2–5)	0.024 (0.005)
Slow[b]	0.5–1.0 (0.020–0.039)	0.55 (0.022)	<1.6		
Slow[d]	0.15–0.35 (0.006–0.014)		1.5–3.0 (<2.0 BEST)		
Rapid[a]	0.3–1.0 (0.012–0.039)		<4.0	1.36–3.40 (2–5)	0.024 (0.005)
Rapid[b]	0.6–1.18 (0.024–0.46)	0.75 (0.030)	<1.6		
Rapid[c]		0.35–0.60 (0.014–0.024)	<1.7		
Recirculating[a]	0.8–3.0 (0.032–0.118)		<4.0	2.04–3.40 (3–5)	0.024 (0.005)

a   engineering.purdue.edu.
b   Ratnayaka, et al.
c   suezwatertechnologies.com.
d   biosandfilter.org.

Data to be collected with an explanation of how they will be collected (Ex.: "Water temperature data for three days using a continuous data logger")
Grain size distribution data will be collected from a sieve set shaken on a standard sieve shaker in accordance with the manufacturer's instructions. Those data will include the weight of each individual sieve prior to shaking, the weight of each sieve with sample after shaking, and the weight of the total sample.

Potential Interferences and Interference Management Plan
There are no known interferences that could infiltrate the data from this experiment. However, failure to use proper care in removing sieves from stacks, spilling material from sieves prior to weighing, or overdoing the shaking period can cause material from one sieve to be mixed with material from other sieves, altering the grain size distribution curve and making an accurate assessment of the suitability of the test sample impossible.

Tools, Equipment, and Supplies Required:
    Standard sieve shaker
    Set of sieves of size: Cover, No. 40, No. 60, No. 80, No. 100, No. 150, and pan
    Sample of sand, approx. 6–8 lb (2.7 to 3.6 kg) minimum
    Scale to weigh the sample, with an accuracy of at least 0.1 lb (0.05 kg)
    Sieve analysis forms

Safety
Sieve shakers are generally safe if they are properly latched and secured to their operating mechanisms and if the sieves are properly secured inside the shaker. Careful checking of latches and other safety features prior to starting the shaker will reduce those risks. Operators should stand away from the door of the unit while it is operating and stand clear of the device while it is running and until it stops completely.

   Dust may be generated by the shaking operation which can be hazardous if respired. A dust mask is required, along with eye protection, when operating a sieve shaker.

Planned Experimental Procedures and Steps, in Order:

1. Gather the equipment and materials together and put on the appropriate personal protective equipment.
2. Carefully weigh each sieve and record those weights.
3. Carefully weigh the sample to be sieved and record that weight.
4. Stack the sieves in the order shown such that the sieve with the largest openings is on the top.
5. Place the sample into the top sieve and place the cover over the top.
6. Secure the stack of sieves inside the shaker in accordance with the manufacturer's directions.
7. Shake the sieve stack for the time recommended by the manufacturer or about 7 minutes.
8. Turn off the shaker and allow it to stop shaking before opening the door.
9. Carefully remove the stack of sieves, weigh each one with the collected sample mass inside, and record those weights.

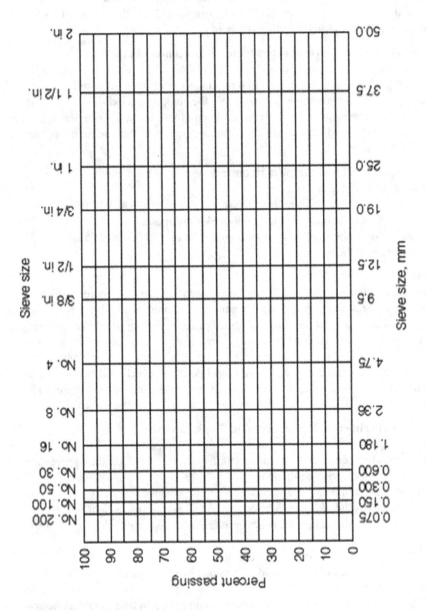

FIGURE 14.1 Form for plotting soil grain size distribution curves.

10. Prepare a size distribution curve using the standard sieve analysis form (See Figure 14.1) and determine the effective size (d_{10}) and the uniformity coefficient (d_{60} / d_{10}) for this sample.

11. Determine what soil sizes need to be added to, or subtracted from the sample to yield an effective size of 0.55 mm (0.022 in) and a uniformity coefficient of <1.7.

Data Collection Format and Data Collection Sheets Tailored to Experiment:
See attached Data Collection Form and Sieve Analysis Form.

Data Analysis Plan:
The data collected from this experiment will be the mass of grains collected on each specific sieve. The mass of material collected is the mass of the empty sieve subtracted from the mass of the sieve with sample after shaking. The sum of those individual sample masses needs to be compared to the original mass of the sample to ensure that there are no significant losses due to spillage or other causes. Assuming that the sum of the individual masses adds up to the total mass, the mass on each sieve, as a percentage of the total mass, needs to be calculated and recorded.

Once the percentages are known, the distribution curve for the various grain sizes can be drawn by plotting the percentages measured and drawing a smooth curve along the line of plotted data points. The d_{10} and d_{60} values are then determined directly from the curve and used to determine the effective grain size and the uniformity coefficient of the sample.

If the sample does not meet the specified criteria, determine what grain sizes need to be added to, or removed from, the sample to bring the sample into compliance. This is basically a trial and error procedure in which variable percentages of specific gran sizes are added to or subtracted from the measured percentages for that sample, the percentages of all the sizes as a function of the new total mass are determined and a new curve plotted. Time and experience will yield improved results with this procedure. Setting up an EXCEL, or similar data management, spreadsheet to help with the calculations may also prove useful.

Expected Outcomes:
It is expected that the initial sample will not meet the specifications. Normally, specifications will allow for a range of d_{10} and uniformity coefficient values, and those are plotted on the same grain size distribution chart as the actual data. The ranges will yield a set of two curves, and the intent is for the accepted sample to fall within the window between the two outside limit curves.

In this example experiment, it is suggested that the d_{10} size be allowed to vary between 0.5 and 0.6 mm and that the uniformity coefficient be allowed to vary between 1.5 and 1.9.

Experiment Data Sheet for Determination of Granular Media Suitability for Use in Granular Media Filters

Sieve No.	Initial Weight (kg)	Weight with Sample (kg)	Total Sample Weight (kg)	Percentage of Sample in this Sieve	d_{10} Size	d_{60} Size	Uniformity Coefficient
30							
40							
60							
80							
100							
150							
PAN							

EXPERIMENT 14.7: ANALYSIS OF SUSPENDED SOLIDS IN WATER

Date: _____

Principal Investigator:

    Name: _____

    Email: _____

    Phone: _____

Collaborators:

    Name: _____

    Email: _____

    Phone: _____

    Name: _____

    Email: _____

    Phone: _____

    Name: _____

    Email: _____

    Phone: _____

    Name: _____

    Email: _____

    Phone: _____

Objective or Question to Be Addressed:

This procedure is designed to evaluate a sample of water for the presence of suspended solids. Suspended solids are the undissolved particles that float around in water making it cloudy. Not all suspended solids create this cloudiness, but all will do so if the concentration is sufficiently high. Two methods are used in this experiment to evaluate the presence of suspended solids in a stream or pond water sample.

Theory Behind Experiment

Surface waters in nature arise from the flow of surface water and groundwater into a relatively low area where the surface of the soil is lower than the surface of the groundwater. Surface runoff into these bodies of water carries small particles of soil, contaminants, and debris with it, and those particles tend to remain suspended in the water column when the density of the particle is very close to, or less than, the density of the water. Turbulence in the water flow will also affect the size and mass of such particles that will remain in suspension.

The ability of light to reflect through a water sample may be hindered or scattered by the presence of suspended solids in the water sample. It is important to note that the visibility through a sample may be impacted by multiple particle types; the differences between suspended solids, dissolved solids, and total solids are important water quality parameters.

There are several treatment processes which remove suspended particles such as filtration. Alternatively, the water may be removed from around the particles by evaporation. The concentration of those particles may also be determined analytically using a turbidimeter. This experiment compares the results from a common source using all three techniques.

Potential Interferences and Interference Management Plan

The mass of material being analyzed is generally low. The volume of water containing the suspended solids to be measured is very small. The results, however, are projected over a large volume of water. Consequently, a small error in the experimental data will translate into a very large error in the field.

Things that can cause errors here include oils from touching the glassware and filter pads with fingers, placing clean filter pads and glassware on soiled surfaces where minute particles can become attached to them, weighing things hot, rather than allowing cooling to room temperature first, and failure to mix the original sample of pond or stream water adequately or consistently immediately before collecting an aliquot for testing. Storage for long periods of time or in areas of high humidity can alter the ability of a filter pad to function properly. Filters that may have been subjected to those conditions may be placed in a desiccator overnight prior to use to significantly improve their performance.

Care in the handling of materials and caution to cool things adequately before weighing will go a long way to resolving most of these potential interferences. Variation in the actual mass of suspended solids in any specific aliquot of the same source water is still possible, however, and some variation in the results is likely.

Data to be collected with an explanation of how they will be collected (Ex.: "Water temperature data for three days using a continuous data logger")

The data to be collected during this experiment include the mass of various pieces of equipment using a calibrated analytical scale capable of reading to 0.001 g.

Tools, Equipment, and Supplies Required:

Approximately 250 mL or more of source water

Calibrated analytical scale capable of reading to 0.001 g

Clean watch cover of sufficient diameter to hold the filter pad

5 µ filter pad of sufficient size to fit the filtering apparatus

25 mL clean glass beaker

100 mL clean graduated cylinder

Filtering apparatus consisting of a filtering flask, filter pad holder with screen, filtering funnel, funnel clamp, vacuum pump, and sufficient vacuum tubing to connect the pump and the filtering flask

Drying oven

Tongs for handling watch cover and filter pads

Safety

A drying oven heated to the boiling point of water is used in this experiment. Heat-resistant gloves and tongs are required for handling glassware that is placed into and removed from this oven.

Latex or similar gloves are required for handling cool materials to avoid contacting glassware and filter papers with hands. This is important to minimize interferences. It is also a safety issue; however, because pond water and stream water are generally not potable and the use of gloves will minimize the risk of accidental ingestion of source water or potential infection through cuts or open wounds on the hands.

As with all lab procedures, eye protection and lab coats are strongly recommended.

In the event of exposure to the skin, wash with warm water and soap as soon as possible. In the event of ingestion, seek medical attention immediately due to the potential for the water source to be contaminated. In the event of contact with the eyes, immediately flush at an eyewash station for up to 15 minutes while seeking immediate medical assistance.

Planned Experimental Procedures and Steps, in Order:

1. Gather all equipment and supplies needed, set up the filtration equipment, and put on personal protective equipment.
2. Weigh a clean, dry, $5\,\mu$ filter pad of a size suitable for the filtering apparatus being used, removed from the package with tongs to avoid touching the pad with fingers or contaminating the pad from any other source. Record that mass as the clean dry mass of the filter pad. Again, note that small variations in the readings for mass may impact results so be sure to level the scale, and if the scale has an enclosed area, slide the enclosure doors closed for more accurate readings.
3. Using gloved hands or tongs, weigh a clean, dry glass watch cover large enough to hold a filter paper of the size required for the filtering apparatus, with the preweighed clean, dry, filter pad on the watch cover. Avoid touching the watch cover or the filter pad with fingers to minimize the potential for oils from hands contaminating, and adding mass to, the watch cover or the filter pad. Record that mass.
4. Subtract the mass of the filter pad from the mass of the watch cover and filter pad and record that value as the mass of the watch cover.
5. Place the clean, dry filter paper into a vacuum filtering apparatus using tongs to avoid touching the pad with fingers, connect the vacuum pump to the filtering flask, and secure the filter holder to the top of the flask.
6. Mix the sample of water thoroughly and immediately measure out a 100 mL (3.38 oz) of sample in a graduated cylinder.
7. Turn on the vacuum pump and pour the sample through the filter, avoiding splashing the sides of the funnel so that the maximum volume of the aliquot will be directed through the filter paper.
8. After a few seconds of vacuum, most of the liquid will have been pulled through the filter and the solids (larger than $5\,\mu$) will remain behind. Turn off the vacuum pump.

9. Remove the filter pad from the filtering apparatus using clean tongs and place it back on the preweighed watch cover.

10. Using gloved hands or tongs, place the watch cover with the filter pad on it into a drying oven at a temperature of 100°C (212°F). Allow the sample to remain in the oven until dry, approximately 4 hours in most cases, depending on how much moisture remains in the pad after filtering.

11. After the pad is dry, carefully remove the pad and watch cover from the oven with gloved hands or tongs, allow them to cool to room temperature, and weigh them together. Record that mass.

12. Subtract the initial mass of the watch cover from the total mass after drying and record that as the mass of the filter pad with suspended solids.

13. Carefully remove the filter pad from the watch cover using tongs and weigh the dry filter pad with the suspended solids. Record this mass and compare it to the value calculated by subtracting the mass of the watch cover from the total dry mass of the watch cover and filter pad. The mass of the filter pad with suspended solids should be the same after both calculations. If it varies, note the variance so that the total mass of suspended solids may be corrected later.

14. Subtract the initial mass of the clean, dry, filter pad from the mass of the dried filter pad with suspended solids and record that mass. This is the mass of solids removed from the original 100 mL sample of water. Multiply this mass by 10 and record the mass in mg/L.

15. Select a clean glass 25 mL beaker and weigh it using gloved hands or tongs to handle the beaker after it is cleaned. Record this mass as the initial mass of the beaker.

16. Mix the sample water well and carefully collect a 25 mL sample in a graduated cylinder.

17. Carefully pour the new sample into the 25 mL beaker and place the beaker into a drying oven set at 100°C (212°F). Allow the beaker to remain in the oven overnight or until it is dry.

18. After the beaker has dried, remove it from the oven with tongs or gloves and allow it to cool to room temperature. Then weigh the dried beaker, handling it with gloved hands or tongs, and record this mass.

19. Subtract the mass of the clean, dry, beaker from the mass of the dry beaker with suspended solids in it and record this mass as the mass of suspended solids per 25 mL of sample. Multiply this value by 40 (there are 40 of the 25 mL aliquots in 1 L) and record the value as the mass of suspended solids in the water in mg/L. Compare that value to the mass determined in Step 14.

20. Calibrate a standard turbidimeter in accordance with the manufacturer's instructions and using standards provided by the manufacturer. (See Experiment 9.18.) Be sure to clean the outside of the standard containers before inserting into the meter and handle standards with gloved hands to avoid touching the glass with fingers.

21. Using the calibrated turbidimeter, determine the concentration of suspended solids in the sample reported by testing the sample with the turbidimeter. Use a clean glass test tube provided by the turbidimeter manufacturer,

handle the tube with gloved hands, fill the tube with a sample of well-mixed test water and record the value. Compare the suspended solids concentration recorded by the turbidimeter to the suspended solids concentration found in the sample as determined in steps 14 and 19.

22. In the lab report, discuss why the three values are not identical, assuming that will be the case, or how closely they align if that is the case.

Data Collection Format and Data Collection Sheets Tailored to Experiment:
See attached Data Collection Sheet.

Data Analysis Plan:
The data are not likely to be identical from all three methods due to the variety of interferences that may occur. A review of the procedures outlined and the manner in which they were carried out will be instructive regarding any variation in the values recorded. A simple comparison of the data from the three methods will be conducted with an opinion provided regarding the source of any variations noted.

Expected Outcomes:
It is expected that the results will be reasonably close for all three methods, depending on how carefully the procedures are conducted. Some variation is likely, however, due to interferences noted.

Data Collection Sheet for Suspended Solids Experiment

Date Collected			
Date Tested			
Principal Investigator			
Water Source			
Mass of clean dry filter pad (mg)		Turbidity Meter Readings (NTU)	
Mass of clean, dry watch cover, with filter pad (mg)		Standard 1	
Mass of clean, dry, watch cover		Standard 2	
Mass of dried watch cover and used filter pad (mg)		Standard 3	
Mass of dried filter pad with suspended solids by subtraction (mg)		Standard 4	
Mass of dried filter pad by weighing (mg)		Standard 5	
Mass of dried suspended solids on used filter pad (mg)		Test Sample	
Mass of suspended solids per 100 mL, converted to mg/L		Suspended Solids Concentration based on standards calibration curve (mg/L)	
Mass of clean, dry, 25 mL glass beaker (mg)			
Mass of dried 25 mL beaker with suspended solids residue inside (mg)			
Mass of dried suspended solids residue inside beaker (mg)			
Mass of suspended solids per 25 mL converted to mg/L			

EXPERIMENT 14.8:   ANALYSIS OF TOTAL SOLIDS IN WATER

Date: _____

Principal Investigator:

      Name: _____

      Email: _____

      Phone: _____

Collaborators:

      Name: _____

      Email: _____

      Phone: _____

      Name: _____

      Email: _____

      Phone: _____

      Name: _____

      Email: _____

      Phone: _____

      Name: _____

      Email: _____

      Phone: _____

Objective or Question to Be Addressed:

This experiment is designed to provide detailed information regarding the dissolved and suspended solids content of a water sample.

Theory Behind Experiment

Water samples, including potable water supplies all the way through wastewater samples, contain varying concentrations of suspended and dissolved solids. Samples subjected to extreme solids removal techniques, such as ultrafiltration, will have essentially all suspended solids removed, but dissolved solids need to be converted to suspended solids before they can be removed. The magnitude of the concentrations of the suspended and dissolved solids are useful tools in determining treatment and identifying potential contaminant sources. Knowing whether the solids in either state are organic or inorganic is also useful in identifying suitable treatment techniques for human risk reduction.

Determination of the suspended solids content (as discussed in Experiment 14.7) is accomplished by filtering a sample of the water through a $0.5\,\mu$ glass fiber filter with a vacuum pump and filter arrangement. It is generally accepted practice that any particle which passes the $0.5\,\mu$ filter is classified as dissolved and those captured by the filter are classified as suspended. The filter is weighed dry, the water sample is filtered through it, and the filter is dried again and reweighed. The difference in dry weight before and after the filtration step, divided by the original sample volume, is considered the concentration of the suspended solids in the original sample. The use of a glass fiber filter is necessary because the filter will later be subjected to significant heating and must not be allowed to melt or otherwise be affected by that heat.

Determining the dissolved solids concentration is done by weighing a suitable clean, dry container, inserting a suitable quantity of the water sample which has been subjected to filtration into this container, and then drying the sample to expel the water and other liquid components of the sample. The residue is then assumed to be the total dissolved solids concentration based on a generally accepted practice that the dissolved solids will revert to a suspended state as the moisture content of the sample is reduced to essentially zero. That moisture reduction is accomplished by evaporation of the water at a temperature of $100°C$ ($212°F$) designed to evaporate the water, but not volatilize any of the solids. The difference in the weight of the clean dry container and the dried container after evaporation of the sample, divided by the original sample volume, is generally accepted to be the total suspended solids concentration of the sample.

To determine the organic and inorganic content of the suspended solids, the dried glass filter with the suspended solids on it is carefully weighed and then placed on a clean, dry, glass, watch cover. The watch cover with the filter on it is then placed into a muffle furnace set at $550°C$ ($1,022°F$) and allowed to remain in that furnace at that temperature for 6 hours, or overnight. At the end of the heating period, the sample is removed, cooled, and weighed. The difference in the weight of the dried filter before and after heating in the $550°C$ muffle furnace is generally accepted to be the *volatile* suspended solids. The difference in the weight of the clean dry filter before filtration subtracted from the weight of the filter after being subjected to the $550°C$ muffle furnace is the *non-volatile* fraction of the suspended solids. It is expected that at a temperature of $550°C$ all organic components will be oxidized and only the nonorganic portions will remain. It is further accepted practice that the volatile fraction is the *organic fraction* and that the nonoxidizable fraction is the *inorganic fraction* of the total suspended solids.

To determine the organic and inorganic content of the dissolved solids, the dried container with the dissolved solids residue in it is carefully weighed and the weight recorded. The container is then placed into a muffle furnace set at $550°C$ ($1,022°F$) and allowed to remain in that furnace at that temperature for 6 hours or overnight. At the end of the heating period, the container is removed, cooled, and weighed. The difference in the weight of the dried container before and after heating in the $550°C$ muffle furnace is generally accepted to be the *volatile* dissolved solids. The difference in the weight of the clean dry container before the addition of the sample subtracted from the weight of the container after being subjected to the $550°C$ muffle furnace, is the *non-volatile* fraction of the dissolved solids. It is expected that at a temperature of $550°C$ all organic components will be oxidized and only the nonorganic portions will remain. It is further accepted practice that the volatile fraction is the *organic fraction* and that the nonoxidizable fraction is the *inorganic fraction* of the total dissolved solids.

Once the four fractions have been determined, it is useful to add the two volatile fractions together and the two nonvolatile fractions together to check the accuracy of the original total suspended and total dissolved solids concentration values. Significant variations should be addressed. If very small aliquots of sample are used for the test, the probability of variation in the values at this stage is greater than if large quantities of original sample are used. Larger quantities take longer to dry and burn in the muffle furnace, however. The experiment outlined here relies on 25 mL (0.85 oz) samples, indicating that very precise measurements are needed to ensure reasonable accuracy of the outcomes.

It is noted that there are many places and ways for errors to be introduced to the data during this experiment. Most of the errors will be undetectable when the data are viewed independently. Consequently, a control sample is carried through the drying and burning processes to provide total solids, total organic solids, and total inorganic solids for the sample. Comparison of the calculated total solids from the test and the sums of the total organic and inorganic fractions from the tests to those from the control should indicate whether significant errors have occurred and, if so, where in the system they happened. That information may be useful in adjusting some of the test data to provide reasonable estimates of the actual values where such estimates are acceptable.

Data to be collected with an explanation of how they will be collected (Ex.: "Water temperature data for three days using a continuous data logger")
This experiment relies for accuracy on very careful measurement of various weights and measures. Accurately calibrated pipettes for liquid measurement and analytic scales calibrated and accurate to 0.001 g should be minimally acceptable measurement devices.

Weights to be recorded using an analytical balance:
Dry glass fiber filter paper, 0.5 μ
0.5 μ glass fiber filter after filtration of sample and drying at 100°C (212°F)
0.5 μ glass fiber filter after burning at 550°C (1,022°F)
Clean, dry, 25 mL (0.85 oz) glass beaker
25 mL (0.85 oz) glass beaker with filtered sample
25 mL (0.85 oz) glass beaker after drying of sample at 100°C (212°F)
25 mL (0.85 oz) glass beaker after burning at 550°C (1,022°F)
Volumes to be measured using graduated pipette:
50 ml (1.70 oz) of original sample

Potential Interferences and Interference Management Plan:
Several things can dramatically influence the outcome of these tests. The samples are very small, and the data are projected to very large volumes. Consequently, a very small error in the test will yield a very big error in the outcome data.

Touching the clean glassware with fingers can add oils to the glassware that will burn off in the muffle furnace. The loss of mass due to that event will manifest as added solids in the final output data. This error will likely lead to an over-indication of volatile organics in the dissolved solids concentration, but can also lead to an over-indication of volatile suspended solids if the filter is handled without the use of tweezers or tongs.

The glass filter and the glass beaker will contain a minute, but potentially measurable mass of water vapor at room temperature. By allowing the samples to cool to room temperature after removing them from the muffle furnace, any inherent moisture should equalize and not affect the outcome.

The glass fiber filter is fragile and an overly high vacuum can fracture some of the fibers, causing them to drop into the filtrate. This will yield a lower than actual measurement of total and inorganic suspended solids and an equivalent increase in the total and inorganic dissolved solids.

Transfer of the filtrate from the vacuum apparatus to the 25 mL (0.85 oz) beaker will inevitably leave some of the filtrate behind inside the filtering flask. This will lead to a consistent reduction in the concentration of total, organic, and inorganic dissolved solids. Taking care to remove as much of the filtrate as possible is the only realistic way to minimize this effect.

Due to the potential for these minor defects to multiply, a sample of the water being tested is run through the system as a control for total solids, total volatile solids, and total nonvolatile solids. Summing the fractions determined from the separated sample and comparing those sums to the values for the control sample should provide guidance on where errors may have occurred and provide a means to correct some of the calculations where reasonable estimates of the actual values are acceptable.

Tools, Equipment, and Supplies Required:

Muffle furnace calibrated at 100°C (212°F) and at 550°C (1,022°F)

Analytical balance calibrated to 0.001 g

Filtering funnel and vacuum filter apparatus

25 mL (0.85 oz) clean glass beaker

50 mL (1.70 oz) clean glass beaker

Clean, dry, 0.5 μ glass fiber filter of a size compatible with the filtering apparatus

Clean dry watch glass sized to fit the 0.5 μ glass fiber filter

Clean, dry tweezers to handle the glass fiber filter

Tongs to handle the glass fiber filter and the hot glassware

Heat resistant gloves to handle hot glassware

Safety

This experiment utilizes samples of water and wastewater that are not suitable for human ingestion. Care is required to avoid contact with the sample or accidental ingestion of sample.

The experiment utilizes a muffle furnace that is heated to 100°C (212°F) initially and ultimately to 550°C (1,022°F). These temperatures will instantly destroy skin tissue on contact. Heat-resistant gloves are required for accessing the muffle furnace and handling hot glassware.

The sample is filtered through a glass fiber filter using a vacuum apparatus. Most vacuum filters are connected to a vacuum pump that also serves as an air pump. It is essential to ensure that the vacuum line is connected to the correct nipple on the pump before adding sample to the filter. Connection to the wrong nipple will result in airflow back up through the filter, dislodging sample into the air where it can contact eyes and mouths of the experimenter.

As with all good laboratory practice protocols, eye protection and a laboratory coat are required safety equipment during this experiment. Latex or vinyl gloves are required when heat-resistant gloves are not in use.

Planned Experimental Procedures and Steps, in Order:

1. Collect all equipment and verify calibration of measuring devices. Put on appropriate personal protective equipment.
2. Weigh a clean dry $0.5\,\mu$ glass fiber filter and record the weight.
3. Preheat the muffle furnace to 100°C (212°F).
4. Assemble the filtering apparatus using the previously weighed glass fiber filter.
5. Carefully pipette a 25 mL (0.85 oz) aliquot of the sample into a clean, dry, 50 mL (1.70 oz) glass beaker, being careful not to touch the beaker with hands. This is the control sample.
6. Weigh the 50 mL glass beaker with the sample in it and record the weight.
7. Place the 50 mL (1.70 oz) beaker into the muffle furnace at 100°C (212°F) and record the time that the beaker is placed into the furnace.
8. Carefully pipette a 25 mL (0.85 oz) aliquot of the sample through the filter using the vacuum assist to ensure that as much sample as possible is drawn through the filter but without breaking the fibers or changing the pore size of the filter.
9. Carefully remove the filter from the filtering apparatus, being careful not to touch the filter with hands, and place it on a clean watch cover.
10. Place the watch cover into the muffle furnace at 100°C (212°F) and record the time that the filter is placed into the furnace.
11. Carefully pour the filtrate from the filtering apparatus into a clean, dry, 25 mL (0.85 oz) glass beaker being careful to ensure that as much of the filtrate as possible is placed into the 25 mL beaker.
12. Weigh the beaker with the filtrate and record that weight.
13. Place the beaker into the muffle furnace at 100°C (212°F) and record the time that the beaker is placed into the furnace.
14. After the glass fiber filter has been in the muffle furnace at 100°C for at least 6 hours, or until the filter is clearly dry, remove the watch cover with the filter on it and set aside to cool.
15. Record the time that the filter is removed from the muffle furnace.
16. After the 25 mL glass beaker has been in the muffle furnace at 100°C for at least 6 hours, or until the beaker is clearly dry, remove the beaker and set aside to cool.
17. Record the time that the 25 mL beaker is removed from the muffle furnace.
18. After the 50 mL glass beaker has been in the muffle furnace at 100°C for at least 6 hours, or until the beaker is clearly dry, remove the beaker and set aside to cool.
19. Record the time that the 50 mL beaker is removed from the muffle furnace.
20. Preheat the muffle furnace to 550°C (1022°F).

21. After the filter has cooled to room temperature, using clean, dry, tweezers, carefully remove the filter from the watch cover and weigh the cool dry filter.
22. Record the weight of the dried filter.
23. Return the filter to the watch cover and insert into the muffle furnace at 550°C (1,022°F).
24. Record the time that the filter is returned to the muffle furnace.
25. After the 25 mL beaker has cooled to room temperature, carefully weigh the beaker being careful not to touch the beaker with hands.
26. Record the weight of the cooled 25 mL beaker and return the beaker to the muffle furnace at 550°C (1,022°F).
27. Record the time that the 25 mL beaker is returned to the muffle furnace.
28. After the 50 mL beaker has cooled to room temperature, carefully weigh the beaker being careful not to touch the beaker with hands.
29. Record the weight of the cooled 50 mL beaker and return the beaker to the muffle furnace at 550°C (1,022°F).
30. Record the time that the 50 mL beaker is returned to the muffle furnace.
31. After the filter has been in the muffle furnace for at least 6 hours at 550°C (1,022°F), carefully remove the filter from the furnace using tongs and heat-resistant gloves and set aside to cool. Record the time the filter is removed from the oven.
32. After the 25 mL beaker has been in the muffle furnace for at least 6 hours at 550°C (1,022°F), carefully remove the beaker from the furnace using tongs and heat-resistant gloves and set aside to cool. Record the time the 25 mL beaker is removed from the oven.
33. After the 50 mL beaker has been in the muffle furnace for at least 6 hours at 550°C (1,022°F), carefully remove the beaker from the furnace using tongs and heat-resistant gloves and set aside to cool. Record the time the 50 mL beaker is removed from the oven.
34. After the filter has cooled to room temperature, carefully weigh the cooled filter and record the weight.
35. After the 25 mL beaker has cooled to room temperature, carefully weigh the beaker and record the weight.
36. After the 50 mL beaker has cooled to room temperature, carefully weigh the beaker and record the weight.
37. Following the guidance of the data collection sheet, calculate the following parameters of the original sample:
    Total solids (from the control data and from the test data)
    Total suspended solids (from the control data and from the test data)
    Total dissolved solids (from the control data and from the test data)
    Volatile suspended solids
    Volatile dissolved solids
    Nonvolatile suspended solids
    Nonvolatile dissolved solids
    Total volatile solids
    Total nonvolatile solids

Data Collection Format and Data Collection Sheets Tailored to Experiment:
See attached Data Collection Sheet

Anticipated Outcomes:
Outcomes will vary depending on the nature of the water sample being tested.

Most drinking water supplies will be very low, in the order of 10 mg/L or less of total solids, most of which will be dissolved solids, with the split between organic and inorganic depending upon the source. Groundwater sources will tend to be higher in inorganic dissolved solids, while surface water will tend to be higher in organic dissolved solids.

Wastewater samples will vary widely depending on where in the system the sample is collected. Samples are collected throughout the system to monitor system health. Samples are collected at the outlet from the plant to monitor regulatory compliance. Discharge limits of 20 mg/L is a standard discharge permit limit for total suspended solids.

Data Analysis Plan:
A lot of data are generated from this experiment. The calculated total, organic, and inorganic fractions of the total sample should be calculated. Then the total, organic, and inorganic fractions of both the suspended portion and the dissolved portion of the total solids will be calculated. The sum of the organic fractions and the inorganic fractions of the suspended solids will be added to the organic and inorganic fractions of the dissolved solids to calculate total organic and inorganic fractions of the total sample. Those totals will be compared to the total organic and inorganic fractions determined from the control sample.

Significant variation between the total of the organic or inorganic fractions from the test, when compared to those of the control, will indicate potential errors in the test procedure. Where accuracy is required, redoing the test may be necessary to better quantify the results. Here reasonable estimates of the actual concentrations are acceptable, the data from the control will be assumed to be correct, and the other fractions will be proportionally adjusted to reflect consistency of the values. If the error is suggested in a specific area of the test, the adjustments to the data may be skewed to reflect those realities. Adjustments to the data need to be fully and clearly described in the ensuing laboratory report.

Data Collection Sheet Analysis of Solids in Water

Principal Investigator:

Dates of Data Collection:

Date of Analysis:　　　　　　　　　　　　　　　　　　Page:

Measurement	Value Identifier	Measured Value	Notes
Initial weight of 0.5 μ glass fiber filter (mg)	A		
Initial weight of 50 mL glass beaker (mg)	B		
Initial weight of 25 mL glass beaker (mg)	C		
Time 0.5 μ glass fiber filter placed in muffle furnace at 100°C			
Time 25 mL glass beaker placed in muffle furnace at 100°C			
Time 0.5 μ glass fiber filter is removed from muffle furnace			
Time 25 mL glass beaker is removed from muffle furnace			
Time 50 mL glass beaker is removed from muffle furnace			
Weight of dry, cooled 0.5 μ glass fiber filter (mg)	D		
Time 0.5 μ glass fiber filter placed in muffle furnace at 550°C			
Weight of dry, cooled 25 mL glass beaker (mg)	E		
Time 25 mL glass beaker placed in muffle furnace at 550°C			
Weight of dry, cooled 50 mL glass beaker (mg)	F		
Time 50 mL glass beaker placed in muffle furnace at 550°C			
Time 0.5 μ glass fiber filter removed from muffle furnace			
Time 25 mL glass beaker removed from muffle furnace			
Time 50 mL glass beaker removed from muffle furnace			
Weight of cooled 0.5 μ glass fiber filter (mg)	G		
Weight of cooled 25 mL glass beaker (mg)	H		
Weight of cooled 50 mL glass beaker (mg)	I		
Calculation of values			

(Continued)

Data Collection Sheet Analysis of Solids in Water (*Continued*)

Parameter	Value Identifier	Equation	Calculated Value
Calculation of total suspended solids	J	$T_s = (a-d) / 0.025$ mg/L	
Calculation of total dissolved solids	K	$T_d = (c-d) / 0.025$ mg/L	
Calculation of organic fraction of suspended solids	M	$T_{so} = (d-g) / 0.025$ mg/L	
Calculation of inorganic fraction of suspended solids	N	$T_{si} = (a-g) / 0.025$ mg/L	
Calculation of organic fraction of dissolved solids	O	$T_{do} = (b-f) / 0.025$ mg/L	
Calculation of inorganic fraction of dissolved solids	P	$T_{di} = (f-i) / 0.025$ mg/L	
Summation of total organic fractions	Q	$T_o = m+o$ mg/L	
Summation of total inorganic fractions	R	$T_i = n+p$ mg/L	
Calculated summation of total suspended solids	S	$T_{sc} = m+n$ mg/L	
Calculated summation of total dissolved solids	T	$T_{dc} = o+p$ mg/L	
Calculated summation of total solids	U	$TS_c = s+t$ mg/L	
Calculation of total solids from control data	V	$T_{cc} = f-b$	
Calculation of total inorganic solids from control data	W	$TS_{cc} = i-b$ mg/L	
Calculation of total organic solids from control data	Z	$TD_{cc} = f-i$ mg/L	
Comparison of Results			**Variance**
Total solids		u versus v	
Total inorganic solids		r versus w	
Total organic solids		q versus z	

Appendix

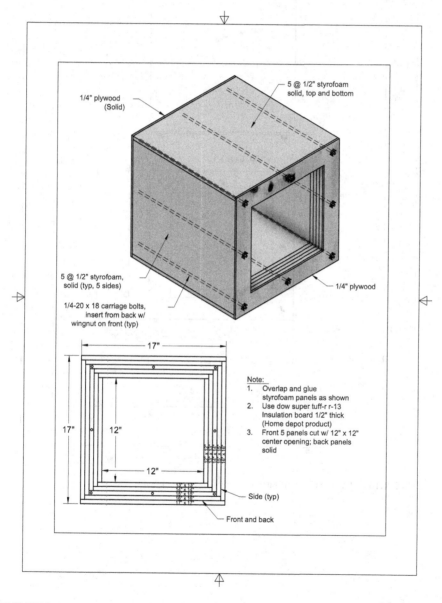

Labels on figure:

1/4" plywood (Solid)

5 @ 1/2" styrofoam solid, top and bottom

5 @ 1/2" styrofoam, solid (typ, 5 sides)

1/4-20 x 18 carriage bolts, insert from back w/ wingnut on front (typ)

1/4" plywood

17"

17"   12"

12"

Note:
1. Overlap and glue styrofoam panels as shown
2. Use dow super tuff-r r-13 Insulation board 1/2" thick (Home depot product)
3. Front 5 panels cut w/ 12" x 12" center opening; back panels solid

Side (typ)

Front and back

FIGURE A.1a   R-value determination test box plan.

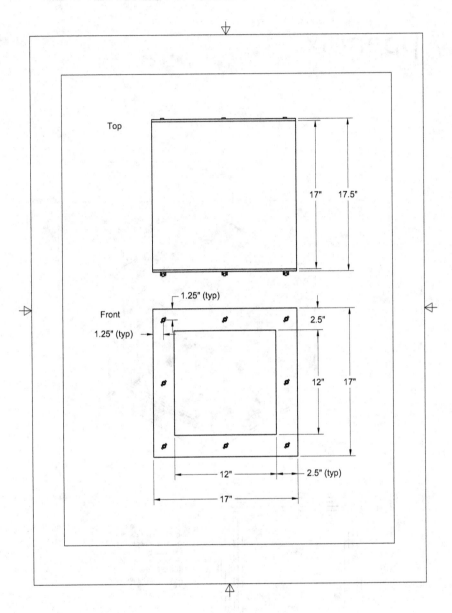

FIGURE A.1b R-value determination test box details (1).

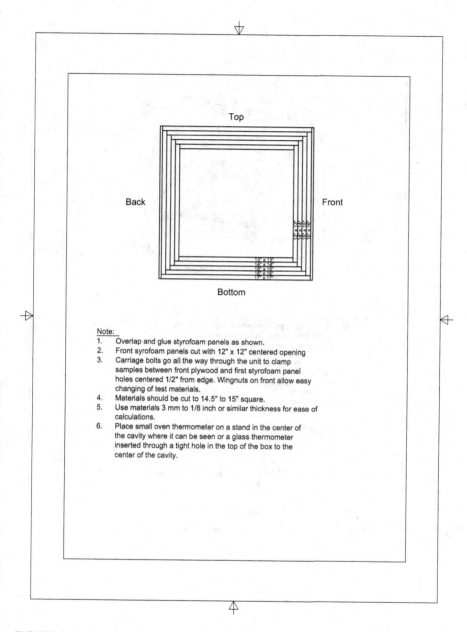

Top

Back   Front

Bottom

Note:
1. Overlap and glue styrofoam panels as shown.
2. Front syrofoam panels cut with 12" x 12" centered opening
3. Carriage bolts go all the way through the unit to clamp
    samples between front plywood and first styrofoam panel
    holes centered 1/2" from edge. Wingnuts on front allow easy
    changing of test materials.
4. Materials should be cut to 14.5" to 15" square.
5. Use materials 3 mm to 1/8 inch or similar thickness for ease of
    calculations.
6. Place small oven thermometer on a stand in the center of
    the cavity where it can be seen or a glass thermometer
    inserted through a tight hole in the top of the box to the
    center of the cavity.

FIGURE A.1c   R-value determination test box details (2).

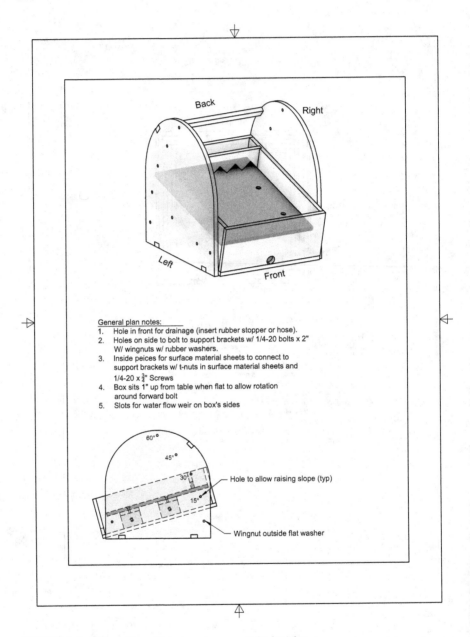

FIGURE A.2a   Runoff coefficient measurement device plan.

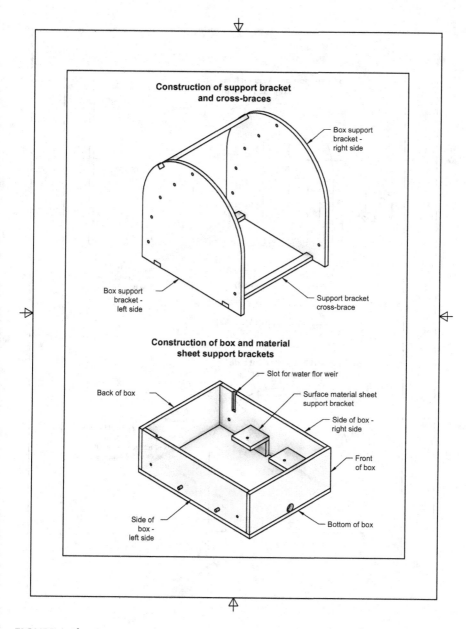

FIGURE A.2b Runoff coefficient measurement device details (1).

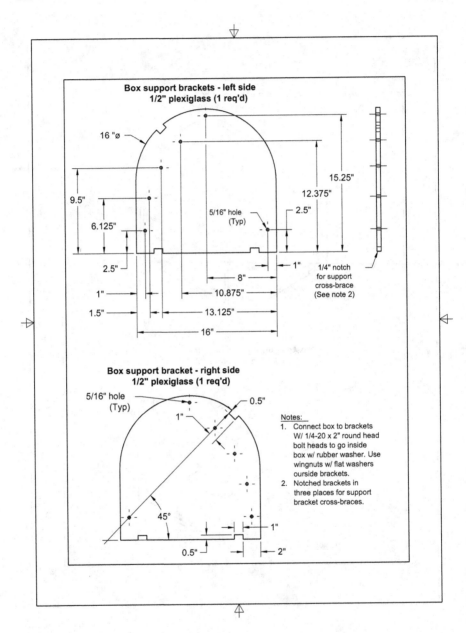

FIGURE A.2c   Runoff coefficient measurement device details (2).

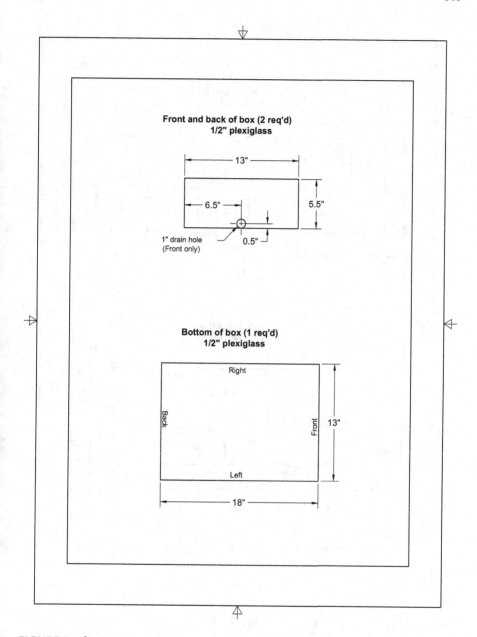

FIGURE A.2d   Runoff coefficient measurement device details (3).

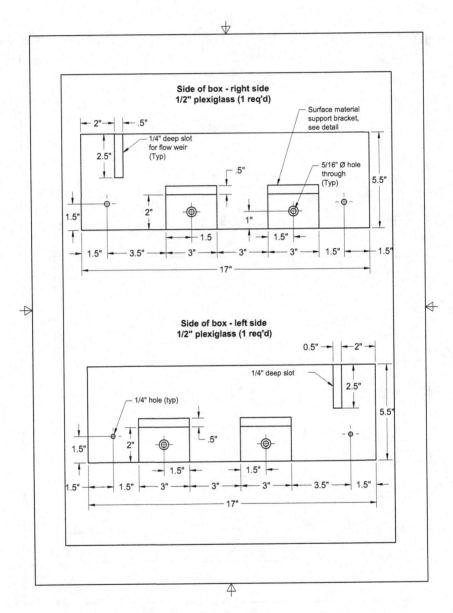

FIGURE A.2e Runoff coefficient measurement device details (4).

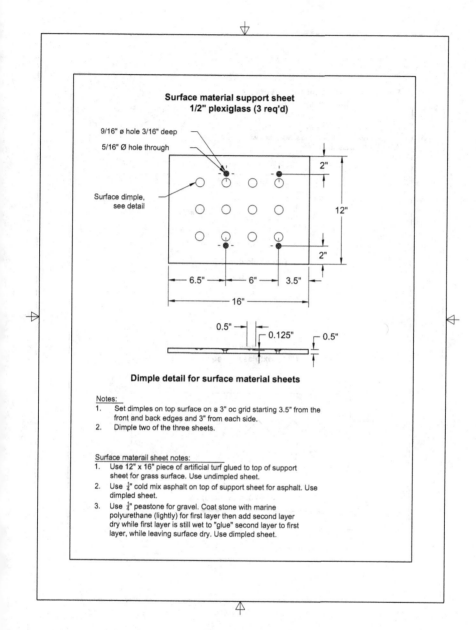

FIGURE A.2f Runoff coefficient measurement device details (5).

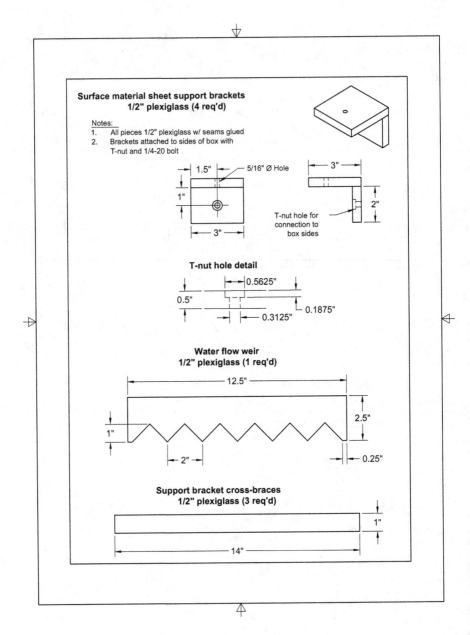

FIGURE A.2g   Runoff coefficient measurement device details (6).

TABLE A.1
Collection, Preservation, and Holding Times for Selected Liquid Environmental Samples

Parameter	EPA Testing Methodology	Container/Volume to Collect	Preservatives, If Any	Transport/Holding Conditions	Holding Times
Acid/base neutral extractables	625	Two 1 L Teflon lined amber glass	Cool to 4°C Add NaSO to pH<2	Cool to 4°C	7 days before extraction
Acid/base neutral extractables	8270C 8270 D	Two 1 L Teflon lined amber glass	Cool to 4°C	Cool to 4°C	7 days before extraction
Acidity	SM 2310B	250 mL plastic	Cool to 4°C	Cool to 4°C	14 days
Alkalinity	SM 2320B	250 mL plastic	Cool to 4°C	Cool to 4°C	14 days
Ammonia	350.1 SM 4500 NH-BH	250 mL plastic	HSO to pH< 2 Cool to 4°C	Cool to 4°C	28 days
Biological oxygen demand	SM 5210B	1 L plastic	Cool to 4°C	Cool to 4°C	48 hours
Boron	200.7 6010C	250 mL plastic	HNO$_3$ to pH<2 Cool to 4°C	Cool to 4°C	180 days
Bromide	300.0	250 mL plastic	None	None	28 days
Chemical oxygen demand	410.4 SM 5220 D	250 mL plastic	HSO to pH< 2 Cool to 4°C	Cool to 4°C	28 days
Chloride	9251 300.0 SM 4500 Cl-E	250 mL plastic	Cool to 4°C	Cool to 4°C	28 days
Chlorine, total residual	SM 4500 Cl-G	250 mL plastic	Cool to 4°C	Cool to 4°C	Analyze immediately
Chlorinated herbicides	8151 A	Two 1 L Teflon lined amber glass	Cool to 4°C	Cool to 4°C	7 days before extraction
Chromium VI	7196 A SM 3500 Cr D	250 mL glass or plastic	Cool to 4°C	Cool to 4°C	24 hours

(*Continued*)

TABLE A.1 (*Continued*)
Collection, Preservation, and Holding Times for Selected Liquid Environmental Samples

Parameter	EPA Testing Methodology	Container/Volume to Collect	Preservatives, If Any	Transport/ Holding Conditions	Holding Times
Cyanide	335.1 9010B SM 4500 CN-CE	250 ml plastic	NaOH to pH>12 Cool to 4°C	Cool to 4°C	14 days
Dissolved organic carbon	5310B	40 mL VOA vial with Teflon lined cap	Cool to 4°C	Cool to 4°C	28 days
Fluoride	300.0 SM 4500 F-B BC	500 mL plastic	Cool to 4°C	Cool to 4°C	28 days
Formaldehyde	8315	1 L amber glass	Cool to 4°C	Cool to 4°C	3 days
Haloacetic acids	552.2	250 mL amber glass jar with Teflon cap	Cool to 4°C Add NH$_4$Cl	Cool to 4°C	14 days
Hardness	SM 2340B	100 mL plastic	Cool to 4°C Add HNO$_3$ to pH<2	Cool to 4°C	6 months
Herbicides	8151 A	1 L amber glass jar with Teflon cap	Cool to 4°C	Cool to 4°C	7 days before extraction
Hexavalent chromium	7196 A SM 3500 Cr-D	500 mL plastic	Cool to 4°C	Cool to 4°C	24 hours
Mercury (TCLP)	1311 7470 A	4 oz (118 mL) amber glass jar	Cool to 4°C Add HNO$_3$ to pH<2	Cool to 4°C	28 days before extraction
Nitrate	300.0 353.2 SM 4500 NO$_3$-F	250 mL plastic	Cool to 4°C	Cool to 4°C	48 hours

(*Continued*)

TABLE A.1 (*Continued*)

Collection, Preservation, and Holding Times for Selected Liquid Environmental Samples

Parameter	EPA Testing Methodology	Container/Volume to Collect	Preservatives, If Any	Transport/ Holding Conditions	Holding Times
Nitrate/nitrite	300.0 353.2 SM 4500 NO$_3$-F	250 mL plastic	Cool to 4°C Add H$_2$SO$_4$ to pH<2	Cool to 4°C	28 days
Nitrite	300.0 353.2 SM 4500 NO$_3$-F SM 4500 NO$_2$-B	250 mL plastic	Cool to 4°C	Cool to 4°C	48 hours
Nitrogen, ammonia	SM 4500 NH$_3$ B, C	500 mL plastic	Cool to 4°C Add H$_2$SO$_4$ to pH<2	Cool to 4°C	28 days
Nitrogen, total kjeldahl	353.3/.1 SM 4500 N$_{org}$-C	250 mL plastic	Cool to 4°C Add H$_2$SO$_4$ to pH<2	Cool to 4°C	28 days
Oil and grease	1664 A	Two 1 L amber glass	Cool to 4°C Add HCl to pH<2	Cool to 4°C	28 days
Oil and grease	1664 B	1 L amber glass with Teflon lined cap	Cool to 4°C Add HCl or H$_2$SO$_4$ to pH<2	Cool to 4°C	28 days
Orthophosphate	SM 4500 P-E	250 mL plastic	Cool to 4°C	Cool to 4°C	48 hours
Polychlorinated biphenols (PCBs)	608	Two 1 L Teflon lined amber glass	Cool to 4°C Add NaSO	Cool to 4°C	7 days before extraction
Polychlorinated biphenols (PCBs)	8082 8082 A	Two 1 L Teflon lined amber glass	Cool to 4°C	Cool to 4°C	None before extraction
Pesticides (organochlorine)	608	Two 1 L Teflon lined Amber Glass	Cool to 4°C Add NaSO	Cool to 4°C	7 days before extraction

(*Continued*)

TABLE A.1 (Continued)
Collection, Preservation, and Holding Times for Selected Liquid Environmental Samples

Parameter	EPA Testing Methodology	Container/Volume to Collect	Preservatives, If Any	Transport/Holding Conditions	Holding Times
Pesticides (organochlorine)	8081 A 8081 B	Two 1 L Teflon lined amber glass	Cool to 4°C	Cool to 4°C	7 days before extraction
Petroleum hydrocarbon identification	8015 B (modified)	4 oz (118 mL) Teflon Lined amber glass jar	Cool to 4°C	Cool to 4°C	14 days before extraction
Phenolics	420.4	1 L glass	H_2SO_4 to pH<2 Cool to 4°C	Cool to 4°C	28 days
Phosphorous, total	SM 4500 P-E	250 mL plastic	Cool to 4°C Add H_2SO_4 to pH<2	Cool to 4°C	28 days
Polynuclear aromatic hydrocarbons (PAHs)	625 8270 D	Two 1 L Teflon-lined amber glass	Cool to 4°C Add NaSO	Cool to 4°C	7 days before extraction
Polynuclear aromatic hydrocarbons (PAHs)	8270C 8270 C-SIM	Two 1 L Teflon-lined amber glass	Cool to 4°C	Cool to 4°C	7 days before extraction
Purgeables using GCMS	524.2	40 mL VOA vial with Teflon lined cap	Cool to 4°C Add ascorbic acid and HCl to pH<2	Cool to 4°C	14 days
Purgeables using GCMS	624 8260C	40 mL VOA vial with Teflon lined cap	Cool to 4°C Add HCl to pH<2	Cool to 4°C	14 days
Salinity	SM 2520	150 mL plastic	Cool to 4°C	Cool to 4°C	28 days
Semivolatiles (TCLP)	1311 8270C 8081 A 8081 B 8151 A	8 oz (237 mL) Teflon-lined amber glass jar	Cool to 4°C	Cool to 4°C	14 days before extraction

(Continued)

TABLE A.1 (Continued)

Collection, Preservation, and Holding Times for Selected Liquid Environmental Samples

Parameter	EPA Testing Methodology	Container/Volume to Collect	Preservatives, If Any	Transport/ Holding Conditions	Holding Times
Silica	200.7 6010C	150 mL plastic	Cool to 4°C	Cool to 4°C	28 days
Sulfate	300.0 9038 SM 4500 SO$_4$-E	250 mL plastic	Cool to 4°C	Cool to 4°C	28 days
Sulfide	9030B SM 4500 S$_2$-AD	Two 250 mL plastic	ZnOAC, NaOH to pH>9 Cool to 4°C	Cool to 4°C	7 days
Sulfite	SM 4500 SO$_3$-B	100 mL plastic	Cool to 4°C	Cool to 4°C	Analyze immediately
Total metals	200.7 200.8 6010B 6010C 6020 6020 A 7000 A	501 mL plastic	HNO$_3$ to pH<2 Cool to 4°C	Cool to 4°C	180 days (28 days for Hg)
Total metals (TCLP)	1311 6010B 6010C 6020 6020 A 7000 A	4 oz (118 mL) amber glass jar	Cool to 4°C	Cool to 4°C	180 days before extraction
Total organic carbon	415.1 9060 SM 5310C	Two 40 mL amber glass VOA vials	Cool to 4°C Add H$_2$SO$_4$ to pH<2	Cool to 4°C	28 days

(Continued)

TABLE A.1 (Continued)
Collection, Preservation, and Holding Times for Selected Liquid Environmental Samples

Parameter	EPA Testing Methodology	Container/Volume to Collect	Preservatives, If Any	Transport/Holding Conditions	Holding Times
Total petroleum hydrocarbons	1664 A	4 oz (118 mL) Teflon-lined amber glass jar	Cool to 4°C	Cool to 4°C	28 days
Total petroleum hydrocarbons	1664 B	1 L amber glass jar with Teflon-lined cap	Add HCL or H_2SO_4 to pH<2 Cool to 4°C	Cool to 4°C	28 days
Total petroleum hydrocarbons-GC/FID	8015 B (Modified)	4 oz (118 mL) Teflon lined amber glass jar	Cool to 4°C	Cool to 4°C	14 days before extraction
Total phenol	420.1 9065 SM 510 ABC	Two 1 L amber glass	Cool to 4°C Add H_2SO_4 to pH<2	Cool to 4°C	28 days
Total residual chlorine	SM 4500 Cl-D	500 mL plastic	Cool to 4°C	Cool to 4°C	24 hours
Total solids	2540 C	250 mL plastic	Cool to 4°C	Cool to 4°C	7 days
Total dissolved solids	SM 2540 C	500 mL plastic	Cool to 4°C	Cool to 4°C	7 days
Total suspended solids	SM 2540 D	1 L plastic	Cool to 4°C	Cool to 4°C	7 days
Total volatile solids	SM 2540 E	500 mL plastic	Cool to 4°C	Cool to 4°C	7 days
Turbidity	180.1 2130 B	500 mL plastic	Cool to 4°C	Cool to 4°C	48 hours
Volatile organics	524.2	Two 40 mL Teflon-lined amber glass VOA vials	Ascorbic acid, HCl to pH<2 Cool to 4°C	Cool to 4°C	14 days
Volatile organics	624	Two 40 mL Teflon-lined amber glass VOA vials	NaSO Cool to 4°C	Cool to 4°C	7 days
Volatile organics	8260 B	Two 40 mL Teflon-lined amber glass VOA vials	HCl to pH<2 Cool to 4°C	Cool to 4°C	14 days
Volatiles (TCLP)	1311 8260 B	8 oz (237 mL) Teflon-lined amber glass jar	Cool to 4°C	Cool to 4°C	14 days before extraction

Consolidated data based on published guidelines from various analytical laboratories. Verification of data with the testing lab prior to sampling is strongly

TABLE A.2

Collection, Preservation, and Holding Times for Selected Soil and Sediment Environmental Samples

Parameter	EPA Testing Methodology	Container/Volume to Collect	Preservatives, If Any	Transport/Holding Conditions	Holding Times
Acid/base neutral extractables	8270C	4 oz (118 mL) Glass jar	Cool to 4°C	Cool to 4°C	14 days prior to extraction
Acid/base neutral extractables Oil/NAPL samples	8270C	4 oz (118 mL) Glass jar	Cool to 4°C	Cool to 4°C	None
Chrome VI	7196 A SM 3500 Cr - D	4 oz (118 mL) Glass jar	Cool to 4°C	Cool to 4°C	21 days prior to digestion; 3 days after digestion
Chrome VI	SW 846 7196 A	8 oz (118 mL) Glass jar	Cool to 4°C	Cool to 4°C	30 days
Cyanide	9010B 9012 A 9014	4 oz (118 mL) Glass jar	Cool to 4°C	Cool to 4°C	14 days
Diesel range organics (DRO)	8015 D (Mod)	8 oz (236 mL) Glass jar with Teflon cap	Cool to 4°C	Cool to 4°C	14 days
Flashpoint	1010 A 1030	8 oz (236 mL) Glass jar with Teflon cap	Cool to 4°C	Cool to 4°C	Analyze immediately
Gasoline range organics (GRO)	8015 D (Mod)	8 oz (236 mL) Glass jar with Teflon cap	Cool to 4°C Add 15 mL CH_3OH	Cool to 4°C	14 days
Herbicides	8151 A	8 oz (236 mL) Glass jar with Teflon cap	Cool to 4°C	Cool to 4°C	14 days
Ignitability	1010	4 oz (118 mL) Glass jar	Cool to 4°C	Cool to 4°C	180 days
Metals	6010B 6020 A 7000	4 oz (118 mL) Glass jar	Cool to 4°C	Cool to 4°C	180 days

(Continued)

TABLE A.2 (Continued)
Collection, Preservation, and Holding Times for Selected Soil and Sediment Environmental Samples

Parameter	EPA Testing Methodology	Container/Volume to Collect	Preservatives, If Any	Transport/Holding Conditions	Holding Times
Metals by TCLP	1311 6010B 6010C 6020 6020 A 7000 A	8 oz (236 mL) Glass jar	Cool to 4°C	Cool to 4°C	180 days prior to extraction
Mercury	7471 A 7471 B	8 oz (236 mL) Amber glass jar	Cool to 4°C	Cool to 4°C	28 days
Mercury by TCLP	1311 7470 A 7474	8 oz (236 mL) Amber glass jar	Cool to 4°C	Cool to 4°C	28 days
Oil and grease	1664 B	8 oz (236 mL) Glass jar with Teflon cap	Cool to 4°C	Cool to 4°C	28 days
Pesticides	8081 A 8081 B	8 oz (236 mL) Glass jar with Teflon cap	Cool to 4°C	Cool to 4°C	14 days prior to extraction
Polychlorinated biphenols (PCBs) homologs or congeners	680 8270 C (M)	4 oz (118 mL) Glass jar	Cool to 4°C	Cool to 4°C	14 days prior to extraction
Polychlorinated biphenols (PCBs) aroclors, homologs, or congeners	8082 8082 A	8 oz (236 mL) Amber glass jar with Teflon cap	Cool to 4°C	Cool to 4°C	14 days prior to extraction
Polynuclear aromatic hydrocarbons (PAHs)	8270 C 8270 C - SiM	4 oz (118 mL) Glass Jar	Cool to 4°C	Cool to 4°C	14 days prior to extraction

(Continued)

TABLE A.2 (Continued)
Collection, Preservation, and Holding Times for Selected Soil and Sediment Environmental Samples

Parameter	EPA Testing Methodology	Container/Volume to Collect	Preservatives, If Any	Transport/Holding Conditions	Holding Times
Polynuclear aromatic hydrocarbons (PAHs) Oil/NAPL samples	8270C 8270C - SiM	4 oz (118 mL) Glass jar	Cool to 4°C	Cool to 4°C	NA
Reactivity	Ch. 7 SW 846	8 oz (236 mL) Glass jar	Cool to 4°C	Cool to 4°C	Analyze immediately
Semivolatiles by TCLP	1311 8081 A 8081 B 8270C	8 oz (236 mL) Glass Jar	Cool to 4°C	Cool to 4°C	14 days prior to extraction
Sulfide	SM 4500 S-AD	4 oz (118 mL) Glass jar	Cool to 4°C	Cool to 4°C No headspace	28 days prior to extraction; 7 days after extraction
Total organic carbon (TOC)	9060	4 oz (118 mL) Glass Jar	Cool to 4°C	Cool to 4°C	28 days
Total petroleum hydrocarbons	8015 (Mod)	20 mL glass vial	Cool to 4°C	Cool to 4°C	NA
Volatile organics	8260B 5035 (High level)	40 mL amber glass VOA Vial (5 g minimum)	Cool to 4°C, Add 5 mL MeOH	Cool to 4°C	14 days
Volatile organics	8261B 5035 (Low level)	Two 40 mL amber glass VOA vial (5 g minimum each)	Cool to 4°C, add 5 mL water	Cool to 4°C	48 hours to freeze, 14 days to analyze if frozen

Consolidated data based on published guidelines from various analytical laboratories. Verification of data with the testing lab prior to sampling is strongly recommended.

TABLE A.3
Specific Heat Capacity of Selected Materials

Material	J/(kg-°K)	J/(g-°C)	BTU/(lb-°F)	BTU/ (lb-°C)
Air[e] (sea level, dry)		1.480		
Air[c] (sea level, dry, 0°C)	1003.5			
Air[c] (typical room temp.)	1012			
Alcohol (ethyl)[b]	2400		0.58	
Alcohol (ethyl)[d]		2.440		
Aluminum[a]	921.096	0.921096	0.220	0.396
Aluminum[b] (at 20°C)	900		0.215	
Aluminum[c]	897			
Aluminum[d]		0.897		
Asphalt[c]	920			
Asphalt[d]		0.920		
Brass (yellow)[a]	401.9328	0.401933	0.096	0.173
Brass[b] (at 20°C)	380		0.092	
Brass[d]		0.375		
Brick[c]	840			
Brick[d]		0.840		
Carbon steel[a]	502.416	0.502416	0.120	0.216
Cast iron[a]	460.548	0.460548	0.110	0.198
Charcoal[d]		0.840		
Concrete[c]	880.000			
Concrete[d]		0.880		
Copper[a]	376.812	0.376812	0.090	0.162
Copper[c]	385			
Copper[d]		0.385		
Cork[d]		2.000		
Ethanol[c]	2440			
Glass[b] (at 20°C)	840		0.20	
Glass[c] (pyrex)	753			
Glass[d] (pyrex)		0.753		
Glass[c] (silica)	840			
Granite[b] (at 20°C)	790		0.19	
Granite[c]	790			
Granite[d]		0.790		
Ice[b] (−10°C)	2050		0.49	
Ice[c] (−10°C)	2050			
Iron[a]	460.548	0.460548	0.110	0.198
Iron[c]	412			
Iron[d]		0.449		
Lead[a]	125.604	0.125604	0.030	0.054
Lead[b] (at 20°C)	128		0.0305	

(Continued)

TABLE A.3 (*Continued*)
Specific Heat Capacity of Selected Materials

Material	J/(kg-°K)	J/(g-°C)	BTU/(lb-°F)	BTU/ (lb-°C)
Lead[c]	129			
Lead[d]		0.129		
Methane[c] (at 2°C)	2191			
Methanol[c]	2140			
Nitrogen[c]	1040	56		
Oxygen[c]	918			
Sandy clay[d]		1.381		
Water[b] (at 20°C)	4186		1.0000	
Water[d] (at 20°C)		4.182		
Water[c] (at 25°C)	4181.3			
Water[c] (at 100°C)	4181.3			
Water[c]	4181.3			
Zinc[a]	376.812	0.376812	0.090	0.162
Zinc[c]	387			
Zinc[d]		0.388		

[a] Engineersedge.com.
[b] Hyperphysics – Tables.
[c] Wikipedia.org.
[d] Engineerstoolbox.com.

TABLE A.4
Thermal Conductivity of Selected Materials at 25°C (77°F)

Material	Adapted from: Hyperphysics		Adapted from: Engineering Toolbox		Adapted from rti.rockwool.com	
	k Value W/(m * °K)	k Value BTU/h/(ft * °F)	k Value W/(m * °K)	k Value BTU/h/(ft * °F)	k Value W/(m * °K) at 10°C	k Value BTU/h/ (ft * °F)
Acrylic			0.2	0.116		
Air			0.026	0.0151		
Air @ 0°C	0.024	0.014				
Aluminum	205	118.53				
Asbestos board	0.8	0.463	0.744	0.43		
Asbestos loose			0.15	0.0867		
Brass	109	63.02				
Concrete					1.6	0.925
Copper	385	222.60				
Cork board	0.04	0.023	0.07	0.0248		
Fiberglass	0.04	0.023	0.04	0.0231		
Fiber insulating board			0.048	0.0277		
Glass (ordinary)	0.8	0.463			1.1	0.636
Glass (window)			0.96	0.5550		
Insulating brick	0.15	0.087	0.15	0.0867		
Iron	79.5	45.97				
Lead	34.7	20.06				
Polyurethane foam	0.02	0.012	0.021	0.0121		
Red brick	0.6	0.347	0.6–1.0	0.3470		
Rock wool insulation					0.033	0.0191
Rubber			0.13	0.0751		
Steel	50.2	29.02			50	28.909
Styrofoam	0.033	0.019	0.033	0.0191		
Vermiculite granules			0.065	0.0376		
Wood	0.12–0.04	0.069–0.023	0.12–0.19	0.0693–0.11	0.12	0.069
Wool felt	0.04	0.023	0.04	0.0231		

TABLE A.5

Typical Soil Porosity and Void Ratio Values for Selected Soils

Soil Type or Description	Uniform Soil Classification System Designation (USCS)	Porosity[b]		Void Ratio[a]	
		Minimum Likely	Maximum Likely	Minimum Likely	Maximum Likely
Well graded gravel, sandy gravel, little or no fines	GW	0.21	0.32	0.26	0.46
Poorly graded gravel, sandy gravel, little or no fines	GP	0.21	0.32	0.26	0.46
Silty gravels, silty sandy gravels	GM	0.15	0.22	0.18	0.28
Gravel	GW-GP	0.23	0.38	0.30	0.60
Clayey gravels, clayey sandy gravels	GC	0.17	0.27	0.21	0.37
Well-graded sands, little or no fines	SW	0.22	0.42	0.29	0.74
Coarse sand	(SW)	0.26	0.43	0.35	0.75
Fine sand	(SW)	0.29	0.26	0.40	0.85
Poorly graded sands, gravely sands, little or no fines	SP	0.23	0.43	0.30	0.75
Silty sands	SM	0.25	0.49	0.33	0.98
Clayey sands	SC	0.15	0.37	0.17	0.59
Inorganic silts, silty or clayey fine sands with slight plasticity	ML	0.21	0.56	0.26	1.28
Uniform organic silt	(ML)	0.29	0.52	0.40	1.10
Inorganic clays, silty clays, sandy clays with low plasticity	CL	0.42	0.68	0.41	0.69
Organic silts and organic silty clays with low plasticity	OL	0.42	0.68	0.74	2.26

(Continued)

TABLE A.5 (Continued)
Typical Soil Porosity and Void Ratio Values for Selected Soils

Soil Type or Description	Uniform Soil Classification System Designation (USCS)	Porosity[b]		Void Ratio[a]	
		Minimum Likely	Maximum Likely	Minimum Likely	Maximum Likely
Silty or sandy clay	(CL-OL)	0.20	0.64	0.25	1.80
Inorganic silts with high plasticity	MH	0.53	0.75	1.14	2.10
Inorganic clays with high plasticity	CH	0.39	0.59	0.63	1.45
Organic clays with high plasticity	OH	0.50	0.75	1.06	3.34

Data adapted from:
[a] Geotechdata.info, Soil Void Ratio, http://geotechdata.info/parameter/soil-void-ratio.html (as of November 16, 2013). Accessed 11/17/20.
[b] Geotechdata.info, Soil Porosity (Soil Porosity, 2013), http://geotechdata.info/parameter/soil-porosity.html (as of November 16, 2013). Accessed 11/17/20.

TABLE A.6
Density Estimates for Various Soil Types

Soil Type	Dry Unit Weight in g/cc	Porosity, Undisturbed in %	Porosity, Repacked in %
Fine sand	1.13–1.99	26.0–53.3	26.7–50.2
Medium sand	1.27–1.93	28.5–48.9	27.2–52.3
Coarse sand	1.42–1.94	30.9–46.4	37.0–42.0
Fine gravel	1.60–1.99		25.1–38,5
Medium gravel	1.47–2.09		23.7–44.1
Coarse gravel	1.69–2.08		23.8–36.5
Silt	1.01–1.79	33.9–61.1	41.0–56.0
Clay	1.18–1.72	34.2–56.9	39.9–52.8

Consolidated from: Summary of Hydrologic and Physical Properties of Rock and Soil Materials, as Analyzed by the Hydrologic Laboratory of the U.S. Geological Survey 1948-60 by D. A. Morris and A. I. Johnson https://pubs.usgs.gov/wsp/1839d/report.pdf. Accessed 11/17/20.

TABLE A.7
Maximum DO Concentration in Water by Temperature

Water Temp in °C	Max Do in mg/L	Water Temp in °C	Max Do in mg/L	Water Temp in °F	Max Do in mg/L	Water Temp in °F	Max Do in mg/L
0	14.60	31	7.41	32	14.6	63	9.61
1	14.19	32	7.28	33	14.35	64	9.49
2	13.81	33	7.16	34	14.13	65	9.39
3	13.44	34	7.05	35	13.92	66	9.28
4	13.09	35	6.93	36	13.74	67	9.18
5	12.75	36	6.82	37	13.51	68	9.07
6	12.43	37	6.71	38	13.33	69	8.97
7	12.12	38	6.61	39	13.12	70	8.88
8	11.83	39	6.51	40	13.08	71	8.77
9	11.55	40	6.41	41	12.75	72	8.69
10	11.27	41	6.31	42	12.56	73	8.59
11	11.01	42	6.22	43	12.4	74	8.51
12	10.76	43	6.13	44	12.21	75	8.42
13	10.52	44	6.04	45	12.06	76	8.34
14	10.29	45	5.95	46	11.89	77	8.24
15	10.07			47	11.75	78	8.15
16	9.85			48	11.58	79	8.08
17	9.65			49	11.44	80	7.99
18	9.45			50	11.27	81	7.92
19	9.26			51	11.11	82	7.84
20	9.07			52	10.98	83	7.77
21	8.90			53	10.84	84	7.68
22	8.72			54	10.71	85	7.62

(Continued)

TABLE A.7 (Continued)
Maximum DO Concentration in Water by Temperature

Water Temp in °C	Max Do in mg/L	Water Temp in °C	Max Do in mg/L	Water Temp in °F	Max Do in mg/L	Water Temp in °F	Max Do in mg/L
23	8.56			55	10.57	86	7.54
24	8.40			56	10.45	87	7.46
25	8.24			57	10.31	88	7.40
26	8.09			58	10.20	89	7.32
27	7.95			59	10.07	90	7.26
28	7.81			60	9.95	91	7.18
29	7.67			61	9.83	92	7.12
30	7.54			62	9.71	93	7.05

TABLE A.8
Density of Water at Selected Temperatures

Temperature °C	Temperature °F	Water Density g/cc	Water Density kg/m³	Water Density lb/in³	Water Density lb/cf
0	32	0.99987	999.87	0.03612	62.415
5	41	0.99999	999.99	0.03613	62.433
10	50	0.99975	999.75	0.03612	62.415
15	59	0.99913	999.13	0.03610	62.381
20	68	0.99823	998.23	0.03606	62.312
22	72	0.99776	997.76	0.03605	62.294
25	77	0.99707	997.07	0.03602	62.243
30	86	0.99562	995.62	0.03597	62.156
35	95	0.99406	994.06	0.03591	62.052
40	104	0.99224	992.24	0.03585	61.949

TABLE A.9
Typical Surface Stormwater Runoff Coefficients

	Soil Type											
	Deep, Well Drained Sandy Soils			Shallow, Sandy Loams			Dense, Clayey Soils			Soils that Swell When Wet		
Typical Infiltration Rates in in/hr (cm/hr)	>0.30 (>0.76)			0.15–0.30 (0.38–0.76)			0.05–0.15 (0.13–0.38)			<0.05 (<0.13)		
Slope in %	Flat <2%	Avg 2% to 7%	Steep >7%	Flat <2%	Avg 2% to 7%	Steep >7%	Flat <2%	Avg 2 to 7%	Steep >7%	Flat <2%	Avg 2% to 7%	Steep >7%
Land Use Characteristics												
Downtown areas, heavily paved areas, and areas with significant impervious cover[a]	0.88		0.89	0.89	0.89	0.89	0.89	0.89	0.90	0.89	0.89	0.90
Downtown areas, heavily paved areas, and areas with significant impervious cover[b]		0.7–0.95			0.7–0.95			0.7–0.95			0.7–0.95	
Streets and paved roadways[a]	0.76		0.79	0.80	0.82	0.84	0.84	0.85	0.89	0.89	0.91	0.95
Streets and paved roadways[b]		0.70–0.95			0.70–0.95			0.70–0.95			0.70–0.95	
Driveways and walkways[a]	0.76		0.79	0.80	0.82	0.84	0.84	0.85	0.89	0.89	0.91	0.95
Driveways and walkways[b]		0.75–0.85			0.75–0.85			0.75–0.85			0.75–0.85	

(Continued)

TABLE A.9 (Continued)
Typical Surface Stormwater Runoff Coefficients

	Soil Type											
	Deep, Well Drained Sandy Soils			Shallow, Sandy Loams			Dense, Clayey Soils			Soils that Swell When Wet		
Parking lots [1]	0.95	0.96	0.97	0.95	0.96	0.97	0.95	0.96	0.97	0.95	0.96	0.97
High-density neighborhoods [a]	0.33–0.70	0.37–0.70	0.40–0.70	0.35–0.70	0.39–0.70	0.44–0.70	0.38–0.70	0.42–0.70	0.49–0.70	0.41–0.70	0.45–0.70	0.50–0.70
Single-family residential areas [a]	0.22–0.50	0.26–0.50	0.29–0.50	0.24–0.50	0.28–0.50	0.30–0.50	0.28–0.50	0.30–0.50	0.30–0.50	0.30–0.50	0.30–0.50	0.30–0.50
Single-family residential areas [b]		0.30–0.50			0.30–0.50			0.30–0.50			0.30–0.50	
Multifamily detached units [a]	0.25	0.29	0.32	0.28	0.32	0.36	0.31	0.35	0.42	0.34	0.38	0.46
Multifamily detached units [b]		0.40–0.60			0.40–0.60			0.40–0.60			0.40–0.60	
Multifamily row houses [a]	0.30	0.34	0.37	0.33	0.37	0.42	0.36	0.40	0.47	0.38	0.42	0.52
Multifamily row houses [b]		0.60–0.75			0.60–0.75			0.60–0.75			0.60–0.75	
General neighborhood areas [b]		0.50–0.70			0.50–0.70			0.50–0.70			0.50–0.70	
General suburban areas [a]	0.28	0.32	0.35	0.30	0.35	0.39	0.33	0.38	0.45	0.36	0.40	0.50
Roofs [b]	0.75–0.95	0.75–0.95	0.75–0.95	0.75–0.95	0.75–0.95	0.75–0.95	0.75–0.95	0.75–0.95	0.75–0.95	0.75–0.95	0.75–0.95	0.75–0.95
Lawn areas [b]	0.05–0.10	0.10–0.15	0.15–0.20							0.13–0.17	0.18–0.22	0.25–0.35
Agricultural land [a]	0.14	0.18	0.22	0.16	0.21	0.28	0.20	0.25	0.34	0.24	0.29	0.41

(Continued)

TABLE A.9 (Continued)
Typical Surface Stormwater Runoff Coefficients

	Soil Type											
	Deep, Well Drained Sandy Soils			Shallow, Sandy Loams			Dense, Clayey Soils			Soils that Swell When Wet		
Industrial areas[a]	0.85	0.85	0.86	0.85	0.86	0.86	0.86	0.86	0.87	0.86	0.86	0.88
Parks and cemeteries[b]		0.10–0.25			0.10–0.25			0.10–0.25			0.10–0.25	
Playgrounds[b]		0.20–0.35			0.20–0.35			0.20–0.35			0.20–0.35	
Disturbed soil areas[a]	0.65	0.67	0.69	0.66	0.68	0.70	0.68	0.70	0.72	0.69	0.72	0.75
Unimproved areas[b]	0.10–0.30	0.10–0.30	0.10–0.30	0.10–0.30	0.10–0.30	0.10–0.30	0.10–0.30	0.10–0.30	0.10–0.30	0.10–0.30	0.10–0.30	0.10–0.30
Forested areas[a]	0.08	0.11	0.14	0.10	0.14	0.18	0.12	0.16	0.20	0.15	0.20	0.25
Forested areas[b]		0.05–0.25			0.05–0.25			0.05–0.25			0.05–0.25	
Meadows[a]	0.14	0.22	0.30	0.20	0.28	0.37	0.26	0.35	0.44	0.30	0.40	0.50
Pastures[a]	0.15	0.25	0.37	0.23	0.34	0.45	0.30	0.42	0.52	0.37	0.50	0.62
Pastures[b]		0.05–0.25									0.15–0.45	

Adapted from:

[a] brighthubengineering.com.

[b] waterboards.ca.gov.

Bibliography

Anscomb, F. (1973). Graphs in statistical analysis. *American Statistician 27*, 17–21.

Baird, R. B., Eaton, A. D., Rice, E. W., & Bridgewater, L. (2017). Standard Methods for the Examination of Water and Wastewater (Twenty-third edition.). Washington, DC: American Public Health Association.

Bevans, R. (2020, July 3). *A Guide to Experimental Design.* Retrieved from Scribbr.com: https://www.scribbr.com/methodology/experimental-design/.

Bevans, R. (2020, October 20). *An Introduction to Multiple Linear Regression.* Retrieved December 9, 2020, from scribbr.com: https://www.scribbr.com/statistics/multiple-linear-regression/.

Biosandfilter.org. (2020). Retrieved January 4, 2021, from Sand as a filter media: https://www.biosandfilter.org/biosand-filter/filter-media/sand-as-a-filter-media/.

Board, T. U. (n.d.). *ucdsb.on.ca.* Retrieved January 29, 2021, from Density of Water: www2.ucdsb.on.ca/tiss/streton/Database/DofWater.htm.

Cecil, S. (n.d.). *P-I-A-N-O Standards for Detailed Hydrocarbon Analyses.* Retrieved January 3, 2021, from sigmaaldrich.com: https://www.sigmaaldrich.com/technical-documents/articles/analytix/p-i-a-n-o-standards.html

Chapter 6-2 Oxygen Transfer. (n.d.). Retrieved January 9, 2021, from https://cbe.snu.ac.kr/sites/cbe.snu.ac.kr/files/board/LectureBoard/Chap%206-2_0.pdf

Charest, A. (2015). *Investigation of Physical Characteristics Impacting Fate and Transport of Viral Surrogates in Water Systems,* Dissertation, Worcester Polytechnic Institute, Worcester, MA.

Chemistry 301. (2020, November 19). Retrieved from ch301.cm.utex.edu: https://ch301.cm.utexas.edu/data/section2.php?target=heat-capcities.php.

Combinations and Permutations. (n.d.). Retrieved December 4, 2020, from Mathsisfun.com: https://www.mathsisfun.com/combinatorics/combinations-permutations.html.

Courtemanch, D. (1979). *Foam - a Cause for Concern?* Retrieved November 23, 2020, from Maine Department of Environmental Protection: https://www.maine.gov/dep/water/lakes/foam.html.

Donev, J. E. (2018). *Energy Education - Hydrocarbon (Online).* Retrieved January 3, 2021, from Energyeducation.ca: https://energyeducation.ca/encyclopedia/Hydrocarbon.

Engineering.Perdue.edu. (1997, November). Retrieved January 4, 2021, from Sand Filters: https://engineering.purdue.edu/~frankenb/NU-prowd/sand.htm#:~:text=Sand%20filters%20usually%20are%20used,is%20usually%20colorless%20and%20odorless.

Engineeringtoolbox.com. (n.d.). *Thermal Conductivity.* Retrieved December 12, 2020, from Engineeringtoolbox.com: https://www.engineerstoolbox.com/thermal-conductivity-d_429.html.

Engineersedge, com. (n.d.). *Insulation Material Thermal Conductivity Chart.* Retrieved December 12, 2020, from Engineersedge: https://engineersedge.com/heat_transfer/insulation_material_thermal_conductivity_chart_13170.html.

Expeimentation. (1997–1998). Retrieved from Yale, edu: http://www.stat.yale.edu/Courses/1997-98/101/expdes.htm.

Foam. (n.d.). Retrieved November 23, 2020, from Clemson.edu: https://www.clemson.edu/extension/water/stormwater-ponds/problem-solving/muddy-turbid-water/index.html.

Foam a Naturally Occurring Phenomenon. (2016, January). Retrieved November 23, 2020, from Michigan.gov: https://www.michigan.gov/documents/deq/deq-oea-nop-foam_378415_7.pdf.

Foam on Water. (2014). Retrieved November 23, 2020, from in.gov: https://www.in.gov/idem/files/factsheet_owq_nps_foam.pdf.

Fondriest Environmental, Inc. (2013, November 19). *Dissolved Oxygen. Fundamentals of Environmental Measurements.* Retrieved January 3, 2021, from fondriest.com: https://www.fondriest.com/environmental-measurements/parameters/water-quality/dissolved-oxygen/.

Geotechdata.info. (2013, November 16). Retrieved November 17, 2020, from Soil Void Ratio: http://geotechdata.info/parameter/void-ratio

Geotechdata.info. (2013, November 16). Retrieved November 17, 2020, from Soil Porosity: http://geotechdata.info/parameter/soil-porosity

Glossary. (n.d.). Retrieved January 9, 2021, from http://techaliove.mtu.edu/modules/module001_alt/Glosasary.htm.

Green, J. (2005). *Distillation.* Retrieved November 24, 2020, from Sciencedirect.com: https://www.sciencedirect.com/topics/biochemistry-genetics-and-molecular-biology/distillation.

Green, J. (2019). Distillation. In *Encyclopedia of Analytical Science* (Third Edition) (pp. 214–219). Amsterdam: Elsevier.

Haack, Sheridan K., Joseph W. Duris, Lisa R. Fogarty, Dana W. Kolpin, Michael J. Focazio, Edward T. Furlong, and Michael T. Meyer. (2009). Comparing wastewater chemicals, indicator bacteria concentrations, and bacterial pathogen genes as fecal pollution indicators. *Journal of Environmental Quality* 38(1), 248–258.

Hach Corporation. (2020, August 18). *support.hach.com.* Retrieved January 14, 2021, from What is the Difference Between the Turbidity Units NTU FNU, FTU, and FAU? What is a JTU? https://support.hach.com/app/answers/answer_view/a_id/1000336/~/what-is-the-difference-between-the-turbidity-units-ntu%2C-fnu%2C-ftu%2C-and-fau%3F-what.

Hopcroft, F. J. (2015). *Wastewater Treatment Concepts and Practices.* New York: Momentum Press.

Hopcroft, F. J. (2016). *Engineering Economics for Environmental Engineers.* New York: Momentum Press.

Hopcroft, F. J. (2017). *Conversion Factors for Environmental Engineers.* New York: Momentum Press.

Hopcroft, F. J. (2019). *Presenting Technical Data to a Non-Technical Audience.* New York: Momentum Press.

Kenton, W. (2020, September 21). *Multiple Linear Regression (MLR).* Retrieved December 9, 2020, from investopedia.com: https://www.investopedia.com/terms/m/mlr.asp.

Lake Stewards of Maine. (2014, January). *Maximum Dissolved Oxygen Concentration Saturation Table.* Retrieved January 16, 2021, from Lakestewardsofmaine.org: https://lakestewardsofmaine.org/wp-content/uploads/2014/01/Maximum-Dissolved-Oxygen-Concentration-Saturation-Table.pdf.

Metcalf & Eddy/AECOM. (2014). *Wastewater Engineering: Treatment and resource Recovery* (Fifth Edition). (G. H. Tchobanoglous, Ed.) New York: McGraw Hill Education.

Missouri Department of Natural Resources. (n.d.). *Maximum Dissolved Oxygen Concentration Saturation Table.* Retrieved January 16, 2021, from dnr.mo.gov: https://dnr.mo.gov/env/esp/wqm/DOSaturationTable.htm.

Morris, D. A. (1967). *Summary of Hydrologic and Physical Properties of Rock and Soil Materials, as Analyzed by the Hydrologic Laboratory of the U. S. Geologic Survey 1948–60.* Retrieved from pubs.usgs.gov: https://pubs.usgs.gov/wsp/1839d/report.pdf.

Nichols, L. (2020, August 14). *5.3: Fractional Distillation.* Retrieved November 24, 2020, from chem.libretexts.org: https://chem.libretexts.org/Bookshelves/Organic_Chemistry/Book%3A_Organic_Chemistry_Lab_Techniques_(Nichols)/05%3A_Distillation/5.03%3A_Fractional_Distillation.

Oxygen Transfer Rate. (n.d.). Retrieved January 9, 2021, from http://techalive.mtu.edu/
modules/module0001_alt/OxygenTransferRate.htm#:~:text=T%he%20rate%20of%20
ixygen%20mass, key%20input%20in%20diffuser%20design.

Peeler, Kelly A., Stephen P. Opsahl, and Jeffrey P. Chanton. (2006). Tracking anthropogenic
inputs using caffeine, indicator bacteria, and nutrients in rural freshwater and urban
marine systems. *Environmental Science & Technology 40*(24), 7616–7622.

Petroleum Hydrocarbon Environmental Forensics. (2020, May). Retrieved January 3, 2021, from
microbe.com: https://microbe.com/wp-content/uploads/2020/05/Petroleum_Hydrocarbon_
environmental_forensics.pdf.

Plastics International. (n.d.). *Optix Acrylic.* Retrieved December 12, 2020, from Plastics
International.com: https://www.plasticsintl.com/media/wysiwyg/Acrylic__PMMA__
Extruded.pdf.

Precipitation by pH (and Viable Alternatives). (n.d.). Retrieved December 10, 2020, from
Water Specialists: https://waterspecialists.biz/?page_id=115#:~:text=To%20convert%
20dissolved%20(ionic)%20metals, the%20pH%20of%20the%20solution.

Protection, M. D. (1994). *Interim Remediation Waste Management Policy.* Boston, MA:
Massachusetts Department of Environmental Protection. Retrieved January 27, 2021,
from https://www.mass.gov/doc/wsc-94-400-interim-remediation-waste-management-
policy-for-petroleum-contaminated-soils/download.

Ramakrishnaiah, C. A. (2011). Hexavalent chromium removal by vhemical precipitation
method: A comparative study. *International Journal of Environmental Research and
Development, 1*(1), 41–49. Retrieved January 15, 2021, from http://www.ripublication.
com/ijerd.htm.

Ratnayaka, D. D. (2009). *Water Supply (Sixth Edition).* Elsevier, Ltd. Retrieved January 4,
2021, from https://www.sciencedirect.com/topics/engineering/sand-filter.

Recommended Containers, Preservation, Storage, & Holding Times. (2016, July 29).
Retrieved November 24, 2020, from Eurofins Spectral Analytical: https://www.
eurofinsus.com/media/447768/appendix-d-section-5-attachment-holdtime-container-
list_2016-july.pdf.

Safe Drinking Water Foundation. (2017, January 23). Retrieved December 31, 2020, from
Conventional Water Treatment: Coagulation and Filtration: https://www.safewater.
org/fact-sheets-1/2017/1/23/conventional-water-treatment.

Sauer, T. C. (2003). *Fingerprinting of Gasoline and Coal Tar NAPL Volatile Hydrocarbons
Dissolved in Groundwater.* Retrieved January 3, 2021, from tandfonline.com: https://
www.tandfonline.com/doi/abs/10.1080/714044376.

Soil Porosity. (2013, November 16). Retrieved from Geotechdata.info: http://geotechdata.info/
parameter/soil-porosity.html.

Soil Void Ratio. (2013, November 16). Retrieved from Geotechdata.info: http://geotechdata.
info/parameter/soil-void-ratio.html.

Specific Heat Capacity of Metals. (n.d.). Retrieved November 19, 2020, from Engineersedge.com:
https://www.engineersedge.com/materials/specific_heat_capacity_of_metals_13259.htm.

Specific Heat of Gases. (n.d.). Retrieved November 19, 2020, from Hyperphysics.phy-astr.
gsu.edu: hyperphysics.phy-astr.gsu.edu/hbase/kinetic/shegas.html#c4.

Specific Heat of Some Common Substances. (n.d.). Retrieved November 19, 2020, from The
Engineering Toolbox: https://www.engineeringtoolbox.com/specific-heat-capacity-d_
391.html.

Specific heats and molar heat capacities for various substances at 20 C. (n.d.). Retrieved
November 19, 2020, from Hyperphysics.phy-astr.gsu.edu: http://hyperphysics.phy-astr.
gsu.edu/hbase/Tables/sphtt.html

Stout, S. A. (n.d.). *11- Chemical fingerprinting of gasoline and distillate fuels.*
Retrieved January 3, 2021, from sciencedirect.com: https://www.sciencedirect.
com/science/article/pii/B9780128038321000118.

Suez Water Technologies. (2021). Retrieved January 4, 2021, from Handbook of Industrial Water Treatment 2021, Chapter 06- Filtration: https://www.suezwatertechnologies. com/handbook/chapter-06-filtration.

Sullivan, L. A. (n.d.). *Simple Linear Regression.* Retrieved December 9, 2020, from Boston University School of Public Health: https://sphweb.bumc.bu.edu/otlt/mph-modules/bs/ bs704-ep713_multivariablemethods/index.html.

Sundararajan, K. (n.d.). *Design of Experiments - A Primer.* Retrieved November 2020, from isix-sigma.com: https://www.isixsigma.com/tools-templates/design-of-experiments-doe/ design-experiments-%E2%90%93-primer/.

Support Services. (2020). Retrieved from Alphalab.com: https://alphalab.com/index.php/ support-services/holding-times#HH0.

Table of Specific Heat Capacities. (2020, November 19). Retrieved from en.wikipedia.org: https://en.wikipedia.org/wiki/Table_of_specific_heat_capacities.

The International Water Association. (2020). Retrieved December 31, 2020, from Coagulation and Flocculation in Water and Wastewater Treatment: https://www.iwapublishing. com/news/coagulation-and-flocculation-water-and-wastewater-treatment.

ThermoFisher.com. (n.d.). Retrieved January 15, 2021, from Atomic Absorption Spectrometry (AAS): https://www.thermofisher.com/us/en/home/industrial/spectroscopy-elemental-isotope-analysis/spectroscopy-elemental-isotope-analysis-learning-center/trace-elemental-analysis-tea-information/atomic-absorption-aa-information.html#:~:text=Atomic%20 absorption%2

Tufte, E. (2001). *The Visual Display of Quantitative Information*, 2nd edition. Cheshire, CT: Graphics Press.

Vail, J. H., Morgan, R., Merino, C. R., Gonzales, F., Miller, R., & Ram, J. L. (2003). Enumeration of waterborne Escherichia coli with petrifilm plates: Comparison to standard methods. *Journal of Environmental Quality*, 32(1), 368.

Yang, C. C. (2017). *Chapter 4- Chemical Fingerprints of Crude Oils and Petroleum Products.* Retrieved January 3, 2021, from sciencedirect.com: https://www.sciencedirect. com/science/article/pii/B9780128094136000047.

Zainuddin, N. A. (2019). Removal of nickel, zinc and copper from plating process industrial raw effluent via hydroxide precipitation versus sulphide precipitation. *IOP Conference Series: Materials Science and Engineering 551*, 012122.

Zueva, S. B. (2018). *Chemical Precipitation.* Retrieved December 10, 2020, from Sciencedirect. com: https://www.sciencedirect.com/topics/engineering/chemical-precipitation.

Index

5-Day BOD test 165
5-day BOD test with determination of exertion rate, k 165

accounting for the effects of interferences 7
air particulates 20
aliphatic hydrocarbons 136
alkanes 136
alkenes 136
alkynes 136
analysis of
    suspended solids in water 283, 297
    total solids in water 303
Anscombe's Quartet 36, 38
Anscombe's Quartet variation 37, 38
anthropological foam 248
aromatic hydrocarbons 136
average parameter value 25, 29
avoiding the effects of interferences 7

Biological Oxygen Demand (BOD) 147, 165–167

calibration of
    DO meter by Winkler method 148
    spectrophotomer 70
    turbidity meter 64
cause and effect 36
characterization of pond, lake, or stream foam 247
chemical testing 20
coagulation 114, 120, 210, 273, 282
coagulation, flocculation, and sedimentation for the removal of organic and inorganic water contaminants 282
coliform 61, 180, 181, 187, 196
Colilert Methodology 180, 187
coliphage 195
coliphage quantification 195
collection of
    gas samples 19–20
    liquid samples 17
    soil samples 18
combinations 27
comparison of disinfection methods 201
comparison of disinfection methods remote area options 209
comparison of experimental output data with literature 49
compositing a sample 18
compositing a volatile sample 18
conclusions and recommendations 36, 50, 53

contaminant removal experiments 253
contaminant removal rate determination 254
contrasting of experimental output data with literature 49
control sample 107
controlled variables 4
controlling the variables 5
conversion of theory to experimental output data 49
correlation 36

data analysis plan 48
data to be collected 47
defining the question 3
defining the variables 4
density of water, table 339
dependent variables 4
design elements 12
design methodology 43
determination of
    contaminant removal rate 254
    dissolved oxygen concentration 160
    dissolved solids 282, 303, 304
    DO exertion rate, k 165
    granular media suitability for use in granular media filters 289
    insulation R-values for various materials 95
    maximum DO concentration in water as a function of salinity 160
    mean cell residence time in a dispersed plug flow reactor 231
    oil solubility in water as a function of salinity 130
    organic and inorganic content of the dissolved solids 304
    oxygen transfer rate 152
    particulates in air 20
    pH as a function of acid/base concentration 224
    porosity and void ratio in soil 140
    solubility of oil in water 130
    specific heat capacity 89
    surface runoff rate and volume calculation 109
    surface water evaporation rate 237
    suspended solids 297
    total coliform and E. coli 180, 187
disinfection 121, 201, 209
disinfection methods, comparison 201
disinfection methods, remote areas, comparison 209
dispersed plug flow reactor 231

dissolved oxygen 3, 5, 8, 160
dissolved oxygen in water, table 337
dissolved oxygen testing 21
dissolved solids determination 282, 303, 304
distillation 268
DO exertion rate, k, determination 165
DO meter calibration 148
Draeger Tube 19
duct tape permeability test 82

E. coli 61, 180, 181, 187
effective size 122, 290
effects of interferences 7
environmental microbiology experiments 179
estimable parameters 24
estimated probability 29
estimates 25
estimating future parameter values 25
estimating probabilities 29
expected outcomes 23, 47
expected value 41
experimental design 1
experimental variables 4
experimentation 1
experiment design format model 43, 46

factors affecting thermal conductivity 96
fecal coliform 62
field testing and quantification of total coliform
        and E. coli by Colilert and Petrifilm
        methodologies 187
finger printing gasoline 135
flame ionization detector (FID) 18
flocculation 210, 282
foam 247–248
Formazin Attenuation Units (FAUs) 65
Formazin Nephelometric Units (FNUs) 65
Formazin Turbidity Units (FTUs) 65
future consequences 25

gas chromatograph 132
gas sampling bags 20
gasoline fingerprinting 135
GC/MS 132
general experiments 59
granular media 123
granular media filter characteristics 290
granular media filters 289
granular media suitability determination 289

headspace 17
headspace analysis for the presence of volatile
        organic compound 17, 104
Health and Safety Plans (HASPs) 21
heat capacity ratio 90
holding times 16, 24

liquid samples, table 323
    soil samples, table 329
Homogeneity of Variance 242

IDEXX Quantitray Method 180
independence of observations 242
independent variables 4
inorganic fraction 304–309
insulation R-values determination for various
        materials 95
interpretation of data 23
introduction to water quality parameters 218
in situ testing 15, 17

Jackson Turbidity Units (JTUs) 65
jar test 75
jar test procedure 75
joint probabilities 27

laboratory report 49
laboratory report template 50
Lee's method 97
linearity 242
linear regression analysis 39, 241
liquid phase component separation 268
liquid sample collection 15
liquid sample holding times 16
liquid sample preservation 16
liquid sample preservation, table 323
liquid testing methodologies 17

mass spectroscopy 132
maximum DO concentration in water as a function
        of salinity and temperature 160
mean cell residence time determination in a
        dispersed plug flow reactor 231
mean parameter value 25
measuring air particulates 20
measuring variables 5
metal ion precipitation from water 260
microbiology experiments 179
minimizing the effects of interferences 7
misuse of probability data 30
model design methodology 43
model format 43
most likely parameter value 25
most probable number (MPN) 180
multiple linear regression 241, 243

natural foam 248
Nephelometric Turbidity Units (NTUs) 95
neutralization calculations 224
non-organic fractions 59, 305
non-oxidizable fraction 305
non-turbulent sampling 16
non-volatile 304
non-volatile fraction 304

normality 242
number of data points needed 31

objective to be addressed 24, 43, 46
oil and petroleum based experiments 129
oil solubility in water as a function of salinity 130
optimistic parameter value 25
organic and inorganic content of the dissolved solids 304
organic fraction 59
outcomes range 25, 176
outliers 37
oxygen and BOD experiments 147
oxygen transfer rate determination 152

particulates in air 20
permeability 83
permutations 27
personal protective equipment 12, 21
pessimistic parameter value 25
Petrifilm Methodology 187
pH
    definition 224
    as a function of acid/base concentration 224
    as a function of acid/base concentration with neutralization calculations 224
    neutralization calculations 224
    testing 15
phage 180, 182, 196
photoionization detector (PID) 18
photometer 71
pin floc 263
plug flow reactor 231
$PM_{2.5}$ and PM_{10} particulates 20
pond, lake or stream foam 247
porosity 83
porosity and void ratio determination in soil 140
porosity table 335
potable water softening technique 274
potential interferences 7
potential variables 4
precipitation of metal ions 260
presentation of data 55
preservation of
    liquid samples 19
    liquid samples, table 323
    soil samples 16
    soil samples, table 329
preservative additions 15
probability 25
probability basis of statistics 26
probability rules 25
purity of the samples 15

quantification of
    coliphages 195
    E. coli 180, 187

total coliforms 187, 192
Quantitray Method 180
question to be addressed 3, 43

random outcome 12, 29
recommended liquid preservatives, table 329
recommended soil sample preservatives, table 323
regression line 39, 68
removal of organic and inorganic water contaminants 254, 282
research vs. experimentation 59
research project design 59
risk 21, 41
R-value 95, 96

safety 12, 21
safety considerations 12, 21
sample containers 16, 19, 323, 329
sample holding times 16, 19, 323, 329
sample volumes 16, 19, 323, 329
sampling
    a monitoring well 17
    air 19
    at various depths in liquid 17
    gases 19
    health and safety plans 21
    liquids 15
    semi-solids 18
    soil 18
    solids 18
    source media 15
    water 15
sand filters 122, 289
Searle's method 97
sedimentation 114, 120, 282
selective use of data 32
sensitivity analyses 8
separation of liquid phase components through a distillation process 268
SilcoCan 20
slow sand filter 122
soil density, table 336
soil porosity, table 335
soil sample containers 18, 323
soil sample volumes 18, 323
soil testing methodologies 16
soil void ratio, table 335
solubility of oil in water as a function of salinity 130
specific heat at constant pressure 90
specific heat at constant volume 90
specific heat capacity 89
specific heat capacity determination 89
spectrometer 71
spectrophotometer 71
spectrophotometer calibration 70
standard deviation 41

standard values of specific heat, table 332
statistical analysis of data 11, 25, 36
surface runoff coefficient, table 340
surface runoff rate determination and volume
        calculation 109
surface water evaporation rate determination 237
suspended solids 6, 65, 126, 220
suspended solids in water 6, 65, 126, 220, 297
suspended solids determination 297

technique for metal ion precipitation from
        water 260
technique for potable water softening 274
Tenax Tube 19
testing of gases for particulates 20
theoretical expectations 23
theory behind the experiment 43, 46
thermal anisotropy 98
thermal conductivity 96
    coefficient 97
    table 334
title of the experiment 43, 46
tools, equipment and supplies 44, 47
total coliform 61, 180, 187
total coliform and *E. coli* by IDEXX Quantitrays
        and Colilert Most Probable Number
        methodologies 180
total coliform and *E. coli* determination
        180, 187
total solids 59, 291
tracer study 231
transport and holding conditions 16, 19, 323, 329
Tufte, Edward R. 36
turbidity 8, 9, 64
turbidity meter calibration 64
turbidity units 64, 95

uncertainty 25, 32
uncertainty considerations 25
uncontrolled variables 4
uniformity coefficient 122
units of specific heat 90
unmeasured interferences 7
unmeasured parameters 5, 6

variables
    controlled 4, 5
    dependent 4
    independent 4
    uncontrolled 4
variable control 5
variance 37, 41
viral indicators 195
viral indicators coliphage quantification based on
        EasyPhage method 195
void ratio 140
void ratio determination in soil 140
void ratio, table 335
volatile organic analysis (VOA) vial 17
volatile suspended solids 304

water
    evaporation rate 237
    filtration media evaluation 114
    filtration media evaluation, remote area
        options 120
    parameters 218
    quality experiments 253
    runoff rate determination and volume
        calculation 109
    softening 274
Winkler method 148

Printed in the United States
by Baker & Taylor Publisher Services